DATE DUE

The Pinochet Effect

PENNSYLVANIA STUDIES IN HUMAN RIGHTS
Bert B. Lockwood, Jr., Series Editor

A complete list of books in the series is available from the publisher.

The Pinochet Effect

Transnational Justice in the Age of Human Rights

NAOMI ROHT-ARRIAZA

PENN

University of Pennsylvania Press

Philadelphia

9558402

Copyright © 2005 University of Pennsylvania Press
All rights reserved
Printed in the United States of America on acid-free paper

10 9 8 7 6 5 4 3 2 1

Published by
University of Pennsylvania Press
Philadelphia, Pennsylvania 19104-4011

Library of Congress Cataloging-in-Publication Data

Roht-Arriaza, Naomi.
    The Pinochet effect : transnational justice in the age of human rights / Naomi
Roht-Arriaza.
        p.   cm. (Pennsylvania studies in human rights)
    ISBN 0-8122-3845-1 (cloth : alk. paper)
    Includes bibliographical references and index.
    1. Pinochet Ugarte, Augusto—Trials, litigation, etc.   2. Operación Cóndor (South
American countersubversion association).   3. Human rights—Southern Cone of
South America.   4. Criminal liability (International law).   5. Criminal jurisdiction.
6. Southern Cone of South America—Politics and government—20th century.   I. Title.
II. Series.
KH966.I57 R64   2004
345'.04—dc22   2004055463

Contents

Preface   vii

1. The Beginning   1

2. The Adventures of Augusto Pinochet in the United Kingdom: A "Most Civilized Country"   32

3. The Investigations Come Home to Chile   67

4. Argentina: Truth and Consequences   97

5. The European Cases   118

6. Operation Condor Redux   150

7. The Legal Legacy of Pinochet: Universal Jurisdiction and Its Discontents   170

8. The Actors Behind the *Pinochet* Cases   208

Notes   225

Bibliography   239

Index   247

Acknowledgments   255

Preface

The arrest of Augusto Pinochet in London in October 1998 electrified the world. Pinochet was, after all, a symbol of the dictatorships that had plagued much of the world during the 1970s and 1980s. All that had gone wrong in that era, in Chile and elsewhere, was captured in a photograph. A stern group of officers flanks General Pinochet, in dark glasses and uniform, arms crossed, who stares implacably into the camera, daring anyone to challenge him. That image, flashed across the world, became the dark symbol of a dark era. Maybe that's why, a quarter-century later, it retains its potency. The story of the general's downfall has the same end-of-an-era resonance.

I was a college student when Salvador Allende, a doctor and a Socialist, was elected president of Chile in 1970. His experiment creating democratic socialism came to a bloody end in September 1973. After months of plotting the military staged a coup, supported by opposition political parties, the United States, the business sector and a good part of the Chilean middle class. Allende killed himself as the presidential palace was strafed by the Air Force; Congress was dissolved, the Constitution was suspended, and a military junta ruled by decree. The Junta soon came to be dominated by General Augusto Pinochet, whom Allende had appointed as army chief. Pinochet centralized control, created a separate secret police under his personal jurisdiction, and eventually had himself named President and head of the Armed Forces. Under his dictatorship, some five thousand people were killed, over a thousand detained and disappeared, tens of thousands were imprisoned and tortured or forced into exile. After the first years of dictatorship, the crimes became more selective. Requests to the courts for writs of habeus corpus routinely went unanswered. Families were told that their loved ones had no doubt left the country, taken new lovers, been mowed down in military confrontations or internecine squabbles of the left. Fear clamped down on Chile. Those who were killed, it was said, had deserved what they got; their families were shunned, neighbors divided, the press silenced. It lasted, in all, seventeen years.

Many of those who fled the Allende debacle found refuge, at first, in neighboring Argentina. But soon, and especially after 1975, the Argentine military took power and began its own campaign of terror. Not content to crush the country's armed insurgencies, they too struck at a broad swath of Argentine society, including left-wing supporters of ex-president Juan Perón, students, professionals, exiles from other Latin American regimes, and anyone who seemed to get in the way. In the end, over 30,000 died, most of them taken away to secret detention centers and camps, tortured, tossed still alive from airplanes into the sea or shot and buried in unmarked graves. Pregnant women gave birth manacled and blindfolded, and were then killed and their babies given to military families. Jews were marked for especially sadistic treatment. The terror eventually engulfed the entire Southern Cone of Latin America, as the militarized regimes of Chile, Argentina, Uruguay, Paraguay, Bolivia, and Brazil coordinated their efforts to find and destroy opponents through Operation Condor, sending dissidents found in one country to another to disappear. Operation Condor was led by Manuel Contreras, Pinochet's secret police chief.

Argentina and Chile eventually reverted to civilian rule, in 1986 and 1990 respectively. The Raúl Alfonsín government in Argentina commissioned a group of notables headed by writer Ernesto Sábato (also known as CONADEP) to report on the fate of the disappeared. Their report, *Nunca Más* (*Never Again*) established the existence of more than three hundred death camps, the names of the disappeared and the geography of terror. It was a best-seller in Argentina. Alfonsín turned to the military courts, believing that the armed forces could purge their own, but after a year of stonewalling the civilian courts took over cases against the military brass. Nine members of the ruling juntas were tried for crimes including torture and murder. Efforts to reach further down into the military ranks ran into threats of mutiny from disgruntled officers. So Alfonsín, afraid of jeopardizing a fragile transition, backed off. He passed laws limiting the time within which prosecutions could be brought. When those laws didn't sufficiently placate a restive military, he followed up with a "due obedience" law that made it practically impossible to indict any but a handful of top officers. The final insult came when his successor, Carlos Menem, in 1990 pardoned the junta leaders along with the few others who were still subject to prosecution.

In Chile, before leaving government the military had exacted a constitutional scheme that reserved a key role for them. The arrangement reserved a percentage of foreign exchange for the military, retained Pinochet as armed forces chief until 1997, and then made him a senator for life along with other nonelected senators. The incoming Aylwin government did not even try prosecutions. Chastened by the Argentine experience, Patricio Aylwin promised the truth, "and as much justice as possible." His Truth and Reconciliation Commission published a three-volume report that included the names of known victims of the dictatorship along with what could be discovered about their fate. But the report named no names of those responsible, and the Commission got little help from the military in finding out what had happened. Although Aylwin encouraged the courts to make use of information passed on to them by the Commission or from other sources, he did not try to overturn a military self-amnesty that immunized them from prosecution for crimes committed before 1978—the bulk of the military's crimes. Rather, he focused on reparations payments to victims, and took the then unparalleled step of publicly apologizing, in the name of the Chilean state, for the crimes committed in its name.

By the mid-1990s, both countries' governments were anxious to move on. Both saw continuing concerns about the disappeared and their children, and about justice for the victimizers, as distractions from the beckoning issues of economic growth and global integration. The human rights movements that had sustained family members and social activists through years of dictatorship were at a loss, reduced in numbers, unable to impose their agenda, and unsure how to combine demands about an accounting of the past with attention to current injustices. The international community, for whom Chile and Argentina were the poster children of repressive regimes during the 1970s, called off its scrutiny and reestablished the flow of loans and trade. The Chilean "economic miracle" was held up as a model for the developing world. No suggestion of ad hoc UN Criminal Tribunals here. A controlled and limited transition from dictatorship to democracy, based on pacts among elites, partial truths, and very partial justice, seemed to have become the template for other Latin American countries, and even for other continents. End of story.

Or was it? What was the road from there to Pinochet's 1998 arrest, and beyond? I set off to find out.

Argentina and Chile were only the first of a parade of countries struggling with the dilemmas of "transitional justice," as it has come to be called. There were the ex-Soviet bloc states, with their extensive secret police files and networks of informers to be exposed and their waves of property seizures to sort out. Soon after, negotiated settlements of long-simmering civil conflicts in El Salvador and Guatemala included UN-sponsored truth commissions, charged with investigating the pattern of (mostly) military atrocities over the preceding decade. In both countries, the "truth" combined with an almost total lack of justice. The Salvadoran legislature passed a broad amnesty three days after the distinguished UN-appointed truth commissioners found the army had carried out hundreds of atrocities. The Guatemalans did little better. A mixed commission of national and foreign dignitaries found that the army had committed acts of genocide against the Mayan population, but its recommendations so far mostly gather dust.

In the mid-1990s, South Africa's formula for transition was heavily influenced by the lessons from the Southern Cone. A Truth and Reconciliation Commission would receive victims' testimony in public hearings and write a report on gross human rights violations committed during the apartheid years. The TRC took statements from more than 21,000 people. Unlike the Southern Cone commissions, it could issue subpoenas and name perpetrators. Unlike any other commission, it could also grant amnesty from prosecution for those who came forward, confessed publicly, and convinced a quasi-judicial panel that their crimes had been politically motivated. Those potential amnesty applicants who remained silent were subject to criminal prosecution. The idea was to get low-level officers to fill in the chain of command, and to focus limited court resources on the unrepentant. The results were mixed: few members of the security forces came forward to the Amnesty committee of the TRC, but those that did provided new information on the fate of victims and the policies of the regime that would have been unlikely to emerge otherwise.

The South African experiment, in turn, spawned its own round of variants on transitional justice, in Nigeria and Peru and Iraq. Country after country moving out of a period of war or repression needed to confront the demons of the past without jeopardizing the possibility of living together in the present or of stability for the future. Although each country found its own path, over time a trend emerged. From a willingness at the beginning of the 1990s to accept amnesia as the price of future peace came an understanding, by the end of the decade, that peace without a reckoning with the past was merely an interlude between conflicts.

The conflicts in the former Yugoslavia and in Rwanda hastened that understanding. The nightly TV images of emaciated concentration camp inmates, reports of mass rapes and ethnic cleansing of whole areas, in the Europe that had sworn "never again," produced public pressure on western countries to act, but both the U.S. and European countries were reluctant to send ground troops. So the United Nations International Criminal Tribunal on the Former Yugoslavia was born. The Security Council resolution establishing the Tribunal declared that the member states believed that its creation would "contribute to the restoration and maintenance of peace" and to "ensuring that . . . violations are halted and effectively redressed." A tall order for a court that had no marshal service or police backing to find or arrest suspects. A year later, a three-month killing spree, carried out by militias armed mostly with machetes and hoes, left more than three quarters of a million people dead in Rwanda. The Security Council decided to establish a similar tribunal; to do otherwise after the Yugoslav precedent would seem callous or even racist.

As the tribunals got underway, they raised dozens of new legal questions, and helped develop the body of international criminal law articulated at the post-World War II Nuremburg tribunals. The question of *international* justice became even more important when, in July 1998, 120 countries created an International Criminal Court to try cases of genocide, crimes against humanity, and war crimes. The court, which will be permanently available and not limited to cases referred by the Security Council, opened its doors on July 1, 2002.

Questions of how much justice is enough, and for whom, are profoundly troubling in post-conflict settings. The questions are not only legal, they implicate our ideas about expiation of sin, reconciliation, forgiveness, and judgment. They touch our views of history, who makes it, who gets to write it, what gets left out, and how the currents of historiography mutate over time. They speak to the balance between responsibility and expediency of political leaders. They challenge us, in the context of globalized economies and communications, to compare domestic, foreign and international venues for truth or for justice. And, most profoundly, they confront the anger, the profound unhealable hurt, at times the obsession of those who suffered the most, not to let those responsible get off without an accounting.

I have lived through civil conflict and repression. The anger I feel watching the ex-Generals responsible for all those deaths and all that suffering live unrepentant lives of comfort and prestige is almost overwhelming. At the same time, I am a lawyer, and believe that simply lining the criminals up against the wall and shooting them solves nothing, for me or for wartorn societies. It's a public accounting I want, the list of crimes, and of victims, read out in the dock, the defendant forced to hear the awful evidence, to hear sentence pronounced by a duly constituted, legitimate, impartial court of law. In my own case, I began channeling the anger into a search for legal constraints on impunity. Then something surprising happened.

On October 16, 1998, Scotland Yard detectives arrested General Pinochet at the London Clinic, where he was recovering from back surgery. Pinochet would spend the next eighteen months fighting his extradition to Spain, where a judge had charged him with genocide, terrorism, and torture, all committed in Chile two decades before. When he was finally released, ostensibly on grounds of ill health, he would return to a different country, in a different world.

Never again could dictators find refuge in their official position to excuse them from charges of torturing and killing their own people.

The venerable British House of Lords, in two separate decisions, found that Pinochet could be extradited to Spain to stand trial for his crimes. A 1984 treaty committed all the countries involved to either prosecute alleged torturers or turn them over to someone who would; this was the first time it had been used to extradite a suspect to a country other than his own to stand trial. With the *Pinochet* precedent, human rights treaties like the 1984 Convention Against Torture took on new teeth. Long seen as well-intentioned but hollow declarations, they became *real*, able, at least for a time, to put people behind bars for heinous crimes of state. By 2001, there were at least half a dozen proceedings pending in different national courts against current or former heads of state, and more against various torturers and *génocidaires*.

This is the story of that transformation, from the mid-1990s until 2003. I have started with the beginnings of the *Pinochet* saga in Spain and the companion Argentine and Chilean investigations. I recount how the cases were put together, and the stories of some of the main actors. I try to give a sense of how legal strategy is plotted, the arguments lost and won, the ways it could have been and the way it finally was. The action then shifts to Britain with Pinochet's London detention and the House of Lords hearings. I follow the ever-spreading ripples of the investigation back to Chile and Argentina and show how human rights-related investigations, prosecutions, and initiatives blossomed in the wake of the detention. I trace the spreading ripple effects through the rest of the Southern Cone and to Mexico, Belgium, France, Germany, Italy, and the United States. Finally, I look at the subsequent evolution of the idea of universal jurisdiction, which gives the courts of any country authority to investigate and judge international crimes no matter where committed and by whom. A final chapter draws some lessons of the *Pinochet*-related litigation for social theory.

The book is based on several years of research. I have traveled to Spain, Italy, Mexico, Belgium, France, and the UK and interviewed many (but not all) of the main participants in these events, some of them several times. I spent the first half of 2000 living in Chile, observing Pinochet's return to the country, and his subsequent domestic legal woes, first hand. I have spent weeks at a time in Argentina, talking to lawyers, activists, and judges, and have observed some of the European hearings as well. I have combined my own observations and interviews with archival research, newspaper and book-length journalists' accounts, scholarly writings and the texts of the indictments and court cases themselves. Some of the material was straightforward; in other places I have picked my way as best I can through a welter of contradictory details and interpretations of events. All the translations are mine unless otherwise noted.

In the end, it is always individuals who make history. These stories are full of the efforts of ordinary—and extraordinary—people who gave up nights and weekends, put themselves into debt, found ways to travel thousands of miles, ignored the skepticism of colleagues and experts, and kept going in the face of delays and setbacks. People like Joan Garcés, who as a twenty-year-old political advisor to President Allende left the burning presidential palace in 1973 as military bombs engulfed it in flames. A quarter century later, Garcés was the Spanish lawyer who brought the complaint against Pinochet. Or like Alcira Rios, a survivor of the Argentine death camps, who now represents the Grandmothers of the Plaza de Mayo in their efforts to jail the abductors of their grand-children. Or again like Baltazar Garzón, the Spanish investigating judge, whose tenacity and ingenuity allowed the investigations to develop. The book is dedicated to these individuals and thousands more like them around the world, who have never given up on justice.

Chapter 1

The Beginning

The Trip

General Augusto Pinochet really wanted to travel. During his seventeen years as head of Chile's military government, he had only been able to make two long trips abroad. Both had been disasters. When Spanish dictator Francisco Franco died in 1975, he had flown to Spain for the funeral, his first trip to Europe. His Spanish hosts gave him forty-eight hours to leave the country. In 1980 he flew to visit fellow dictator Ferdinand Marcos of the Philippines, but at the first stop, Fiji, he had trouble disembarking because the airport workers' unions refused to move the stairs into place. The next day it got worse: the plane had to turn around when Marcos, under pressure, rescinded the invitation. Since stepping down as president, he had made short trips abroad for shopping and business reasons—the family has been persistently tied to arms dealing in news reports—but none had lasted more than a few days. He had a permanent invitation from Margaret Thatcher to make an extended visit to England, a place he considered among the world's most civilized.

The opportunity for a longer trip presented itself in October 1998. A herniated disc in his back required surgery, and a trip to the exclusive London Clinic seemed just the thing. He could combine a medical visit with a little shopping in Paris, see old friends, and pursue an invitation from the Royal Ordnance company to look into arms purchases. What is more, none of the doctors at the Military Hospital in Santiago seemed eager to perform the operation. "Nobody wanted to operate here, because if they botched the operation or he died it would mean their military career," Verónica Reyes of the Chilean legal aid group FASIC recounted. "Some of his doctors even offered to bring in British specialists to operate here, but he didn't want that." He wanted to travel.

There was a single, slight worry in the back of his mind, however. Two years earlier, in June 1996, a criminal complaint had been filed in a Spanish court accusing him, along with most of the military high command and their civilian allies, of genocide, terrorism, and torture. The Chilean press had duly reported the suit, but no one seemed to give it much chance of success—another harebrained leftist scheme, was the general opinion. Nevertheless, Pinochet had asked his lawyers about the risks. Both the Foreign Ministry lawyer and his own family attorney urged him not to go in light of the Spanish investigation. The military lawyer, however, had been to Spain to see about the case and thought otherwise. His view, that no law of a faraway land could touch the powerful senator-for-life, prevailed. Perhaps his advice was a fitting metaphor for the military's disdain for civilian institutions, sense of its own power, and refusal to see how much the post-cold war world had changed.

In any case, on September 23, 1998, Pinochet flew to London. It would be 503 days before he would see Chile again.

The First Complainant

Carlos Castresana wasn't thinking about Augusto Pinochet in March 1996. He wasn't thinking about Chile at all, but about its neighbor, Argentina. Castresana was a Spanish anti-corruption prosecutor and head of the Union of Progressive Prosecutors (UFP), a professional association. With the twenty-year anniversary of the March 24, 1976 Argentine coup, no chance of prosecutions in Argentina, and a twenty-year statute of limitations on crimes in Spain, Castresana decided someone had to do something. "I watched the news of hundreds of thousands of demonstrators against impunity in Buenos Aires, and the thought that soon those torturers would be beyond the reach of the law here as well as in Argentina made me indignant," he recalled. Castresana, a mild-mannered, soft-spoken type, scoured the Spanish law books looking for a legal hook. He remembered an obscure statute, previously used in drug-dealing cases, that allowed Spanish courts jurisdiction over non-Spaniards for crimes committed abroad. On March 28, Castresana presented a criminal complaint to the Spanish national court, Audiencia Nacional, based on names of victims he had gleaned from press reports and those of Amnesty International and other human rights groups. The complaint named 38 Spanish victims, and accused Generals Jorge Videla and Antonio Bussi, Admiral Emilio Massera, and a number of lower-ranking well-known torturers as perpetrators. It charged them with genocide against a national group, terrorism, air piracy (for illegal death flights over the ocean—a charge later dropped), illegal detention, disappearances and child kidnappings.

March 24, 1996 was a Sunday. Castresana presented his complaint to the judge on call for the weekend, Baltazar Garzón of the Fifth Chamber of the Audiencia Nacional. Normally, cases fall to the judge who receives them. Because the events described happened outside the time in which he was on call, Garzón accepted the case but turned it over to the chief judge to be reassigned by lot. By sheer chance, it came back to him. "I didn't look for this case," Garzón told Spanish journalist Pilar Urbano. "I had plenty to do at that moment. But a judge deals with the cases that come before him."[1] And now a potentially explosive one had come his way.

Baltazar Garzón was well known to Spaniards at the time as, variously, a fearless Elliot Ness, a publicity hound, a turncoat to his party, a super-judge. Born in 1955 in Jaén, the hot, dry, poor hinterland of southwestern Spain, Garzón at one point studied to be a priest. His father ran a gas station. Upon graduating from law school, he married his high school sweetheart; they have three children. Garzón began working as a provincial judge, and in 1988 took up his current position in the Audiencia Nacional. He is a big-living sort, partial to bullfights, soccer tournaments (he plays goalie), and flamenco. In 1993, he briefly detoured into national politics, winning office on the Socialist party slate after Socialist leaders agreed to clean up the party and root out the corruption that was eating away at its integrity and popularity. He quit less than a year later, feeling used and disgusted at the continuing scandals. He has been a political adversary of Socialist party ex-president Felipe González ever since.

The Audiencia's role in Spain's decentralized trial court system is to deal with cases relating to more than one province; treason, piracy, aircraft hijacking, and other international offenses; and complex or serious smuggling, money laundering, or drug cases. It sits in a single high-security building in central Madrid, with six chambers. Garzón's large office includes a comfortable couch, desk, and a photograph of his colleague public prosecutor Carmen Tagle, killed by Basque separatist ETA (Euzkadi Ta Askatasuna) members as she worked on a case.

Over the years, the judge has made more enemies than any one person should have, and, as a result he has more bodyguards than any one person should need. He has investigated drug, arms, and money laundering rings stretching from Syria to Argentina to Spain and back again. His decades-long investigation of the financing and organization of ETA led to the arrests of many top ETA leaders, who have publicly threatened to kill him. He was the first Spanish judge to travel to France to interrogate ETA leaders detained there, and the first to investigate the financing of ETA terrorism and the links between ETA and its aboveground political supporters. He is adamant that ETA is not a liberation movement but a criminal, terrorist group to be smashed. His hard line on ETA has given him an aura of heroism among many ordinary Spaniards, especially as the group has stepped up its terror tactics over the last few years. He has also investigated the activities of anti-ETA death squads run by the Socialist Party government. He prosecuted high ranking members of the Socialist government, including the interior minister, for sponsoring the death squads, known by their Spanish acronym GAL (Grupo Antiterrorista de Liberación), a move widely credited with helping push the Socialists out of office. He is no friend of the conservative Popular Party either, and has investigated businessmen close to the party leadership for corruption. He is active in international anti-drug and anti-money laundering efforts, as well as in efforts to protect indigenous peoples. After September 11, 2001, he was the judge charged with investigating Al-Qaeda suspects found in Spain.

Joan Garcés read about the filing of the Argentine case buried in the interior pages of the newspaper. Garcés was a young academic from Valencia when he arrived in Santiago in 1970, enchanted by Chile's vibrant democracy. Through a twist of fate, he met Salvador Allende, then chairman of the Senate. When Allende became Chile's Socialist president later in 1970, Garcés became his political advisor, working in La Moneda presidential palace directly with the president. When the coup came, he was one of the last to leave the embattled president's side. He only left the palace, minutes before it was bombed and Allende died, when the president told him to escape because "someone has to tell the world what happened here." He walked out unarmed, which probably saved his life. After hiding in Santiago for two days, he made it to the Spanish ambassador's residence, and eventually returned to Europe.

Garcés is now in his mid-fifties, a professorial man with a mild demeanor and a mustache that makes him look a little like the photos of Allende. He is given to tweed jackets and speeches peppered with erudite references to French political philosophy and seventeenth-century history. He spent several years teaching political science at Paris's most prestigious university, writing books about Chile, geopolitics, and the significance of the end of the Cold War. There followed a stint in Washington at the Institute of Policy Studies, where Orlando Letelier (the Chilean ex-ambassador assassinated in 1976) had worked.

Garcés and his Chilean-born wife returned to Madrid when they realized they wanted their children to grow up speaking Spanish. He eventually established a relatively prosperous law practice. One of his specialties as a lawyer was defending people who were wanted for extradition. He learned the ins and outs of extradition law, including one case where he successfully applied Spain's new law on universal jurisdiction. He stopped doing extradition cases by 1986, focusing instead on a general civil and criminal law practice. His practice was thriving, but he always kept in touch with events in Chile and remembered Allende's last request. Castresana's complaint in the Argentine case precipitated Garcés's phone call to the Union of Progressive Prosecutors, whose president, Miguel Miravet, was also from the eastern city of Valencia. They agreed to hold off with another complaint to see what Garzón would do. They also wanted to see whether the Chilean courts would allow investigation into Spanish diplomat Carmelo Soria's death (soon after, the Chilean Supreme Court closed that investigation). In July, three months after Castresana filed his complaint, and days after Judge Garzón declared his jurisdiction proper in the Argentine case, his colleagues at the Association of Progressive Prosecutors in Valencia filed a similar complaint against Pinochet and the military and civilian command of his dictatorship. This time the case was assigned, again by lottery, to Judge Manuel García-Castellón.

The Argentine Complaint

Spanish law is peculiarly well suited for pursuing criminal complaints brought by ordinary citizens. In the U.S., criminal charges must be brought by a government prosecutor, who can decide whether or not to bring charges after investigating, no matter what the wishes of the victim of the crime. If a prosecutor decides not to press charges, there is little the victim can do. In Spain, not only can victims bring a complaint directly to an investigating magistrate and ask him to pursue it, but the victim then becomes a party to the case and is able to follow the course of the investigation and any subsequent trial. Even if the public prosecutor disagrees, if the victim can convince the investigating magistrate that there is a valid case, that's good enough. The public prosecutor and the investigating judge usually work hand-in-hand to look into and prepare the case, but sometimes (as in this case) the public prosecutor can take an independent or even adversarial role with respect to the judge. Plaintiffs can pursue civil damages in the course of the proceedings, and they rarely bring separate civil cases where criminal behavior is at issue. It's much easier (and cheaper!) to get the investigating magistrate to do much of the evidence gathering.

Even more expansive, Spain has very broad rules allowing people who are not directly connected to an alleged crime to file complaints. These "popular accusers" have to be reputable nongovernmental groups concerned with the public interest. They can file complaints, become party to cases, and even have privileged access to the files and an ability to intervene at many stages of the proceedings. The investigating judge acts as a prosecutor, interviewing witnesses and possible defendants, assembling documents, and deciding whether or not there's enough evidence to charge particular individuals with particular crimes. Only after all the evidence is assembled and indictments are issued does the case move forward to a second, trial phase. The actual trial, which unlike those in some other European countries requires the presence of the defendant, is held before a three-judge panel (not including the investigating judge), and witnesses must testify again, with the defendant able to cross-examine as well as testify himself.

The implications of this arrangement are profound. Complainants have much wider latitude than in the U.S. to go forward. There is no need to have individual victims as complainants, avoiding worries that family members back home in Argentina or Chile could be harassed (or worse). And complainants don't need any help from the executive branch of government at the beginning. Even if the political branches are opposed to beginning an investigation, so long as there's an investigating judge who will go forward that will be good enough. The state prosecutor is free to challenge the judge's decision before a higher court. Meanwhile, witnesses can be called, requests sent abroad, indictments and arrest orders issued, and the Foreign Ministry is mandated to forward the judge's requests to other governments. To do otherwise would unjustifiably interfere with the independence of the judge, a hallmark of a democratic system.

Castresana's complaint began with a recounting of the outlines of the repression in Argentina. He recalled the tens of thousands of disappeared, killed and imprisoned. He listed 340 secret detention camps. He focused especially on the Navy Mechanics School (ESMA), where up to 4,500 people were killed and at one point 14 electroshock torture chambers operated simultaneously, and on the provinces of Buenos Aires, Córdoba, and Tucumán. He named those publicly responsible for military activities in those areas, those who ran the detention camps, and other well-known torturers. He mentioned some 500 children, born in captivity or kidnapped with their parents, who were later adopted by military-related families and their real identities hidden. Two subsequent revisions added more facts and victims, focusing on those born in Spain or of Spanish parents. For most cases, the complaint listed only the name, origin, age, and the circumstances of the person's detention. For all these crimes, he concluded, no one is now serving time; the Punto Final and Due Obedience laws in Argentina have foreclosed punishment there.

Castresana's complaint argued that the Spanish courts had jurisdiction under Spanish law over the crimes of the Argentine military officers, even though they were committed in Argentina and against Argentines. He cited Article 23.4 of the Organic Law of State Power, which allows for prosecution of certain crimes committed by non-Spaniards outside Spain, including genocide, terrorism, and other crimes recognized in international treaties ratified by the Spanish government. Article 23.4 was incorporated into Spanish criminal law in 1985, but an earlier version went back to the 1870s. Thus, while both the complaint and the decision accepting it used international law liberally in justifying the court's ability to exercise its power, the case was firmly grounded in Spanish national law.

How could a court have power to try people who were not even present in Spain, for crimes committed in far-off countries, against mostly non-Spaniards? This question goes to the heart of the changes in international law over the last half century. Generally speaking, courts have always had jurisdiction over crimes committed in their territory (the territoriality principle), by their citizens abroad (the nationality principle), or by others who affect the country's national interests (currency counterfeiters, for instance—the protective principle).

Beyond these widely accepted bases, the age-old rule was that, in general, courts had no power to act outside their own territory—it was the sovereign power over their territory that gave states the right to exercise power over individuals in the first place. Any other rule would undermine state sovereignty and lead to chaos. Even so, there have long been two other possible situations in which courts can act. One involves cases where citizens of the country have been the victims of a crime, known somewhat curiously as "passive personality" jurisdiction (as opposed to active personality or nationality jurisdiction). The other potential jurisdictional grounding, universal jurisdiction, is the most controversial. Under this type of jurisdiction, the connection to the prosecuting state is not made through any particular connection of the state to the criminal event, but rather to the nature of the crime itself. Certain crimes are so universally agreed to be heinous, so potentially disruptive of international peace, and so difficult for any one state to adequately prosecute, that all states have the right to try anyone accused of them.

The emblematic case, until recently, of universal jurisdiction, was the trial of Adolf Eichmann in Jerusalem. Eichmann had made the Nazi death trains run on time, organizing the massive deportations of Jews and others to death camps. He had escaped from Germany after the war, and in 1960 he was kidnapped from his Argentine refuge by Israeli agents and tried for "crimes against the Jewish people" in an Israeli court, the court of a state that had not existed when the crimes were committed. The universality of the Eichmann case was always ambiguous: he was convicted of both crimes against humanity (including the deportation of Poles, Slovenes, and Roma) and crimes against the Jewish people.[2] Nonetheless, states generally acquiesced in the Eichmann prosecution, although they had doubts about the legality of kidnapping.

In the years following, there were few prosecutions in national courts based solely on the universality principle. A number of the treaties created after World War II to deter international crimes did involve a type of universal jurisdiction. The 1949 Geneva Conventions on war crimes, for instance, provide that the courts of any party must try suspects accused of certain war crimes or extradite them to somewhere that will. Later conventions on other crimes of international concern, like air piracy, hijacking, taking of hostages, and the like, also committed any country that found a defendant on its territory to extradite or prosecute. In 1984, as we will see later, the Convention Against Torture did the same. Some states also allow universal jurisdiction, under certain circumstances, over ordinary crimes like murder and kidnapping. More than a hundred and twenty countries, according to an Amnesty International study, now provide for a form of universal jurisdiction over at least some crimes. But the model was not embraced everywhere: the 1948 Genocide Convention, for instance, only provided the courts of the place where the crime took place, or an international criminal court, with the ability to try suspects. This limitation, explained further on, would vex the Spanish courts.[3]

The crimes of the Argentine military, Castresana argued, constituted genocide against a national group, which was prohibited under both Spanish and international law. They further constituted acts of terrorism, part of a common plan carried out by armed bands belonging to the state, and as such a violation of article 174 bis (b) of the Spanish Penal Code. Spanish courts were not limited by the Argentine amnesty laws. It was important to file the complaint at that moment, Castresana added, because it was just about twenty years after the reign of terror began, and the statute of limitations for serious crimes in Spain is generally twenty years. He asked to be able to add more events and potential defendants later; for now, he asked the judge to begin an investigation. The whole complaint was some ten pages long.

Of course, none of the Argentine military in the original complaint were then to be found in Spain. But an investigating magistrate could look into the acts, and eventually issue international judicial assistance requests and arrest warrants and ask for their extradition. Even if Argentina ignored or denied the warrants (as all agreed was likely), the case would still serve several goals: it would bring attention to the crimes of the defendants, increase pressure within Argentina to take some action against them, allow the victims to tell a judge their story, and create a more complete factual record. It would also keep the defendants from spending their retirement going on shopping sprees to Europe and elsewhere, turning Argentina into a vast open-air prison. Even that much would bring some measure of satisfaction. In 1996, General Pinochet's detention in London seemed the sheerest fantasy.

Gregorio Dionis, an Argentine economist living outside Madrid, was surprised to see a small story about the lawsuit in the local paper. A group of Argentine exiles in Madrid had been discussing the possibility of a lawsuit with visiting members of Argentine human rights groups, especially SERPAJ, the Peace and Justice Service group headed by Nobel Prize winner Adolfo Pérez Esquivel. Laura Bonaparte, a member of the Mothers of the Plaza de Mayo, the white-kerchiefed women who had for twenty years walked around the main square of Buenos Aires demanding the return of their disappeared children, had visited Madrid in 1995, sponsored by Amnesty International. After her visit, Dionis, together with another Argentine exile, labor lawyer Carlos Slepoy, and a few others had reactivated the Argentine Human Rights Association in Madrid, and begun discussing possible strategies for a trial. In February 1996 they held a conference on impunity in Latin America, where ideas flew back and forth.

Dionis had left Argentina in the early 1970s after finding, by chance, secret documents that tied the Argentine navy to the impending Chilean coup and to U.S. navy exploration of the Argentine continental shelf. These discoveries had led navy officials to try to kill him. In Spain, he ran a web-based human rights news and documents service focused on Latin America from his living room. Slepoy had also seen his share of trouble: after graduating from law school, he was detained in 1976 in a street roundup of student activists. He was taken to the notorious Navy Mechanics School and other torture centers, where he spent twenty months before being exiled to Spain. Once there, he developed a labor law practice. In 1982, a drunk Madrid police officer shot him when he interfered in the cop's abuse of a group of street children. The bullet tore through his spinal cord, leaving him with a heavy limp and unable to walk far. The two men had very different temperaments: Dionis saw political conspiracies everywhere, and had a well-honed sense of strategy; Slepoy was sunnier and a visionary, even a bit of a dreamer. These two men, allies at the start, ended up espousing different strategies and paths for the Spanish trials. Their growing personal animosity would make everyone's life more complicated. But both played key roles in the subsequent litigation.

Carlos Castresana of the Prosecutors' Union caught both men by surprise. Who was Castresana anyway? According to Dionis, some of the names in the complaint were misspelled, others could not be found in the Sábato Commission's *Nunca Más* or on any other list, the dates were wrong, as were some of the facts. A premature and badly done complaint, he thought, could only be aimed at sabotaging the case under preparation. The coincidence was just too much. But now that the die was cast, the human rights activists scrambled. As Carlos Slepoy recalls: "Castresana wasn't in contact with anyone. We went to see him, to find out what he was up to. He was very happy to see us." From that point forward, the Argentine exile group and Castresana worked together.

A team was quickly assembled in Argentina to sift through the complaint and correct the errors. Among them were Ana Chávez of SERPAJ, Graciela Lois and Mabel Gutiérrez of Family Members of the Disappeared in Argentina (Familiares), and Horacio Ravenna of the Permanent Association of Human Rights (APDH). Amended complaints, adding additional Spanish citizens and Argentines descended from Spanish citizens, were filed on April 9 and 16. On April 10, the Association of Free Lawyers (Asociación Libre de Abogados, ALA—the progressive alternative to the Madrid Bar Association) joined the complaint. The ALA lawyer, José Luís Galán, brought to the legal team expert knowledge of Spanish criminal law and experience bringing cases against police misconduct and the operation of death squads against Basque separatists. He joined Carlos Slepoy, Dionis (a business manager by training), and a team from the Izquierda Unida (the United Left, IU) political party. Fran Pérez and Isabelo Herreros ran the party's Human Rights Secretariat while Angel García Castillejo was the party's lawyer. A subsequent addition to the team, Enrique Santiago, son of a Spanish Guardia Civil, had a small legal practice representing cooperatives and refugees. There were other early supporters: Carlos Nieto, a young Spanish judge interested in international law who was a member of Judges for Democracy, put on seminars and training sessions in international law for his fellow judges. Marga Durán, a gravel-voiced, chain-smoking, no-nonsense woman in her sixties whose husband was a NASA scientist, brought in the local Amnesty International group. The local AI group, in turn, brought in Federico Andreu, of Amnesty International's central office. Andreu, a Colombian-born legal expert, provided expertise in international criminal law.

So it was that the Union of Progressive Prosecutors, the United Left Party, the Association of Free Lawyers, and the Argentine Human Rights Association of Madrid became the "popular accusation" in the nascent Argentine litigation. A number of individual family members of victims and victims themselves would later sign on as individual complainants. Throughout the summer of 1996, the plaintiffs' lawyers added names to the list of victims. By October there were almost 300 cases, almost all of Spanish descent. Around 30 had been born in Spain and moved to Argentina, others were spouses, children, or grandchildren of Spaniards (like Italy, Spain allows descendants of Spanish citizens to maintain dual Spanish nationality under some circumstances). The work of compiling Spanish-origin victims had to some extent already been done: in 1982, a Spanish congressional committee had investigated the disappearances of Spanish subjects in Latin America, finding hundreds of cases. By

October too, the list began expanding beyond victims with ties to Spain, to encompass the tens of thousands of Argentines killed or disappeared during the junta years. But this presented its own set of dilemmas.

"We argued a lot about the proper legal strategy," says Dionis, and Slepoy agrees. The issues were related: what was the proper basis for asking the courts to act, and how wide or narrow should the litigation be drawn?

The first question was key: how to get a Spanish court to accept the idea that it could investigate cases involving Argentine defendants, who committed crimes in Argentina, against both Argentines and Spaniards? The only possibility under Spanish law was to base the suit on universal jurisdiction, which allows courts in any country to hear cases involving certain very limited—and very awful—crimes. Although the lawyers agreed that this was the only possible legal avenue open, they disagreed about the implications. For one group, the case had to be grounded in Spanish penal law, utilizing local precedents and codes, in order to be taken seriously by a Spanish judge. They focused on specific murders and torture cases, and looked for models to earlier cases in France and Italy that charged Argentine military officers with crimes against French and Italian citizens respectively. For others, the key was to focus on the international law that makes certain crimes—genocide, crimes against humanity, torture, disappearance, and a few others—subjects of international concern. They wanted the focus to be on the overall plan or "criminal conspiracy." They looked for models to Nuremberg.

Another bone of contention was the scope of the case. For some, the case should be about creating an overall picture of the magnitude of the Argentine disaster—bringing as many victims as possible to testify, without distinctions between those Argentines descended from Spaniards and those who were not. After all, the repression had made no such distinctions, and the bulk of the victims were simply Argentines. It would distort the historical case to focus just on one subset of people, and a major goal of the case, at least at the beginning, was to compile a broad historical record. Especially if one didn't think the case would get far in the courts, it was important to put on the best possible case in the court of public opinion. Creating a compelling public record early on would increase pressure on the government not to close the investigation down. That meant bringing in as many victims as possible, presenting hundreds of witnesses, and emphasizing the sheer breadth of the military's crimes.

No, argued other lawyers, broadening the case too much would make it flabby and unmanageable. First, even though the legal basis of the case was not primarily the victims' nationality, it was important both legally and politically to ground it in a Spanish context. Legally, the

Spanish constitution requires judges to do justice for Spanish citizens, which might make an investigating judge more willing to take on what was likely to be an unconventional, difficult and time-consuming case. Moreover, a judge who needed to explain to colleagues or the public why Spain had any business getting involved in far-off, long-ago events would have an easier time of it if he could point to Spanish victims as well as relying on more abstract legal principles. Conversely, the political branches of government would find it more difficult to explain why Spanish courts shouldn't be getting involved, when Spanish citizens had been hurt. It was this political imperative, not any legal requirement, which eventually led to an initial focus on the Spanish victims.

"Españolización" of the case had two corollaries. First, it was better to concentrate on preparing evidence on a small number of crimes, and doing it really well, rather than to try to encompass the whole scope of the Junta's activities. What was needed was to focus on the existence of a criminal conspiracy, involving elements of the army, navy, air force, and police, which permeated the military structure. If the investigation could produce evidence of how the conspiracy worked, and who was in it, it would contribute to the store of historical knowledge now being compiled and make a repeat performance more difficult. This strategy would rely on fewer victim witnesses and pay more attention to lines of command and control. It also fit in nicely with a focus on international criminal law. After all, a good part of the Nuremberg prosecutions had been aimed at showing the existence of criminal organizations within the German state.

Second, the case had to involve a Spanish political party in the proceedings. Dionis, SERPAJ, and others arguing for this view were motivated by analysis of the earlier experience of Italian colleagues, whom they had met through conferences on impunity. For years they had seen cases involving Argentine victims of Italian descent languish in local courts because there was no political will to crank up the investigation. (That eventually changed: the story is told in Chapter 5.) There had to be a domestic political constituency, or the slightest political pressure might be enough to ruin everything. Two candidates seemed feasible: the Socialist Party and the United Left (IU). The Socialist Party, then in power for fourteen years under the leadership of Felipe González, was suffering through a series of corruption scandals and defections and showed no interest in supporting a case that might jeopardize commercial relations with Latin America. That left the United Left, at the time trying to figure out how to increase its meager base. After a series of meetings with party leadership and lawyers, IU signed on as co-plaintiff. Dionis took a job in the party's human rights secretariat. In an uneasy coalition with Slepoy and his team, they began putting together the evidence and witness lists they would present to Judge Garzón.

Like the Argentine, the Chilean complaint alleged genocide, terrorism, torture, and illegal detention followed by disappearance, all between 1973 and 1990. It was sent to Manuel García-Castellón, another investigating magistrate of the Audiencia Nacional, who accepted the complaint in July. The guiding forces behind the complainants' case were Joan Garcés and Manuel Murillo, a Spanish criminal lawyer, representing the (also Spanish) President Allende Foundation. Chilean human rights organizations, including the Association of Family Members of the Disappeared and of those executed, as well as a number of individual victims, joined as co-complainants.

"The Chilean case from the start was different from the Argentine, in a few ways," Garcés recounts. "First, we had far fewer suspects, never more than thirty. The Argentine case at one point had over a hundred suspects. That's because we focused on a Nuremberg-type strategy. We wanted to get the guys at the top, not the shooters, and we figured that since the court had limited resources to put into investigations, we shouldn't dissipate its energy." Dionis agreed: "The Chileans weren't interested in developing a theory of criminal conspiracy of the military, they wanted to focus on Pinochet and his group." He thought they were worried about antagonizing the Chilean Socialist Party, which at the time was a likely contender for the presidency (Socialist Ricardo Lagos became president in 2000).

Strategy wasn't just a matter of preference. The different structures of repression also counseled different investigative tacks. The repression in Chile had been centralized, with clear lines of command from Pinochet through the military and, eventually, the secret police (known first as the DINA and, as of 1978, as the CNI). The head of the DINA, Manuel Contreras, had boasted that he breakfasted every day with Pinochet to keep him abreast of progress in the fight against subversion, and Pinochet himself had remarked that not a leaf moved in Chile without his knowledge. In Argentina, in contrast, the country was divided into military zones, and the commanders of each zone had a large degree of autonomy. Each "working group" in charge of detentions within the zone picked its own targets and decided on their fate. So there a broader range of military and police suspects made sense.

"Second, we were far less public with the legal documents," Garcés continued. "We issued summaries, but not the actual documents. The investigating judge also had a far lower profile, and seemed to like it that way. While Judge Garzón issued indictments running into the hundreds of pages, García-Castellón tended to write three paragraphs. According to Fernando Mas, who covered the case for the Spanish and Argentine papers, this made the Chilean investigation maddeningly hard to cover. A third difference, which made the Chilean investigation more agile, was that there was a unified legal team. Garcés and his partner Murillo represented all the complainant organizations and individuals, no matter what their political stripe. The differences of opinion, sniping, and personal antagonisms that took up so much of the Argentine legal teams' time and energy were absent from the Chilean case.

As in the Argentine case, the Chilean complaint included several cases involving Spanish citizens killed or disappeared in Chile. Antonio Llidó and Juan Alsina were Spanish priests. Alsina was detained and shot by the army in September 1973, his body dumped into the Mapocho River that traverses Santiago. Llidó was tortured and disappeared by the DINA in 1974. Members of the Chilean church hierarchy testified in Spain as to the circumstances of their detention. Carmelo Soria was a UN official working in the Santiago offices of the Economic Commission for Latin America. Soria's status as an internationally protected person did not stop the DINA from kidnapping, torturing, and assassinating him in 1976. The Chilean Supreme Court had closed the investigation into his fate on grounds that the case was covered by the amnesty law. García-Castellón got a copy of the case file.

The Spanish Government's Position

Judge Garzón (and soon after, Judge García-Castellón) sent the complaint off to the Public Prosecutor's office for comment, as required under Spanish law. The prosecutor's office in Spain acts as a kind of independent state counsel; according to the constitution, the prosecutor is to "promote the course of justice in defense of the legal order, of the rights of citizens and of the public interest" (art. 124). As the human rights lawyers had feared, the prosecutor was initially inclined to oppose the case. To change his mind, Slepoy and Matilde Artés, grandmother of a kidnapped baby and now living in exile in Spain, went to see then chief prosecutor Carlos Granados. Artés told her story: her daughter Graciela and nine-month-old granddaughter Carla had been kidnapped by Bolivian security forces and transferred to the Automotores Orletti concentration camp outside Buenos Aires. There, according to eyewitnesses, Graciela was killed and Carla given to a member of a pro-military death squad named Eduardo Ruffo. Eight years later, improbably, Carla happened to be watching TV in the Ruffos' home when she saw a picture of herself as a baby, carried by a woman she had never seen in a demonstration of the Grandmothers of the Plaza de Mayo. "Who's that lady and why does she have my picture?" she asked Mrs. Ruffo. As Matilde and the Grandmothers closed in, the Ruffos fled, changing houses, disguising Carla and preparing to take her out of the country. Soon after, the Ruffos were arrested for baby-snatching and Carla was reunited with her grandmother after years of desperate searching. The two had moved to Madrid.[4]

It was a moving story. Moreover, Granados worked for the Socialist government, and the Socialist party had just lost the elections. For a lame-duck official, the risks of being branded in the press (as a story in the paper *La Vanguardia* suggested) as the person who obstructed justice for the disappeared in Argentina seemed to outweigh the headaches of allowing a controversial case to proceed. The headaches, of course, would belong to his successor. The complainants' lawyers sent Granados reams of arguments about why the case should continue. In a meeting of prosecutors, Castresana recalled, no one was willing to defend the case; then one of the senior prosecutors spoke out in favor and the balance shifted. Granados agreed to remain agnostic as to the legal merits of the case. The investigation could continue and the jurisdictional issues would be sorted out later.

It seems incredible, with the value of hindsight, that the Spanish government did not step in at the beginning to head off cases with the potential for causing endless diplomatic nightmares. In part, the issue was one of timing: the case slipped through during the transition period from the Socialist to the Popular party government, when official eyes were turned elsewhere. In part, no one saw a threat because the legal theory seemed outlandish, doomed to failure, a set of mere shots in the dark by exiles and activists desperate for attention. "The lawyers weren't taken seriously at first by anyone, no one paid attention to Castresana," confirms Fernando Mas. The lawyers themselves weren't sure where the cases might lead. Academic opinion in Spain at first almost uniformly thought they were doomed.

Paradoxically, the election of José María Aznar of the conservative Popular Party actually helped legitimize the case. Aznar could hardly be accused of being a leftist or sympathetic to the exile community. Indeed, Spanish journalists had noted his ties to Argentina: four days after his inauguration, he invited the Argentine chief of military intelligence to dinner. So it was difficult for the Argentine (or later Chilean) governments to hold the Spanish government politically responsible for judicial investigations. At the same time, however, Aznar, unlike Felipe González of the Socialist Party, had no history to defend. González had advised then president Raúl Alfonsín of the center-left Radical Party to placate the military by passing limits on prosecutions and was worried that any unraveling of deals promising impunity would sink the Socialists' chances of winning elections in Chile and the Radicals' chances in Argentina. Aznar had no such worries.

The political climate in Spain at the time also made it harder to interfere with a case before the courts. The memory of Franco's rule was still
raw enough, and admittance to the European Union club of democracies still new enough, for Spaniards to jealously guard the independence
of their judges in both appearance and reality. One of the major tasks
of the post-Franco transition had been the total revamping of the judiciary, both to modernize it and to guarantee its independence from the
executive branch. The GAL anti-ETA death squad investigation, with its
overtones of military dictatorship and abuse of power, was still ongoing.
The revelations around the GAL, together with corruption scandals and
the toll of fourteen years in power, had led to the Socialist loss of power.
Anything that smelled of abuse of executive power vis-à-vis the courts was
off limits under those circumstances.

Popular opinion was solidly in favor of the investigations. The media
reported on them, showcasing the stories of sympathetic witnesses.
Argentina and Chile have always had close ties to Spain. Thousands of
Spaniards migrated to Argentina early in the twentieth century, and the
two countries have had close economic and cultural ties. Spanish investments in both countries reach into the billions, including utility companies, hotels, and Argentina's oil industry. Fifty thousand Argentines and
a smaller but still large number of Chileans live in Spain, many of them
exiles from the days of the military who decided to stay on. Most of them
are middle-class urban professionals or workers, who look just like the
Spanish and have learned to "work the system" in their new homeland.
Thus there was a good deal of sympathy for the investigations among
ordinary people.

Whatever the combination of reasons, once Aznar's public prosecutors took office they acted incoherently, probably because the attention
of the top prosecutors was elsewhere. The state prosecutor in the Argentine case, Pedro Rubira, opposed Judge Garzon's investigation from the
start, but appealed some of his decisions and not others. In the Chilean
case, state prosecutor Javier Balaguer initially decided that the Spanish
courts had jurisdiction (based in part on fact that the Chilean dictatorship continued past 1985, the date when the current Spanish jurisdictional regime became law). Only much later, in March 1998, did the
public prosecutor ask for dismissal of the Chilean case. Meanwhile, the
investigations were underway.

The first step was to organize the evidence gathering. Testimonial evidence could come from exiles who lived in Spain and throughout
Europe, from survivors, family members, journalists, lawyers, and others
living in Argentina. In addition, the Sábato (CONADEP) investigatory
commission in Argentina and the prosecutors who had tried the junta
members and built up files on other high-ranking military had files that

needed to be introduced and pored over. For a group of lawyers and activists working mostly part time and a judge juggling a half-dozen high-profile investigations, it seemed like an overwhelming task.

One of the first steps was to increase awareness of the investigation, and its potential, within Argentina. From the start, certain Argentine human rights groups had been in on the case—indeed, one of the catalysts was a visit from one of the Mothers of the Plaza de Mayo. But much more help was going to be needed. Two of the IU team, Fran Pérez and Isabelo Herreros, traveled to Buenos Aires in the summer of 1996. There they met with most of the human rights organizations and with the opposition political parties, including that of ex-president Alfonsín. The Buenos Aires Lawyers Association promised their support. Carlos Slepoy also visited in the early days, receiving good press coverage and giving seminars and talks to academics and lawyers. He too lined up support from human rights groups, including the association of survivors of the detention camps. There were tensions from the beginning, however. The association of survivors did not work well with some of the other groups. Plus, the message was mixed: IU came to talk about justice for Spanish victims, while Slepoy invited all Argentines to participate. "They confused everybody," recalls Castresana.

The Argentine human rights groups took on the task of getting public support for the investigation. All those involved knew that the Spanish government's early hands-off attitude would not last and that public pressure would be needed to keep the case alive. SERPAJ head and Nobel Peace Prize laureate Adolfo Pérez Esquivel, who had been one of the first to testify in Madrid, wrote to fellow Nobel laureates asking for support. Letters to Garzón from Desmond Tutu of South Africa (writing as chair of South Africa's Truth and Reconciliation Commission) and the Dalai Lama followed, as did other letters of support.

A coordinating group was set up to work with the IU lawyers on testimony. Ana Chávez of SERPAJ was part of that group. "The Spanish trial made us go back and recompile the available information in a way that hadn't been done either by CONADEP or during the trial of the military commanders. We had lots of information on victims, but it wasn't cross-referenced with that of nationality, detention centers, military zones and perpetrator. We had to go back and create a matrix that the lawyers could use, figuring out which testimony on which victim would pertain to which possible defendant," she told me.

The matrix SERPAJ and the other groups put together matched up victims, nationality, and detention center and then correlated that information with the names of those military and police who had benefited from the amnesty laws and the information that had come out from existing trials. They began to reconstruct the chain of command from the bottom up, in an ironic mirror image of the military reconstruction of insurgent organizational charts a quarter century before. That this had not been done before reflects the specific priorities and needs of criminal prosecutions: unlike larger historical memory exercises or truth commissions, which look at overall patterns and results, criminal investigations must focus on proving the specific acts of specific individuals, something not always easy to do if the evidence-gathering focuses on what happened to the victims. The trial of the Junta members had relied on some 700 emblematic cases, but thousands of cases had never been prepared for trial. In the early 1980s, Argentine prosecutors and human rights lawyers had begun this process, but it had been cut short by the full stop and due obedience laws. Now it had to be taken up again.

Chávez went on: "We added in information from files in the Interior Ministry, the Episcopal Conference, and elsewhere that hadn't been available during the earlier trial. Many people had been reluctant to testify before, out of fear. The fact that the trial would take place elsewhere, and political confidence in Garzón, made people come forward now who had never testified before."

One of the key goals of the IU lawyers' visit was to arrange for the many people who could not travel to Madrid to be able to provide testimony. Sympathetic personnel at the Spanish embassy were happy to oblige, and agreed to send the testimonies taken at the embassy directly to Garzón via diplomatic pouch. Over two hundred people gave testimony at the Embassy in Buenos Aires in addition to another two hundred who talked to Garzón in Madrid. The testimonies were based on questionnaires developed by the lawyers in Spain working with the Argentine human rights groups, and revised back and forth over the Internet. In addition, as word spread, unsolicited letters began arriving at Garzón's office. One seventy-three-year-old woman wrote from Sweden asking the judge to include her family members as private plaintiffs and telling the story of their disappearance. Others wrote from Luxembourg, France, and all over Spain.

The lawyers were convinced that documentary evidence, no matter how compelling, needed to be backed up by live witness testimony. From a political and public relations viewpoint as well, a parade of witnesses would keep the investigation in the public eye and forestall the inevitable political pressures on Garzón to desist. But there was no money in the kitty to pay for witness travel. The lawyers were almost all working on a pro bono basis, and financing for costs was scraped together from human rights groups, provincial and city governments in Spain, and some contributions. The only solution was to piggy-back on other trips to bring witnesses to Madrid. An elaborate choreography of visits was the result. Julio Strassera, ex-chief prosecutor at the trials of the junta members, stopped into Garzón's office on his way to Geneva to meet his new grandchild. He brought with him the entire prosecution file. Emir Sader, whose Brazilian-born wife Regina Maconde had disappeared in Argentina, came on his way back from London, where he had attended a meeting of sociologists. Other witnesses, especially those active in the Mothers or Grandmothers, came invited by Amnesty International or local human rights groups to give talks or participate in conferences. Garzón juggled requests from dozens of people who could only be in Madrid for a two- or three-day window. The lawyers and human rights groups on both sides of the Atlantic struggled to keep some order in the witness parade. As the investigation progressed, it became harder.

The first witnesses before Garzón had no travel problems: they lived in Madrid. Esperanza Labrador was born in San Esteban de la Sierra, an arid agricultural town near Salamanca, Spain. She and her husband Victor moved to Rosario, in the industrial heartland of Argentina, and raised three children. In 1976, one of her sons, Miguel Angel, was picked up by a group of "armed men" and never heard from again. Victor began a fruitless search for his son. A week after a visit to the local police station, a group of some twenty men invaded his house and told him that they had just come from killing his other son, Palmiro, and his daughter-in-law. His daughter, Manuela, who survived to testify alongside her mother, recalled that the same group of men invaded her house, forced her husband to sign a series of blank checks, and left. Her father, Victor, went to see if the death of Palmiro was true. The next day, his body appeared alongside his son's. The survivors, mother and daughter, fled back to Spain.[5]

But first they notified the Spanish consul in Rosario, Vicente Ramírez Montesinos, of their plight. Ramírez, invited to testify, took the train in from Alicante, where he had retired, and told the judge that he remembered the Labradors well. Soon after Miguel Angel Labrador disappeared, the consul had gone to the military base and asked the commander, Leopoldo Galtieri, for information. He returned asking about Victor Labrador's death. Galtieri, he testified, looked at a list of names that included the two sons, but indicated that the father's killing had been a mistake. Galtieri then pulled out a purse taken from the family's leather workshop and showed the consul that it had a false bottom where papers could be hidden. This evidence, intended to show the consul that his compatriots were subversives, instead convinced him of the link between the "armed thugs" who had invaded the Labradors' residences and the army base. Afraid for his safety, the consul left Argentina soon after.

Other witnesses followed. Adolfo Pérez Esquivel, the Nobel laureate, testified about the pattern of repression. María Isabel Perón, who had been the figurehead president during the years preceding the 1976 "Process of National Reorganization," was called to testify. She knew nothing, she said, and had no power at all over events. During the final months in office, she testified, "it was as though she were not president but rather a kind of decorative figure."[6]

By March 1997, after hearing some nine months of testimony and receiving rooms full of documentary evidence, Garzón had enough evidence to proceed. He issued the first international detention order in the case against Leopoldo Fortunato Galtieri, ex-head of the Second Corps of the army, in charge of the city of Rosario and the northern provinces between 1976 and 1979.[7] Eyewitness testimony placed Galtieri, head of the military in the zone, commanding operations against suspected subversives, including the secret detention of disappeared persons.

Collaborators and Collaboration

A year after the case started, differences in approach blew up the already uneasy alliance among the lawyers on the Argentine investigation. The detonator was the July 1997 testimony from survivors of the detention camps. Few people had survived their incarceration, but those that did were key witnesses, able to provide eyewitness accounts of the fate of victims, identify individual perpetrators, and explain the pattern behind the disappearances and deaths. Their stories, reported in often gruesome detail in the Spanish press, also helped build up sympathy for the case among ordinary Spaniards.

While some torture centers killed almost all their victims, others were more complex. Many of the survivors who testified had been held in the Navy Mechanics School. ESMA had been one of the most notorious torture centers, where people were held for months or even years. Most of the prisoners there were eventually killed and the bodies buried in clandestine graves or at sea, but a larger number than usual survived, due to the camp's peculiar nature. ESMA had some special facilities. There was an operating room where pregnant prisoners would give birth, often chained to tables. The prisoners were then killed and the babies given to military or pro-military families in an effort to cleanse the nation of potential subversives. It also had a large number of workshops and offices where prisoners with special skills were kept as forgers, electricians, cryptographers, and the like. For example, Mario Villani, a physicist by training, testified that he had been ordered to fix radios, TVs, and other electronic devices stolen in the military's raids. One day he was told to fix the electroshock machine used to torture the prisoners (he told the judge he had managed to limit its potency while fixing it). In addition to these specialized workers, known as the "staff," other prisoners worked as slave domestics and laundresses for the torturers.

One of the leaders of the navy, Admiral Massera, had political ambitions of his own in the new, cleansed Argentina. To carry out those ambitions, he ordered the torturers to try to "turn" detained left-wing activists, especially those from the Montoneros, radical Peronists who were Argentina's largest armed guerrilla group at the time. Those who "turned" became his political analysts and advisors. They also, according to other survivors, did dirtier jobs as well: pointing out their old comrades on the street, directing the army to safe-houses, even, according to some witnesses, participating themselves in torture. These turncoats were known within the ESMA as the "ministaff."

None of the lawyers and activists in the case opposed the testimony of those survivors who had been part of the "staff," or, more generally, who had made it through the system alive through sheer luck or fortitude. Those who had been accused, either within Argentina or in the exile community (where rumors flew fast and furious) of being members of the "ministaff" were a different matter. Not only were they vilified by a large part of the ex-left as traitors complicit in murder, persistent rumors whispered that some were still on the military's payroll, charged with infiltrating and sabotaging the investigation. One witness in particular, Juan Gasparini, had been a treasurer for the Montoneros before being captured. After his release, he moved to Europe and became a journalist. In his testimony before the military courts, Jorge "El Tigre" Acosta had boasted that Gasparini had been turned into an intelligence agent and continued to act as a double agent; other torturers had also mentioned his name as a turncoat. Some activists, including Dionis, were convinced (not unreasonably) that he was still somehow connected to Massera. On the other hand, Gasparini since his release had testified against the military whenever and wherever possible and investigated the tentacles of their financial dealings with some skill. Carlos Slepoy and others thought (also not unreasonably) that an ex-agent would be unlikely to act this way. Slepoy insisted there was no evidence of any current connection to the military and that ex-detainees should be treated as victims of the repression unless unambiguous evidence proved otherwise. For him, the boasts of a torturer were not credible. The feud quickly degenerated, with each side accusing the other of endangering the whole prosecution project. It ended up spreading from the exile community in Spain to the Spanish lawyers on both sides and then to Argentina, where each side worked with different human rights groups. Many friendships were lost, and bitter feelings remain to this day.

The question of collaboration has bedeviled many inquiries into periods of acute repression or war. Is the prisoner tortured into denouncing her comrades a victim, a collaborator, or both? How should we treat such people at the hour of justice?

One response has been to compare those who collaborated in order to survive with those, stronger and braver, who preferred martyrdom, and to find the former wanting. Perhaps absolute condemnation of anything less than total resistance is necessary to deter turncoating, in the same way the rule against negotiating with hostage-takers is seen as unfortunate but necessary to deter hostage-taking. But a certain smug self-righteousness of those who never faced torture can creep into such absolute condemnation. According to Slepoy, "it depends on what the person does with their life afterwards. Here these people were coming forward to provide evidence against their torturers, exposing themselves." Shouldn't that count for something?

The ambiguities and gray areas that haunted the Argentine case came to a head around the visit to Madrid of Adolfo Scilingo. Scilingo was notorious in Argentina. In 1995, just before the Argentine investigation was getting underway, journalist Horacio Verbitsky published an interview with the former navy captain. Scilingo, who had been assigned as head of the automotive workshop to the Navy Mechanics School during the worst years of repression, was upset that certain military officers and not others were being promoted. He had a chilling tale to tell. He detailed secret detentions and tortures; most spectacularly, he confessed to participating in "death flights." Many of the ESMA's prisoners were disposed of by being dumped, alive, from airplanes into the sea. The prisoners were kept docile during the process of "transfer" by telling them they were being transferred to a legal prison and giving them heavy doses of tranquilizers. Thus drugged, they were "sent up" on airplanes and, once over the ocean, stripped and pushed out the door to their deaths. Scilingo told of his own participation in such flights, and recounted how officers were regularly rotated through these duties, to make sure all were complicit. He also recounted how he had written to his military superiors, asking them to take responsibility for these actions and to publish a list of those killed, but had never received an answer.

The story caused a sensation in Argentina. The military accused Scilingo of fraud and extortion and attempted to have him jailed. Three weeks after his revelations, some forty thousand people demonstrated against impunity on the twentieth anniversary of the coup, surprising everyone including the organizers. Politicians began calling for new investigations. Scilingo was attacked by thugs and his face was disfigured. He received regular death threats. His wife was terrified of remaining in Argentina.

Isabelo Herreros, on his first visit to Argentina, met with the Scilingos and asked Adolfo to come to Spain to testify. "We weren't just working with Scilingo," recounts Gregorio Dionis. "We had some ten military officers we worked with for over a year to entice them to Spain. We got one as far as Brazil, but then he wanted too much money and it fell through. Scilingo was the only one who came."

The IU team had two main reasons for wanting Scilingo to come to Madrid. First, they thought an insider could testify better than anyone about the existence of a criminal organization among the military. It was important to the case to show that torturers and even military zone leaders had acted not on their own but as part of an overall plan to use the institutions of the Argentine state to kill, brutalize, and steal. Although much of the organizational chart of terror was now known, Scilingo could fill in gaps. Second, given the lack of cooperation from the Argentine authorities, and thus the slim possibilities of extradition, eventually the investigation would hit a wall. There is no such thing as trials in absentia under Spanish law. Without a live defendant, in custody in Madrid, the case could never proceed to trial. While the investigation itself was proving invaluable in political and moral terms, it would be incomplete justice without at least some convictions.

The Slepoy/Galan team, on the other hand, was opposed to bringing Scilingo to Madrid. They too had their reasons. They worried that Scilingo would attempt a plea bargain with the judge, trading his testimony for some degree of immunity. It would be a sad day, they thought, when the torturers of their clients walked free in Spain as well as in Argentina. Second, having absent defendants had some advantages: defendants "in rebellion" could not name lawyers or appeal the judge's rulings. Plus, they were afraid that having a live defendant would energize the public prosecutor's opposition to the case, which during the first year was still lukewarm (They turned out to be right on that point.). Finally, they didn't think Scilingo's testimony would add much. It would shift the focus from listening to the victims to taking the word of their victimizers, and it could retraumatize witnesses. And there was, perhaps, an even more delicate reason: Scilingo, who knew the inner workings of the ESMA intimately, could testify about the identity and role of the ex-prisoner collaborators. If those who had already testified before Garzón were identified as members of the "ministaff" who fingered their ex-comrades, it might discredit their testimony and increase the already acrimonious infighting among the different groups. The result might be a loss of legitimacy for the entire investigation.

One option might have been to take Scilingo's testimony at the Spanish consulate in Buenos Aires, as had been done in many other cases. But not only would that not provide a live defendant, it could not be done. In his enthusiasm, Scilingo had written to Judge Garzón, telling of his role in the "death flights" and providing details about the functioning of the ESMA. That made him a suspect, not a witness, and the consulate could not take depositions from suspects.

Scilingo, harassed at home and with his expenses to Madrid paid by a Spanish TV station that wanted an exclusive interview, decided to fly to Spain. It is not clear what he thought would happen to him, whether he would be jailed or hailed as a hero; it is clear that Garzón had made no deal with him in exchange for his testimony. He arrived on October 6, 1997, with two Argentine lawyers and a satchel full of documents for the judge.

Judge Garzón then asked Scilingo about the death flights. The ex-official described his participation and explained why orders for the flights could only have come from the top ranks of the navy. "Did you participate?" the judge asked. "Yes," came the answer. At that point, Garzón gathered up his papers, told Scilingo he was under arrest, and left.[8] Scilingo spent the night at Carabanchel prison.

In the end, Scilingo's visit proved a mixed blessing. He provided Garzón with more detailed information than that available to date about the internal structure of the ESMA, and traced the history of the institution as a "criminal organization" starting in 1975. But he also eventually energized opposition to the case by both the public prosecutor and his own defense lawyer, and ended up enmeshing the case in speedy trial issues brought on by his detention.

Many of the stories Garzón began to hear from survivors and family members involved pillage and extortion. Survivor Mario Villani told of fixing electrical appliances stolen from the apartments of the disappeared. Family members told of being forced to sign over deeds to houses and businesses in a vain attempt to save captured relatives. Others told of being driven into ruin by the military. What happened to all the money stolen?[9] Garzón decided early on to see how much of it was stashed in secret bank accounts. In October 1996 he sent a rogatory commission (request) to Switzerland, asking the Swiss attorney general, Carla del Ponte, for information on possible bank accounts of over a hundred military officers. The same Del Ponte would soon take over as Chief Prosecutor of the UN Ad Hoc Tribunals for ex-Yugoslavia and Rwanda. According to journalists, she looked into some 360 local banks. Sixteen months later, she reported that six bank accounts had been found. The Argentine press reported that one of the accounts belonged to Jorge Acosta of ESMA fame; another had the name of retired admiral Mario Arduino, recently deceased.

Along with Scilingo, Garzón issued international detention orders (valid everywhere but Argentina) for nine naval officers, including Admiral Emilio Massera, Luís María Mendía, Jorge Raúl González, Jorge

Vildoza, Adolfo Mario Arduino, Jorge "El Tigre" Acosta, Jorge Enrique Perren, and others associated with the ESMA. The arrest orders, like the one for Galtieri, detailed the general history of the repression, and then detailed the role of each individual within the structure of the ESMA. All were accused of genocide, terrorism, and, as part of those crimes, causing the disappearance of individuals. Within the next few months, Garzón would expand the number of indictments, eventually reaching some 150 officers. He would issue, in all, sixty-six arrest warrants.

Chile

The Chilean investigation also proceeded apace before Judge García-Castellón. One of the first tasks here too was to create effective lines of communication to Chile. "We heard from Garcés, who some people knew had managed to escape after the coup through the Spanish Embassy," recounts Verónica Reyes of the legal aid organization FASIC. "We thought it was a bit crazy, when he started sending us lists of things he needed, among them things that were impossible to find. But the Association of Family Members of the Disappeared began to believe in him. They started going to the Spanish embassy in Santiago to give their statements for transmission to Madrid." Witnesses began making the trek across the Atlantic. As in the Argentine case, there was no money for witness travel, so they came on their own dime or invited by others.

Support began arriving from Europe and elsewhere. The European Parliament passed a resolution supporting the investigations. The Italian courts forwarded their files on the assassination attempt against Socialist Party leader Bernardo Leighton and his wife in Rome, including a conviction in absentia of Manuel Contreras for the crime. Chilean exiles across Europe sent letters detailing their stories and asking to testify.

The Chilean government at first paid little attention, although the local press had mentioned the case and even, in December 1996, published interviews with some of the lawyers involved. A turning point came in 1997 when García-Castellón asked the United States government for the results of official investigations into the murder of Chilean Orlando Letelier in Washington, D.C. and other documents related to Chile. The U.S. investigators in the Letelier case had testified in Madrid, including federal prosecutor Lawrence Barcella, and as a result of their testimony García Castellón sent a request to the U.S. for cooperation. Barcella's testimony was key not only to the Chilean investigation, but to Garzón's eventual expansion of the Argentine case to cover Operation Condor. Barcella testified that the Chilean DINA had conspired to commit terrorist acts in Spain, France, Italy, Portugal, the U.S., Mexico,

Costa Rica, and elsewhere, with Pinochet's knowledge and participation. Documentation from the Letelier investigation also indicated Pinochet's involvement in the murder of his ex-commanding officer, General Carlos Prats, and other crimes. To everyone's surprise, U.S. Attorney General Janet Reno agreed to seek material from CIA and FBI files and send it to Spain to collaborate with the investigation. The State Department and National Security Council pledged their cooperation with the Spanish courts. The U.S. not only knew about the Letelier case: the Nixon administration had played a major role in undermining Allende and supporting the junta. (By 2001, both Argentine and Chilean judges would send requests for information about his knowledge of the repression directly to Secretary of State Henry Kissinger.) In 1996, opening this potentially giant can of worms made the Chilean government sit up and take notice.

"Chile has its own laws, and lives in democracy, it has jurisdiction and does not recognize the jurisdiction of the courts of other countries to judge events that occurred here," declared foreign minister José Miguel Insulza.[10] "I'm sure the information will be useful to clarify many things that have happened here in the last thirty years," he added. The local press began a war of words for and against the investigation. A socialist senator asked that the Chilean government request copies of the declassified files, and several congresspeople traveled to Spain to testify before García-Castellón. María Adela Maluenda Campos, for example, president of the Chilean lower house of Congress, testified about Pinochet's receipt of funds from outside the country, the declarations of the ex-minister of defense that he had followed Pinochet's orders, and the detention and strangulation of her own son by the security forces. Roberto Garretón, one of the early human rights lawyers and an ambassador in the early 1990s, talked about the planned nature of terror as well as about the impossibility of finding justice within Chile. Meanwhile, the right wing accused the government of complicity in a scheme by Marxist lawyers, judges, and governments to harass General Pinochet.

On March 13, 1998, Garcés and Murillo asked Judge García Castellón to issue arrest warrants for 39 military and civilian officials of the ex-dictatorship, including Pinochet, Contreras, and the leadership of the DINA. Among those accused were the operatives believed to be responsible for the deaths and disappearances of Carmelo Soria, the missing and shot priests, and a number of other Spanish citizens.

The military, meanwhile, were receiving regular reports on the progress of the investigations from the Chilean military attaché in Madrid. They were especially concerned about the presentation of sworn witness statements from a number of ex-military officers about the tight chain of command in Chile. One air force general, Sergio Poblete, testified in

Spain about his own detention and torture as well as about Pinochet's role. Others sent copies of declarations they had given in local investigations of Pinochet's control over the Caravan of Death (see Chapter 3) and of military decrees establishing that "only the President of the Junta [Pinochet] can arrest people and detain them in places that are not recognized as prisons." The reports were worrisome enough that the military set up a team, headed by military Auditor General Fernando Torres Silva, to monitor developments, express concern to the government, and try to find sympathetic ears within the Spanish military and government for quashing the case.

If any one person can be credited with General Pinochet's subsequent arrest in London, General Torres Silva may be the one. Not that this was his intention: Torres Silva was one of the general's trusted advisors, and the auditor general of the army. He had apparently proved his worth to Pinochet by finding and prosecuting those members of the leftist MIR who had attacked Pinochet's convoy in 1985, an attack from which the General miraculously emerged unscathed. Now Pinochet authorized him to go to Spain, to find out how serious a threat the case in the Audiencia Nacional actually was.

Torres Silva contacted judge García Castellón, who courteously but firmly advised him that if he wanted to provide information, he was free to appear before the judge and present his testimony like anyone else. Torres Silva did so on October 3. He apparently intended to show that Pinochet and his officers had acted according to law and not as criminals. But more important from the point of view of the Chilean press, by appearing before the judge he had validated the Spanish court's jurisdiction over the affair. Indeed, Torres Silva began his testimony by declaring that "given that Your Honor's competence is the investigation of alleged penal acts, it is judicially possible for your Honor to receive information and background to clarify the accusations."[11] Upon his return to Chile, Torres Silva recognized his error. He hadn't been on an official mission, he insisted; he had acted on his own, during his vacation. The foreign minister agreed that the mission wasn't official. The sub-secretary of the Army disagreed, announcing that the army had officially informed him of Torres's trip. Amid the government's evident confusion, some pro-military voices began calling for Torres's resignation.

One explanation of Torres Silva's acts (he was an experienced lawyer, and must have known that his appearance would be tantamount to acceptance of jurisdiction) is that during his stay in Madrid he met with the public prosecutor for the Audiencia Nacional, Eduardo Fungairiño. Lawyers close to the case speculate that Fungairiño must have assured Torres that the case was on a fast track to nowhere, so that his putting in exculpatory evidence would have positive publicity value for the general, without in the long run harming him. After all, the case would have to be dismissed within a matter of months, if not weeks. Fungairiño had come to a similar conclusion in the Argentine case, especially after the Argentine government's intelligence chief visited Madrid. Torres Silva duly reported these views to Pinochet, who took them to heart.

Fungairiño had expressed his skepticism about investigating cases where the crimes were committed far away from the beginning, but had never actually appealed Garzón's denials of his motions to dismiss the case to a higher court. In part he no doubt thought the case would just go away, and in part he had no marching orders from above. His non-oppositional opposition was driving Garzón crazy: the judge told Spanish journalist Pilar Urbano: "for two years, the prosecutors have had a passive, disinterested attitude, and they've been incoherent: they oppose some things, but let others slip by . . . one day I told [Fungairiño] to just decide, instead of making so many public statements against the case just challenge my damned jurisdiction once and for all, and let's let the Criminal Appeals Chamber [of the Audiencia Nacional] decide."[12]

Fungairiño is a somber character, bald and wheelchair bound, heavy-browed and jowly. A merit citation from the FBI and a large cross adorn his office. Lawyers for the complainants consider him a leftover supporter of Franco. He has been a public prosecutor since 1980, and worked closely with Baltazar Garzón on any number of cases involving ETA Basque terrorism: indeed, they express themselves with very similar vehemence against ETA. Fungairiño was alive because he decided not to open a letter bomb presumably sent by ETA. He was, however, controversial among the public prosecutors service, which is charged with bringing cases to the courts, including the Audiencia Nacional. In 1997 he was one of a trio of candidates presented to the AN Prosecutors' Council for promotion to chief prosecutor. Despite receiving no votes, he was confirmed by the newly elected conservative Aznar government as chief.

Fungairiño's vision of international law dated from the classic, pre-Nuremberg texts. "International law is about relations among states," he told me. "We have no business going off and investigating these cases." Eventually, spurred by Torres Silva's visit and a similar one from the Argentine military, Fungairiño appealed the issue of jurisdiction to the Criminal Appeals Chamber of the Audiencia.

Once the battle was joined, Fungairiño and his staff relentlessly opposed every decision. With Garzón, it became personal. The judge waited resignedly for the opposition to each *auto* (decision); after a while both opposition and response became obvious cut-and-paste jobs, filed merely to maintain a record. In October 1997 a memo purported to be from Fungairiño's office caused a small firestorm. The memo, unsigned, was submitted (perhaps by mistake) to the Prosecutors' Council, which was deciding whether to support Fungairiño in his appeal. It largely repeated the same arguments, but then added a ringing defense of the Argentine and Chilean dictatorships. "Regarding the argument that the objective of exterminating political dissidents was to subvert public order, it is worth remembering that the Military Juntas only aimed at the temporary substitution of the established constitutional order, through institutional acts aimed at overcoming the insufficiencies inherent in each constitutional order for purposes of maintaining public peace."[13]

This bald justification for the crimes of the military was too much for large parts of Spanish society. Newspapers, lawyers and judges groups, and associations of prosecutors protested loudly. Socialist party spokespeople as well as the Communist party denounced Fungairiño as the presumptive author of the memo and called for his removal. The complainants' lawyers sought his recusal for having mischaracterized Torres Silva's visit as "informal," and, more generally, for bias. Their complaints resonated in a Spanish society where the judiciary had been one of the main targets of post-Franquista reform, and where there were substantial groups of progressive prosecutors, judges, and attorneys. The leaked memo helped swing the country's public opinion solidly in favor of pressing on with the investigations, and made it more difficult for the Aznar administration to intervene to limit them without seeming to align itself with the likes of Pinochet, Contreras, Galtieri, and Massera.

Operation Condor

As Garzón's investigations progressed, he began hearing more and more cases of kidnappings and disappearances that crossed national boundaries. Early on, for instance, he heard testimony from Matilde "Sacha" Artés, the Argentine grandmother who had convinced the public prosecutor not to oppose opening the investigation. Artés reminded Garzón that her daughter had been arrested in Bolivia by Bolivian police and had later been seen in a Buenos Aires detention center. She also provided some leads into the death of Juan José Torres, a left-wing Bolivian general who mysteriously turned up dead in Argentina in the 1970s. Her testimony provided the first window for Garzón into the continent-wide consortium of terror known as Operation Condor.

As Garzón dug deeper, he found that the military intelligence services of Chile, Argentina, Uruguay, Paraguay, Bolivia, and Brazil, alarmed by the continental spread of revolutionary groups, in the 1970s decided to form a counter-revolutionary alliance of their own. Starting in 1973, they agreed to share information, exchange captives, and coordinate their activities both bilaterally and on a regional level. A December 1975 "intelligence meeting" formalized the agreement. As a result, Chilean activists who had fled to Argentina after the September 1973 coup were picked up by Argentine security forces and turned over to the Chilean DINA; Argentine and Uruguayan activists were picked up in Paraguay, Uruguayans in Brazil and Argentina, Bolivians in Brazil. They were either killed outright or turned over to their respective security forces, then tortured and disappeared. The coordinator of Operation Condor was Manuel Contreras of the Chilean DINA. Its main strategist was Augusto Pinochet.

Information on Condor began arriving from a number of different witnesses. Martín Almada of Paraguay brought the relevant contents of the "Archives of Terror" to Garzón. Almada, who had been a political prisoner, had filed a freedom of information request for his police file in 1992, three years after the Stroessner dictatorship was overthrown. He had gone to a police station outside the Paraguayan capital, accompanied by a local judge, José Agustín Fernández, to search for his records, and instead found boxes and boxes of abandoned files, over half a million documents including over 9,000 files on suspected government opponents, surveillance reports, and minutes of meetings of the security forces. Worried about the safety of the records, Judge Fernández and a colleague, together with reporters and human rights activists, formed a human chain to move the records to a courthouse in Asunción for safekeeping. They also found documents from the legal division of the police department, which were similarly stored and have been made available to researchers. Among the most interesting documents were minutes of meetings of the intelligence services of the six countries as well as bilateral meetings among them. The archive also contained evidence of transfers of prisoners from one country to another: Argentines and Uruguayans detained in Paraguay and then disappeared at the hands of Argentine security forces, Paraguayans picked up and disappeared in Argentina. To cover up the transfers, the security forces invented local gun battles, internecine warfare among the left, or deaths abroad.

Other witnesses also mentioned Operation Condor. Juan Gelman, one of Latin America's best-known poets, told the judge about how his son and daughter-in-law were taken from Uruguay to the detention camp at Automotores Orletti outside Buenos Aires, which served as the main Argentine camp for those picked up elsewhere and transferred as part of Condor. The investigators in the Letelier bombing referenced Condor as well. From all this testimony, Garzón decided to divide his burgeoning investigation into three parts: one on Argentina, one on stolen children, and a third on Operation Condor.

The Operation Condor segment expanded the scope of Garzón's investigation far beyond Argentina, to encompass the crimes of six Latin American security forces. The Argentine investigation now began to overlap with the Chilean inquiry into the crimes of General Augusto Pinochet and his subordinates being investigated by Judge Garcia-Castellón in the trial chamber next door. But García-Castellón's inquiry was progressing slowly.

Then, in early October 1998, Joan Garcés received a phone call from Amnesty International. Augusto Pinochet was in London.

Chapter 2

The Adventures of Augusto Pinochet in the United Kingdom: A "Most Civilized Country"

London—The Arrest

Andy McEntee, chair of Amnesty International's UK section, had been following General Pinochet's trip to London in 1998 with great interest. This was not the first time he had thought about seeking an arrest warrant for the Chilean dictator. "He had been here a number of times before, but he always came for short periods and left before we could get the authorities to act," he told me. On the first trip, in 1991, he had come in relation to official British Aerospace arms sales to Chile, and had left the same day. In 1992, the lawyers' network connected to Amnesty in the UK and the Netherlands had set up study groups to see what could be done, but had come up with little. In 1994, the Dutch group had tried to get the local prosecutor to issue a warrant when the general arrived in the Netherlands, but the prosecutor had declined. He had argued that Dutch courts had no jurisdiction, Pinochet had immunity, and that there was no Dutch public interest in prosecution. Similarly, when Pinochet again visited the UK in connection with an arms fair, AI asked Geoffrey Bindman, a well-known civil liberties lawyer, to attempt to obtain an arrest warrant. "We tried to use section 134 of the Criminal Justice Act, which is the British law that implements the Convention Against Torture, but had never been used. The law requires the Attorney General's permission to proceed, so we went to the AG with a dossier of cases, and he told us to take our evidence to the police, so we did, but by that time Pinochet had left," Bindman recalled.

The British human rights lawyers tried again the next year. This time, the police told them they needed sworn declarations from witnesses. "I knew the Chilean human rights groups well because before coming to AI I worked for five years with a development agency-funded NGO called the Chile Committee for Human Rights," said McEntee. "So I called the human rights lawyers in Chile and they got us declarations that detailed their detention and torture or that of family members and stated that they were willing to come to the UK to testify. But the Metropolitan Police were overworked and had higher priorities, the desk officer who worked on the Americas didn't speak Spanish, and altogether it was hard to get them to act. They kept saying we didn't have enough evidence, but they wouldn't tell us what more was needed. It's a real problem with section 134—it leaves complete discretion to the police." In addition, domestic prosecution for torture committed outside the UK requires the Attorney General's approval.

Because of this limitation, the section had been rarely used. There was one precedent: a case involving a Sudanese doctor living in Scotland, who was accused of torture. In that case, after launching a prosecution in September 1997, the Scottish Advocate General had decided to drop the case, adducing a lack of evidence.[1] In other cases, the authorities had refused to prosecute even when they were given reams of evidence.

Civil cases were no more promising. In 1996, the Court of Appeals had refused to allow a civil suit against the Kuwaiti government for alleged acts of torture against a citizen with dual UK-Kuwaiti citizenship who had incurred the wrath of a relative of the royal family. The government, the court ruled, had immunity from civil liability even for acts that violated the Torture Convention. By 1998, that case, *Al-Adsani v. United Kingdom*, was on appeal to the European Court of Human Rights (the court eventually upheld the decision).[2] Because of this negative precedent, as well as the fear of Chilean exiles whose families were still in Chile and who therefore didn't want their names on a complaint, no civil case was ever brought.

"Pinochet came in 1997, but again left before we could get the police to act. It became a kind of standing joke in human rights circles—'here comes Pinochet again'. So when we got word that he would be coming again, and this time to have surgery, we thought this might be an opportunity. We were thinking about domestic prosecution at the time," recalls McEntee. "Then we started thinking that if the Spanish courts requested judicial cooperation on their investigation, we might get the courts involved and get over the hurdle of the police having complete discretion whether to act." McEntee talked to Joan Garcés about the status of the Spanish case. So did Federico Andreu of AI's International Secretariat. Garcés started thinking about how to ask the Spanish courts to question Pinochet during his visit to London.

Garcés quickly framed a request to Judge García-Castellón asking him to ask the British authorities to detain Pinochet long enough for him to be questioned in the Chilean case. But by then Garcés had his doubts about whether the judge would take such an audacious step. So, to increase the chances of success, he went to see Enrique Santiago, the lawyer for The United Left in the Argentine case. Operation Condor was the key link between the two cases. Because the Chilean DINA secret police, which reported directly to Pinochet, was the lead agency for the transcontinental kidnapping and disappearances consortium of Condor, Pinochet was at the least a useful witness in Garzón's investigation as well. According to Santiago, he and Garcés agreed that they would also submit a request to Judge Garzón, asking him to request that the British help him serve a "letter rogatory" on Pinochet asking questions relevant to his Operation Condor investigation.

That Tuesday, October 13, Garcés and Santiago presented their briefs to Judge Garzón and Judge García-Castellón. The briefs outlined the evidence that Pinochet had been the mastermind behind Operation Condor and detailed some of the crimes committed by that conspiracy. On Wednesday, in response, both judges wrote up requests, sent via Interpol to London, asking the British authorities to allow them to personally question Pinochet when he recovered from surgery, and meanwhile asking them to guarantee his presence in the country until he could be questioned. The next day, the complainants' lawyers presented additional evidence, including cases involving hundreds of Chilean victims killed or disappeared in Argentina. The lawyers, Enrique Santiago recalled, were trying to give the judges as much ammunition as possible to allow them to act—and quickly.

When the request arrived in Scotland Yard, it set off a flurry of inquiries within the British police. The police asked the Foreign Office and the Home Office whether Pinochet had diplomatic immunity; the answer came back that he was present on a private visit, and they had no knowledge of any diplomatic immunities. In addition, the Foreign Ministry was aware of Pinochet's presence in the UK because it had approved the arms carried by the Chilean security detail that accompanied him to the hospital. While the general's exact location was a secret, the fact that he was in the UK was not. He had publicly taken tea with Baroness Thatcher, and gone to see a munitions plant, before checking into a private clinic for surgery.

On Friday, October 16, as Garzón was about to leave town for the weekend, he received an urgent fax back from the UK police. The police could not guarantee Pinochet's presence for any interrogation. Pinochet was free to go whenever he wished, and in fact, according to police information, was planning to leave the next day. The only way to stop him, the police helpfully added, was to issue an arrest order.

Garzón must have taken a deep breath—an arrest order for Pinochet was a daring step into uncharted territory. At the time, the higher courts had not yet ruled on whether Spanish courts even had jurisdiction to look into the Southern Cone cases; furthermore, he had enormous amounts of other work. The Chilean case wasn't even his but belonged to Judge García-Castellón—his only connection was through the Operation Condor cases. The political fallout could be enormous, and he would be held responsible if the case became a diplomatic disaster. But . . . this was also a once-in-a-lifetime opportunity, and if he turned it down, what was the point of all the hard work that had gone before? This could mean a breakthrough in the law. Garzón decided to take the plunge.

It was late in the afternoon, and almost all the court staff, the complainants' lawyers, and his fellow judges had left for the weekend. Garzón sat down and wrote out an order of arrest for Augusto Pinochet for the crimes of genocide and terrorism, based on a number of the Operation Condor cases. He specified only one: Edgardo Enríquez, one of the leaders of the Chilean leftist party MIR, had been seen in a number of Argentine detention camps, where he disappeared. Garzón asked the British authorities to execute the international arrest order. The order was transmitted through Interpol and eventually reached the British police. It was by then late in the day, but the police were still able to get in touch with Magistrate Nicholas Evans of the Bow Street Courts, who could approve an arrest warrant. Luckily as well, when Magistrate Evans called the Home Office to ask whether the subject of the warrant had diplomatic immunity, there was someone still there who was able to inform him that as far as the British government was concerned, there was no diplomatic immunity involved. Late that evening, Evans, acting from his home, swore out a warrant for the arrest of one Augusto Pinochet, Chilean.

At around 11 p.m., a delegation from Scotland Yard arrived at the London Clinic to serve the warrant. Pinochet's own security detail at first thought they were there to protect the patient from protesters. When they realized their mistake, they briefly resisted, but then stepped aside. Pinochet was half asleep. The Scotland Yard translator read him the detention order, which woke him up. Upon hearing that the order had originated with Judge Garzón, Pinochet (perhaps referring to Joan Garcés, who he saw as his nemesis) reportedly exclaimed "That Communist!"[3]

A few days later, Judge García-Castellón moved to consolidate the Chilean and Argentine cases under Garzón's investigation, in effect bowing out of the case. This made sense from the standpoint of Spanish law: Garzón's investigation had started first, and so he in effect had seniority. From now on, there would be a single investigation, under Judge Garzón. The human rights lawyers were pleased.

Once the warrant was issued, there was little the British government could do to protect its visitor from arrest. But still, a government determined to protect Pinochet would have acted differently. The Home Office could have slowed down its response to Scotland Yard until well after the close of business Friday: by Monday, Pinochet would have been gone. Indeed, having apparently gotten some inkling of problems in the making, Pinochet's retinue had already booked him on a Saturday flight out of the country. Or they could have fudged the immunity issue, leaving it for resolution on Monday. Why did neither of these things happen? In part, there was already a great deal of sympathy for the Chilean cause within British society, and the civil service was no exception. This was a new Labor government, recently installed after eighteen years out of power, and it had promised an "ethical foreign policy." Many of its top officials, including Home Secretary Jack Straw, had protested against the military coup in 1973. Pinochet was the very symbol of brutal dictatorship for the generation now in power. Peter Mandelson, a top adviser to Blair, in the days after the arrest remarked that "the idea that such a brutal dictator as Pinochet should claim immunity, I think for most people in this country would be pretty gut-wrenching stuff." In addition, Geoffrey Bindman and Amnesty had been sending evidence of the crimes of the Chilean military to the police and Attorney General at regular intervals; *someone* in those offices had read the files.

On the other hand, there were significant constraints. Britain was a major supplier of arms to the Chilean military, and members and associates of the Pinochet family were partners in arms deals with powerful UK interests.[4] The British right, starting with Thatcher, lionized Pinochet as the savior of the Chilean economy and Britain's ally during the Falklands (Malvinas) war. There was also the effect on Chile's current government to think about. The government at the time was headed by Eduardo Frei Ruíz-Tagle, a Christian Democrat, but the ruling coalition included the Socialist party. By 1998, a Socialist was widely expected to be the coalition's candidate in the upcoming Chilean presidential elections. The Socialist party had close ties to Tony Blair's Labor party. Both had been out of power for a generation, both were members of the Socialist International, both espoused a "third way" combination of free markets and social programs. There were long-standing contacts among the Laborites, the Chilean Socialists, and Spain's PSOE, then headed by Felipe González, and González opposed the Spanish investigation.

British public opinion on the arrest was predictably divided, with the Conservatives decrying the Spanish court's intermeddling and the left cheering. The media were divided as well. In the rest of the world, initial reactions were overwhelmingly favorable. The French, German, Australian, Norwegian, Dutch, Danish, Swedish, Italian, and even Luxembourg ministers expressed their satisfaction and agreed that Pinochet should be tried for his crimes. The European Parliament passed a resolution on

October 20 supporting the principle of universal jurisdiction and urging extradition.[5] The United Nations Committee on Torture weighed in on November 20, pointing out the "extradite or prosecute" obligations of the Convention Against Torture.[6] German Foreign Minister Joschka Fischer summed it up: "Dictators are not above the law."[7]

When he heard of the arrest, then-President Frei was at a meeting of Ibero-American presidents in Portugal. His immediate reaction was to ask why, if the Spanish were so quick to judge others for genocide, they had never judged anyone in relation to the crimes committed during the Spanish Civil War?[8] Other Chilean politicians were also quick to invoke sovereignty and the need for a domestic solution. On the other hand, some members of the Chilean Socialist Party supported the action. Pro-Pinochet groups began protests outside the Spanish and British embassies. "Ingleses piratas, devuélvannos al Tata" (loosely: "English pirates, give us back our Leader"), they chanted.[9]

Under those conditions, the government decided that the most prudent course of action was to leave the matter to the courts. Most likely, the courts would quickly quash any extradition proceedings on immunity grounds, thus allowing the government a graceful way out. And as for a domestic prosecution, investigation into the charges would take some time. Without a pending arrest warrant, it was unlikely that the General would wait around to find out the results.

The Piquete de Londres

Ever since Pinochet's arrival, the British human rights groups had mobilized. "At first, we thought this was another short visit, like the previous ones, so we weren't thinking about detention. We wanted the government to declare him *persona non grata* (as the French government had done shortly before) and throw him out," recalls Nicole Drouilly, a Chilean exile living in London. At the same time, Amnesty International sent a public letter to the British government, reminding the government of its international obligation not to shelter those who had committed crimes against humanity. The British government, the letter suggested, should either prosecute Pinochet or extradite him to a country that would.

The exiles and Amnesty staff set about trying to find out which clinic was hosting the general. On other visits, they had at least managed to picket his hotel. "We had a general idea what kind of operation he would be having, so we began asking around at all the most expensive private clinics," continued Drouilly. "There were Chileans and other Latin Americans working as janitors, nurses, and nurses' aides at all these places, and we asked through the grapevine whether anyone had seen Pinochet. Many Chileans worked in social services, and they also began to ask around with their clients. Pretty soon, one of our contacts told us they had seen a patient who looked like Pinochet, registered under the name Ugarte. That's his mother's name. The government wouldn't confirm his location. So we went down to the London Clinic, with flags and banners and signs, and we began to form a picket line. This eventually became known as the London picket"—the Piquete de Londres.

The Chilean exile community worked hard to sway public opinion in the days after the arrest. They knew that with public opinion strongly on their side, they could lessen the chances of government action to protect Pinochet. Although dispersed throughout the UK, many of the exiles who had decided to stay after an elected government returned to power in Chile had kept in touch over the years. "During the dictatorship years, we created a fabulous support network throughout Europe, including artists, unions, politicians and the like. We had been organizers in Chile, so we knew how to organize," explained Jimmy Bell, another Piquete activist. "What's more, many of us had been political prisoners, and to be accepted into a European country as an asylee you had to fill out a long questionnaire with your education and job history. It tended to be the better-educated people who ended up here. We knew each other all over Europe because we had either been prisoners together, or knew someone who had. So as we learned English, got jobs, and developed good contacts in British society, we kept in touch with others throughout Europe."

This exile network had known about the Spanish investigation because of fundraising visits from Sola Sierra, head of the Association of Family Members of the Disappeared (AFDD) earlier in 1998. They had been in touch with Joan Garcés because Garcés had represented the sister of a Chilean exile based in London before the Spanish courts. And they knew Andy McEntee at Amnesty because of his prior Chile-related work. They also knew people in the press, Parliament, unions, and academe. This network went into high gear with the news of Pinochet's arrest.

"We called the AFDD in Chile, which hadn't yet heard, and asked them to send a press statement. Then we started calling each other, and soon people more or less spontaneously converged on the London Clinic, carrying Chilean flags, candles and the large photos of the disappeared that Sola Sierra had left with us," recalls Drouilly. The vigils outside the clinic became a daily occurrence. Groups of Chileans and other Latin Americans began arriving from all over Europe, anxious to see where the dictator had been brought to bay. The London-based exiles took on housing, feeding, and organizing the new arrivals.

The exiles and their supporters were from a range of political groups. They soon needed to decide on an approach to answering press queries. They agreed that the bottom line was that they wanted justice, and the truth about the fate of the disappeared. Political slogans were unwelcome. At one point, a local Trotskyist group tried to burn Pinochet in effigy, but the Chileans stopped them. They were afraid the Chilean military or its supporters would try to provoke violence among the protesters, and so were very careful to keep the protests nonviolent and to maintain good relations with the police.

While the Chileans brought with them organizing skills, they also learned from the social movements around them. "We learned from the gay rights movement, from the anti-nuclear movement, from a variety of European social movements," recalled Roberto Vásquez (a third organizer, along with Drouilly and Bell). "We personalized the issue, by using crosses, sending up balloons, changing the text on billboards. Even though no one is allowed to demonstrate in front of Parliament, we stayed there for months. We kept looking for creative and fun ways to get our message across." Supporters brought coffee, chocolate, Swedish massages, money. Protesters got sheets for banners from the hospitals where some of them worked. "At one point, we sent 70,000 faxes and e-mails to Jack Straw asking him to deny bail to Pinochet. Later, we hand delivered letters for members of Parliament. We gave them to a secretary there who we didn't know: we found out later that she had stuffed each Member's personal mailbox, which was against the rules. That's the kind of sympathy and support we managed to generate."

The exiles also served a vital communications function. They sat in on all the court hearings, took copious notes, and every evening transcribed them, translated them and sent them to Spain, Chile, and journalists around the world. They helped put Chilean human rights lawyers in touch with British civil liberties lawyers. "We would go to our regular jobs in the morning, in the afternoon we would divide up the meetings that needed to be covered, then we would go and picket for a few hours, and then stay up until two a.m. e-mailing and calling people. We were obsessed. We knew that the detention had been the result of a lot of little actions by many people, and by failing to take some little action, we could lose it all," said Nicole Drouilly.

The Chileans living in the UK formed a key part of the coalition of legal and human rights groups that eventually formed to press both for extradition and, in the alternative, for domestic prosecution. The Chilean human rights movement eventually participated formally through the Santiago-based AFDD. Chileans were also brought into the case through the Medical Foundation for the Care of Victims of Torture, which worked with a number of Chilean torture victims. "I got a call from Geoffrey Bindman, asking if we wanted to get involved," recalls Sherman Carroll, policy director of the Foundation. "At first, I said no. I couldn't see what extradition had to do with us. But then it became clear that we could play a useful role in making the case for domestic prosecution as an alternative to extradition." The Medical Foundation began collecting affidavits of Chileans who had been tortured or whose close family members had been killed or disappeared. Eventually, they collected more than sixty statements, from France, Belgium and Russia and the U.S. as well as the UK. People wrote in asking to participate in the case in some fashion. "For the political people, the case was great, they were really energized. For the less political, it was quite traumatic. For example, we had one client who in all these years had never told his Chilean wife what had happened to him, much less anyone else. Now it all came out," recalled Carroll.

From the beginning, the emerging coalition of groups followed a two-track strategy. The emphasis was on extradition to Spain, where the investigating judge was obviously sympathetic, the evidence was most developed, and the chances of reaching the trial stage most favorable. But at the same time, domestic prosecution was always an option. After all, the Convention Against Torture, ratified by the UK in 1987 and enacted into British law in 1988, required states holding an alleged torturer either to prosecute him themselves or to turn him over to a state that would do so. So if the extradition request foundered for any reason, the human rights groups wanted to be ready to push for a British trial of Pinochet.

There were, moreover, British citizens who had been victimized by Pinochet. Dr. Sheila Cassidy, for instance, had been tortured by the DINA while detained after the 1973 coup. William Beausire's sisters joined because their brother had disappeared. The British citizen victims, it was thought, would help assure that the human rights lawyers had standing to challenge government action in a domestic prosecution; they were also important to consolidate the British public's support for action against Pinochet.

Once the legal battle was joined, other actors became part of the human rights coalition. Amnesty International, of course, had been there from the start. Amnesty is a large and complex organization, and several different Amnesty components, including the International Secretariat and the British section, played important roles as legal advisors as well as spokespersons. Bindman's private law firm, with a practice ranging from immigration to personal injury to civil liberties law, was also in the center. Human Rights Watch, the New York-based advocacy group, sent a delegation to attend the proceedings and played a key role in legal research and drafting. Another British human rights group, the

Redress Trust, specialized in representing torture survivors in court proceedings. Redress had been involved in the earlier case involving torture by a Sudanese doctor living in Scotland, as well as in the *Al-Adsani* civil case against the Kuwaiti government and cases challenging the export of equipment that could be used for torture. Fiona McKay, then the group's legal officer, recalled the vertigo of those first days. "We pulled together a group of people, including academics, lawyers and NGO people. It was all happening very quickly, within a matter of a few days."

Pinochet, incensed by his treatment at the hands of what he had considered a friendly, even a model, country, hired the best legal talent money could buy. Clive Nicholls, an expert on extradition law, and Clare Montgomery, a criminal law specialist, argued before the court. Montgomery was also active in civil liberties work, and was not associated with the political right. She took the case, she said, out of a sense that it was important, especially in high-profile cases, for all sides to benefit from good lawyering. Pinochet's solicitor was Michael Caplan of the high-priced firm of Kingsley-Napley. (In the UK, there is a division between barristers, who are appointed to do court appearances, and solicitors, who act as legal advisors to their clients.) While the barristers drew praise from the other side for their professionalism, Caplan came in for criticism for his hard-ball advocacy. According to British journalist Hugh O'Shaughnessy, Kingsley-Napley's work as solicitor cost 4,500 pounds sterling a day, while Clive Nichols charged £500 an hour and Montgomery £350.[10] Pinochet's supporters also hired a British public relations firm.[11]

Extradition cases in the UK are handled by the Crown Prosecution Service (CPS), which represents the government requesting extradition. The CPS, in turn, hires experts to go into court on its behalf. Alun Jones, Queen's Counsel, a private lawyer and another of the country's foremost extradition experts, was designated to represent the Spanish government.

Legal obstacles came up soon enough. Judge Garzón's warrant charged Pinochet with genocide and terrorism. It was up to the British authorities to translate those charges into English law, according to the terms of the extradition treaty. In the press of events, the provisional arrest warrant issued on Friday October 16 charged that Pinochet did "murder Spanish Citizens in Chile."[12] There was only one problem, and Pinochet's lawyers soon pointed it out. While murder is a crime under British law, murder outside the UK is not, unless the perpetrator is British. If it was not a crime under British law, it was not an "extradition crime," so the warrant was no good. Moreover, the lawyers added, Pinochet was immune from prosecution as a former head of state. They asked Jack Straw, the home secretary, to cancel the provisional warrant.

(Under English law, a provisional warrant does not need to be approved by the home secretary, but he does have the power to cancel it.) When the problem was explained to Garzón, he quickly wrote out another warrant. Metropolitan Magistrate Ronald Bartle approved that provisional warrant, over the strenuous objections of Pinochet's lawyers, on October 22. It now charged Pinochet with torture and conspiracy to torture from 1988 to 1992, with hostage-taking and conspiracy to take hostages from 1982 to 1992, and with conspiracy to murder from January 1976 to 1992. The starting dates of the offenses were pegged to the dates when the relevant international treaties became part of British law.

The warrant snafu illustrated some of the difficulties inherent in going from one country to another and from international to domestic law. On the most basic level, translation was a problem. Judge Garzón recalled: "I would receive faxes in English at 10 p.m., and needed to respond by the next morning at 10. I don't speak English, so I would take them home and have my daughter, who knew English, do an unofficial translation. Then I would write out the answer in Spanish and, first thing the next morning, an English-speaking staff member would translate it and fax it out through the Spanish Foreign Affairs ministry." It was a cumbersome and stressful process—and there was no way of knowing how much was lost in translation.

Beyond simple language, there was a conceptual problem that extended to judges and lawyers alike. When countries ratify international treaties criminalizing certain behavior, part of the commitment they take on is to effectively make that behavior criminal under their own domestic law. However, often they neglect to do so. In some places, those that follow a "monist" view of international law as being part of the same legal system as domestic law, theoretically it doesn't matter much, because the treaty itself automatically becomes part of domestic law. But in an extreme "dualist" country like the UK that completely separates international from domestic law, anything not in the local penal code cannot be used to prosecute. Even in more "monist" civil law countries, judges are often reluctant to put people in jail on the strength of treaty provisions alone, which may not be detailed enough for the protections of the criminal law. (The U.S. follows an intermediate position, by which only certain treaties considered "self-executing" can be directly used by domestic judges; in practice the U.S. applies international criminal law treaties once they have been transposed into our penal code.) The extent to which international law can be applied directly by the domestic courts has bedeviled all the cases considered in this book.

Andy McEntee of Amnesty recalls: "I talked to Joan Garcés, and he kept insisting that Pinochet be charged with genocide. I kept trying to explain that, even though the UK is a party to the Genocide Convention, genocide was never defined in our penal code, so our judges won't use it as the basis of a prosecution. The only option was to rely on section 134, which translated the Torture Convention into domestic law." By the time of the second provisional warrant, it was obvious that Garzón had received the same advice. Still, it is within the province of the requested country to decide how it wants to translate the charges from foreign law into its own law. If the charges are based on international law, and the crimes described have been completely and faithfully transferred into each country's penal code, they should be the same and translation should be no problem. That is rarely the case. In its absence, there is a great deal of leeway in the system to characterize the underlying facts in many different ways—some more favorable to successful extradition than others.

With the second provisional warrant approved by Magistrate Bartle, Pinochet's lawyers moved to challenge both warrants in the High Court, which convened barely five days later, on October 28. Three judges, led by Lord Bingham of Cornhill, Lord Chief Justice of England and Wales, were to consider the arguments that one or both provisional warrants were bad, and that Pinochet was immune from prosecution. The human rights lawyers watched from the gallery, but only Mr. Jones of the CPS argued the case for continued detention. "We thought about trying to intervene at that stage, but it would have been very difficult to get standing to intervene on such short notice, so we decided to watch and wait," recalls Fiona McKay of Redress. The first issue went relatively well for the CPS. The court decided that the first provisional warrant was bad (no surprise, given that the request for a second warrant implied at least some doubts about the validity of the first). They upheld the second provisional warrant, finding no reason why two judges could not approve two separate warrants. They also approved the torture and hostage-taking counts in that warrant, although they threw out the conspiracy to murder count.

One interesting point of the High Court judgment foreshadowed a key issue for the House of Lords. Mr. Nicholls, one of the lawyers for Pinochet, argued that the charges were no good because some of the allegations covered a time period before the offenses had become incorporated into English law. While Lord Bingham thought a ruling on the matter could be left until later in the proceedings, he added that in his opinion the conduct alleged need not have been criminal at the time the crime was committed abroad, but only at the time of the extradition request. That meant that pre-1988 torture charges and pre-1982 hostage-taking charges would be valid.

Turning to the question of immunity from prosecution, the High

Court panel found that under English law, Pinochet, as a former head of state, would have immunity only for his official functions. But could the crimes alleged be considered "official functions"? The court found that they could. After all, if a head of state was clearly entitled to immunity for *some* criminal acts carried out as part of his official functions (which was uncontested) then there was no logical way to distinguish the most serious criminal acts, like torture, from less serious ones. The Genocide Convention, which says that "constitutionally responsible rulers, public officials, or private individuals" are equally subject to punishment, was of no help because that language had never been transferred to English law. To the argument that such heinous crimes could never be carried out as official functions, Justice Collins had a stinging reply:

> Unfortunately, history shows that it has indeed on occasions been state policy to exterminate or to oppress particular groups. One does not have to look very far back in history to see examples of that sort of thing having happened. There is in my judgment no justification for reading any limitation based on the nature of the crimes committed into the immunity which exists.[13]

In other words, just because it is morally bad doesn't mean a head of state cannot do it. This was the traditional international law position: states had no business telling other states how to treat their own citizens. The last fifty years of development of a human rights canon has been a challenge to that traditional view.

On that note, the hearing ended. The only recourse for the prosecution was to appeal to the House of Lords, Britain's final legal authority. Alun Jones requested, and got, an order requesting the House of Lords, "having regard to the obvious public importance and international interest in the issue," to review the decision on immunity. He also got the court to agree that any order quashing the provisional warrant would not take effect while appeals were pending—a crucial point that left Pinochet under arrest for the duration. Pinochet's lawyers, for their part, got the court to agree that the English taxpayer should foot the bill for his court fees.

Spain: After the Arrest

Pinochet's detention in London gave a whole new urgency to the question of whether the Spanish courts actually had jurisdiction over the Chilean and Argentine cases. As you will recall, that question had been appealed (by public prosecutor Fungairiño) to the full Criminal Appeals Chamber of the Audiencia Nacional, which acts as the equivalent of a U.S. federal appeals court. Now Fungairiño appealed Judge Garzón's arrest order, and the complainants' lawyers responded. The appeals ended up consolidated for argument and were quickly scheduled for the end of October. Amid the maneuvering in London, the complainants' lawyers also prepared to argue their case in Spain.

The oral arguments in Madrid on October 29 had some of the same circus air around the courthouse as the London proceedings in the same season. Outside waited the demonstrators, the police, the press, the public that couldn't get an invitation to attend. Inside were the solemn, robed lawyers and the eleven judges of the court, nine men and two women.[14]

The prosecutor, Pedro Rubira, opened, rehearsing the arguments he had made in writing. The case, whatever its merits, did not belong in a Spanish court: Spain had no jurisdiction, the crimes charged did not fit the facts, and in any case the statute of limitations had expired. Then it was the complainants' lawyers turn. Carlos Slepoy began, speaking from memory, detailing the evidence of terrible crimes in Argentina that had been presented to the judge. He laid out the international treaties, some of them incorporated into Spanish law, that formed the basis of the complaint. The Spanish court, he concluded, by unanimously affirming Garzón, could fittingly mark the upcoming fiftieth anniversary of the Universal Declaration of Human Rights. When Slepoy sat down, the public applauded. The president of the court remarked with a smile that it was not customary in Spain to applaud the lawyers—although it was occasionally all right to applaud the judges.

Enrique Santiago, lawyer for the United Left, followed, detailing the investigation process over the previous two years. He ended by saying that international public opinion would never understand how these crimes could remain unpunished, especially now, after a criminal investigation had begun. After him came Manuel Ollé. Then it was Pepe Galán's turn to lay out the case under Spanish penal law. After a short break, the family members of the Chilean victims took the place of the Argentines in the public gallery. The public prosecutor, and then Joan Garcés, argued the Chilean case, making most of the same arguments as in the Argentine hearing. No one knew how long it would take for the judges to agree on a decision. It could be days, or even weeks.

The very next day, around mid-morning, the court clerk announced that, contrary to normal custom, the judges would announce their decision from the bench. The judge in charge of writing the decision, Carlos Cezón, could barely get the first words out of his mouth, "We have decided to declare inadmissible . . ." when cheers and shouts erupted from the chamber. The public prosecutors' appeal was inadmissible, which meant that the Spanish court had jurisdiction. The lawyers, family members, ex-prisoners, and even much of the press broke into tears.

In two nearly identical decisions,[15] the appellate court upheld the jurisdiction of the Spanish courts over crimes of genocide, terrorism, and torture committed in Argentina and Chile. The decisions turn on three main issues: the definition of the crimes involved under international and Spanish law, the applicability of the current universal jurisdiction and torture provisions of law to events that took place before the laws were enacted, and the effect in Spain of the amnesty (or, in the Argentine case, due obedience) laws that shielded the defendants from prosecution at home.

The court began by considering whether the charge of genocide could be fairly laid against these defendants. The prosecutor argued that it could not. In international law terms, the closest fit to the facts involves characterizing them as "crimes against humanity."[16] The Statute of the International Criminal Court, in article 7, defines the crime as "widespread or systematic attacks against a civilian population." But this definition was not available to Garzón. Spanish universal jurisdictional law lists genocide and terrorism, as well as offenses for which treaties give jurisdiction, as the only relevant crimes the courts can consider.

The word genocide did not exist until the 1940s. Polish international lawyer Raphael Lemkin coined it to describe what the Turks did to the Armenians, and to warn that the Nazis could do the same to the Jews and other "inferior" minorities. The Holocaust remains the paradigmatic example of the crime. The 1948 Convention on the Prevention and Punishment of the Crime of Genocide set out the definition of the crime still used today: any of a series of acts, committed with the "intent to destroy, in whole or in part, a national, ethnical, racial, or religious group, as such" through killing, causing serious bodily harm, forcibly transferring children of the group to another group, or other means. Two issues arose: was there jurisdiction under the Convention (and Spanish law, which implemented it) in a Spanish national court, and did the facts fit the definition of the crime?

The Convention obligated states that signed on to punish genocide, but its article 6 only mentioned two places where the crime should be tried: the place where the acts had occurred or an international criminal tribunal. The public prosecutor's office argued that, because Spain was neither, there was no jurisdiction to prosecute under the Convention. The Audiencia Nacional made short shrift of the argument: just because the treaty listed these two kinds of jurisdiction didn't mean it excluded others.

It is not easy to prove a charge of genocide. Not only do you have to show killing, harming, or the other acts, but you have to show that the perpetrators specifically intended to destroy the victims as a group. And not just any group: the language of the convention limits its reach to "national, ethnical, racial or religious" groups. These limitations mean that even large-scale murder isn't genocide if the aim isn't to eliminate a group defined as such, a group that comes within the four categories.

Garzón had grounded the case on a broader vision of what is meant by genocide, one disdained by most Spanish (and other) academic opinion. In substantiating this broader view, Garzón got help from, among others, Federico Andreu of AI's International Secretariat and Professor Richard Wilson of American University in Washington, D.C. Wilson had been at a number of anti-impunity conferences, and was interested in involving his clinical law students in the case. He brought Garzón some interesting documentation on English-language debates over genocide in Cambodia and elsewhere, which allowed the judge to piece together a viable theory of genocide.

Garzón adopted the ideas put forward, among others, by UN Special Rapporteur Benjamin Whittaker. He argued that, as in Cambodia, a kind of auto-genocide had been committed in both Chile and Argentina. A "national" group was simply a subset of the national population singled out on the basis of some common, defining characteristic. In this case, the common characteristic was active or even passive opposition to the new vision of a "nation" and a "national project" espoused by the military governments. As the Audiencia Nacional put it in approving Garzón's views on the subject, the victims of the regime were "contrary to the understanding of national identity and national values supported by the new government." Even if the Convention text was limited to the four listed groups, the text had to be seen as a living document, to be interpreted in light of later practice and sensibilities.

In the Argentine case, Garzón added another possible ground. Using evidence of both anti-Semitism and military statements decrying the "atheistic, anti-Christian" nature of subversion, Garzón argued that the military had engaged in a "crusade" intended to destroy Jews, atheists, Christians who did not follow the official church line, or anyone else who did not fit their image of a proper Christian, and that this was equivalent to persecution of a religious group. The intent was to destroy the group in order to impose a given type of Christian ideology.

In considering whether the killings, disappearances, kidnappings, and torture of the Southern Cone regimes fit within the "genocide" definition, the Audiencia Nacional had the benefit of a peculiarity of Spanish law. When Spain ratified the Genocide Convention in 1968, it had to make genocide a crime under its national law. It did so in 1971, but changed the wording of the convention slightly, so that it read "intent to destroy a national ethnic, social or religious group." This reflected the Spanish legislature's view of genocide as a crime against groups, whatever their nature, which corresponds with the widespread popular meaning of the term, the Audiencia Nacional held, and without which the concept is incomplete. Did Spain mean to change the outlines of who was protected? It is not clear. A number of countries have done just that in their national laws, protecting political groups, social groups, or, in the case of France, any group identified by an arbitrary criterion. In 1983 Spain changed the code section to mirror the language in the Genocide Convention. But during the dates when the crimes were committed, the "social group" definition was in place.

The biggest omission of the Genocide Convention, and the one that caused Garzón and the Audiencia Nacional the most trouble, is the exclusion of political groups. Apparently, they were included in the definition of protected groups up to the very last moment, and then taken out because the Soviets objected, and a number of countries thought their neighbors would be more willing to sign on to the treaty if there was no ambiguity about whether political insurgents could be covered.

In more recent times, there has been less pressure to include political opponents as potential victims of genocide, presumably because the concept of crimes against humanity, which is now codified in the Rome Statute creating an international criminal court, does the job. And yet, given the narrow range of options before the Spanish courts, it is reasonable to ask why a limitation introduced over fifty years ago for purely tactical reasons should govern today's interpretation of the Convention. Professor William Schabas gives one reason: the Convention asks states to prevent as well as punish genocide. If we are asking states to take the prevention obligation seriously, the number of times in which they will have to act will need to be both clear and limited.[17] On the other hand, though, it seems that it is the intent to wipe out a group simply because of who it is (or is perceived as), to erase a group of people *as such*, that makes genocide so much worse than other crimes. It targets not just the individual, but the whole of the social fabric. Perhaps the interest in diverse human groupings, or historical precedents, justifies the focus on ethnicity and religion. If the narrow rather than the social view of genocide prevailed, the court noted that systematic killings of AIDs sufferers, or old people, or foreigners of different nationalities, would all be (unjustly, in the court's view) excluded from prosecution.

Terrorism provided a less controversial handle on which to hang Garzón's investigation, but one that was key to the complainants' strategy. The definition of terrorism in Spanish law refers to acts aimed at subverting the constitutional order. The public prosecutor argued that the law covered only those trying to subvert the *Spanish* constitutional order, something far from the minds of the Chileans and Argentines. The court disagreed. A terrorist was someone who tried to subvert his own constitutional order; otherwise extraterritorial jurisdiction would make no sense. Moreover, the Criminal Appeals Chamber found that it was not the Argentine (or Chilean) state as such that was terrorist, but those individuals who took advantage of state structures and resources to act like a criminal organization from within the state. It was these secret groups, epitomized by the DINA in Chile and the Grupos de Tareas in Argentina, that were the targets of the investigation.

The court then turned to the question whether it could properly investigate crimes that happened before all the current definitions of the law were in place. A cardinal maxim of international criminal law says "no crime without law," *nullum crimen sine lege*; sometimes Americans talk about the same idea as "no ex post facto law," or law made after the facts. A slightly different version of this rule applies to how states deal with each other. When states accept a treaty, they generally do so only concerning acts that take place after the treaty comes into force. The combination of these two rules has proved to create all kinds of dilemmas for judges in cases involving kidnappings, disappearances, torture, and mass killing.

The public prosecutor argued that the Spanish court could not hear the cases because the law allowing the court jurisdiction dated from 1985, well after the events of the 1970s at issue in both Chile and Argentina. Only in the Chilean case, he allowed, might there be a few post-1985 acts that would qualify (the Pinochet government stepped down in 1990). To apply a 1985 law to pre-1985 facts would violate the *nullum crimen sine lege* prohibition.

The Criminal Appeals Chamber looked at the underlying crimes, and found that the behavior to be punished had clearly been criminal by the 1970s. The 1985 law had not created new crimes or penalties, had not punished anyone or restricted anyone's rights; it had merely created the jurisdictional scheme under which trial could take place. That was a procedural norm, not a substantive one, and as such applying it retrospectively violated no due process rights.

The same issue arose with regard to torture, since the Torture Convention only came into force for Spain in the mid-1980s. (A variant of this issue would consume much of the debate in the British House of Lords.) The Spanish court avoided the problem, at least at this stage, holding that the torture charges were subsumed under the genocide charges; torture was one of the ways in which the group at issue was destroyed.

Finally, the Audiencia Nacional touched on the issue of the Argentine (and Chilean) amnesty laws. Judge Garzón had found that the existence of amnesty or due obedience laws was irrelevant to his investigation, both because Spanish law doesn't recognize general amnesties and because the laws at issue had been condemned by the Inter-American

Commission on Human Rights and the UN Human Rights Committee as violating the victims' rights. If the amnesties were invalid under international law, there was no reason why a judge outside Argentina or Chile should give them any weight. The Audiencia Nacional found that, independent of whether the laws violated treaty norms, they could not be seen as an acquittal or pardon which would preclude retrial in Spain, and so were irrelevant to the proceedings.

At the House of Lords

The House of Lords is a venerable institution. Twelve of its members are not only legislators but also sit as the highest court of appeal for the United Kingdom. In their guise as the Privy Council, they also serve as the ultimate arbiter for disputes from other British Commonwealth countries. Unlike the U.S. Supreme Court, the House of Lords in its judicial capacity sits in panels rather than as a whole, and judges give individual opinions rather than a majority view. Knowing what the law is, then, requires counting the number of votes for each argument. A panel of five Law Lords was chosen at random to hear the appeal in Pinochet. Of the five, two were noted commercial lawyers. Two had been born in South Africa.

On November 4, just a day after Spanish judge Garzón asked formally for Pinochet's extradition, the five panel members met to hear argument on whether Pinochet should be extradited. Representing Pinochet were Clive Nicholls and Claire Montgomery. Alun Jones again represented the Crown Prosecution Service, in its capacity as lawyer for the Spanish seeking extradition. But this time he had help. The human rights groups had decided to sit out the High Court hearing and had been disappointed in the treatment of the international law issues there. They wanted these arguments given a full airing in the higher court, and could bring in the experts to do so. Amnesty International, the other human rights groups, and the British victims jointly requested intervenor status before the court, which would allow the organizations to appear before the judges, argue, and file briefs. "There was no precedent for intervention in the House of Lords except one: in a child abuse case, the Society for the Protection of Children intervened," recounts Geoffrey Bindman. "Pinochet was the first for a human rights organization. Who knows if it will be the last." A half hour after submitting the petition for intervention, Bindman got a call from one of the Lords informing him that the judges had decided to accept it. The House of Lords also agreed to accept written representations from Human Rights Watch, which later proved influential to several Lords. In addition, the court appointed Mr. Lloyd Jones as *amicus curiae* (friend of the court) to advise on the precedents. The decision to allow Amnesty International into the case was soon to prove fateful.

Argument over the eight days of hearings focused on the question of Pinochet's immunity as a former head of state. The judges concentrated on the arcane provisions of the 1978 British law that governed the immunity of diplomats, because no specific provision referred to former heads of state. The law said that a diplomat (and by extension a former head of state) had immunity for "official" acts performed as part of his functions, but not otherwise. Could the crimes of torture, hostage-taking, and genocide be considered part of a head of state's official functions?

On the morning of November 25, the Lords announced their decision to a packed chamber, before the assembled journalists and television cameras.[18] Baltazár Garzón watched the decision on Madrid TV, with a TV announcer who breathlessly narrated the scene as though it were a question of penalty kicks at a soccer match, and who could not keep straight what a yes or no vote meant.[19] The judges spoke in order of seniority. The first two judges to speak, Lords Slynn and Lloyd, summarized their decisions: Pinochet had immunity from extradition as a matter of customary international law, and none of the treaties requiring prosecution of human rights-related crimes explicitly removed that immunity. Then came Lord Steyn and Lord Nicholls: they found no immunity for conduct that, because it was an international crime, could not possibly be an official function. It was 2-2. Nicole Drouilly and the other Chileans sitting in the gallery held their breath. Lord Hoffman rose to speak. Hoffman's speech was one sentence long. "My lords, I have had the advantage of reading in draft the speech of my noble and learned friend Lord Nicholls of Birkenhead and for the reasons he gives I too would allow this appeal." The gallery erupted into cheers; people hugged each other, crying. On the streets of Santiago and Madrid, people celebrated. Pinochet was not immune from extradition. It must have been a rather glum eighty-third birthday for him.

Two weeks later, Home Secretary Jack Straw issued an authority to proceed, setting in motion the formal extradition process. In light of the intense public interest in the case, Straw made public his reasons for issuing the authority. He noted that Pinochet was accused in Spain of offenses equivalent to those of attempted murder, conspiracy to murder, torture, conspiracy to torture, hostage taking, and conspiracy to take hostages. Even though Spain had included genocide charges, he found that genocide could not be considered an "extradition crime" (because genocide committed abroad was not part of the British penal code) and so threw those charges out. He also repeated the Divisional Court's statement that the offense should be a criminal offense in the UK at the time extradition is requested, not the time the conduct alleged occurred. There were no bars to extradition because of immunities, political offense exceptions, or the passage of time.

Straw included consideration of the political and humanitarian factors. "It does not appear that the Senator is unfit to stand trial and . . . in all the circumstances it would not be unjust or oppressive for him to stand trial in relation to the offenses with which he is charged." With regard to the Chilean government's argument that Pinochet could stand trial in Chile, Straw pointed out that Chile had not asked for his extradition. He added that the possible effects on the stability of Chile and its future democracy did not amount to sufficient grounds not to proceed. The exhaustive discussion was obviously aimed at quashing any attempts by Pinochet's lawyers to seek judicial review based on arguments that Straw had not adequately considered one or more factors.

Once the authority to proceed was granted, extradition hearings per se could commence. On December 11, Pinochet appeared for the first time in public, in the local Belmarsh court. He used a wheelchair and spoke only briefly. Pulling himself up to as close to military bearing as he could muster, he announced, in Spanish, that he did not recognize the jurisdiction of any courts but the Chilean to try him for anything. He was held over for extradition proceedings and returned to his gilded cage, a rented mansion in Surrey where he remained under house arrest.

Straw had also rejected a request from Pinochet's lawyers to set the House of Lords judgment aside on grounds of alleged bias on the part of one of the law lords. But days after he signed the authority to proceed, the bias issue exploded in the courts. To the dismay of the human rights activists, the House of Lords decision was set aside. A new panel of judges would rehear the case. It was back to square one.

Lord Hoffman and the Issue of Bias

It has long been a maxim of law that "no man can be a judge in his own case." Over the years, rules developed about when judges had to withdraw, or recuse themselves, from a case before them. Most obviously, judges could not be a party to a case before them. Nor could a judge sit on a case in which he or she had an obvious interest: the criminal trial of a father-in-law, or a civil trial involving a company in which she or he owned a controlling share. But how far did this rule extend? Pinochet's lawyers, a month after losing the extradition appeal in the House of Lords, argued that it extended this far: Lord Hoffman, the judge who had cast the deciding vote, should have been barred from the case because he was on the board of directors of a charity connected to Amnesty International. Even though everyone, including Pinochet's lawyers, conceded that his link to AI had not actually influenced his decision in the case, the defense contended that the appearance of impropriety was enough. His vote should not be counted or, at least, the judgment should be thrown out and redone. On December 17, 1998 (followed by a written decision a month later) the House of Lords agreed.

How could this have happened? How could a case this notorious, with high stakes and experienced lawyers, have gotten this far without the conflict of interest issue being raised and resolved? The answers, predictably, depend on whom you talk to. Pinochet's lawyers insisted they had first heard of a link when a Chilean senator mentioned ties between Lady Hoffman, the judge's wife, and AI on the BBC news. The lawyers followed up, sending a note to Geoffrey Bindman, Amnesty's solicitor, asking for information on Lady Hoffman's position within the organization. Bindman replied that she had worked in administrative positions at Amnesty since 1977, and since 1994 had worked in the media department. She had no substantive role in the Pinochet litigation. Why, Bindman asked, did Pinochet's lawyers want to know?

Pinochet's lawyers, looking for an angle to improve an unfavorable position, now smelled a possible strategy. They asked Bindman for more information about both Lord and Lady Hoffman's links to the organization, and added that they were considering the question of actual or apparent bias. On December 7, Pinochet's lawyers got a break. They, they said, received an anonymous tip, in which a man telephoned to tell them that Lord Hoffman was a director of the Amnesty International Charity Limited (AICL). The next day, Bindman confirmed that link. AICL is a registered charity, set up to allow AI's research, publication, and relief efforts to earn normal tax benefits under UK law. Lord Hoffman and Peter Duffy, Q.C. were the only directors. These kinds of arrangements are quite common among large non-profits. They do not generally require a large commitment of time or energy on the part of the charity's directors.

It is easy to see, in retrospect, why Lord Hoffman would have neglected to mention the link to AICL, or why, if he did so, his fellow judges might have found it unnecessary to pursue the issue or to ask for his recusal. The hearing had come up very quickly, and everyone involved felt a sense of urgency to decide the matter as soon as possible. There had never before been a situation where a non-economic interest in a case was considered enough to disqualify a judge. Most of the law lords supported various charities, some concerned with human rights issues. Indeed, Lord Hoffman had worked on a fundraising appeal for AI's new London offices along with Lord Bingham, who had ruled in favor of Pinochet's immunity at the High Court. Pinochet's lawyers, as Bindman pointed out, had themselves contributed some £1,000 to that appeal.

Why Amnesty International itself failed to catch the potential problem is more difficult to determine. AI is a big organization, however, and AICL was a rather obscure financial mechanism known to few staffers, so it probably just fell through the cracks. Time pressures and the lack of clear precedent affected Amnesty as well. In addition, many people may have felt that disqualifying a judge on the basis of a purported ideological link was dangerous. Lord Hoffman had made his reputation as a brilliant commercial lawyer, not an activist.

Many of the activists and human rights lawyers involved in the case are convinced that Pinochet's lawyers had known at least about Lady Hoffman's job for months, and were holding onto the information to be pulled out of their sleeve should they lose the appeal. After all, the information was public, as were Lord Hoffman's fundraising solicitation letters. If that had been proven to be the case, the Lords could easily have rejected the bias claim as untimely. If it were known before, why did the defense team wait until after they'd lost to raise the issue? But there was no such proof.

In any case, the December revelations created an unprecedented situation for the House of Lords. It was not even clear whether they could set aside an earlier decision, let alone whether they could do so on grounds of apparent, not actual, bias. Montgomery argued that if the country's highest court couldn't invalidate its own decision on bias grounds, who could? On December 17, 1998, the Lords found that they had no choice but to set aside their earlier opinion.[20]

The decision triggered a number of legal debates within the UK. The House of Lords rarely received the intense press scrutiny it now endured. Perhaps, as some argued, the House of Lords itself was now an outmoded vestige of the British past.[21] Parties with cases before the Law Lords began raising bias issues left and right.[22] Eventually, the government's senior legal officer stated that he was looking at the possibility of a Register of Interests for judges, in order to defuse future potential conflicts of interest.

The decision exacerbated existing tensions within the NGO groups fighting for extradition, including the various Amnesty International entities. Lady Hoffman's employment was well known, but for most of those involved in the legal strategizing this was the first time they had heard of the Amnesty-related charity. For Amnesty activists, the commotion had the clear advantage of identifying the prosecution of Pinochet with Amnesty as an organization. Support poured in from the grass roots. For some of the other NGOs, there was concern that AI had jeopardized the whole case by wanting to be in the forefront and by not doing a better job of checking out possible conflicts.

Beyond the issue of Lord Hoffman's role, there were more profound differences among the intervenors. In every high-profile public interest case, tensions are bound to arise because everyone is trying to meet more than one objective. It is important to win, and to win the way your clients want, but it is also important to make good law for the future and to educate the public about the larger issues involved. Sometimes these goals conflict. Here, for instance, Amnesty was trying to be a dispassionate, objective expert on international law for the Law Lords, but also an effective activist organization swaying British and world public opinion and supporting the Chilean victims of the Pinochet regime. The legal arm needed a low public profile and a focus on the international law arguments, not on Pinochet's guilt or the debate over where best to try him. The activist arm needed lots of publicity and a clear moral stance. It was hard to do both at once, especially when different parts of the organization were in charge of the two different tasks. Other tensions arose: some members of the team wanted to rely on UK statutory law, which was more familiar to the judges and more likely to win, while others thought it important to set a precedent based on international law. On top of these tensions, there was the sheer exhaustion. Other work had to be dropped; families were neglected. On the other hand, being in the eye of the hurricane around the case was exhilarating.

In any case, the decision to set aside the House of Lords decision gave those involved a little more time to refine their arguments. A new panel of judges was chosen, consisting of the seven Lords who had not heard the first appeal. Argument was set for January 18, 1999.

With more time to prepare, all sides reevaluated their strategy over the holiday break. The major issue in *Pinochet I* had been Pinochet's immunity as a former head of state. Pinochet's defenders had focused on immunity because it was a threshold issue: if there was immunity, there was no need to proceed. The House of Lords decision, by a bare majority, that torture could not constitute the kind of official act protected by state immunity, now presented a problem. It was possible to convince a new panel of judges to go the other way, but not likely. The judges would be influenced by the institutional imperative to maintain uniformity between different panels of the same court, to avoid appearing arbitrary. With this in mind, the defense team began looking for other possible arguments.

The CPS and the intervenors also started rethinking the immunity arguments. The decision in the first round had been too close for comfort. What if the whole immunity question could be avoided? The Chilean groups and their lawyer Joan Garcés in Madrid reminded the British lawyers of the history. Pinochet had actually begun plotting the military coup that brought him to power well before September 11, 1973, including provisions for arrest of Allende supporters if the coup was successful. If there was a conspiracy to torture (as Alun Jones, the CPS lawyer, urged the judges to read the factual allegations), it had started before Pinochet became head of the military junta. What is more, being a member of a four-person junta was different from being head of state. Pinochet had actually only assumed that title nearly a year after the coup, in June 1974. Many of the worst cases of torture and disappearance (as well as murder) had taken place during those first months. This issue had been tentatively raised before the first panel, but none of the judges had paid much attention to it. Jones traveled to Madrid to meet with Garzón and Garcés. Together they put together a new slant on the question of immunity. When the hearings started again in January, Judge Garzón was sitting at the prosecution table, just behind the lawyers for the Crown Prosecution Service.

The hearings took twelve days in all. Throughout, the various lawyers and experts expounded and the Law Lords asked questions, went around in circles, and bounced from fine points of law to basic queries about the nature of customary law and international crime. Lord Browne-Wilkinson, for example, admitted that "you are going to have to tell me when things do become part of international law and when they do not. It is a point I have never understood since I was at Oxford."[23] Before them sat "bundles" of documents, pages and pages of them, which the lawyers referred to in order to back up one or another point. In the bundles were not only each side's briefs and memorandums, but case decisions from almost a dozen countries, international decisions and treaties, and the works of international organizations and scholars. It was an almost overwhelming mass of information to digest.

On March 24, 1999, the Lords announced their decision to a packed chamber.[24] In the English tradition, each judge gave his own opinion and it was up to the spectators to add up the votes. It was not easy to do in this case. Several things were clear. By a vote of six to one, the Lords decided that Pinochet had committed extraditable crimes and that his immunity as a former head of state did not extend to these crimes. Torture could be prosecuted, even if the person ordering it was a once a high-ranking official. Furthermore, under the Torture Convention, states had an obligation, not just an option, to act against allegations of torture. These holdings represented major steps forward in international criminal law.

The judges agreed by a clear majority on the basics. Beyond that, the judgments take various paths. Common to most of them is that they rely on the intricacies of UK, not international law. To the extent international law comes into play, a majority of the Lords looked to treaty law, in this case the Torture Convention, rather than to the more nebulous (and harder for judges to understand) concepts of customary international law. Only Lord Millet looked to customary law as the basis of his discussion. In terms of the development of international law, this decision was far more conservative than that of the first panel. Wherever the judges had a choice, they took the more limited route.

The judgment focused on two points: the "double criminality" issue and the immunity of an ex-head of state. Even though the language of the UK Extradition Act and the discussion in the lower courts seemed to indicate otherwise, the judges found that the conduct at issue had to have been a crime under UK law at the date it happened, rather than at the date extradition was requested. The result was that the judges decided to limit Pinochet's extraditable crimes to those that occurred after 1988, although they disagreed about the exact date in 1988. Three picked the date the UK ratified the Convention Against Torture (December 8), while two chose the date the domestic implementing legislation came into force (September 29) and one picked the date of Chile's ratification (October 30). In any case, the upshot was to exclude almost all the charges against Pinochet: what remained were one act of post-1988 torture and conspiracy to torture.

On the immunity question, a majority of the Lords found that while a sitting head of state has personal immunity, a former head of state's immunity is limited to his official acts. Three of the Lords then found that torture and conspiracy to torture could not be part of a head of state's official functions. Lord Browne-Wilkinson grounded this rule in the Torture Convention, Lord Hutton in customary law that made torture an international crime, and Lord Phillips in a rule that said former heads of state never have immunity. Lords Hope and Saville thought that there was immunity under international law, but that Chile had waived that immunity by ratifying the Torture Convention. Lord Goff thought that while immunity could be waived, it had to be done explicitly and not by implication through ratifying the treaty; thus, for him alone, Pinochet still had immunity. Lord Millet found that torture had been a crime under customary international law long before 1988, and so there was no immunity for any of the charges. In this, his explanation more closely matched that of the majority in *Pinochet I*, which had relied much more on general, broad principles of international law.

The Lords seemed to be looking for the narrowest possible way to satisfy everyone involved. The intervenors got a declaration that there was no immunity for torture even by a former head of state. The Crown got to proceed with extradition, although on a vastly reduced slate of charges. Pinochet's defense got statements from almost all the judges, pointing out that discarding most of the charges put the case into a whole new light, and inviting the Home Secretary to reconsider the authority to proceed. But in attempting to satisfy these multiple constituencies, the Lords also highlighted the limitations of deciding important cases by panels of less than the whole. The reasoning in this case differed significantly from that of the first panel, even though the overall result—a go-ahead to extradition—was the same.

Once the Lords rendered their decision, the ball was back in Jack Straw's court. Would he accept the court's open invitation to reject the extradition request because it now encompassed far fewer charges? Pinochet's lawyers pressed their advantage. The new charges, they argued, no longer amounted to a massive or systematic practice of torture, and the House of Lords had tied its immunity finding to that kind of torture, which amounts to a crime against humanity. This was a flatly untrue reading of the decision, although certain individual opinions did seem to lean in that direction.

On April 5, Straw reissued the authority to proceed. He didn't need to look into the number or quality of charges, he found, because the European Convention on Extradition did not require the extraditing state to consider whether there was enough evidence for trial; that was up to the state requesting extradition. Any other questions arising from the nature and quality of the charges could best be considered during the court stages of the extradition proceedings. For the same reason, Straw would not consider any new material from Spain, except to conclude that there was no reason to think (as Pinochet alleged) that the Spanish charges were not made in good faith. He again rejected assertions that Chile would be a better forum or that Pinochet's health should exempt him. After all, he would get a final chance to consider the matter after the case had gone through the extradition hearing and the expected subsequent appeals, which could take over a year.

Finally, after three appeals dealing with the preliminary question of immunity, the British courts could begin the actual extradition hearing. Meanwhile, as summer approached, the diplomatic maneuvers were about to intensify.

End Game in London

With the extradition hearing set for September, the spring and summer of 1999 were a time of intense diplomatic and legal maneuvering. On the legal front, the Crown Prosecution Service asked Garzón to submit any other post-1988 cases within his dossier that could bolster the case. The attorneys for the Spanish complainants moved into high gear to find information to bring before the judge. There had been, from the beginning, some worries that the date of ratification of the Torture Convention might prove important, and so Amnesty London and the other human rights groups as well as the attorneys in Spain had long before begun looking for more witnesses and documents on torture during Pinochet's last years in office. After March, the search intensified. Lawyers at the Chilean legal assistance groups received urgent e-mails from Spain. The Chilean lawyers at CODEPU, FASIC, and other legal groups began combing through case files and through lists of clients of their related social service and counseling arms. They tracked down people who had complained of mistreatment by security forces in 1989 and 1990 and sent the case histories on to Spain.

By September, Garzón was able to add 34 new cases to the indictment and send them to London to beef up the extradition request. In addition, Garzón pointed out that well over a thousand people had disappeared in Chile. Because they had never reappeared, the crime of their kidnapping continued, and for some of them there was evidence of torture after they were detained. Furthermore, the families suffered the mental anguish of not knowing whether they were dead or alive. According to a recent case at the European Court of Human Rights involving Turkish disappearances, the effect on the families could constitute mental torture, and it too would continue beyond 1988.[25] Garzón sought to add these cases as well.

As it became clear that a legal win for Pinochet was no longer a foregone conclusion, the diplomatic battle escalated. From the beginning, the Chilean government had taken the position that Chilean sovereignty was at stake here and that the detention was invalid. When the House of Lords announced their March decision, Foreign Minister José Insulza traveled first to London and then to Madrid to meet with Prime Minister Aznar and Abel Matutes, the Spanish foreign minister. The Chilean military, in addition to making pilgrimages to Surrey to see their chief, began sending missions to Madrid. For months Pinochet had declined to name a lawyer before the Spanish court, not wanting to appear to recognize Garzón's jurisdiction as legitimate, but now he began assembling a legal team.

Aznar began expressing his reservations publicly: "I don't want Spain to become an International Criminal Court," he told reporters.[26] At the same time, Aznar was cautious in his criticism. He had no close ties to the governing coalition in Chile, and the discomfiture of the Socialist Party cannot have been all bad from his perspective. Aznar, moreover, headed a minority coalition government, and the case had attracted broad support within Spain, including from the Spanish Parliament.

Meanwhile, on April 23, 1999, Chile's foreign minister announced that Chile was seeking arbitration of the matter, either under the Torture Convention or, when that turned out to be problematic, under a 1927 arbitration treaty. Initially, Spain was interested. On August 1, the new Chilean foreign minister, Juan Gabriel Valdés, told the press that "we have clear signals that the Spanish government, in very good faith, is . . . studying the idea of arbitration."[27] When the idea hit the Spanish media, however, it caused an outcry. The daily *El País* editorialized: "the principle of judicial independence cannot be destroyed in the name of reasons of State."[28] When the Spanish government asked Spanish Socialist party (PSOE) leader Joaquín Almunia to support arbitration should the issue come before Parliament, Almunia refused. At that point, the influence of Felipe González, a staunch opponent of Garzón's investigation, had waned considerably, and the PSOE was not about to be seen as undermining the judiciary. Three days later, the PSOE demanded on the floor of Congress that the government explain its actions. The lawyers and judges associations were, almost unanimously, opposed to arbitration. In the face of this ferocious opposition, the Aznar government backed off. The promise of a quick resolution of an unwanted conflict with Chile was not worth the price of a domestic battle over the prerogatives of the courts.

The summer recess over, all the players turned to preparing for the extradition hearing to be held in late September before Judge Ronald Bartle back at the Bow Street courthouse in Central London. The hearing began on September 27. Pinochet was excused from the hearing because of his poor physical health. His defense counsel, however, went on the offensive. New charges, he argued, could not be introduced at this stage, and without them there was no proof of the systematic torture needed to convict the defendant. No, replied the Crown Prosecution Service, the new charges were perfectly proper, and the judge could consider them even if the Home Secretary had not needed them to make a decision. What's more, a single act of torture would suffice for extradition, and there was much more than that in the record.

After a week or so of deliberation, Magistrate Bartle delivered his opinion.[29] Compared to the convoluted House of Lords decisions, his was a model of simplicity and clarity. He must have thought that some clarification to the public was necessary, because he began by explaining the role of the court in extradition proceedings, what the proceedings were meant to do, and what his own role in them was. Like the Torture Convention, international treaties "represent the growing trend of the international community to combine together to outlaw crimes which are abhorrent to civilized society, whether they be offences of the kind to which I have referred or crimes of cruelty and violence which may be committed by individuals, by terrorist groups seeking to influence or overthrow democratic governments or by undemocratic governments against their own citizens. This development may be said to presage the day when, for the purposes of extradition, there will be one law for one world."

This stage of the process was not supposed to evaluate guilt or innocence, only determine if the prerequisites for extradition were met. He allowed in the new charges, found they constituted extraditable offenses, and added two considerations that, if and when the case arrived in Spain, would be crucial. First, "information relating to the allegation of conspiracy prior to 8th December 1988 can be considered by the court, as conspiracy is a continuing offence." Second, "whether the disappearances amount to torture; the effect on the families of those who disappeared can amount to mental torture. Whether or not this was intended by the regime of Senator Pinochet is in my view a matter of fact for the trial court."

These last two rulings meant that the Spanish courts could look at all the evidence, not just that after 1988, in deciding Pinochet's guilt or innocence. They made the case potentially much easier to prove, allowed the witness testimony already gathered to be used at trial, and avoided the criticism that the whole course of crimes during the military dictatorship had been reduced to a couple of halfhearted acts at its tail end.

About a year of further appeals could have followed, but the legal issues remaining to the defense were getting thinner by the day. The General, depressed by the turn of events, suffered two small strokes during the fall. By November the question of Pinochet's fitness to stand trial had taken center stage.

Pinochet's lawyers had been reluctant to raise the health issue, in part because the general himself still preferred to fight on legal grounds. The Chilean government had no such reluctance, however, and sent evidence of medical deterioration to Straw, pleading for Pinochet's release as a humanitarian gesture. The Chilean army took control of Pinochet's daily routine at his Surrey residence, and discouraged visitors. There followed a period of negotiation with Pinochet's lawyers to obtain his consent to be examined by a team of doctors chosen by the UK. The agreement included assurances of confidentiality. A panel was duly appointed, including two eminent geriatric medicine specialists, a neurologist, and, as a consultant, a Spanish-speaking neuropsychologist. Their findings, after a morning of physical tests and an afternoon with the neuropsychologist, were that Pinochet was unfit to stand trial. He had "memory deficit for both recent and remote events, limited ability to comprehend complex sentences and questions owing to memory impairment and consequences; inability to process verbal information appropriately; impaired ability to express himself" and was easily tired. "With these impediments he would be unable to follow the process of a trial sufficiently to instruct counsel . . . and would have difficulty making himself heard and understood in replying to questions." What's more, the doctors added, these conditions could not have been faked.[30]

On January 11, 2000, Jack Straw announced that, based on the medical evidence, he was "minded . . . to take the view that no purpose would be served by continuing the . . . proceedings."[31] He gave the interested parties a week to comment on his proposed decision. The Spanish government, no doubt immensely relieved, promptly declared that they would not contest the British decision. Judge Garzón, in Spain, fumed that the decision whether to contest was for the judge, not the Foreign Ministry, to make, and wrote to Straw arguing that denying him at least access to the medical reports that underlay the decision "rendered illusory the guarantees . . . of equality of arms."[32] He asked for copies of the medical reports, to be allowed to depose Pinochet himself, and to use his own doctors to do a second medical exam. But to no avail. On January 17, the Spanish ambassador wrote to the Home Secretary that Spain would accept his discretionary decision.

The Belgian government, however, decided to fight. On January 19, two days after it became clear that Spain would back down, Belgium asked to be able to do its own medical examination. The complainants' lawyer announced that Belgium was preparing to take the case to the International Court of Justice. On January 24, the Belgians backtracked a little, asking merely to be able to see a copy of the existing report and question its authors. The Home Office replied that General Pinochet had politely refused to release the report to the states requesting extradition. On January 27, the Belgians sued in British court, along with the intervening human rights organizations.

Why the Belgian insistence? I asked that question of parliamentarians, lawyers and government officials. All had a similar set of explanations. Legally, a 1993 law, which I discuss in Chapters 5 and 7, provided a clear legal basis for Belgian jurisdiction, and Belgian law had no exemptions for health reasons. Internal politics also mattered: the Belgian coalition government was new, and had come into office (in June 1999) as a "Rainbow Coalition" of Liberals, Socialists, and Greens on the heels of an administration dogged by scandals over its handling of serial murders and dioxin contamination of the food supply. Prosecuting Pinochet would give the government a chance to show off its new pro-human rights agenda. In part, the government's stance reflected its costless nature. Belgium came after Spain, France, and Switzerland on the extradition calendar. It was unlikely ever to gain possession of the accused and actually have to try him.

Three days later, the trial court dismissed the suit, holding that neither Amnesty nor the Belgian government had standing to challenge the government's decision not to release the report. The Belgian government (along with Amnesty and the other human rights groups) appealed. On February 15, Britain's High Court reversed the decision and ordered Straw to release the report to Belgium, Spain, France, and Switzerland, all the countries that had pending extradition requests.[33] The medical report was duly released to the four countries.

Doctors, like lawyers, often disagree with one another, and it was not long before criticisms of the medical examinations started coming in, especially after the results of the exams were leaked to the Spanish press. A group of eminent Spanish doctors, consulted by Judge Garzón, complained that the tests were insufficient and inappropriate for older patients, that there were no psychological exams, that Pinochet's eleven different medications were not factored in, and that the neurological examination results were within the normal range for a man of his age. "From the evidence drawn from the analyzed reports, it can be deduced that Mr. Pinochet presents both a physical and mental condition sufficiently normal to face any uncomfortable situation, such as presence at a trial."[34]

But by then the die was cast. On March 2, 2000, Jack Straw issued a final decision not to proceed with the extradition. Before the assembled House of Commons, Straw explained his decision. He pointed to the medical evidence to conclude that "the trial of an accused in the condition diagnosed in Senator Pinochet, on the charges which have been made against him in this case, could not be fair in any country." He acknowledged the 70,000 letters and emails he had received about the case, almost all in favor of extradition, and nodded to the "importance of the principle that universal jurisdiction against persons charged with international crimes should be effective."[35] But, he concluded, given the evidence, he had had no choice. There were boos from the floor of the Commons, but also, more discreetly, a sigh of relief that the Home Secretary had found a graceful way to get Britain off the hook.

At that point the chances of a successful appeal were slim, and none of the complainants had the stomach for a further fight. For the Belgians, who had been under considerable diplomatic pressure from the UK, Spain, and Chile to forgo their appeal, challenging Straw's decision would have meant arguing, in essence, that a fellow European Union country's fair trial procedures were inadequate. The Belgian Foreign Ministry, though deeply disappointed in the outcome, was not willing to go that far. For Amnesty and the other human rights groups, pressure to desist came from a worry that at some point they would be seen to be hounding an old man past the bounds of propriety, no matter what he had done. If this was about justice, not vengeance, then it would not do to be seen "chasing him down the runway" as one activist put it. It was more important to focus on the gains for international law, not just for this case. Even if the activists had their doubts about the veracity of the medical findings, they admitted that, should they be true, international human rights norms as well as common sense forbid trying someone who is not able to understand and participate in the proceedings.

Why did Jack Straw change his mind? After all, he had twice given the go-ahead for extradition proceedings, by issuing an "authority to proceed." He had gone forward even when the House of Lords decision in *Pinochet III* gave him an easy out, one explicitly invited by the judges when they reduced the number of charges. His foreign secretary, Robin Cook, had consistently maintained the government's commitment to an "ethical foreign policy."

By early 2000, however, the balance of costs and benefits had shifted. Media attention had waned. The Labor government's commitment to international law and justice had been established, and the law had been allowed (with exception of final habeas corpus appeals) to take its course. The outcome would send Pinochet home a free man, but as a recipient of pity, not a legal victor. Within Chile, the government line had changed from a ringing defense of sovereignty to a public commitment to try Pinochet at home. Criminal investigations of high-ranking military officers were advancing after years of foot-dragging.

And, of course, pressure was building on the other side. The social democratic parties of Europe and Latin America were concerned that Pinochet's continuing detention might jeopardize the chances of Ricardo Lagos, the first Socialist since Allende to seek the Chilean presidency. According to several journalists' reports, the deal to release Pinochet was struck at a Euro-Latin American conference in Brazil that summer.[36] There, Foreign Ministers Cook and Valdés agreed that Chile would push forward on a humanitarian strategy for releasing Pinochet before the end of Frei's term in office. Abel Matutes agreed that the Spanish government would not contest a decision by the Home Secretary to send the general home. Frei and Tony Blair also cemented a "back-channel," opened earlier that year, relying on contacts related to the Socialist Party.

The rest, according to journalists and some of the Chileans involved in the case, was the playing out of a "done deal" to release Pinochet. Even without such a "deal," the continuation of normal diplomatic contacts among the three states is, in fact, evidence that the affair was handled without creating a sense of crisis or breakdown of normal political channels.

Despite the fears of each of the three governments, the damage to interstate relations turned out to be ephemeral. True, there were harsh statements exchanged on all sides, bilateral official meetings between Chile and both the UK and Spain were suspended, and the Chilean ambassador in London was recalled temporarily. Chilean flights to the British Falkland Islands (Malvinas) were stopped and the Chilean military mission in Madrid was downgraded. The Spanish and British embassies in Santiago maintained barriers and police protection. The Chilean government sought the solidarity of fellow Latin governments and got a declaration against the extraterritorial application of law by national courts that could be interpreted to refer to the Spanish prosecution of Pinochet—or, as easily, to the U.S. Helms-Burton laws applying U.S. sanctions to European and Latin American companies doing business in Cuba. In Latin America, only the Argentines, facing their own set of extradition requests from Judge Garzón, vociferously decried Spain's overreaching.

On the economic front, the damage seems to have been temporary and minor. The most important effect was on military sales. The Chilean military, guaranteed a portion of the country's copper revenues, had become an important importer as well as regional exporter of military equipment. As you will recall, part of the reason for Pinochet's trips to London was to browse British ordnance factories. Spain too was a major source of arms. From 1982 to 1998, Spain sold Chile $740 million in military equipment. With Pinochet's arrest, sales were suspended (but not canceled), including a $35-million French-Spanish deal for the sale of transport planes to the Chilean military that eventually went through.[37]

Economic relations continued pretty much unchanged. Spanish exports to Chile declined some 12 percent from 1997 to 1998, but apparently due more to the effect of the Southeast Asian economic crisis than to the Pinochet case.[38] In 1998, as before, Chile was the second largest recipient of Spanish direct investment and Spain was the largest foreign investor in Chile. Spanish investments tended to be large, and long-term, in telecommunications, banks, electricity provision, and agriculture. A "thunderstorm" (Spanish academic Remiro Brotóns's term) like the detention of Pinochet was not about to stand in the way of these long-term plans.

Of course, in many ways the circumstances of this case were ideal for minimizing conflict. There was, for instance, never any question about the ability of the Chilean government to inflict serious economic or military retaliation on either Spain or the UK. The three governments involved were all centrist, committed to an independent judiciary and a subordinate military. The Chilean Concertación coalition, while it felt obliged to defend Pinochet, surely bore him no great affection, and many of its members were privately pleased at the turn of events. A multitude of public and private channels of communication existed to smooth over difficulties. Most other governments, to the extent they expressed themselves at all on the subject, supported the Spanish right to seek extradition, and the British right to carry out the extradition proceedings.

With Pinochet's homecoming, attention shifted to maneuvers in the Chilean courts. The British extradition attempt had left a lasting legacy: the notion, confirmed by one of the world's most venerable legal institutions, that torture and conspiracy to torture are not protected by former state position. Retired state officials and military commanders began factoring the precedent into their travel plans. Guatemalan ex-strongman Efraín Rios Montt blustered but finally canceled a planned trip to Paris. Other potential suspects suddenly found medical treatment at home to be more than adequate. The Israeli military issued instructions for officers planning to travel abroad on how to avoid arrest. Even if nothing else, Pinochet's detention had given new teeth to international law.

Chapter 3

The Investigations Come Home to Chile

Homecoming

Jack Straw's decision to let Pinochet go home set in motion the long-standing plans of the Chilean military. Not about to take chances on a last-minute Interpol warrant, the air force plane carried enough fuel to ensure reaching Chile nonstop. Pinochet celebrated in his flying hospital, no doubt savoring Margaret Thatcher's parting gift of a silver plate originally crafted to commemorate the British victory over the Spanish navy in 1588. "I know you'll appreciate and enjoy the symbolism," she wrote him. At home, the head of the army worked on his welcoming speech, while incoming President Ricardo Lagos told journalists that any pending issues were for the courts, a position he would repeat many times over the next months. Lagos was a Socialist who spent the early years of the dictatorship outside the country. He participated in a number of opposition initiatives during the 1980s, but the moment that made him famous came during the 1989 plebescite on Pinochet's rule. Lagos, in the name of the "No" vote, challenged Pinochet on national TV, pointing his finger into the camera like an exasperated school-teacher, and exclaiming "it seems inconceivable to me that any Chilean could be so thirsty for power that he would try to keep it for twenty-five years!"

Outgoing president Frei Ruíz-Tagle, who had made Pinochet's return one of his administration's promises, thought he had negotiated a low-key homecoming for the General. In exchange for the government's help in getting him home, Pinochet was to go quietly to his hacienda in the country, stay out of politics, and generally act like someone deserving of medical and humanitarian leave. Frei wanted to put the incident behind him and to turn over a government unencumbered by the past. At the same time, he had promised a number of European governments that local courts would try Pinochet. Indeed, he had staked the country's prestige on the argument that local courts not only could but would do justice.

As the airplane touched down on the morning of March 3, about 100 people were waiting on the tarmac. They included the top brass of all the Chilean security forces, the businessmen who had paid the bills in London, family, and political supporters of the general. As a military band played his favorite marches, Pinochet descended from the plane. But the decrepit, pitiable figure of Jack Straw's invocation had disappeared. Instead, a rosy-cheeked Pinochet left his wheelchair behind, walked from the plane, lifted his cane to show he could walk unaided, and strolled through the crowd, greeting supporters by name. He headed to the waiting Super Puma helicopter and took off for the Military Hospital.

Accusations quickly flew: Pinochet had tricked the doctors; the foreign minister had tricked the British; the general's lawyers had tricked both the foreign minister and the British; the Chilean, British, and Spanish governments had conspired to trick the world into thinking the general was sicker than he now seemed. The head of Congress worried that the welcome would hurt the country's image. Talks between the military and human rights lawyers collapsed when the lawyers walked out, enraged by the spectacle. The British press headlined "Pinocheat!"[1]

For the incoming Lagos government, Pinochet's choice not to come home quietly confirmed their earlier decision to frame the issue strictly as one for the courts. Until January 1998 there had never been a complaint naming Pinochet as a defendant. Gladys Marín, secretary general of the Chilean Communist Party, made the first, charging Pinochet with the disappearance of the Party's Central Committee, including her husband, Jorge Muñoz. Eduardo Contreras, Marín's lawyer, was exiled for fifteen years and returned in 1990. He told me, "When I came back to Chile, I would go to meetings of human rights lawyers and suggest that we file complaints against Pinochet. I figured, if they're rejected, it'll be clear to the whole world that there's no justice available in Chile. Everyone told me I was crazy, that it was impossible. Not even the [Association of] family members of those killed or disappeared would sign on."

The 1996 Spanish investigation planted the idea that Pinochet could be taken on, at least abroad. Then Pinochet resigned as commander-in-chief, not before assuring his immunity from criminal process by becoming a senator for life (a provision of the 1980 constitution). His arrival in the Senate created a "moment of national indignation," according to Contreras. Twenty-four hours later, Gladys Marín came to Contreras's office and the first complaint was filed.

It was the breaching of a dam. With Pinochet in London, complaints against him multiplied. Many added him as an additional defendant in cases of disappearance, murder, and torture that implicated high-ranking members of the armed forces. By the time the plane touched down on March 3, 2000, there were more than 60 complaints; two months later there were more than a hundred. Every day saw a new parade of lawyers march down the halls of the Santiago court to register a complaint, accompanied by somber family members of the victims. The Socialist party of Ricardo Lagos filed a complaint on behalf of its assassinated members; the teachers' union and Medical Association filed complaints on behalf of teachers and doctors killed or disappeared; humble farmers and housewives came forward with information about missing husbands, parents, and children. By 2004, the complaints numbered almost 300.

Early Cases in the Chilean Courts

This was not the first time lawyers had tried to use the courts in cases involving human rights violations. Criminal complaints against members of the military and security forces for killings, disappearances and torture went back to the very first days after the military coup.

Like Spain, Chile operates on a civil law system derived from Napoleonic days. Criminal complaints go to an investigating judge-magistrate, who pursues leads, interviews witnesses, confronts witnesses when they provide inconsistent testimony, and assumes many of the functions performed in the U.S. by a prosecutor. Under the system used for Pinochet-era cases, the magistrate decides whether there is enough evidence to charge specific individuals with a crime, holds a separate trial to rule on the accused's guilt or innocence, and passes sentence.[2] Also as in Spain, private complainants as well as prosecutors may bring cases before an investigating magistrate. Civil damages against individuals for the most part depend on a prior finding of criminality. The separation of criminal and civil law, which allows, say, a criminal jury to acquit O. J. Simpson while a civil jury finds him liable for damages on the same facts, does not exist. There is no jury and no plea bargaining. Judges, generally speaking, choose a judicial career path straight out of law school, and because judging is badly paid, the best and brightest often go elsewhere. Higher-ranking judges can discipline and control the careers of lower-ranking ones, leading to a good measure of caution among trial court judges. Unlike the situation in the U.S., the decisions of the courts are only binding in the particular case and have no precedential value. Judges tend to pay less attention to prior holdings and more to the language of statute and academic commentary.

During the years of military government, with few exceptions judges were at best complacent, and at worst complicit, with the abuses committed. Alejandra Matus in her book *The Black History of Chilean Justice* recounts case after case of venality, cowardice, and complicity of judges from the trial court level up through the Supreme Court.[3] Even honest judges could come to believe that ducking was the only way to survive: "If the courts had not agreed to mold ourselves to the power of the military, the judiciary would have disappeared as a state power. You have to understand the limitations we were working under," one Appeals Court judge told me somewhat plaintively.

With no cooperation from the armed forces, no investigative resources, and a climate of fear and intimidation, most judges quickly closed cases without looking too far into the facts. Judge Juan Guzmán recalls that when a habeas corpus petition came into the courts the judges would stamp it "denied" without even reading it. Even in the few cases where a courageous panel of judges granted a habeas petition, the executive branch refused to cooperate and the judges had no choice but to close the case.

Human rights lawyers aimed at temporary closure, which might allow for reopening once times had changed, rather than permanent closure. The difference became important, because with temporarily closed cases the presentation of any new evidence within three years reset the clock on the statute of limitations, even if the case progressed no further. Thus lawyers managed to keep many cases alive. And no matter how useless it seemed, human rights attorneys always put together the available information, sent the habeas petitions to the courts, and created a file on the victim. Verónica Reyes of FASIC explains: "from the beginning family members went to the courts. The courts would make inquiries at the Interior Ministry, which would send back a mimeographed sheet with the name of the missing person written in, saying the government had no information. Of nearly ten thousand habeas corpus petitions filed, we got answers on about ten. But the documentation was there." Those files, carefully guarded over the years at the Vicaría de la Solidaridad, would prove a treasure trove of information when political conditions changed.

An even greater obstacle was (and is) the 1978 self-amnesty law. Decree-Law 2191 of April 18, 1978 applied a global amnesty to "all persons who committed . . . criminal offenses during the period of the state of siege, between 11 September 1973 and 10 March 1978." This initial period was when most of the crimes took place. A few crimes, including theft, rape, fraud, and incest, were excluded, but murder, kidnapping, and assault were not. Only one case was explicitly left out of the amnesty, under pressure from the U.S. government: that of Orlando Letelier and Ronni Moffitt, killed by a car bomb in Washington in 1975. Because of this exception in the amnesty law, the Letelier case is one of the few political crimes ending in a conviction. In 1995, the ex-director of Pinochet's secret police (DINA), General Manuel Contreras, and his deputy,

Brigadier Pedro Espinoza, were sentenced to seven and six years in prison respectively for the crime.

In the presidential campaign of 1990, candidate Patricio Aylwin promised to overturn the military's self-amnesty. This turned out to be harder than it seemed. The 1980 Constitution, put in place by Pinochet by agreement with the political parties, could not be touched; under it, senators appointed by the military maintained a balance of power, so legislation could not be passed without their approval. Nor could the law be annulled based on its undemocratic origins, as President Alfonsín did when he nullified the Argentine military's self-amnesty law in 1983. The concept of a null *ab initio* (from the start) law does not exist in Chilean law. Others argued that repeal of the law, even if it were politically feasible, would be fruitless, because the courts would apply the more favorable law to the accused whenever the law had changed. Aylwin, fearing for the outcome if a still fragile democracy challenged the military, decided not to raise the issue directly. It could only be dealt with by reinterpretation, but legislative proposals to reinterpret the law one way or another over the course of the 1990s had been vetoed by one or another political faction. That left the courts as the only recourse.

Until the late 1990s the courts were not very receptive to imposing limits on the amnesty law. The overwhelming majority of courts, civil and military, held that as soon as it seemed like an investigation might pertain to human rights violations committed during the 1973–78 period, investigation should not even begin and the case should be closed. There were a few exceptions. Carlos Cerda, for example, later president of the Santiago Appeals Court, as an investigating magistrate back in the mid-1980s refused to close a case involving disappearance. Around Christmas 1976, thirteen Communist party members had been picked up by security forces, never to be seen again. Family members complained to the courts, but the local judge closed the case when police showed him a border crossing registry indicating that the thirteen had gone to Argentina. Judge Cerda became determined to find the truth and to make the legal system do its job. Working nights and weekends, he discovered that the border registry had been doctored and that the victims had been picked up by the "Joint Command," an Air Force-led rival to the DINA. He named 38 people as suspects in the crime. They included air force and police generals and colonels, who quickly appealed based on the amnesty.

The decision to pursue the case led to emergency government meetings. The Santiago Appeals Court agreed with the defendants that the amnesty law protected them from investigation, but Cerda refused to back down. "This investigation is far from finished," he wrote, and until there were formal charges against specific defendants, application of the amnesty law was premature. In effect, he said, the amnesty law as written required the court to identify the defendant(s), and to specify when, how, and what crimes had been committed. Only at the very end of the investigation could the judge decide whether the law applied.[4] Two days later, the Supreme Court reversed, telling Cerda his decision showed "absolute ignorance of his obligations and a grave lack of judicial discipline."[5] He was suspended for two months. "I was absolutely alone in 1986," Cerda recalls. "Only one justice, Rafael Retamal, supported me. But I was fully convinced I was right." Other judges took the Supreme Court's broad hint. But Cerda's theories would come back to haunt the military.

The first chink in the wall of the amnesty came when President Aylwin turned over a copy of the 1991 Truth and Reconciliation Commission's report to the Supreme Court, with an exhortation to the courts to investigate the violations described in the report despite the court's inability to bring suspects to trial. How could the courts know whether the amnesty applied, Aylwin and his legal advisors asked, if they didn't know what had happened and when? The aim of investigation became simply finding out the fate of the disappeared person, not putting anyone in jail. What a cruel irony for the families! So long as they were kept in dreadful uncertainty, the case could go forward, but as soon as they found proof of the death of a loved one, those responsible would go free.

But a majority of the Supreme Court would have no part even of the Aylwin doctrine, arguing that amnesty meant that no crime ever existed, and so there was nothing to investigate. By 1996, when the Spanish investigations into the Chilean military's crimes began, it appeared that a larger Supreme Court majority than ever before was in favor of simply shutting down investigations. "Although last year we reported that the courts were divided over how and whether to apply the amnesty law, we now have to conclude that the backsliding over the last year points to the consolidation of a sinister jurisprudence for the goals of truth and justice," read a summary of cases from the Archives of the Vicaría de la Solidaridad.[6] A balance of judicial results at the time showed 15 members of the armed forces in jail, but dozens more investigations frozen or thrown out of court. It would take changes in the courts themselves and in the international scene to reverse the trend.

For almost twenty years, the courts had been made up overwhelmingly of supporters of the military, but by the 1990s the old guard were getting old. Unable to dismiss them outright, the new civilian governments did the next best thing: they bribed them into leaving. In 1998, a series of reforms offered generous retirement packages to judges, coupled with mandatory retirement at age seventy-five. The Supreme Court was expanded from 17 to 21 members, giving new appointments to the government, including several from outside the career judiciary. Younger judges less beholden to the military government came into the lower ranks of the courts as well. A few Pinochet-era judges were accused of corruption or dereliction of duty, and one was impeached. By the end of 1998, more than half the Supreme Court was made up of post-Pinochet appointees. The political fortunes of these judges and of those who aspired to join them no longer depended on toeing the military line.

The government also created specialized chambers. The five-person Criminal Chamber of the Supreme Court was in charge of hearing all appeals against case closures and other criminal law matters. It had a persistent minority in favor of investigating and against turning cases over to military courts. By 1998 that minority had become a majority.

A third change involved the relationship between civilian and military courts. The military courts had been the repository—or, more accurately, the graveyard—of most complaints against the armed forces for acts against civilians. Military judges, officers on active duty, refused to investigate and applied amnesty or prescription to the cases quasi-automatically. Sometimes a civilian acted as a military judge, but these actions could be blocked by military superiors. Now the higher courts began turning over at least some military court cases to civilian investigators, who unfroze the cases and began seeking indictments. This happened, for example, in the "Operation Albania" case involving the murder of thirteen young political activists in 1987, apparently as retaliation for an attempt on Pinochet's life months before. After years of inaction, the Supreme Court turned the case over to magistrates Hugo Dolmesch and, later, Milton Juica, who within a year had procured indictments against officials of the CNI (the secret police, successor of the DINA).

The effects of these changes had only begun to be felt in 1998. On September 9 of that year, a Supreme Court panel for the first time, approved reopening a case based on the superiority of international law over the amnesty law. The case, called *Poblete Córdova*, had been closed by the military courts. The panel decided that international treaties have supremacy in Chilean law under article 5 of the constitution. The applicable treaties included the 1949 Geneva Conventions, which required (under article 3) humane treatment of those who were unarmed and the imposition of penal sanctions against those who commit grave breaches of the Conventions. The amnesty law could not be an obstacle to Chile's international legal obligations.[7]

The applicability of the laws of war to Chile had always been controversial. Some human rights lawyers and progressive judges had not liked the theory because it required positing that a state of non-international armed conflict had existed from 1973 on. Armed conflict requires two sides, and what had happened in Chile was largely a one-sided campaign against unarmed opponents and perceived opponents.[8] Still, the military had declared the country in a state of war as of September 12, 1973. If the regime considered itself in a state of war, argued the proponents of this theory, they were obliged to act accordingly and respect the laws of war, and were estopped from now arguing those rules did not apply. Moreover, using the Geneva Conventions as the applicable law solved the knotty problem of timing: while the Chilean state had only ratified most of the relevant human rights treaties after 1980, the state had been party to the Conventions since 1950. Other Supreme Court panels had rejected the applicability of human rights treaties to the issue on grounds that treaties were not applied retroactively.[9] It also obviated the need to use customary international law concepts which were more difficult for the courts.

The *Poblete* case gave arguments to the lower courts allowing them to pursue investigations. It was not, however, the unanimous view of the courts. In the same year (1998), other panels of the Supreme Court threw out requests to reopen military court cases on amnesty grounds and on grounds that the statute of limitations had run.[10] The Court allowed the reopening of two disappearance cases on grounds that disappearance is a continuing crime, so neither the amnesty law nor the statute of limitations could apply until the body was found, a view soon to be the basis for the most famous prosecution in recent Chilean history.[11]

The Caravan of Death

The Puma helicopter touched down in cities all over the south and north of Chile in the 40 days after the 1973 coup. Wherever it went, a trail of death followed. Inside was General Sergio Arellano Stark, personal delegate of the Commander in Chief, Augusto Pinochet, and a group of his men. Arellano's mission left a total of at least 75 prisoners dead: 4 executed in Cauquenes on October 4; 15 in La Serena and 16 in Copiapó on October 16; 14 in Antofagasta on October 18; and 26 in Calama a day later. The prisoners were taken from their jail cells in secret and shot. Nineteen of the bodies were left in the desert and never found.

Those killed either were awaiting military court martial or had already been sentenced, often for minor infractions. Many were jailed simply because they had been mayors, union officials, managers, bureaucrats, or journalists under the prior government. Many of them had turned themselves in after hearing their names on military radio, never believing their lives were in danger. They were killed, it seems, to send a message to both the citizenry and the military. To the citizenry, the message was terror. To the military, the message was that the hardliners in the institution were in charge and there was no room for those who were soft.

The modus operandi of the Caravana de la Muerte (the Caravan of Death) was always the same. The Puma would land and General Arellano would present himself to the commanding officer as the personal representative of the Commander in Chief, which gave him temporary command of the base. His mission, the orders read, was to coordinate, revise, and expedite the trials of prisoners. After reviewing the files of the prisoners and marking off several names, Arellano would go off to meet with local officers, attend gala lunches, and review troops. The rest of his party would pull the chosen prisoners out of their cells. In La Serena, they were killed inside the barracks; in Calama they were taken to the desert. There, the bodies were hacked apart, and never returned to the families. The local military commanders were never told of the executions. According to the military bulletin, those executed were part of the Zeta Plan, a supposed conspiracy hatched by military propagandists to justify mass detentions. Meanwhile, the bodies of all but 19 victims were buried in mass graves or returned to the families with orders not to open the caskets or arrange a public funeral. Several of the local military commanders, outraged by the lack of respect for military and legal procedure and by the arrogance of the Caravana group, protested to their superiors. Those who did saw their military careers ruined, while the Caravana members were promoted.

On the morning of October 20, 1973, two army officials came to tell Carmen Hertz that her husband had been shot while trying to escape. He was thirty years old at the time, an attorney and jounalist. Less than a month before his death, he had moved to Calama as the director of the radio station for the giant Chuquicamata mine. He had been sentenced to 60 days in jail for keeping the radio station going during an official news blackout, but the military prosecutor had already agreed to let him out early in exchange for paying a fine. He was one of the 19 victims of the Caravana whose body was never found.

Only days after Gladys Marín filed her complaint naming Pinochet as a suspect, the family members of victims of the Caravana filed their own complaints. On January 28, 1998, Patricia Silva filed a complaint against Augusto Pinochet and anyone else who might be responsible for the death of her husband, Mario Silva Iriarte, shot in Antofagasta. In June, the family of Maguindo Castillo, one of those taken away in Copiapó whose body was never found, added seven more defendants: Sergio Arellano Stark, who had headed the Caravana, and six of its members. More complaints followed, in October, November, and on into 2000. At first the complaints alleged murder, illegal burial, and violations of the Geneva Conventions of 1949. Later complaints added kidnapping and illegal association (conspiracy) to the charges. Carmen Hertz represented a number of the complainants as well as herself. Hertz was one of the first people to agree to testify in the Audiencia Nacional in Spain.

The cases normally would have gone to a local investigating judge. But once a person with special immunity like Pinochet was one of the defendants, only a specially named Santiago Appeals Court judge could head the investigation. That judge would then centralize all the complaints involving Pinochet, including those that also contained allegations against other potential defendants. Because the cases all named Pinochet, they were assigned by lottery to Judge Juan Guzmán Tapia of the Santiago Appeals Court.

Guzmán was determined to investigate. Guzmán, the son of a famous Chilean poet, is a patrician, multilingual, well traveled, and cultured. He comes across as sincere, gentle, an old-fashioned gentleman. His politics had always been quite moderate: initially he supported the military coup. But as relatives of the disappeared began appearing in his office, he found himself moved by their stories, and ashamed of his own inaction during the bad years. He would now make up for lost time. Guzmán was tireless. Once assigned to the case, he traveled around the country with a team of forensic anthropologists, looking for the remains of those disappeared or executed. He visited the military bases where the prisoners had been kept, taking testimony from family members, eyewitnesses, and the military.

In the case of Cauquenes, four prisoners had been the victims of the Caravana. Claudio Lavín's body had been found, but the other three remained missing. Guzmán took testimony from Juan León, who had worked with Lavín and who watched from his own jail cell as Lavín was taken away. In a 1986 interview, León told how a fifth detainee, Ricardo Ugarte, a distant cousin of the dictator, described the "court-martial" to him. The five were taken before a group of heavily armed military men who yelled at them and insulted them. One of the soldiers knocked Ugarte out and dragged him to a bathroom, and when he woke up he was returned to his cell. He was certain he had been hidden because of a telegram from Pinochet asking whether he had been detained. Claudio Lavín's wife testified that she saw the four remaining prisoners leave the base in a military jeep, together with police lieutenant Enrique Rebolledo, a trip from which they never returned. Rebolledo was also called to testify, as was Colonel Rubén Castillo White and others. Castillo White, head of the local regiment, confirmed that Arellano had been in Cauquenes on the day of the murders and had personally marked off the names of the four prisoners and ordered his subordinates to interrogate them. Rebolledo told how he had accompanied the group as they drove the prisoners to a nearby farm, where they left him at the entrance and returned shortly to tell him the prisoners had been shot while trying to escape.

Judge Guzmán found that it was fully proven that the four had been taken to a farm outside town, where Lavín was killed. About the other three, he wrote, "it is not conclusively known where they were taken, nor their current whereabouts, a situation which subsists until today, giving rise to the crime of multiple aggravated kidnapping perpetrated against Miguel Enrique Muñoz Flores, Manuel Benito Plaza Arellano, and Pablo Renan Vera Torres."[12] Eventually the bodies of the three were found in an unmarked grave, so the charges were modified to aggravated murder.

In Copiapó he found that of the 16 prisoners removed from the public jail, 13 had been killed and the bodies found, while three, whose deaths had never been established, had been kidnapped. In Calama there were 13 kidnap victims. The evidence was similarly overwhelming, including numerous eyewitnesses, reports from forensic anthropologists, testimony by the commanders of the local military bases, media interviews over the years, the evidence gathered by the Truth and Reconciliation Commission, and accounts by family members of those killed and missing.

As a result, on June 8, 1999, Judge Guzmán issued preliminary arrest orders for ex-General Arellano Stark, ex-Colonel Sergio Arredondo, ex-Brigadier Pedro Espinoza, ex-Colonel Patricio Díaz Araneda and ex-Major Marcelo Manuel Moren Brito. (A fifth member of the Caravana, Armando Fernández Larios, was not then ordered arrested, although on appeal his arrest order was affirmed.) Several of the defendants were already known to the Chilean justice system. Espinoza, already sentenced to six years in the Letelier car bombing, had also been found guilty of an attack, in Rome, against Christian Democratic leader Bernardo Leighton. Moren Brito was under investigation as the chief of Villa Grimaldi, one of the most notorious DINA torture centers. Arellano was placed under house arrest and the rest sent to military jails to await trial.

Guzmán's June 1999 decision did not directly challenge the legality of the 1978 amnesty law. Indeed, in those cases where bodies had been found after the executions, Guzmán characterized the crimes as first degree murder and then initially dismissed the charges because the crimes had been completed within the amnesty period. But it blasted a large hole in the amnesty's coverage. By characterizing those cases where no body had been recovered as continuing crimes, "kidnappings" "which persist until now," he neatly sidestepped the need to close pre-1978 cases. After all, if the victims had been taken away and no one knew where they were, who was to say that they were not still alive, and in the hands of their captors, on March 11, 1978, or indeed in 1979 or 1999? Thus, Guzmán put the onus on the defendants: if they wanted the amnesty applied, they needed to come up with proof of where, quite literally, the bodies were buried. If they couldn't or wouldn't, they would stand trial.

With respect to Pinochet, Guzmán wrote that he would not issue an arrest warrant, "since, for now, the prerequisites of processability are not yet met." In other words, Pinochet could not be subject to trial while he had his senatorial immunity. It was an open invitation to ask for removal of that immunity.

Guzmán's decision to proceed at least against some suspects was not that surprising, considering the wealth of evidence against the members of the Caravana. What followed was more surprising. The Criminal Chamber of the Supreme Court, on the defendants' appeal of their arrest, unanimously upheld Guzmán.[13] It held that because proof of the victims' death and of the date of death had not been entered into evidence, the crimes constituted kidnappings, which were of a continuing nature. As such, they were not subject either to amnesty or to the statute of limitations. Furthermore, they accepted the view that the facts, crimes charged, and individuals responsible had to be known before the amnesty law could be applied.

The army and the right were outraged. "It's not good to keep digging [into the past]" said two unelected senators who represent the armed forces. The heads of the four armed forces branches met with the defense minister to express their displeasure with the judge's actions.

Meanwhile, Guzmán sent interrogatories to Pinochet in London, asking him to specify his relationship to the DINA, the orders he had given Arellano, and his knowledge of the operation of Villa Grimaldi and of other crimes. In November 1999, Pinochet responded. He wouldn't answer the questions, he declared, as a protest against Britain and Spain. Moreover, he said, he suffered from various ailments that affected his health and meant that he was not in condition to analyze the legality of the proceedings. He did, however, hire a lawyer in Chile.

On March 2, 2000, with Pinochet's return from the UK imminent, lawyers for the victims of the Caravan of Death took the next step. They asked Judge Guzmán to solicit revocation of Pinochet's parliamentary immunity to allow him to be indicted for ordering the kidnappings. On March 7, only days after the ex-general's return to Chile, Guzmán agreed. The case automatically passed to the full Santiago Appeals Court for a decision, shifting the political pressure off Guzmán and onto that court. The stage was set for the most important legal battle of recent Chilean history.

Desafuero

Two months after Pinochet's triumphal return to Chile, a May 2000 poll showed that 57 percent of the Chilean people thought he was guilty of human rights violations. For the first time ever, human rights lawyers had a chance to prove it. The loss of parliamentary immunity, or *desafuero*, involved a kind of pre-hearing: the complainants would have to show that there was probable cause (*sospechas fundadas*) to believe he had participated in—or covered up—crimes. A judicial finding to this effect would be a huge moral victory, even if, as almost everyone admitted, it was unlikely for reasons of age and health that the eighty-three-year old general would ever stand trial. Verónica Reyes of FASIC was pessimistic: "I don't think they'll strip him of immunity," she said. "On the other hand, the eyes of the world are on the courts, they'll have to justify their decision. Maybe they'll take the route of his health problems."

Chilean law grants legislators limited immunity from legal process. In order to investigate them for possible criminal activity, the court of appeals has to find that there are good reasons for thinking they have been involved. The purpose of this immunity is to make sure legislators are not bothered by frivolous accusations or politically motivated finger-pointing. The decision is left to the courts, to take it out of the political arena. The finding of probable cause is preliminary, and does not require proof of guilt. By passing the case on to the Appeals Court, Judge Guzmán indicated that he had well-founded suspicions that Augusto Pinochet had participated, in some fashion, in the crimes of the Caravana de la Muerte. This in itself was a huge breakthrough for the justice system.

On April 26, 2000, the Court of Appeals heard argument in the petition to strip Pinochet of his immunity. The days leading up to the hearings were hectic. Human rights dominated the headlines and the lawyers for the victims found themselves explaining their legal theories again and again. There was the question of what standard the courts should use to judge Pinochet's ties to the Caravana's acts. The court had before it a fair amount of evidence: Arellano's authorization as the "personal representative" of the commander-in-chief, General Joaquín Lagos's description of how Pinochet had personally altered Lagos's report of the deaths to obscure the killings ordered by Arellano, the promotions of the Caravana members, and the demotions of the officers who questioned its doings. But was it enough? Yes, said the lawyers, because at this stage only well-founded suspicions were needed, not proof beyond a reasonable doubt. Proof would come later, once the judge was allowed to investigate fully.

No, said the defenders of the general, even if there was proof of orders, the orders were to speed up trials, not to kill, and still less to kidnap anyone. They argued further that "kidnapping" was a legal fiction, since everyone knew the disappeared were dead. Letters to the editor flew back and forth in the local papers. Inventing a legal fiction to allow the courts to bypass the amnesty was a travesty of justice and showed the political influence on the courts, said Pablo Longeira, head of the pro-Pinochet UDI. Well, replied human rights lawyer José Zalaquett in his published response, "everyone knows" that Pinochet was responsible for thousands of killings, torture and disappearances, but that doesn't mean you don't have to prove it in court. In the same way, he added, the fact that "everyone knows" the disappeared are dead doesn't mean the courts can declare it so without having the "body of the crime" before them, as required by Chilean law.

Perhaps the most ironic aspect of the swirling controversy was that the issue of due process of law took center stage. Right-wing politicians and spokespeople for the retired military, many of whom had never been too worried about the due process rights of those they summarily executed and disappeared, suddenly discovered the virtues of fair trials and the ability of defendants to confer with their lawyers. From one day to the next the international human rights treaties ratified by Chile became the darlings of Pinochet defenders. That these same treaties contained provisions that have been interpreted as requiring prosecution for certain grave violations, like those alleged against Pinochet, was of no import.

The due process arguments focused on Pinochet's deteriorating health. British medical exams had clearly shown that he was unable to stand trial. How could the Chilean government argue he was unfit to stand trial in a foreign country, but allow him to stand trial at home?

Unlike the British law that allowed Jack Straw to let Pinochet go because his health problems allegedly made him unfit to stand trial, Chilean law does not automatically release suspects for health reasons. The criminal procedure code does require that every defendant over seventy be subjected to examinations of physical and mental health, but the only reasons specified in the code for releasing a defendant are insanity or dementia. And of course at that point neither the general nor his defenders wanted to have to admit the old man was demented. Instead, they argued that Chile's international human rights commitments, which have the force of constitutional law, provide that people have the right to adequate time and means to prepare their defense and to have the effective assistance of a lawyer. Because of Pinochet's problems talking and understanding, as well as his medical woes, he was unable to communicate with his lawyers. "That's funny," mused Hiram Villagra, one of the lawyers for the victims, to the local press: "he can get together with his children, meet with generals, receive delegations [of politicians]. But he can't talk to his lawyers?"

At around 9:30 on April 26 the hearing began.[14] On one side were the seven lawyers representing the victims and the lawyer for the State Defense Council, Clara Szczaranski. Across from them was Pinochet's legal team, headed by Ricardo Rivadeneira. In the back sat four members of the press, a family member for each of the complainants, Gladys Marín as the lead complainant, and the heads of the Associations of Family Members of the Disappeared and of Those Executed for Political Reasons. Facing them all, in three rows of high-backed wooden chairs, sat the twenty-two members of the Santiago Appeals Court. The public was excluded. On either side of the imposing courthouse in downtown Santiago, on separate streets with barricades and police in between, were knots of pro- and anti-Pinochet demonstrators, the pro-Pinochet group waving flags and posters of the general as benevolent grandfather, the anti-Pinochet forces holding up photos of the disappeared. All day the competing chants of the demonstrators could be faintly heard in the courtroom. By evening, the two groups, after a few quick scuffles, had melted away. Many from both sides merged into the crowds that formed around the downtown Plaza de Armas to cheer on the national soccer team, playing Peru that night. (They tied 1–1.) The next morning, the crowds were smaller.

The decision came down little more than a month later, on June 5, 2000.[15] By a vote of 13 to 9, the Santiago Appeals Court decided to strip Augusto Pinochet Ugarte of his parliamentary immunity, opening the way for his trial. Neither the outcome nor the reasoning of majority and dissent were much of a surprise, although many observers expected the vote to be closer (indeed, when the results were first leaked the lineup had been 12–10). The majority opinion, written by the most recent addition to the court, Jaime Rodríguez Espoz, mirrored many of the complainants' arguments. This was only a preliminary proceeding, and an adequate investigation into the facts would follow. Nonetheless, investigation to date, confirmed by the courts, showed that the crime was indeed one of kidnapping and that the Caravana members were involved. "In conclusion," for the majority, "the evidence gathered to date makes it necessary for this court to declare that there are grounds to proceed in relation to Senator Pinochet. This is the only way of allowing both the complainants as well as the accused, legislators and the other persons subject to indictment, to discuss and prove, through the gradual development of the legal proceedings, whether or not the events that form the basis of the many complaints constitute the crimes described, and whether the court can find that the participation of the Senator in these events is more than mere suspicion." The dissent stressed the lack of evidence that the disappeared were not dead, and of proof that Pinochet was involved in these particular deaths.

The general's defense team promptly appealed. Three months later, a similar two-day hearing took place with the same cast, this time before the Chilean Supreme Court. Here again, while there were clear pro- and anti-*desafuero* factions, the middle group of judges were a great unknown. The Court handed down its judgment on August 8, 2000. A majority of the court, 14 to 6, ratified the lower court decision and its reasoning. The proceedings were preliminary and required no definitive showing of guilt. Because they were not a legal "proceeding," full due process norms did not apply, but even if they did, they had been fully complied with. The acts charged were crimes, not political "acts of administration" that could be dealt with through a political impeachment process, as Pinochet's defenders argued. No such legislative impeachment process could apply, since at the time of the alleged crimes Pinochet had dissolved Congress, and his later constitutional reforms made sure no subsequent Congress could consider anything done during his time in office.

The Court ratified the aggravated kidnapping, homicide, illegal association, and illegal exhumation charges, detailing the highlights of the evidence that supported each charge. Even if the kidnappings later turned out to be homicides, it would only matter at the trial stage. Likewise, amnesty and prescription were not to be automatically applied but could only be considered at the end of the trial stage. Judge Guzmán was to investigate *all* the crimes, including murder, at this stage. Only then could the amnesty law (and the statute of limitations) be considered. It had taken fifteen years, but Judge Carlos Cerda's view of the amnesty law had finally prevailed at the full Supreme Court.

Judge José Benquis's concurring opinion raised for future consumption the further argument that the amnesty law was no obstacle to prosecution under the provisions of the Geneva Conventions, which required prosecutions of "grave breaches." The dissent reiterated the already raised arguments on due process, automatic application of amnesty, and lack of adequate proof.

The Supreme Court's decision gave Judge Guzmán the green light he had been looking for. At the same time, it presented him with a difficult series of investigative strategy issues. He had authority to proceed against Pinochet only in the Caravana case, but he also confronted almost 200 other pending complaints, alleging a wide range of criminal activity involving not just Pinochet but hundreds of military and secret police. He had two investigators and a tiny budget. How to organize his investigations, with extremely limited resources and personnel, was a challenge.

Guzmán decided to concentrate on getting indictments in the Caravana case, which was the earliest in time after the coup, while sorting the rest of the complaints into related incidents by date. A number of cases, for example, concerned people detained and/or disappeared at one of four Santiago area clandestine detention centers: Villa Grimaldi, Cuatro Alamos, José Domingo Cañas, and Venda Sexy. Guzmán did what no judge during the dictatorship years had dared to do: he went to see the clandestine detention centers for himself, collecting evidence and asking political prisoners who survived to give him guided tours. He took shovels to clandestine gravesites, made ex-officials with contradictory stories confront each other (these "careos" or "face-to-faces" are an integral part of Chilean legal process), and asked local trial judges to help him gather testimonies. The indictments piled up: against DINA officials for disappearances at the four detention centers, including that of William Beausire, whose British family was one of the intervenors before the House of Lords. Another indictment, also against DINA officials, concerned the disappearance of a single individual, David Silberman, head of the huge nationalized copper mine under Allende. There were suspects in the Calle Conferencia kidnapping of the Communist Party leadership (Gladys Marín's husband was one of them) and in the Pisagua disappearances. But most of Guzmán's efforts went into preparing an indictment against the Caravana members.

Indictment

By December 1, 2000, Guzmán was under enormous pressure. It was clear the government was not interested in an indictment of Pinochet and was looking for a graceful way out. The judge was receiving threats. The human rights organizations expected action. The Supreme Court was getting impatient: it twice censured Guzmán for talking to the press. The defense team was pushing for medical exams, and complaining very publicly that the general's health was getting worse by the day. It was not clear how long the investigation could continue before the health arguments and political pressure overwhelmed it. Guzmán leaped ahead. He issued an indictment against Pinochet, charging him as a direct participant in 18 kidnappings and aggravated homicides in the Caravana cases. He refused to indict on the torture, illicit association, and illegal exhumation causes of action. He ordered Pinochet confined to house arrest.

Amid the uproar—family members of victims dancing in the streets, the armed forces and their supporters protesting, government ministers calling for calm—Pinochet's defense team filed an emergency appeal to the Supreme Court. The proper steps had not been followed, they claimed. The judge had not questioned the suspect, as required for an indictment. Nonsense, replied Judge Guzmán: Pinochet had answered a written set of interrogatories he had sent to London while the general was detained there, and the judge could decide what constituted questioning. Even though Pinochet had not said much in his answer, Judge Guzmán thought it was good enough. "My conscience is clear," he told the Chilean press.

The Supreme Court disagreed, holding that questioning of suspects had to be done in person, and that, moreover, before Pinochet could be questioned his health status must be ascertained.[16] Medical tests followed, and on January 22 Judge Guzmán appeared at the general's residence to take his statement. Pinochet answered the judge's questions lucidly. According to press reports, he said he had never ordered anyone shot, and if Arellano had committed crimes, it was up to the head of each military base to investigate them. If those killed had not been returned to their families for burial, it was only because they were unidentified terrorists whom no one came forward to claim, he added defiantly.

Meanwhile, Judge Guzmán received the medical examiners' reports, which indicated a "light to moderate" degree of dementia. As if to underscore his fragility, on January 27 Pinochet, with great fanfare, checked into the hospital for a day. Despite the obvious pressure, Guzmán reissued his indictment on January 29, on the same charges as in December. As to the medical arguments, he found that due process was met, that according to the medical evidence the defendant was able to exercise his rights and direct his defense, and that in any case he would be given every possibility to prove his innocence. He ordered Pinochet to remain under house arrest.

The next step after an arrest warrant is issued is the photographing and fingerprinting of the defendant. This too proved highly contentious, with the complainants arguing that Pinochet should be treated just like everyone else and his defense alarmed that the indignity of it all would kill the old man. Judge Guzmán, in a mix of gentlemanly courtesy and political caution, decided against fingerprinting; the justice system certainly knew who the defendant was, and there was no need for gratuitous humiliation. Instead, he allowed archival photographs and fingerprints to stand in for the real thing.

After the Indictment

Within the space of a less than a year, Pinochet had gone from untouchable to the most complained-against man in Chile, facing years of charges. How did it happen? Everyone I asked in Chile agreed in citing two main factors: judicial reform and the case against Pinochet in Spain (and his subsequent detention). But they differed as to how the changes had operated. I have already described some of the judicial reforms. Garzón's investigation affected Chile's political and judicial processes profoundly, speeding up and strengthening already existing tendencies and serving as a catalyst for change. It affected the government, the judges and lawyers, the human rights groups, the press, and the military.

For the ruling Concertación alliance, the case was embarrassing and troubling. It put the limited and partial nature of the democratization process on the front pages of the world's newspapers. While many government ministers and officials secretly rejoiced at the sight of their old adversary in the dock, the official position was to argue, first, diplomatic immunity and, when that proved specious, that the issue was not guilt or innocence but the prerogatives of state sovereignty. Why did they not simply abandon Pinochet to his fate, on grounds that he had disregarded government warnings not to travel? It was a pre-electoral period, and the official parties feared creating sympathy for Pinochet that could tip popular support to the right. The right, on the other hand, worried that too close identification with the ex-general could make them look unmodern, throwbacks to the past. The argument that it was better to try the ex-general at home allowed both sides to take the "high road."

It also put the Chilean government into something of a bind. Once the government had staked its international prestige on trial at home, it could hardly object when the courts and complainants took the message seriously. "The courts decide cases in front of them," Judge Sergio Muñoz of the Santiago Court of Appeals insisted to me. "If the courts didn't act before, it's because no one brought cases involving Pinochet to them. It was not the law but the vision of potential complainants that changed. Plus, the focus on Pinochet allowed the courts to centralize an investigation that otherwise would have been decentralized. Here, unlike other places, we have had to start at the bottom of the chain of command and work our way up. We could now work with a more global vision of what happened."

"The arrest of Pinochet made the domestic cases possible," Nelson Caucoto, a human rights lawyer who has brought dozens of complaints against Pinochet, told me. "There was a new concern about human rights in society, and among the judges. They both realized that there was unfinished business here, and the judges became painfully aware that the judiciary hadn't taken seriously its role during the dictatorship." Roberto Garretón echoed Caucoto's comments: "The 'Garzón effect' was very important in giving the judges courage. Those judges who had already begun pushing investigations felt vindicated." They also, no doubt, felt a little miffed that a foreign judge was getting the publicity and ability to define a case that should by rights have been theirs.

The Spanish case and the wide international publicity it generated also changed the Chilean polity's and judiciary's view of international law. The Chilean legal tradition is Napoleonic, relatively closed to new influences and ideas. Judges had paid little attention to treaties and treaty bodies. With the detention of Pinochet in London, international law assumed a flesh-and-blood reality, capable of frustrating the will of the most powerful person in the country. Its validation by the House of Lords made it clear that Judge Garzón's views on the subjects of universal jurisdiction, torture, and crimes against humanity were far from idiosyncratic: they represented mainstream views in the world. Chileans, always a little worried about their isolation, found themselves out of step with what seemed to be widely shared legal norms.

The Spanish prosecution gave the human rights groups a new visibility as well as an infusion of energy. "When Pinochet was arrested, the foreign press flocked to Chile," recalls Viviana Díaz, head of the Association of Family Members of the Disappeared. "Once they started interviewing us, the national press had no choice but to follow. I had been unknown before this, but now because of the TV coverage my face was known and people began stopping me on the street to tell me their stories."

Talking to the Enemy

The right-wing parties and the military saw Pinochet as a hero who had liberated the country from Communism and ushered in an era of economic vitality. It was a shock to see that much of the rest of the world failed to share this view, indeed, was convinced that the hero was a criminal. The initial reaction of these sectors was that the Spanish case was a new colonial enterprise, masterminded by resentful leftovers from the left.[17] But it was harder and harder to maintain this argument as first the higher Spanish courts and then the British, Belgian, French, and Swiss courts seemed to share the view that the evidence merited further proceedings. For the army and the right wing, the European cases were a kind of vaccination, one judge remarked. They saw that it wasn't out of the ordinary for people to think about Pinochet as having committed crimes. That made it easier to proceed at home.

Pinochet's detention in London also changed civilian-military relations, convincing the heads of the armed forces that time alone would not make the issue of past human rights violations go away. Ricardo Izurieta, the new army chief, had been appointed by Pinochet only the year before the arrest and was still trying to step out from under his predecessor's shadow while remaining true to his legacy. Even though officially retired from the military, Pinochet still wielded a great deal of informal power, as did other retired military officers. For the younger army brass, the arrest was a distraction from the current military leadership's preferred modernization agenda. It also meant that Pinochet was unavailable to make, or veto, decisions.

President Frei's defense minister, Edmundo Pérez Yoma, proposed a dialogue. Why not sit military representatives down with human rights lawyers, religious figures, and civil society representatives and have them hash out the issues face to face? At first, no one liked the idea. Frei, near the end of his mandate, didn't want to risk failure. The family members of the disappeared and most of their lawyers were sure the initiative was really aimed at facilitating Pinochet's return and would result in a "punto final" law ending judicial investigations. After all, two previous attempts to negotiate an end to investigations had ended up being vetoed by Socialist Party legislators because they would have curtailed judicial action. Eventually, however, five well-known human rights lawyers—Héctor Salazar, Pamela Pereira, Jaime Castillo, Roberto Garretón and José Zalaquett—each with many years of activism to his or her credit, agreed to talk on condition that whatever came out of the roundtable could not interfere with the action of the courts.

Unlike their counterparts in Argentina, the Chilean military had walked away from the years of dictatorship undefeated, with a stable economy and the support of a sizeable segment of the population. And being undefeated meant never having to say you're sorry. When the 1991 Truth and Reconciliation Commission's report confirmed widespread killings and disappearances by the military, the army rejected the report's findings. None of the armed forces had ever publicly acknowledged any institutional responsibility for the crimes, attributing military participation to individual aberrations. Nor had the military cooperated with the Rettig Commission or the courts in the search for the disappeared, denying that they had any information on the subject.

The first meeting of the Dialogue Roundtable (Mesa de Diálogo) in August 1999 was less than auspicious. Pamela Pereira, a human rights lawyer, refused to shake hands with General Juan Carlos Salgado, the army representative. "Because my father believed in the word of honor of a military man," she said, "he disappeared. I refuse to shake your hand because I don't believe in the word of the military." Her father had been arrested at his home in October 1973 after an army colonel assured him he would not be detained.

Still, the participants kept meeting. For the military, the roundtable offered a chance to end the transition. If some agreement on the fate of the disappeared could be found, it would stop the parade of military officers before the courts and perhaps even do away with the theory of kidnapping as a continuing crime that was largely responsible for putting them there. And it would show the world that Chile could come up with its own solutions to human rights issues. For the human rights lawyers and their allies, discovering the fate, and the bodies, of the disappeared had always been an important goal, although they were not willing to close off access to the courts in order to get it. So was institutional recognition of the responsibility of the armed forces for the human rights violations and a public commitment of the military to never engage in such acts again. The religious leaders were looking for national reconciliation.

An agreement was on the verge of completion by March 2000. That agreement, according to participants, would have created "carrots and sticks" aimed at coaxing informants to come forward. Withholding information on the disappeared would be criminalized, while providing it would result in reduced or suspended sentences for those who came forward. The armed forces would admit their responsibility for the disappearances and would promise never to resort to unconstitutional means or to use any national security doctrine to excuse violations of human rights. Only the finishing touches remained.

Then Pinochet touched down in Santiago to a hero's welcome from the armed forces. The human rights lawyers walked out of the roundtable in disgust. "Actions speak louder than words. The armed forces' welcome of Pinochet shows they remain anchored in the past," said Héctor Salazar, one of the lawyers. The armed forces backed away from their initial agreement to strong language on their responsibility for the violations, apparently pushed by right-wing politicians who felt marginalized and worried that the current military leaders were giving away the (ideological) store. The military now wanted reference to the amnesty law, full immunity for those who gave information on the disappeared, an explanation that the coup was a reaction to the climate of violence engendered by the Popular Unity government, and recognition of the military regime's economic success. For a while it looked like the whole roundtable initiative would fail. It took a strong push from incoming president Ricardo Lagos to get it back on track.

Lagos began a round of quiet meetings with the military and with

Pamela Pereira, a long-time Socialist Party ally. In a ten-hour marathon session that almost broke up several times, the final language was hammered out. At the end, to the applause of the participants, Pamela Pereira shook hands with the army representative, General Salgado. The photo, a symbol of the roundtable's achievements, made the front page of the newspapers on June 13, 2000.

The public declaration of the roundtable is rather short. Part of it reads:

We reaffirm that it is inherent to a state based on rule of law that the legitimate exercise of force belongs exclusively to the competent organs in a democratic system, and we absolutely reject violence as a method of political action. . . . We also hold that the defense of the rule of law, and especially respect for the fundamental rights of all the inhabitants, always and in any circumstances, is the ethical basis of the nation's institutions. . . . The solution to the problem of the detained-disappeared involves finding their remains when possible, or in any case establishing their fate. If we do this, we will have met the obligation to give—to some extent—peace of mind to their families. But the need to know the whereabouts of the detained-disappeared goes further; it also aims at allowing the country to become aware, in a concrete fashion, of that which should not be repeated.

The fact-finding mechanism involved the creation, by law, of a "professional secret" covering those who receive information on the fate of the disappeared, so that they cannot be forced to reveal the identity of their source. Those who violate the "professional secret" can be legally sanctioned. That is the full extent of the legal changes. The law does not provide any legal sanction for hiding information, although it states that such conduct is morally reprehensible and anti-patriotic and may also constitute perjury, false testimony, or obstruction of justice under existing law.

The armed forces and police solemnly committed themselves, within a six-month period after the law's passage, to exert the greatest possible effort to find useful information on the remains of the detained-disappeared or to establish their fate. On the touchy point of whether the armed forces already have this information in hand, the document states: "The roundtable takes note of the affirmation by the heads of the armed forces and police that their respective institutions do not now have that information, but are willing to help obtain it." This, of course, left open the question of whether individuals within the institutions already knew what had happened but were unwilling to come forward.

The information received was to be turned over to the president. The religious and ethical institutions also committed themselves to receive information and turn it over to the president, protecting the identity of the source. The roundtable also asked the Supreme Court to provide high-level investigating judges to follow up on the information received, in cases where no judge already had the events in question under investigation. It asked the judges to work as quickly as possible to find the remains and turn them over to the families. The declaration ended: "With this declaration we hope to come to terms with our past. We understand that it is unfair to pass on to the young the conflicts and divisions that have hurt the country. We hope to pass on to the new generations of Chileans a culture in which we live together based on liberty, truth, tolerance and respect."

President Lagos received the declaration in an official ceremony before top government, military, religious, and political party representatives. "We're taking a huge step forward on the road towards our reconciliation as a nation," he said. The president of the Supreme Court hailed the agreement as "producing a light of hope in this tunnel we're in."

The human rights community divided sharply over the significance and wisdom of the accord. For the lawyers who participated, the roundtable had produced concrete results, by publicly committing the armed forces to come up with information. "I'm taking a big chance here," acknowledged Pamela Pereira to the press. "I went into this dialogue with two goals: find the detained-disappeared, and make the armed forces condemn the human rights violations. Both those goals were met." The accord could have been more explicit in characterizing the violations and what they meant, she admitted, but the drafting, even with an "ecclesiastical touch," was clear enough. Héctor Salazar stressed the learning process involved. "We discovered we spoke different languages and understood the same words differently. We had to learn to communicate. . . . I learned that the armed forces also condemned the violations, it was a negative experience for them as well. That perverse vision of the good guys on one side, and the bad guys on the other, disappeared."

Those human rights lawyers who had not participated in the roundtable condemned the accord as a veiled out for Pinochet, a way to convince the Supreme Court that the issue was now being dealt with and then to allow the courts to apply the amnesty law on grounds that the bodies had all been thrown into a volcano or the sea.[18] So did the associations of family members of the disappeared and those summarily executed. Viviana Díaz of the AFDD pointed out that "the problem of human rights is not just about finding the remains. It is also about judging and condemning those responsible." The lawyers who signed the agreement "don't represent us," she added. And indeed, a group of family members withdrew their authorization for Héctor Salazar to represent them before the courts.

The Armed Forces Investigate Themselves

Congress moved quickly to pass the "professional secrets" law. Investigations began. Six months later, on Sunday, January 7, 2001, President Lagos presented the results on television. Of 180 disappeared detainees about which the armed forces had obtained some information, 130 had been killed and their bodies thrown into lakes, rivers, or the sea. Some twenty more bodies could be found in a common grave near Santiago. Lagos thanked all those who had worked for the truth starting from the earliest days of the dictatorship, and noted that the information provided was insufficient. He commended the armed forces for "daring to look at the truth, recognizing the horrors committed by their members." The information obtained was to be forwarded to each individual family.

Soon public doubts began seeping in. Why was it, for example, that among the cases where bodies had been thrown into the sea were the family members of the head and former head of the AFDD and of the human rights lawyers, as well as a large number of cases that came within Judge Guzmán's investigations?

On April 24, the Medical Legal Service (the official forensic anthropologists) confirmed that a skeleton they had identified in an old military installation, Fort Arteaga, belonged to communist leader Juan Luis Rivera Matus, who had been detained in 1975 and disappeared. There was only one problem with this information: Rivera Matus's body was listed in the armed forces report on the disappeared as having been thrown into the sea. His children, now living in France, had come to Chile in January to participate in a symbolic burial by the seaside. Now, in May, an embarrassed Lagos invited them to return, to rebury their father in the memorial park to the disappeared in Santiago. Six days after the funeral, another body was identified, dug out of the patio of a military base. It belonged to Samuel Lazo Quinteros, another of the disappeared persons whose bodies had been, according to the armed forces, thrown into the sea.

The mounting evidence that the armed forces had lied, or at least not adequately checked the information they had made public in January, lost them any goodwill the exercise might have generated. The human rights lawyers who had supported the dialogue now spoke of a "fracture" in the armed forces' credibility and refused to participate in efforts to validate the information. Human rights lawyers and the Rivera Matus family filed obstruction of justice complaints against the military high command. The army replied that it had taken the risk of error in the interest of getting the information out fast, but that it was up to the courts to verify the facts.

Crazy or Demented

In the changed political climate, the courts considering the Pinochet indictment began to backpedal. The pressure on the courts to bring the case to an end was overwhelming. The world's eyes had turned away from Chile, the government wanted investor stability above all, and the point had been made that Pinochet was not above the law. While a broad cross-section of Chilean society told pollsters they'd like to see justice done, only a small group was willing to keep pressuring and agitating for that result. The mass media had tired of the story. The Mesa de Diálogo process was wrapping up the last remnants of the human rights issue. It was time to move on, according to a broad consensus of the powerful.

A panel of the Court of Appeals held that Pinochet suffered from a "subcortical dementia" which made him unfit to stand trial. The Court did not exactly find the ex-General "crazy or demented" as the law required, but found that his health problems included a kind of dementia. It therefore "temporarily" suspended the case, at least with respect to the Caravana prosecution. A series of motions to reconsider and appeals followed. On July 1, 2002, the Supreme Court confirmed the permanent closure of the case,[19] due to the suspect's "moderate" and progressive dementia, which was substantial and irreversible. This case in particular, dealing with long-ago events, would require extensive declarations from the suspect, which he was not in a condition to give. Therefore, the case was to be permanently closed, without closure implying any finding on guilt or innocence. Pinochet was a free man.

Ironically, the Pinochet family and the human rights lawyers who had litigated against Pinochet coincided in their view that the old general was not at all crazy. "I heard the other side's lawyer, Hugo Gutierrez, and he seemed to me to say the most sensible thing . . . my father isn't crazy," insisted Augusto Pinochet, Jr., in a press interview. "He remembers everything," the son added on another occasion. The president of the Socialist Party told the press that "while the world watches with approval the trial of criminals like Slobodan Milosevic, Chile demonstrates her inability to do justice and allows Pinochet to seek refuge in a supposed senile dementia to avoid answering for the atrocities that he committed." Other Socialist congress members pointed out that Chilean law doesn't normally allow for a subsequent dementia to preclude trial.

Victims' attorneys insisted that the medical diagnosis was wrong. Twice more in 2003, judges tried to strip Pinochet of immunity, for the Prats and Calle Conferencia murders, but the courts would have none of it. Even though Pinochet had withdrawn from the Senate, his senatorial immunity remained intact. A few months later, the general gave an interview to a Miami TV station in which he called himself an "angel" of democracy who had done nothing wrong. Judge Guzmán argued that this was new evidence that Pinochet was fit for trial, and soon after indicted him for 20 disappearances in conjunction with Operation Condor. On August 26, 2004, the Supreme Court, by a 9–8 vote, agreed to again strip him of his immunity and allow that investigation to proceed. This time, beset simultaneously by new investigations of his secretly amassed fortune, Pinochet had few friends willing to defend him, and he faced the prospect of multiple legal troubles.

No matter the final outcome, Pinochet would go down in history as an indicted criminal not an anti-Communist savior, pitied not feared. There would be no possibility of proving, as he insisted, that he never approved of or ordered the crimes done in his name. His days as a political force were over. And other cases, involving his closest lieutenants, would continue.

A meeting between the government and the human rights lawyers who had been part of the Mesa de Diálogo led to an agreement that the government would ask the Supreme Court to assign a number of judges exclusively to the task of investigating the remaining disappearance cases. By mid-year, the Supreme Court had assigned nine such judges, along with 51 assigned to give these cases preferential treatment. The judges were on a short leash—they had to report on their progress once a month. Many of the judges were new and a striking number were women. They began criss-crossing the country, digging up more mass graves, and calling former military and police officials in for questioning. The Supreme Court also devolved almost all the cases in Judge Guzmán's investigation back to lower court judges, on grounds that, without Pinochet in the picture, there was no need for a special Appeals Court judge.[20] Soon after, Judge Guzmán announced he was retiring and writing a book about his experiences.

Results began to appear in a number of the "emblematic" cases, including the disappeared and killed prisoners in Pisagua, whose bodies had been found in an abandoned mine (one general and a subofficial arrested); the 26 people disappeared in Parral in September 1973 (an ex-army colonel indicted); the disappearances of the Communist Party leadership from Conferencia Street in spring of 1976 (four DINA agents arrested); and others.[21] Cases from the 1980s, less complicated legally because the amnesty law did not apply, advanced particularly quickly. Investigation into the murder of union leader Tucapel Jiménez in 1982 yielded 20 defendants, including four ex-generals, two ex-colonels, and our old friend Fernando Torres Silva, the ex-army Auditor General who visited Spain on Pinochet's behalf. The Jiménez case had languished in the courts for eighteen years; the union leader's family complained that the investigating judge had a son in the secret police. In 2000, they convinced the Supreme Court to appoint a new, energetic magistrate. In August 2002, Judge Sergio Muñoz sentenced twelve of the defendants to prison terms ranging from life for an ex-CNI colonel, eight to ten years for the rest of the participants, and suspended sentences for Torres Silva and others accused of covering up the crime.[22] The state also paid civil compensation claims to the families.

Nineteen defendants, including a retired major general, prepared for trial in the "Operation Albania" case, a well-known assassination of twelve young leftists whose bodies were found on the Argentine border and whom the army accused of killing each other in an internecine firefight. Two of the defendants, attempting to extricate themselves, pointed fingers at Pinochet as the one who ordered the operation. The Chilean cases against Spanish citizens, including Fathers Llidó and Alsina and UN diplomat Carmelo Soria, were finally reopened.

Not all cases progressed equally. Even as the Supreme Court and the Santiago Appeals Court insisted that full investigation must precede the application of the amnesty laws, the military courts continued to close cases on grounds that amnesty was absolute. The civilian courts occasionally backtracked, for example, finding that *res judicata* barred prosecution of DINA head Manuel Contreras for the kidnapping of the Communist Party leaders from the Calle Conferencia in 1976, even though the previous dismissal of the case had been by a military court without investigation or trial.[23] The Santiago Appeals Court in December 2003 overturned another disappearance indictment against Contreras, rejecting the characterization of disappearance as aggravated kidnapping altogether.

By 2004, around 300 cases were pending.[24] As the investigations drew to a close and sentencing hearings began, the amnesty issue again came to life. On a political level, President Lagos proposed a package deal to close the issue once and for all. The government would provide some (largely symbolic) reparations for torture survivors and would name a commission to investigate the practice of torture under the military government. In exchange, Congress would pass a law providing for reduced or suspended sentences for officers who provided useful information to the courts (the courts were to decide what was useful). Low-level conscripts who voluntarily came forward and could show they had no choice but to follow orders were to receive amnesty; the proposal exempts those who gave orders or induced others to commit crimes.[25] Predictably, a group of human rights lawyers denounced the proposal as yet another attempt to declare the disappeared to be dead and thus apply the amnesty or statute of limitations, while others supported it as a balanced way of finally putting the issue to rest.

The doctrine of investigating first before applying the amnesty merely postponed the problem until the end of the judicial process. Once time came for sentencing, the amnesty's legality could no longer be side-stepped. In the first Court of Appeals judgment on a sentence for crimes during the amnesty period, the Santiago Appeals Court held, on January 5, 2004, that forced disappearances were non-amnestiable aggravated kidnappings. The Court relied extensively on a broad range of international human rights law. It cited the Inter-American Convention on Forced Disappearances, signed but not yet ratified by Chile, and found that Chile was bound not to defeat the object and purpose of that treaty by failing to prosecute and punish disappearances. Furthermore, forced disappearances constituted a crime against humanity, and the Inter-American Court of Human Rights (in the *Barrios Altos* case) had disapproved amnesties.[26] The Court read Article 5 of the Chilean constitution, amended in 1989 (under Pinochet!) to assign human rights treaties constitutional status, superior to other treaties and a limit on state sovereignty. Finally, the constitutional provisions were binding on judges above all because of "the primary duty to protect the citizenry and honor the oath with which they undertook the exercise of the sacred trust of administering justice."[27] It was a far cry from the supine judiciary of yesteryear.

With Pinochet gone from the political scene and other cases quietly winding their way through the courts, human rights again faded from the front pages and from public consciousness. Human rights groups struggled to survive. Ironically, the emphasis on the fate of the disappeared as synonymous with human rights may have weakened the long-term prospects for the human rights movement, by defining "human rights" too narrowly. In the public's mind, the fate of the Mapuche indigenous people threatened by huge hydroelectric dams, or censorship laws, or even remedies for torture survivors, were not in the same league. It will take persistence and determination to reverse that perception.

By the time the Pinochet affair closed, and despite the profound disappointment of human rights lawyers and family members in the outcome of that case, a different political and legal landscape existed in Chile. A kind of rough and partial justice, perhaps the only kind of justice available after such terrible crimes, seems to have prevailed. Manuel Contreras, Pedro Espinoza, Marcelo Moren Brito, Sergio Corvalán, and a handful of other notorious DINA and CNI operatives will spend the rest of their lives either in jail, under house arrest, or subject to prosecution for one crime after another. The much-vaunted "pact of silence" among the armed forces has been broken. A good number of younger officers have come to understand, and even support, respect for human rights and the need for justice as prerequisites to a modern, democratic Chile. Some of the generals and colonels will die before they can be indicted. Other military and police officers will get off with a slap on the wrist, a suspended sentence, the public knowledge of the accusations against them. A rough kind of justice, certainly, not all the families hoped for or demanded, not all that could be done. But no longer constituting a wall of impunity either.

Chapter 4

Argentina: Truth and Consequences

Setting the Stage: Argentina in the Mid-1990s

The start of the Spanish investigation coincided with a rebirth of interest in the dictatorship's crimes, including Adolfo Scilingo's 1995 revelations about the death flights, public admissions by officers that the military had used torture, and the public apology and admission by General Balza, head of the army, that the security forces used unacceptable tactics during the 1970s.

Pinochet's arrest in London electrified the entire Southern Cone. By 1998, the renewed public interest in the fate of the "dirty war" victims and their torturers had begun to find an echo in the Argentine judiciary. Even more than in Chile, judges in Argentina have generally been poorly respected in recent times. As in Chile, the judiciary was largely silent during the dictatorship years, ignoring pleas for *habeas corpus* and justifying the suspension of civil liberties. Indeed, President Alfonsín had hoped to use the trials of junta leaders to improve the rock-bottom prestige of the judiciary.[1] The junta trials did indeed boost the judiciary's standing, as radio and TV carried images of the judges sternly confronting members of the military. The trial and convictions of five junta members created a factual record that has served as the jumping-off point for later prosecutions.[2] Only one other trial arising from the campaign of disappearances and deaths resulted in convictions, that of the heads of the Buenos Aires police.[3] Alfonsín's subsequent backpedaling on prosecutions, through the *punto final* and due obedience laws, again undermined the independence and short-lived prestige of the institution.

In 1987, a majority of the Supreme Court upheld the *punto final* and due obedience laws in a case involving the prosecution of former Buenos Aires police chief Ramón Camps.[4] The latter law created an absolute presumption in law that anyone under the rank of lieutenant colonel, and anyone else except heads of military zones or security forces, was acting under orders and could not be held criminally or civilly liable for his actions. The majority opinion held that, first, the court had no power to review the wisdom of an act of Congress, a co-equal branch of government, so long as the act was reasonable. Second, if the legislature was free to impose criminal penalties, it followed that it was equally free to decide not to penalize some acts. Third, according to concurring judge Carlos Fayt, it was not the judge's role to usurp the legislature's political job of deciding what recourse was required in a given historical moment.

Judge Enrique Petracchi concurred in the judgment but dissented from the analysis. He found that the due obedience law could not be a law of general application because it was beyond the legislature's power to impose an absolute presumption on the judiciary. Rather, he found that Congress could enact a general amnesty and had done so. Because the amnesty was generally applicable to everyone in the same circumstances, it passed legal muster.

One judge, Jorge Antonio Bacqué, dissented. Citing the landmark U.S. case *Marbury v. Madison*, he reminded his colleagues that it is the province of judges to "say what the law is" in a constitutional democracy. Congress had no power to tell judges how to rule on facts. Because the law established an irrebuttable presumption that certain facts were true, under article 29 of the Argentine Constitution it exceeded the powers of the legislature. Nor could the law stand as a permissible amnesty because it extended to civil suits and to conduct, like torture, that could not be amnestied. The Court's approval of Alfonsín's amnesty laws and its later refusal to overturn Menem's presidential pardons confirmed its partiality—or at least irrelevancy—to many Argentines.

Carlos Menem, elected president in 1989, envisioned ambitious court reforms, but ended up sapping the courts' legitimacy even further. He tried to do away with the nagging problem of human rights violators by pardoning, in stages over a little more than a year, those who had already been convicted in the few trials, as well as some 50-odd officers still under indictment. He then declared that the subject of human rights violations during the dictatorship was now closed.

Menem went on to announce plans to modernize the court system by introducing oral testimony into criminal trials and increasing the number of judges to reduce backlogs. He expanded the Supreme Court from five to nine judges. The new judges were Menem's business associates, friends or members of his political party, and none had had particularly distinguished legal careers. He created a new appellate court and doubled the number of judges in the capital province, with his supporters and cronies in key positions.[5] By 1998, however, Menem's hold on the judiciary was loosening. "If a judge had tried to put Videla back in jail in 1990, Menem would have cut his head off," Martín Abregú, then head of the Center for Legal and Social Studies, told me. "But by 1998 neither the military nor Menem had the same power as before." Indeed, the widespread perception of judicial corruption had led to a further loss of prestige and legitimacy for the judiciary, and had reached the point that it was scaring away potential foreign investors.[6] As Menem's presidency drew to a close amid mounting economic uncertainty, high-profile corruption and public cynicism, even some of the judges who were products of the Menem machine started seeing a need to distance themselves from it, using as a cover the rhetoric of human rights.

Constitutional reform also set the stage for new judicial activism on human rights. Both Alfonsín and Menem agreed that the constitution should allow presidential reelection, and that was the primary political motivation for the 1994 reform. However, a progressive group of delegates to the 1994 constitutional convention pushed through a clause that made clear the supremacy of Argentina's international human rights obligations over contrary domestic law. Article 75 of the new constitution gives constitutional rank to the basic human rights treaties and instruments ratified by Argentina, starting with the Universal and American Declarations of Human Rights and including treaties on genocide and torture and the American Convention on Human Rights. It provides that a two-thirds vote of the legislature will raise future ratified treaties to constitutional rank. Thereafter, if a law conflicts with a provision of one of these treaties, the treaty trumps the law no matter which one came last.

Article 75 prompted more domestic judges to learn something about international law, since now they would have to apply it regularly. The Supreme Court had held years earlier that self-executing treaties could override contrary domestic law, starting at least from Argentina's becoming a party to the Vienna Convention on the Law of Treaties in 1980,[7] but putting the rule into the actual constitutional text gave it much greater prominence. Seminars, books, and academic forums began training judges, prosecutors, and lawyers in the content and implications of the international human rights treaties.

The legal groundwork for a subsequent resurgence of legal activism also came from an unexpected source: Argentina's role as a safe haven for Nazi war criminals. After World War II, Argentina issued 40,000 visas to war refugees. Among those who made Argentina their new home were Adolf Eichmann, kidnapped in 1960 by Israeli agents and eventually tried in Jerusalem, Ante Pavelic, head of the Croatian proto-Fascist Ustasha, and Joseph Mengele, resident doctor at Auschwitz. Also part of this exile community was Joseph Schwammberger, a mid-level S.S. officer and head of a small concentration camp in Poland that served as a transit point to Auschwitz and Belzec. In 1989, the La Plata Federal Court agreed to extradite him to Germany to stand trial for some 5,000 murders. Schwammberger's lawyer argued that the passage of time barred the case. The court disagreed. The Supreme Court approved the extradition in 1990, without reaching the international law or statute of limitations issues.[8] That decision paved the way for the subsequent extradition of Erich Priebke.

Priebke had participated in the 1944 massacre of more than 300 civilians, including 75 Jews, at the Ardeatine Caves outside Rome in reprisal for the deaths of German soldiers. After the war, he lived quietly and anonymously as a schoolmaster in Bariloche, an upscale ski resort in southern Argentina. There he would probably have stayed, except that someone tipped off a visiting U.S. television crew as to his whereabouts, and he was foolish enough to give them an interview admitting his crimes. The Italian government promptly filed a request for extradition (eventually, so did the German government) and the case made its way to the Argentine Supreme Court.

Priebke's lawyer argued that the crimes occurred so long ago that they were barred by the statute of limitations, and to override the statute would violate basic principles of legality. There was no treaty-based reason to do so, as Argentina was not then a party to the UN Convention on the Non-Applicability of Statutes of Limitations to War Crimes and Crimes Against Humanity. Nonetheless, in 1995 the court ordered Priebke extradited.[9] The court noted that Priebke was being charged with war crimes, genocide, and/or crimes against humanity (the judges differed on the exact characterization). These crimes under customary international law differed from "mere" homicides under national law, the court said, and by their very nature were not subject to either amnesty or a statute of limitations. Priebke was eventually tried in Italy and sentenced, at the age of eighty-three, to five years in prison.[10]

The *Priebke* case established that crimes against humanity, even those that happened long ago, were subject to prosecution. There was a catch, however. The court's ruling had taken place during an extradition proceeding, which meant that the defendant's guilt or innocence was not at issue. It also meant that an Italian, not an Argentine court, would have to impose sentence. Therefore, it didn't matter that the customary law of crimes against humanity did not specify the appropriate penalties. (A dissenter used exactly this fact to argue that without specific penalties there was no double criminality and so no way to extradite.)[11] It was not clear how well the customary international law argument would fare in a domestic criminal proceeding, where a sentence would have to be specified. Nonetheless, it was an encouraging precedent and a powerful political argument. After all, if the statute of limitations could not stand in the way of fifty-year-old crimes, much less could it torpedo more recent ones. And international law mattered.

The Truth Trials

Despite the seeming finality of the Supreme Court's decision on the amnesty laws, judges, legislators, and lawyer/activists began almost immediately looking for loopholes in the law. The first line of attack came in 1995, soon after Scilingo's declarations on the ESMA. The Center for Legal and Social Studies included among its leadership Emilio Mignone and Carmen Lapacó, both of whom had daughters who were disappeared. Alejandra Lapacó had been arrested with her mother and both had been taken to the Club Atlético detention camp. Carmen Lapacó was released, but Alejandra was never seen again. The CONADEP report made no mention of her fate. Mignone's daughter had last been seen in the ESMA. The bereaved parents petitioned the federal court to ask the Ministry of Defense for any information within their control about the fate of persons detained and disappeared within the Buenos Aires area. The Federal Court of Appeals initially denied Mignone's petition. A strong dissent cited extensively from an *amicus curiae* brief from a coalition of international human rights groups, which was later published in full in the local legal papers.[12] The brief may have set the stage for the subsequent treatment of Carmen Lapacó's complaint.

Lapacó argued that, even though the due obedience law might have shut the door to criminal prosecutions, that had nothing to do with her rights to information and to access to the remains of her loved ones. These were obligations of the state and no amnesty law could impede them. The court agreed, and the Ministry appealed. The Buenos Aires Appeals Court affirmed, finding that the state had violated the plaintiffs' rights to the truth and to mourn their dead.[13] The right to truth existed in both Argentine and international law, where it was framed as an obligation on the state to investigate, for instance, in the landmark *Velásquez* case of the Inter-American Court of Human Rights. The right to mourn the dead was one of the most deep-seated fundamental needs in all human cultures and could not be abridged by decree. It required that the location of the loved one's remains be known and that the mourners have a body to mourn. Even though no one could be jailed on the basis of the information provided, the courts still had the independent obligation to back investigations. The court ordered the state to carry out more serious investigations and to provide the plaintiffs with answers.

At that point, the Ministry changed tactics, responding that it had no information to provide. The navy also told Emilio Mignone that it had no information about his daughter or the other approximately 5,000 people detained in the ESMA. When Carmen Lapacó insisted that the court then require other agencies to provide the information, the Court of Appeals reversed course, refusing to act. Lapacó appealed to the Supreme Court.

The Court took three years to write a 14-line opinion, in which they denied Lapacó's appeal by a 5–4 vote.[14] The whole point of judicial investigations was to identify the facts and authors of a crime, the majority wrote. There would be no point in accumulating evidence of crimes for which no one could be tried. The dissent, in arguments similar to those used in Chile and elsewhere, maintained that "only a full investigation could determine whether these acts were carried out by people covered by the [amnesty laws], or by others, or under circumstances not covered by such laws."

Stung by the resulting public criticism, the court backtracked somewhat a few months later, upholding the right to *habeas data* or access to information. Facundo Urteaga had asked for access to military files about the death of his brother, who had been shot in a supposed "armed confrontation" in 1976. The lower court dismissed the request on grounds that the constitutional right to *habeas data* allowed access to information about oneself, not about others. The Supreme Court unanimously reversed, noting that the right to information or *habeas data* implied "the rights to identity and to reconstruct one's own history, which are closely aligned with human dignity."[15]

Unsatisfied by the concession of *Urteaga*, in October 1998 Carmen Lapacó and the other complainants took their case to the Inter-American Commission on Human Rights (IACHR). The IACHR has played a long and important role in nudging Argentina toward respect for human rights. The Commission is part of the Organization of American States and comprises seven experts from different states of the Americas. The Commission's 1979 visit to Argentina is widely credited for helping to stop the massive disappearances and isolating the regime internationally. The resulting report was a powerful indictment of the military's methods, embarrassing the government and providing both cover and encouragement for domestic human rights advocates.

The Commission also serves as a forum of last resort when national courts do not adequately protect the rights guaranteed under the inter-American human rights scheme. Individuals who believe their rights have been violated, and that they either have not gotten justice through the local courts or cannot do so, can file complaints with the Commission. The Commission reports on whether the state is complying with its treaty obligations. It does not issue binding court judgments but it can, under certain conditions, refer a case to the Inter-American Court of Human Rights, based in Costa Rica, which can hold public hearings and award damages.

After Alfonsín's government passed the due obedience and *punto final* laws and the *Camps* decision closed domestic appeals channels, relatives of the disappeared took their cases to the Commission. The Commission found that the amnesty laws violated the petitioners' right to a remedy, the right to a hearing with due guarantees before a competent tribunal, and the state's obligation to ensure rights.[16] The Argentine government argued that the torture and disappearances at issue happened before 1984, the year Argentina ratified the American Convention, and that therefore the petition was inadmissible. Not so, said the Commission. The violations complained of were not the underlying torture and other crimes of the dictatorship years but the rights to redress and fair trial, which were tied to the promulgation of the amnesty and pardon laws after 1984. The Commission came to the same conclusion regarding amnesty laws in Uruguay, Chile, and El Salvador.[17] In 2001 the Inter-American Court agreed with the Commission that blanket amnesty laws violate the American Convention on Human Rights, in the *Barrios Altos* case involving killings by security forces in Peru.[18]

The Lapacó family now asked the Commission to step in and demand that the Argentine government tell them what happened to their daughter. Little more than a year later, in November 1999, the government settled the case. If the petitioners agreed to drop their claims, the government in turn "accept[s] and guarantee[s] the right to the truth, which involves the exhaustion of all means to obtain information on the whereabouts of the disappeared persons . . . the Argentine Government shall adopt the necessary laws to ensure that the national federal criminal and correctional courts throughout the country have exclusive jurisdiction in all cases to determine the truth regarding the fate of persons who disappeared prior to December 10, 1983, with the sole exception of cases involving kidnapping of minors and theft of identity, which shall continue on the basis of their status."[19] The government also agreed to assign special prosecutors to help consolidate and interpret the information found.

Judge Leopoldo Schiffrin of the Federal Appeals Court in La Plata, a small city about an hour outside the capital, was encouraged by the appellate decisions upholding a "right to the truth." Schiffrin went into exile in Germany during the worst years of dictatorship and studied international law there. On his return to Argentina he became secretary (the equivalent of permanent law clerk in the U.S.) to the Supreme Court, and helped write the dissent in the *Camps* case. "As punishment, they sent me here [to La Plata]," he told me half jokingly. Schiffrin is an erudite, intense man. He is a biblical scholar, prone to sprinkling his opinions with teachings from the Talmud. A map of the biblical Middle East adorns his chambers, as do handicrafts of the indigenous groups of northern Argentina. His stay in Germany came in handy when, by sheer chance, the extradition case of Nazi camp commandant Joseph Schwammberger came before him. He wrote a long, learned concurrence in the

Schwammberger case, finding crimes against humanity to be imprescriptable under customary international law, which, he added, was
directly applicable in Argentina.[20]

Judge Schiffrin was looking for a way to use the "right to truth" idea
when he received a complaint from the La Plata Human Rights Association. The Association wanted the La Plata Appeals Court to hold hearings on what had happened to the disappeared and who was
responsible. After much internal debate, the court agreed, 5–4. In April
1998, Schiffrin, along with two other judges, began hearing testimony in
the "truth trials" (Juicios de la Verdad).

I attended the La Plata "truth trials" one overcast day in June 2000.

The three judges sat on a raised podium under a large cross and an
Argentine flag and listened to witnesses describe the disappearances of
their children more than twenty years before. There was no defendant,
and the local human rights group had its own prosecutor, who sat at the
front table together with the official public prosecutor. The room was
full, mostly older women but also some young people, on a Wednesday
afternoon. Martina Elba de Peña told of her desperate search to find
her daughter, Graciela, who disappeared in July 1976. She recounted
her trip to Spain and her hope that Judge Garzón would include her
case in his investigations. She couldn't see the judge in Spain, she
recalled, but she gave her testimony at the consulate. Now she had come
here, still looking for answers. She read a memoir of her daughter, who
loved singing and painting, and burst into tears. The judges, obviously
moved, called for a recess. When they returned, Roberto Morcini told
how his brother was kidnapped and disappeared, and how he later
found out that he had been held at Pozo de Banfield, a suburban detention center, by a policeman nicknamed "Pepi Rey." The judges asked
how he knew what he knew, and wanted the names of his sources. They
were to be subpoenaed to testify. As witnesses rather than defendants,
they could not refuse to come, although they could not be forced to
incriminate themselves. The amnesty laws ensured that none would
serve jail time, regardless what he admitted.

This is the first time many of these stories had been told. The Commission (CONADEP) that compiled lists of those killed and disappeared
during the military "years of lead" held no public hearings. The public
trial of the junta members used 746 "emblematic" cases as evidence,
leaving tens of thousands of stories untold. Those stories with some link
to the area under the jurisdiction of the La Plata federal court were now
told every Wednesday in these hearings. So far, the judges have held
some 400 hearings and heard 2,000 cases of deaths and disappearance.

In La Plata, the local Human Rights Association had three full-time
lawyers participating in the hearings as full parties. "The truth is a right

belonging to the whole society," Marta Vedio of the Association told me. "So we got involved. We acted for two reasons: first, a legislative project to annul the amnesty laws failed [in 1998]. Second, that project, in turn, was partially a product of the Spanish court investigation, which pressured the politicians to do something. It also changed the idea of the judges about the limits of what could be done. It was like a breath of fresh air for them. So we wanted to take advantage of that opening." Vedio saw two purposes to the trials: to make the truth known and to accumulate evidence for possible future criminal prosecutions. Along with the Association, some fifty groups and institutions, including the local university, the Bar Association, professional associations of all kinds, and the local school board, supported the hearings.

Truth trials soon began in other cities: San Martín and Mar del Plata on the outskirts of Buenos Aires, the industrial heartland cities of Córdoba and Rosario, the southern port town of Bahía Blanca, home to a major naval base, Mendoza in the west, and Neuquén in the south. Each took a distinct form. The San Martín hearings were considered civil proceedings and focused mostly on collating existing files and identifying the remains of victims buried as "no name" in local cemeteries. The others were conducted under the aegis of criminal investigations, some in federal appeals courts and others in federal trial courts. Those in Córdoba and Mendoza were held behind closed doors, without public hearings.

The "truth trials" blurred the line between truth commissions and trials, while sharply posing the question of whether trials without defendants, verdicts, or sentences can provide justice. Given these inherent limitations, will such hybrid procedures be, at best, a prelude to a changed calculus of prosecution and a way of getting at long-buried facts, or, at worst, end up being an inconclusive teaser? Many of those involved have found themselves in uncharted territory, trying to determine the consequences of truth.

Judge Schiffrin and his colleagues had to decide how to follow up on the testimony they were hearing from eyewitnesses, family members, and friends of the disappeared. They personally visited the police stations, cemeteries, and houses around La Plata known to have functioned as detention centers. They began calling to testify former police officers, army chaplains, and doctors who signed certificates or performed autopsies. Those who might eventually face indictment were allowed their own lawyers. The question of what to do with information that led to specific suspects became urgent, pointing up the contradictions and limits inherent in the process.

The uncomfortable hybrid nature of the proceedings became clear when Judge Schiffrin tried to get his colleagues to agree to subpoena

Miguel Etchecolatz as a possible suspect. Etchecolatz had been second in command to General Camps in the Buenos Aires police and was convicted of murder and committing torture before he benefited from the amnesty and pardon decrees. More and more evidence in the "truth trials," evidence involving crimes not previously charged, pointed at him. What now? The judges were confused and thoroughly divided. Schiffrin and two colleagues pushed for an indictment. Schiffrin summed up the achievements of the truth trials by 1998: rescuing the memory of events and saving and organizing documents (although much documentary evidence has been lost or destroyed). He continued:

> But these investigations are above all made more difficult by a closed conspiracy of silence, a wall of defiant impassivity that, hearing after hearing, smashes against the legitimate desires to know a minimum of truth . . . , using the guarantees provided by the rule of law, and thus seeming to deny such guarantees to the victims. . . . The direction that this investigation is taking I fear could be seen as a second and definitive burial of the victims. . . . Our function differs from that of the historian, who preserves and narrates the collective memory and, with it, the identity of a society. The judge deals with current acts, she is an actor in the social drama—in this case, the social tragedy—and should decide the future, not just recollect the past. This explains the extent of justifiable impatience that pervades the hearings and the publications, saying to us, if not now, when?[21]

Despite his concerns for the effect on victims of inconclusive hearings, Schiffrin's arguments failed to persuade a majority of his colleagues. Among these, some wanted to declare that the truth trials had no competence to explore penal sanctions, while others held that it was up to the Prosecutor's Office (Ministerio Público) and not the court to pursue the penal aspects of the investigation. Four judges held that the courts could investigate, but that the Buenos Aires court that had originally looked into charges against Etchecolatz (before the amnesty laws were passed) still had primary jurisdiction over the case.[22] In light of the divided vote, Etchecolatz remained undisturbed. (He was arrested and detained in 2000 on baby-snatching charges.)

The related problem of whether the courts could force unwilling witnesses to testify brought the issue to a head. Theoretically, military and police officers could be subpoenaed to testify as witnesses without fear, since they were not considered suspects and, in any case, could not be prosecuted under the amnesty laws. But there were other risks to testifying. Miguel Angel Ferreyro, for example, a police corporal, had testified as a witness in La Plata at the end of 1999 in a disappearance case, denying any knowledge. At the end of the session, an ex-detainee named Nilda Eloy approached the bench, distraught. She knew that voice, she told the judges. When she had been in a detention center named "Hell" in late 1976, she had been blindfolded the whole time, but she could recognize Ferreyro's as one of her jailers from his voice and expressions. The judges then decided to call Ferreyro back, this time as a suspect, not a witness.

Former and current police and military who lied under oath were charged with perjury. In Bahía Blanca and Córdoba, those who refused to testify were held in contempt of court and arrested until they reconsidered. Public prosecutor Hugo Cañón of Bahía Blanca, for example, ordered the arrest of an active officer, Lt. Colonel Julián Corres, who had run a notorious detention center in a former school ("La Escuelita"), and a number of other retired officers for refusing to testify. Cristina Garzón, a judge in Córdoba, ordered the indefinite arrest of ex-General Luciano Menéndez, former head of the Third Army Corps, for refusing to recognize the court's jurisdiction. These officers and others protested that they were being forced to incriminate themselves, if not in Argentina then in investigations that were already, or could in the future, take place outside the country. This possibility would not have occurred to anyone a scant five years before. Now prosecution abroad (and perhaps, eventually, extradition) was a real danger, with investigations and indictments ongoing in Spain, France, Italy, Germany, and elsewhere. Eventually, the Argentine Supreme Court held that because the officers could become criminal suspects they could not be forced to testify under oath or held indefinitely in contempt of court for failing to do so.[23]

As a strategy, the truth trials' success in uncovering new evidence highlighted its contradictions. In part, these derived from the lack of any precedent, which meant that judges were in essence making up procedure as they went along. More fundamentally, the tension created by judges hearing in public credible evidence of chargeable crimes without being able to take the next logical steps to question and detain suspects made the exercise a frustrating one for victims' associations as well as the judges themselves. As more evidence emerged, the pressure to act on it mounted and the judges began responding, either opening criminal investigations themselves or passing evidence of crime on to other courts. Furthermore, times had changed from 1998 to 2002. Mirta Mántaras, one of the complainant lawyers in Bahía Blanca, explained in a press interview: "When the Truth Trials began, we had no possibility of demanding trial and punishment of the guilty, because Pinochet was not then detained, the House of Lords had not yet ruled, Baltazár Garzón had not yet asked for the extradition of the Argentine military officers. All of this created a universal judicial consciousness, an understanding that crimes against humanity can be prosecuted anywhere in the world."[24]

The "right to the truth" soon took on other forms as well. The navy, in a fit of bravado, decided to demolish the grounds of the ESMA and to put up a military academy in its place. Graciela Lois, a long-time member of the Association of Families of the Disappeared, promptly filed suit. "A soldier told me there were bodies under the tennis courts at the ESMA. He had never testified publicly, nor did he want to. But to let the navy just bulldoze it would have been an outrage." Lois's husband disappeared in the ESMA. A Buenos Aires court issued an injunction prohibiting the demolition of the site because evidence of crimes might be found there and because the place was an expression of the nation's memory.[25] In March 2004, it was declared a national museum. In La Plata as well, judges refused to let the army modify the site of a former detention camp out by the lighthouse, which had been leased to a private company for an amusement park.

Stealing Children, Theft, and Other Cracks in the Wall of Impunity

Silvia Quintela was a doctor who ministered to the sick in shantytowns around Buenos Aires. She was abducted by security forces in 1977 and gave birth to a baby boy at the army's Campo de Mayo detention camp. She was never heard from again, but her partner, Abel Madariaga, fled to Sweden and returned to Argentina in 1983. He began to suspect that a military doctor, Norberto Atilio Bianco, had kidnapped the boy and changed his identity. In 1987, he demanded DNA testing of both of Bianco's children. Bianco, his wife, and the two children fled to Paraguay. The children refused to be tested. After a ten-year extradition battle, Bianco and his wife were finally returned to Argentina.[26] Investigating magistrate Judge Roberto Marquevich charged them with child kidnapping, falsification of identity documents, and suppression of the identity of a minor.[27]

Madariaga's attorney, Alcira Ríos, is a thin, intense, middle-aged woman with dark circles under her eyes. During the 1970s, she herself was arrested and held in various secret detention centers before being formally charged and imprisoned, which under the circumstances saved her life. She recalls that she was charged with terrorism based on an incident involving arms smuggling that allegedly occurred two months after her family had already filed habeas corpus petitions denouncing her abduction. She was eventually expelled. In Brazil, she met some of the Grandmothers of the Plaza de Mayo, who were seeking to identify and recover children born in captivity or stolen shortly after birth from mothers who disappeared, like Silvia Quintela. Some of the missing children were given up in formal adoption, others were claimed by their new families as their own. While a few were given to ordinary couples who had no knowledge of their provenance, most went to military or police-related families. According to the Grandmothers, there were over 400 of these children, of whom fewer than a hundred had been found and made aware of their birth families by 2002. Ríos began collecting evidence and eventually brought a complaint against Bianco. "The Paraguayan government refused to extradite him and his wife, but we complained to the Inter-American Commission on Human Rights, which put pressure on the government. We had testimony from midwives and military personnel of the Campo de Mayo about a secret birthing center. Once we got Bianco back, we had a suspect and the investigation could really take off."

"The first task in these cases was to depoliticize them," Ríos recalled. "We kept emphasizing that these children were innocent victims and had the right to know their true identity. We got to the point where no one would defend the practice of child-stealing. When the amnesty laws were written, they specifically excluded these crimes because they were so politically and morally unjustifiable."

Ríos's strategy involved finding those who were holding the stolen children. She and the Grandmothers wanted to identify as many of the children as possible and reunite them with their real families. She also hoped to use evidence obtained from low-level police and military families to move up the chain of command to those who had set the baby-stealing machine in motion. Cases were not hard to find. Mariana Zaffaroni Islas had been less than a year old when she was taken away from her parents, who were detained at the Automotores Orletti detention camp. She was given to Miguel Angel Furci, an agent of the State Information Agency who visited the camp. Furci and his wife were eventually sentenced to five and eight years prison, respectively, for having kept the baby as their own. Carlos D'Elia was born in another detention camp to two disappeared prisoners. The police medic in charge had him handed over on a street corner to his new family, who registered him as their own. It was not until 1995 that his grandparents discovered his true identity. María Sol Tetzlaff was born in the Campo de Mayo to unknown parents and given over to Hernán Tetzlaff, an army officer who worked at the military base.[28]

In identifying the kidnapped children, the courts relied heavily on blood compatibility tests and, later, on DNA testing procedures that could skip a generation, establishing the genetic ties between a child and his or her grandparents. In the 1990s, Argentina pioneered the creation of a DNA databank that would allow matching of DNA across three generations. In 1992, the government created a National Commission for the Right to Identity, charged with finding the missing children.

Some of the children, by this time young adults, came forward to ask for testing that would confirm or deny their suspicions. Others, however, refused to have a sample taken. They could not see the point, they told the court, of jeopardizing the only parents they had ever known, who in many cases had given them loving, middle-class homes. Those who did discover their identities did not always choose to live with their true relatives; often, complicated visitation agreements were necessary. In a few cases, adoptive parents and children were forced under court order to undergo testing.

Until 1997, the goal of Judge Marquevich's investigation had been to find the children and punish those directly responsible for taking them. Then new evidence appeared from a number of sources. The chief medical officer of the Campo de Mayo military base, Julio César Caserotto, under subpoena testified that there were written and verbal orders to give the children away to military families. When asked who gave the orders, he named General Videla, at the time president and head of the army. Other survivors corroborated the existence of a maternity clinic at the camp, in which women who were subsequently disappeared gave birth, often while blindfolded and shackled. The maternity ward was known as an "epidemiology unit." Women were transferred to this unit from detention centers in other parts of the country, including centers run by other branches of the security forces, something that could not happen without high-level coordination. Also, Judge Garzón opened a specific investigation in Spain into the baby-snatching cases, calling witnesses and collecting testimony. Recall, for instance, Matilde Artés's testimony about her granddaughter, found after the girl saw her baby picture on television. Many of those who came forward in Spain had not brought their cases before Argentine courts.

In July 1998, Marquevich ordered the arrest of Jorge Videla on charges of child kidnapping and concealment, forgery of birth certificates, and suppression of the civil status of a minor. The indictment was based on kidnappings from Campo de Mayo, Automotores Orletti, and Pozo de Banfield, all army-run detention centers. Shortly thereafter, Marquevich issued charges against other top army officers, including the head of the Campo de Mayo, ex-General Santiago Omar Riveros, and the commander of the First Army Corps, Carlos Guillermo Suárez-Mason.

Marquevich concluded that the baby-snatchings were part of a systematic plan ordered by Videla to separate from their families those children whose parents were considered linked to "subversion." The aim of the plan was both to sow terror and to ensure that the children did not grow up in subversive households, contaminated by an environment contrary to the prevailing system. "The goal was to demoralize, break and disorganize any remnants of solidarity in the social fabric," he wrote. "The most subtle and refined expression of this strategy consisted in taking control of newborn babies—the most defenseless of human beings—and removing them from those who should care for them, protect them and watch them grow."[29]

Videla objected on grounds that he had already been tried in 1985, in the junta trials, and on grounds that the statute of limitations had expired. The judge replied that the court in the earlier trial specifically declined to rule on the existence of a systematic practice of kidnapping children and changing their identities, and had only considered evidence in two specific child kidnapping cases. In addition, baby-snatchings and denial of identity were continuing crimes until the children were found and their original identity was restored, so the statute of limitations would only begin to run at that point. Even without the continuing crime doctrine, concluded the judge, in this context the crimes at issue constituted crimes against humanity. The *Schwammberger* and *Priebke* cases had already established that such crimes were not subject to statutes of limitations. Videla's appeal was denied and the denial upheld by the Federal Appeals Court.[30] It is now before the Supreme Court.

The investigations in the children's cases quickly expanded. Judge María Servini de Cubría detained nine navy noncommissioned officers accused of taking babies whose mothers had been held at the Mar del Plata naval base. Armed with search warrants, the judge marched into naval hospitals and medical clinics, found suspicious-looking birth certificates, and demanded information from the navy commander-in-chief. There were some twenty cases of child misappropriation before the courts as of 2002.

Buenos Aires lawyer Alberto Pedroncini had a different strategy. Rather than begin with the appropriators of the lost children and work his way up, he wanted to build on existing evidence to start at the top, and to focus solely on the systematic nature of child-stealing. Judge Bagnasco, who received Pedroncini's complaint, focused on the ESMA and on the existence of a plan to bring women from different detention centers to give birth there. The complaint accused Admiral Massera, head of the navy, and most of the top personnel at the ESMA of carrying out a plan to kidnap the children and deny them their identity. It also accused members of the last military junta, including General Reynaldo Bignone, Lieutenant General Cristino Nicolaides, and Naval Commander Rubén Franco, of covering up the crimes.

As part of his investigations, Judge Bagnasco visited Switzerland and Spain in June 1998. He talked to exiles and ex-detainees about their experiences in the camps and their contacts with pregnant prisoners. Eduardo Freiler, the public prosecutor working with him on the case, met with Judge Garzón. Bagnasco eventually indicted and jailed a dozen of the accused pending trial.[31] This case, too, raised the issue of double jeopardy. The defendants argued that even if individual cases had not been aired at the trial of the juntas, the court there had considered and rejected the allegations of a systematic plan. That issue, like the others, is now on appeal to the Supreme Court.

The children's cases, with their strong moral and emotional tug, became one of the wedges prying open the door to renewed prosecutions of the top military brass and some of the worst torturers. The other wedge involved prosecuting the cases where security force members used their practically unlimited power over detainees to kidnap and extort for personal gain. They not only took as "war booty" whatever they could find when raiding people's houses, but also sometimes forced the detainees to sign over property and bank accounts. Desperate relatives sometimes emptied their bank accounts or mortgaged their homes to pay ransom for prisoners who never reappeared. Sometimes they did so just to see their loved ones one last time.

A case in point was the kidnapping and subsequent disappearance of Conrado Higinio Gómez, a wealthy Mendoza businessman suspected of ties to the left-wing Montoneros. Gómez's son testified before Judge Garzón in Madrid. The Buenos Aires Court of Appeals, in reviewing the case, quoted the facts directly from Garzón's summary.[32] Conrado Gómez was kidnapped in January 1977 from his offices by a group of 15 to 20 armed men. His office safe was robbed of almost a million dollars and deeds to expensive properties, and shortly thereafter the family found that checks were written on their bank accounts. Military officers appeared as the new owners of the family's prize racehorses and rural properties, using fake names and a real estate company controlled by Admiral Massera. Gómez called his family and told them he was being held by the military, and that for their own safety they should forget about his business and worldly goods. The last time the family heard from Gómez was in March 1977, when he told them he thought he was going to be sent out of the country. He has not been seen since.

In 1999, the family asked a judge to begin a local investigation, but the judge refused. The family appealed, and the appeals court noted that while General Videla and other high-ranking officers had been acquitted of Gómez's disappearance during the trial of the Juntas, defendants like Captain Alfredo Astiz had never been charged in the case. (Recall that Astiz was one of the navy's most notorious operatives, accused, among other things, of a role in the murder of two French nuns and a Swedish teenager.) The big obstacle, of course, was the existence of the amnesty laws.

The court noted earlier Supreme Court jurisprudence holding that the relevant law should be narrowly interpreted. The amnesty laws covered those members of the security forces who had acted "in the operations carried out for the alleged purpose of repressing terrorism." The Court looked to the purpose of the amnesty laws—which it defined as reconciliation—and found that kidnapping for purposes of extortion was a question of personal benefit, not part of the repression of terrorism. It was not, therefore, covered by the laws. In this case, the appeals court found that only further investigation would determine whether Conrado Gómez's kidnapping and disappearance were carried out for personal, extortive reasons and so fit within the exception.

The court also had to confront the issue of the statute of limitations. Here, the court engaged in a little judicial sleight-of-hand: while the crimes under investigation might be extortion and kidnapping for personal gain for purposes of the amnesty laws, they were in essence a forced disappearance for purposes of the statute of limitations. And, as established in earlier cases, disappearances, as a species of crimes against humanity, were not subject to a statute of limitations under customary international law. As a result, Judge Bonadío indicted Massera and four ESMA operatives—Juan Carlos Rolón, Jorge Radice, Jorge Acosta, and Francis Whamond—for criminal association, extortion, and illegal detention. The Court of Appeals later affirmed for all the defendants except one.[33]

In addition to exceptions to the amnesty laws for kidnapped children and for extortive kidnappings, there were other loopholes. Civilians who were not members of the security forces could be prosecuted, and judges could investigate events prior to the military coup. Cases began involving these exceptions as well. By 2001, the exceptions had come to undermine the rule. The courts came up against the manifest absurdity of being able to investigate what had happened to the children or the goods of the disappeared, but not to look into the disappearances themselves. The result was a spate of decisions holding that the *punto final* and due obedience laws are unlawful under international and Argentine law. The wedges driven into the amnesty by truth trials, trials abroad, and investigations under the loopholes in the amnesty law itself eventually opened the door to its complete repudiation, at least by the lower courts, and eventually by the legislature.

The Demise of Due Obedience?

Claudia Victoria Poblete was eight months old when she was kidnapped together with her parents and held in the El Olimpo detention center. Her father, José Liborio Poblete, was a Chilean disability rights activist who used a wheelchair. Her mother, Gertrudis Marta Hlaczik, was a psychology student. The couple were told that the baby would be given to her grandparents, but instead she was turned over to a police lieutenant colonel, Ceferino Landa, and his wife. After years of investigation, the Grandmothers found Poblete living with the Landas. Alcira Ríos filed suit, Landa and his wife were jailed, and Claudia's real name was restored.

But then something more happened. The Center for Legal and Social Studies, along with the public prosecutor, asked the courts to issue additional arrest warrants for two notorious torturers, Juan Antonio del Cerro (alias Colors) and Julio Héctor Simón (alias Julian the Turk), and seven other military officers for the kidnapping of Claudia Poblete and the disappearance of her parents. On November 1, 2000, del Cerro and Simón were arrested for the crime. The court noted that it was absurd to investigate what happened to the child, who after all was still alive, but not look into the deaths of the child's parents arising under the same set of facts. For that, of course, the amnesty laws had to be brushed aside. In March 2001, Judge Gabriel Cavallo declared the *punto final* and due obedience laws null and void.[34]

Cavallo's 150-plus page decision relied on both Argentine and international law. First, Cavallo established that the disappearances were part of a systematic practice that constituted a crime against humanity. The judge drew on facts established both in the Argentine junta trials, in Judge Garzón's investigation in Spain, and in the U.S. extradition proceedings against General Suárez-Mason.[35] He also referred to the civil cases filed in the U.S. against Suárez-Mason, and to criminal investigations pending in Germany, France, Italy, and Switzerland, to show that "these events affected a large part of the organized international community, becoming the subject of analysis in different countries."[36] He traced the history of the concept of crimes against humanity in international law. Earlier cases, he noted, had established that Article 118 of Argentina's constitution gave customary international law domestic status, including the concepts of crimes against humanity and universal jurisdiction.[37]

Cavallo drew extensively on jurisprudence from other national courts as well as from treaties and UN documents. He cited from U.S. cases brought under the Alien Tort Claims Act and from the House of Lords decision in the *Pinochet* case to show that the crimes at issue were of international concern. He reproduced whole pages from Judge Garzón's *autos* and from the Criminal Appeals Chamber of the Audencia Nacional decision of November 1998. He concluded that "by judging and condemning those responsible for these acts, the state acts in the interests of the whole of the international community."

Unlike the House of Lords majority in *Pinochet*, Judge Cavallo did not require that the jurisdictional or substantive contours of the crime be part of preexisting domestic penal law. It was enough that they were common crimes like murder and kidnapping under domestic law. International law gave them the special gravity that required prosecution despite any limits imposed by local law. Prosecution was a matter of Argentina's international legal obligations under both customary law and treaties duly ratified. The judge quoted at length the Inter-American Commission on Human Rights finding that the two impunity laws violated Argentina's treaty commitments. In addition, the laws violated the constitutional precept that the executive cannot wield "special powers" that put the "life, honor, and fortunes of Argentines at the mercy of any government or person." And by creating irrebuttable presumptions of fact, the law stripped the judiciary of its proper fact-finding role and violated article 29 of the Argentine constitution. This argument was not new: the Supreme Court's majority had rejected it in the *Camps* decision.

Cavallo shrugs when asked why Argentine judges waited for so long to overturn the amnesty laws. "For one thing," he points out, "none of the complainants had raised the unconstitutionality argument before me. It took the CELS initiative to put the issue squarely into play. For another, these weren't new arguments. Academics who worked with victims' groups had been making them for some time, the external and internal pressure was growing, and public opinion was changing. Then foreign judges began making concrete detention requests, and those of us working in the area began to think 'this won't be considered a serious country until we solve this problem.' Foreign governments didn't want to be bothered with having these cases in their courts, and they put pressure on the Argentine government to not stand in the way of the local trials so that foreign judges would not end up doing these investigations. That changed the pressures on judges."

In effect, Judge Cavallo's decision, hailed by human rights groups inside and outside the country, seemed to unleash long-building changes. It was followed by a similar decision by Judge Claudio Bonadío in the case of Conrado Gómez, the businessman whose properties, horses, and money were stolen by the military when he was disappeared.[38] Like Cavallo, Bonadío found it absurd that he could jail the perpetrators for extortion, but not for kidnapping and murder. Both cases were appealed to the Buenos Aires Appeals Court. On November 9, 2001, the appeals court upheld both decisions.[39]

The appeals court decision was obviously written with an eye toward future review by a Supreme Court that had already once upheld the amnesty laws. It traced the jurisprudence, focusing on the dissents in *Camps*, the truth trials, and the loopholes in the law for extortion and for baby-stealing. The court then addressed the claim that invalidating the amnesty laws at this point would both constitute ex post facto criminalization of de-criminalized conduct and a violation of the rule that the most favorable law applies in criminal cases. Neither of these arguments applied here, as the conduct at issue was a crime under customary international law long before it took place. The appeals court pointed out that human rights treaties now had constitutional status, superior to that of mere statutes, which meant that the impunity laws were invalid from the beginning. Treaty law clearly established that the crimes at issue could not be the subject of amnesty. The panel concluded: "in the present context of development of the constitutional law of human rights, the invalidation and declaration of unconstitutionality of the laws [of *punto final* and due obedience] is not an alternative. It is an obligation."

Similar decisions followed from lower federal courts in Salta and Santa Fé and then the Salta Appeals Court, notable because they come from the ultraconservative north and not the capital.[40] The Salta case involves the 1976 torture and subsequent murder of prisoners in the town of Salta. Another case involving the murder of prisoners comes from Chaco province. In May 2001, CELS brought a complaint for the 1976 "Massacre of Margarita Belén," in which 22 prisoners were tortured and killed, and the incident was later justified as an armed confrontation with delinquents. Among the suspects named in the complaint is General Ricardo Brinzoni, until 2003 the army chief of staff. In March 2003, a federal judge once again declared that the amnesty laws were no bar to prosecutions in that case.[41] The country's prosecutor general, Nicolás Becerra, has sided with these courts.[42] A lower court also found Menem's pardons to be unlawful, for similar reasons.

President Kirchner's Changes

Argentina elected a new president in 2003. Néstor Kirchner disavowed the policies of his predecessors and supported efforts to obtain justice. The changes were evident on several fronts. In the courts, while the Supreme Court had still not decided on the constitutionality of the amnesty laws, its composition changed substantially after the election. Several judges retired or were ousted on corruption charges, and some of the new judges have human rights backgrounds.[43]

President Kirschner early on publicly stated that the laws should be declared unconstitutional, and retired the remaining active military and police officers likely to face prosecution. In August 2003, Congress took him up on the suggestion, annulling the *punto final* and due obedience laws. The laws had initially been repealed in 1998, but the repeal made little practical difference because it did not apply retroactively. At that time, a majority of legislators had concluded that to annul the laws would violate principles of *res judicata* (no reopening of already judged cases) and the prohibition on retroactive law. Now, debate centered on another problem: under Argentine penal law, guilty parties benefit from application of the law most favorable to them (sometimes known as the law of lenity). In this case, it was argued, the most favorable law would be the amnesty, so any change would have little practical effect. Nonsense, replied the law's supporters. First of all, President Alfonsín had successfully annulled the military's self-amnesty in 1983.[44] How was this different? Second, if the amnesty laws were a violation of both the Argentine Constitution and international law, they were void from the start and so never attained the force of law. Thus there was no more favorable law to apply. While some thought the annulment would be declared unconstitutional, others argued that its passage made the pending court cases moot. It remained, as of this writing, a convoluted problem for the new Supreme Court's agenda. Meanwhile, lower court judges have reopened two major criminal investigations that had been foreclosed by the amnesties, into crimes committed at the ESMA and by the Army's First Corps (under command of Suarez Mason), and more arrests are announced every week. However the legal battle concludes, the public view of the need for, or inevitability of, the trade-off of amnesty for peace has been forever changed.

Chapter 5
The European Cases

Pinochet's arrest in London also provoked ripples throughout Europe. Many European countries harbored large South American exile populations, and, like Robin Cook in the UK, many of the politicians, judges and lawyers in those countries had as students protested the coup in Chile. Charges against Pinochet were quickly filed across the continent, including Belgium, France, Switzerland, Sweden, Germany, and Italy. I talked to some of those bringing the charges.

Belgium Takes a Stand

Rosario Aguilar remembers what she was doing when she heard that Pinochet had been arrested, the way people in the U.S. remember what they were doing when President Kennedy was shot or the World Trade Center attacked. Aguilar, a small woman in her fifties with a shock of dark hair, moved to Brussels in 1979 after being forced into exile by the Chilean government. Her first husband was killed by the military. Her second husband's brother disappeared. Her husband spent ten years in jail, and when he was offered the choice of more jail or exile, she went with him, leaving her children behind in Chile with her parents. "My children never grew up with their mother and father. Nothing was ever the same. We're still suffering from the aftereffects," she mused.

Aguilar continues:

Most of us [Chileans in Belgium] came here as political activists, but as the years went by we started losing touch with each other. It was the detention of Pinochet that brought us together and made the unthinkable become thinkable. When I heard about it, I began to call around for a lawyer, to see if we could file a case against him here. I got nowhere until, through a contact at Oxfam, I found the League of the Rights of Man. Its president, Georges Beauthier, met with me. He said he would help, but we needed to move fast, that I should gather a group of potential complainants and he would meet with us the next day, which was a Saturday. I was up until two in the morning calling people.

The next day Aguilar and five other people went to see Beauthier. They spent the day drafting statements on the deaths, disappearances and torture of loved ones in Chile, and then went to see the local magistrate on call. "He told us this was too delicate a matter and to come back on Monday. We decided to insist, and went back the next day. Luckily, Judge Vandermeersch was on duty that Sunday. He agreed to accept our complaint. The six of us were the complainants, the *parties civiles*, but some 30–40 other people gave declarations and helped out. We limited the number of complainants because you have to post a bond, and also because the complainants have access to the case file and can work closely with the public prosecutor, so we wanted a small, manageable group of people."

"We spent the next whole day at the police station, answering the investigators' questions. It was terrible. They asked details about events that we hadn't talked about for years, some things we had never talked about before. They asked for documentation in French about the coup and about the Pinochet government, so that they could understand. Sometimes they had a hard time grasping the concepts. At one point someone asked for an explanation of losing people. It became clear to us that the whole idea that a government could deliberately disappear its own people was so strange to them."

As in Spain, several peculiarities of Belgian law made it relatively easy at the time for private parties to bring prosecutions. Judge Vandermeersch explains: "If a criminal case came directly to a prosecutor, the prosecutor could turn it down. If, however, the complainant went directly to the investigating magistrate (*juge d'instruction*) as a complainant (*partie civile*), the magistrate just had to figure out if he had jurisdiction. If he did, he could not turn down the case, but must investigate." The effective check on the investigating magistrate's action came when he sought funds to investigate. If the prosecutor (and through him, the executive branch of government) did not see the merits of the prosecution, no money would be forthcoming. That process applied to cases involving crimes that took place outside Belgium until 2003, when a new procedure was approved, a tale told in Chapter 7.

Damien Vandermeersch, the investigating magistrate who accepted Rosario Aguilar's complaint, was already well known in Belgium. Slim, bearded, unassuming, and professorial, Vandermeersch is an expert in international criminal law. He was already acquainted with the law that could allow prosecution of Pinochet. He was at the time in the midst of an investigation of the crimes committed during the course of the 1994 genocide in Rwanda. That investigation ended in the jury trial and conviction of four Rwandans in 2001. The experience offered Vandermeersch the expertise necessary to understand how to proceed with Rosario Aguilar's complaint.

Before Judge Vandermeersch could even contemplate an investigation into the allegations against Pinochet, he had to decide whether he had jurisdiction. Under the 1993 law, the Belgian courts had jurisdiction over those committing certain war crimes, no matter where the crimes occurred or the nationality or location of the victims or the accused. The Belgian courts' universal jurisdiction could be triggered at the time by a victim acting as complainant, and did not require the defendant's presence in Belgium to open an investigation (this issue is also discussed in Chapter 7). Immunity was also not a problem, as the Belgian law clearly stated that no immunities to investigation applied in cases involving war crimes. Belgian law differed from that of the UK on this score, as we have seen.

There were other problems, however. First, like many of the cases applying these relatively recent laws, Judge Vandermeersch came up against the problem that the crimes alleged had occurred before the 1993 law came into effect. Would applying later law to earlier facts violate the rules against ex post facto lawmaking? No, Vandermeersch decided, the crimes alleged had long been crimes under domestic law, where they were called murder, assault, and the like. So long as the penalties involved were no more severe than the penalties for those common crimes, there was no violation of the principles of legality in investigating them now. He came to the same solution, that is, as Judge Garzón in Spain and Judge Cavallo in Argentina.

How to bring the case within the requirement that the crime be punishable under both Belgian and Chilean law (the "double criminality" requirement for extradition) proved more difficult. At the time the Belgian law covered only grave breaches of the Conventions and Protocols. The Spanish judge had charged genocide, but neither genocide nor crimes against humanity were then codified in the Belgian penal code. The judge therefore either had to find that Chile was in the midst of an armed conflict when the crimes took place, or arrive at some other solution. This same dilemma had fueled endless debates in Chile.

Vandermeersch refused to label the Chilean conflict an internal armed conflict under the language of the 1949 Geneva Conventions and their Protocols. After all, the government's use of force was aimed at disarticulating a domestic opposition which, after the first month or so after September 1973, was almost entirely unarmed. But that did not end the story, he continued. Even though they were not war crimes, the acts alleged in the complaint were clearly crimes against humanity as defined by customary international law. They did not need to be explicitly set out as such in the penal code, because certain acts within the definition of crimes against humanity—murder, manslaughter, hostage-taking, and the like—were covered by the regular criminal law. (Recall this was also Judge Cavallo's solution in Argentina.) Customary international law can be directly applied in Belgian law, Vandermeersch found, and the concept of crimes against humanity already existed in that law.

Anticipating criticism of this sweeping view of the law, the judge chided:

> National judicial authorities often seek legal reasons to avoid prosecuting crimes against humanity instead of ascertaining whether they can prosecute them under international and national law. . . . Concerning the enforcement of international humanitarian law, too, the risk is not that domestic authorities may overstep their competence but rather that by looking for excuses to justify their alleged lack of jurisdiction, they condone the impunity of the most serious crimes. . . . The struggle against the impunity of persons responsible for crimes under international law is, therefore, a responsibility of all states. National authorities have, at least, the right to take such measures as are necessary for the prosecution and punishment of crimes against humanity.[1]

Calling the murders and disappearances at issue crimes against humanity solved other problems. The running of the statute of limitations, for instance, was not a bar because, the judge found, crimes against humanity are imprescriptable—they can have no statute of limitations due to the heinous nature of the crime and the continuing international interest in its suppression. As a result, the investigating magistrate found he could proceed to investigate. He began accumulating witness statements and documents. On December 15, 1998, the Belgian government issued an extradition warrant for Pinochet's arrest. In mid-November, after the Spanish extradition request was filed, France and Switzerland also filed requests.

The unhappy fate of the Belgian extradition warrant in the British courts has already been recounted. Rosario Aguilar, nonetheless, is satisfied that the case got national attention, and brought the scrutiny of the world to the crimes of the Chilean dictatorship.

The "Victims' Nationality" Cases: France, Italy, Germany

The Spanish and Belgian cases broke new ground in international law because they were based on a theory of universal jurisdiction. But long before those cases, European courts began investigating the deaths and disappearances in Argentina and Chile when the victim was a citizen of a European country or a dual national. Cases where courts take jurisdiction based on the victims' nationality differ in several ways from universal jurisdiction cases. The idea of such "passive personality" jurisdiction is an outgrowth of the (colonialist) notion that states had a legal claim for acts against their nationals. Not all countries recognize such jurisdiction as valid, and then not for all crimes. The cases have to focus on victims of the forum state's nationality. This risks creating a partial or distorted picture of events, because these may be a small percentage of the total number of victims and may not be representative. On the other hand, the cases involve charges of regular crimes under national law like murder or kidnapping, rather than crimes with hard-to-prove elements like genocide. They also share a series of problems including difficulties in obtaining evidence, statutes of limitations and variations among countries in the permissible characterization of the crimes.

In the Argentine case, victims with European nationality were not hard to find because of the country's large immigrant population and because Spain, Italy, France, Germany, and some other countries allow dual citizenship for the children (and sometimes grandchildren) of those who emigrate. Other European victims were priests, nuns, and aid workers. A few of these cases, like the investigation of Argentine navy captain Alfredo Astiz for the disappearance of two French nuns, and the Italian disappearance cases, far predate the Pinochet affair. With Pinochet's arrest, a new wave of cases swept through the courts. In addition to those profiled here, there was the investigation by a Swiss military court of the disappearance in Buenos Aires of Alexis Jacquard, a Swiss-Chilean student. In Sweden, the family of Dagmar Hagelin, a seventeen-year-old student shot, dragged off, and disappeared in Argentina's ESMA, insisted again on their extradition request for Astiz and others responsible for her death.

France

Captain Alfredo Astiz was known among prisoners at the ESMA detention camp in Buenos Aires as the Blond Angel. His boyish good looks served him well as a member of Argentina's naval investigations unit. He had been able to infiltrate the Mothers of the Plaza de Mayo in Buenos Aires, then in its infancy. As women found themselves making the same rounds to hospitals and police stations looking for children who had disappeared, they coalesced in a loose organization. Its main activity was the weekly marches of white-kerchiefed women around the central town plaza, mutely holding pictures of the missing. Astiz posed as Gustavo Niño, the brother of a disappeared activist. As a result of his efforts, a number of Mothers and their supporters were themselves detained and disappeared. Among the supporters were two French nuns, Sisters Alice Domon and Léonie Duquet. They were seen last alive in the ESMA in 1977.[2] The Argentine courts twice refused to prosecute Astiz for the crime because of the due obedience law, so the families of the two nuns brought a complaint before a French investigating magistrate, asking him to look into the disappearances.

The families belonged to an Association of Relatives and Friends of

French Citizens Disappeared in Argentina, formed in 1977. Their circumstances varied: in some cases, like the nuns, the victims had moved to Argentina to pursue work, studies, or a vocation. In others, the family had emigrated years ago but kept dual citizenship. The Association found lawyers, among them Sophie Thonon. Thonon was a litigator and head of the French-Latin American Association. She grew up visiting Argentina and, as a student, had lived in Allende's Chile. She left the country two days before the coup in September 1973.

The relatives' association decided it made sense to focus their efforts on an emblematic, "sacred" case. They chose both victims and accused carefully. The nuns had clearly not been armed insurgents—they had merely worked with the poor and the Mothers—and Astiz was clearly a despicable type, but not a commander. "We needed a clear case of Good versus Evil," recalls Sophie Thonon. They decided the nuns' case was the right initial focus.

French courts may investigate crimes against French citizens, no matter where they are carried out. As in Spain, the victims or their relatives can trigger an investigation as *partie civile* if the prosecutor declines to do so, and the investigating judge decides who can act as *partie civile*. Under French law, moreover, a suspect who is notified of indictment but neither is arrested nor shows up for trial, can be tried in absentia (in contumacy, in the French phrase). The absent defendant is found in contempt of court, and the court may proceed to hear the prosecution's case. It decides both guilt or innocence and the damage claims of the *partie civile* without a jury. If the absent defendant surrenders or is brought into custody before the punishment is barred by the statute of limitations, the in absentia judgment is set aside and the defendant gets a new trial complete with defense counsel and full appeal rights.

The French got a chance to put Astiz in the dock when British troops took him prisoner after he surrendered during the 1982 Malvinas/Falkland war. The French requested he be turned over to them for trial, but Margaret Thatcher's government refused, citing Astiz's status as a prisoner of war under the Geneva Conventions.[3] Astiz went home a free man. He was tried in a French court in 1990 and convicted in absentia to life imprisonment.[4] Argentina refused to extradite him. As long as he stayed on his home soil, he was untouchable. Indeed, the Blond Angel's sense of invulnerability eventually caught up with him. In 1998, he was finally briefly jailed in Argentina, not for murder but for boasting to a local paper that he was the most highly skilled person in the country at killing a politician or a journalist. France asked again for Astiz in 2001, and by that time an Italian court wanted him for crimes against *its* citizens as well. The Argentine government refused, and the nuns' case remains pending, although at this point it may be heard first by an Argentine court along with the many other charges against Astiz.

The Argentine cases came to Paris investigating magistrate Roger Le Loire. Le Loire had been an anti-terrorist judge from 1990–95, and had worked with Judge Garzón of Spain on ETA (Basque separatist) extradition cases. Le Loire decided to treat the investigation as he would any other criminal case before him. Eventually, his Argentine investigation would cover 13 cases, including a French priest, Gabriel Longueville, killed in detention in July 1976. Most involved disappearances, which Le Loire found—in a case of first impression in France—should be treated as kidnappings with torture. As such, kidnappings are continuing crimes, so the statute of limitations does not begin to run until the missing person is found, dead or alive. Two of the Argentine cases involved prisoners who had been killed in detention and their bodies recovered. Judge Le Loire ruled that those cases had to be closed because the prescription period had run. On appeal, the Chambre d'accusation (Accusations Chamber) of the Paris Appeals Court reversed on March 15, 2000, on grounds that the investigating magistrate still had to study the case and decide whether there were grounds for finding that the statute of limitations had been tolled or interrupted, for example, on the basis of legal proceedings outside France. (Notice that the Chilean Supreme Court found the same solution under similar facts.) If no such evidence of tolling was found, however, the murder cases could not be brought to trial.

International law was of less help than it might have been. The Torture Convention initially seemed a promising legal avenue, but it turned out to be not very useful in the Argentine cases. Extraterritorial jurisdiction over torture was only made part of French law in 1986, so prior conduct was not covered. Until the criminal procedure code was revised in 1994, torture committed outside France could not be investigated. Indeed it was only in 2002 that the French Cour de Cassation (Supreme Court) for the first time decided to allow an extraterritorial torture prosecution, in a case involving Mauritanian army captain Ely Ould Dah. And due to particularities of French law, higher courts had found that the concept of "crimes against humanity," although it exists in the country's jurisprudence, was not applicable outside the World War II context.[5] The definition of crimes against humanity was amended in 1994, but the new, broader definition could apply only to conduct taking place after that date.

There were French victims in Pinochet's Chile as well as Argentina. Georges Klein, a doctor and close advisor to Chilean Socialist President Salvador Allende, disappeared on the day of the 1973 coup. Chemist

Jean-Yves Claudet-Fernández, student Alphonse Chanfreau, and priest Etienne Pesle also disappeared, as did Marcel-René Amiel-Baquet.

When word came of Pinochet's arrest in London in 1998, at the request of the families, Paris investigating magistrate Le Loire quickly filed a criminal complaint seeking his arrest and extradition in the Chilean disappearance cases. The French government, which had just denied Pinochet a visa to enter France, was quick to back the judge. France has faced recurrent criticism for its own role in human rights crimes in Algeria and its training of repressive military forces around the world (including Argentina); this must have seemed a cost-free way to burnish its human rights credentials in a situation in which the French extradition request was safely behind the Spanish one. Public sentiment in France overwhelmingly supported extradition. Here, too, many of the ruling Socialist Party members had long ago protested the Chilean coup. A Chilean exile community vociferously called for trial. When Jack Straw sent Pinochet home, the French government issued a statement of "regret."

Even though the star suspect had escaped, Judge Le Loire's investigation continued. The judge heard witnesses and accumulated documents. Half the witnesses lived in Europe, and they testified before local judges in their country of residence, answering questions written by the French judge. French citizens abroad could also go to a French consulate to give their statements, but unlike in Spain, noncitizens could not. The French embassy in Santiago nonetheless was sympathetic to the judge's efforts and helped where possible.

Neither the Chilean nor the Argentine government cooperated fully with Le Loire's efforts, although Chile did eventually accept Le Loire's rogatory commissions (formal inquiries). To compensate for the noncooperation, the judge used a number of strategies. He asked Chilean attorney Roberto Garretón, who had testified in the Spanish investigation, to transmit requests for information to the Chilean courts. He contacted people in the foreign ministries in both Chile and Argentina who could help speed up the paperwork. He gathered names and phone numbers from the victims' lawyers and from his own investigations, hired a Spanish interpreter, and telephoned witnesses in Chile, offering to pay their airfare to come to France and testify. Almost all those he invited came, including survivors who had seen the victims in custody, an ex-member of the DINA secret police, and human rights group members. Peter Kornbluth of the National Security Archives, a group based in Washington, D.C., also came, bringing the judge declassified U.S. government documents that shed light on some of the cases. As Le Loire saw it, neither these tactics nor the expense differed greatly from what an investigating magistrate would be expected to do in a local criminal investigation of crimes of this magnitude—everything just took longer because it was international.

Le Loire also turned to fellow European investigating magistrates working on similar cases. He called Judge Garzón in Spain, his old colleague from his anti-terrorism days, and they compared notes on Operation Condor, especially as it concerned the Claudet-Fernández case. Through the complainants' lawyers he got in touch with Italian Judge Giovanni Salvi, who had investigated the near-assassination of Chilean politician Bernardo Leighton and his wife in Rome. Salvi gave him access to the case file, including testimony from DINA operative Michael Townley on Operation Condor. Salvi eventually visited Argentina to get documentation for Argentine cases then before the Italian courts, and sent copies to Le Loire. The two judges lent each other their offices when they were in town.

Facing continuing Chilean and Argentine government foot-dragging in executing his letters rogatory, Judge Le Loire decided that a little additional self-help was in order. He called Judge Guzmán, the Chilean judge in charge of the cases involving Pinochet. Guzmán invited him to visit Chile as a private citizen. Over dinner and drinks his first night in Chile, the two judges and their investigators discussed how to share information appropriately on their respective cases. They compared notes, and Le Loire made up a list of exactly what kinds of documents in the Chilean case files would be of use to him. He then requested those documents through formal channels. This faster informal track paralleled the slower formal one.

In October 2001, Judge Le Loire issued arrest warrants for seventeen people in the Chilean case. According to the French press, they included Manuel Contreras, ex-head of the DINA secret police, four Chilean ex-generals, and Pinochet himself (a case against Pinochet had already been opened in the Chanfreau disappearance). The defendants also included José Osvaldo Ribeiro, an Argentine retired colonel. Ribeiro, also known as Rawson, is accused of kidnapping Claudet-Fernández from Buenos Aires and turning him over to the Chilean DINA, a common scenario under Operation Condor. (Ribeiro had a subsequent career as the officer in charge of a group of Argentine officers who trained Nicaraguan "contras" and Honduran, Salvadoran and Guatemalan security forces in torture, kidnapping, and other "counterinsurgency" tactics.)

In September 2002, the Chilean case got a lucky break, all because of Luis Joaquín Ramírez Pineda's bargain-hunting. Ex-general Ramírez Pineda was the commander of the Tacna regiment in 1973, in charge of prisoners arrested at the Moneda presidential palace on the day of the coup. Among the prisoners were Allende's close advisers and security guards, including Georges Klein. The prisoners were beaten, tortured, and killed. A few of their remains were dug up in 1978 from the military's base at Peldehue, but twelve of the bodies have never been found. Klein's name was on a list of 131 disappeared prisoners brought to the Chilean courts in 1974. The case was closed in 1990 on the basis of the amnesty law, reopened on appeal, but never until 2002 seriously pursued by the domestic authorities.

Ramírez Pineda was sent as military attaché to Argentina in 1974, where, according to press reports, he was involved in the car-bombing of General Carlos Prats. After that, he held a number of high level posts under Pinochet: head of the telephone company, ambassador to South Africa, chancellor of the University of La Serena. He retired in 1990. In September 2002 he decided to visit his old haunts in Buenos Aires, taking advantage of the bargain-basement prices the country's economic crisis had generated. He gave his address to immigration officers as the Hotel Claride. That is where police found him, and took him into custody on the French arrest warrant. He was placed under house arrest in Buenos Aires (at seventy-seven, he could avoid jail based on his age). The Argentine government seemed open to extraditing him to France, which promptly filed an extradition request.

At that point, the Chilean government filed its own extradition request. Argentina and Chile are both parties to a 1936 regional extradition treaty, while there is no such treaty between France and Argentina. Ostensibly on that basis, according to the Argentine lawyer for France, Alberto Zuppi, the Argentine judge decided that the Chilean request, although filed after the French one, had priority. Ramírez Pineda is now home in Chile, under indictment for the Tacna murders.

Judge Le Loire has now been promoted and no longer heads the investigation, but two other judges are separately pursuing the Chilean and Argentine variants. Eventually, they will publish the evidence of alleged crimes and perpetrators. The families will have a chance to challenge the findings. At that point, the prosecutor will have to decide to proceed to the Cour d'Assizes (felony criminal court) for trial *in absentia*, or explain a decision not to proceed. Only at that point could Pinochet face trial in France. The chances of his actually seeing a French jail are, however, remote.

The Strange Case of Jorge Olivera

The difficulties of fitting crimes against humanity into a traditional domestic criminal law framework came dramatically to light when Judge Le Loire tried to detain and extradite the alleged killer of Marie Anne Erize Tisseau, a French citizen. Erize was kidnapped from San Juan Province, Argentina, on October 15, 1976, by soldiers commanded by army major Jorge Olivera. Erize was twenty-two years old, a part-time model who worked with radical priests in poor shantytowns; she was last seen alive at La Marquesita detention center, where Olivera was stationed. Survivors of the camp accused Olivera of torture and of giving orders to disappear prisoners, but because of the due obedience law, he never had to confront the charges. Olivera went on to become a lawyer and developed a successful practice representing, among others, ex-Nazi Erich Priebke and ex-general Suárez-Mason. He became a leading proponent of the "theory of two devils" in which the insurgents and military were equally responsible for the crimes of the dirty war, even asking for government compensation for soldiers and police killed in the course of fighting subversion.

In July 2000, Olivera and his law partner traveled to France, to the European Court of Human Rights. Their mission: to file a complaint against Great Britain for sinking an Argentine ship during the 1982 Falklands (Malvinas) conflict, and to request the extradition of Margaret Thatcher, among others, for the crime. According to Olivera's law partner, Jorge Appiani, they got legal help from supporters of Jean Marie Le Pen's National Front and other extreme right-wing activists. The complaint was duly thrown out and Olivera proceeded to Rome to celebrate his wedding anniversary with his wife.

During the month he was in France, giving press conferences on his complaint, the lawyer for the French victims of the Argentine military was busy. Sophie Thonon checked with Argentine groups, discovered Olivera's repressive past, and brought the evidence before Judge Le Loire. To anyone's knowledge, Erize was the only citizen of French (or other European) nationality for whom there was evidence of Olivera's participation in her disappearance. Le Loire decided to act, just before the August summer holiday. On August 7, 2000, Olivera was detained at the check-in counter of the Rome airport on a French arrest warrant, accused of the kidnapping and forced disappearance of Marie Anne Erize Tisseau.

Olivera began calling in favors. Although the details are still fuzzy, he apparently got friends in Argentina to obtain a blank form requesting a copy of a death certificate, fill in false information, add official stamps, cut out and add seals from other documents, and fax it off to Italy. The forged document purported to be the death certificate of Erize, dated November 11, 1976. It still is not known why the Italian Appeals Court accepted a fax rather than the original document or authenticated copy Italian law requires. It is known that Olivera had powerful friends in the Italian far right, including those close to the semi-secret Loggia P-2, which included among its members the former papal nuncio in Argentina and several Argentine generals.[6] Whatever his methods, they were effective. The Court accepted the fake death certificate as proof that Erize had died in 1976, and that therefore the twenty-two-year statute of limitations on kidnapping began to run as of that date. Since the statute had expired, the double criminality requirement for extradition was not met. Olivera, after 42 days in jail, was set free. By the time representatives of the Buenos Aires local government and the Foreign Ministry arrived the next day with proof of the fraud, Olivera was gone.

With Olivera safely back in Buenos Aires, the Italian and Argentine courts opened investigations into his falsification of a public document. Eight months later, the Italian Supreme Court of Cassation overturned the lower court's decision to free Olivera. The court recognized that there had been a mistake. Moreover, they said, even if the fax was authentic, that didn't necessarily mean that the statute of limitations required Olivera's release. "This was . . . a crime that could be considered the kidnapping of a person in order to interrupt the democratic order. It is well known that the arrival and maintenance in power of the Argentine military junta was carried out with the systematic commission of crimes that, according to the Italian constitution, constitute the physical elimination of the regime's opponents."[7] These crimes are subject to a thirty-year statute of limitations. Thus, if the crime had been characterized differently under Italian law, Olivera could have been sent to France for trial.

Italy: An Italian Jury Delivers the First Convictions

Argentina and Italy have long had a special relationship. Some 40 percent of Argentina's population is of Italian origin, most arriving during the same turn-of-the-century immigrant waves that brought Italians to Ellis Island. Italy makes it easy for immigrants to retain their ties to the old country: anyone who can prove a grandparent was an Italian citizen can obtain Italian citizenship. So it is not surprising that some 600 Italian citizens are thought to have perished at the hands of the military in the 1970s. Taking into account second and third generations, the number is much higher.

The Italian case really began in 1982, when the military was still in power in Argentina. An Italian named Juana Betanin brought a complaint in the Rome courts regarding the murder, torture, and rape of family members by the Argentine security forces. The complaint was backed by the League for Peoples' Rights, an Italian group that provided a place for the growing group of Argentine refugees to meet, and helped them find housing, jobs and political asylum representation. The League also compiled a list of disappeared Italians and Italo-Argentines and turned it over to the press, the legislature, and the government. In 1983, after checking with the Ministry of Justice as required by law, the prosecutor accepted the case under Article 8 of the Penal Code. Article 8 gives the Italian courts jurisdiction over "citizens or foreigners who commit a political crime on foreign territory." A political crime is defined as "any crime which offends a political interest of the State, or a political right of citizens. An ordinary crime which is wholly or partly driven by political reasons shall also be regarded as a political crime." Here, Italian citizens abroad had been victims of politically motivated assassination and kidnapping. This was the easiest statutory basis for jurisdiction. Italy will not recognize crimes against humanity in its domestic law until it passes implementing legislation for the International Criminal Court.

Shortly thereafter, in December 1983, Raúl Alfonsín was sworn in as civilian president of Argentina. The investigation came to a halt as the prosecutor waited to see whether the Argentine courts would take up the cases, but once it was clear that the *punto final* and due obedience laws would foreclose the domestic option, the investigations in Italy resumed, albeit slowly. By 1986 there were 117 pending cases and more were added with each passing year, eventually implicating over a hundred Argentine military and police officers. In 1987, Marcello Gentilli, a mournful-faced Italian criminal lawyer, joined the legal team, and two years later his colleague Giancarlo Maniga signed on. Both lawyers worked through the 1990s, on a pro bono basis, at times neglecting their own practices. The driving force behind the cases, however, was not a lawyer at all, but an Argentine activist. Jorge Iturburu had fled Argentina in fear of his life and settled in Rome. He supported himself through a series of ill-paid part-time jobs, but his passion was bringing the military to justice. Friends told me that at one point he was so poor that he and his wife and child shared a single rented room.

As the years dragged on, it became more and more unclear whether the case would ever come before a jury (the Italian penal system, reformed in the early 1990s, has an investigating magistrate during the investigatory phase and a mixed panel of judges and "lay judges" during a second, trial phase). In 1993, a new investigating magistrate came onto the case. He sent a series of interrogatories to an Argentine federal judge, Gustavo Literas, asking for witnesses to testify using the international rogatory procedure, but he got no results. "All the Argentine governments have been uncooperative in helping witnesses to testify. We get documents through informal channels, through family members we know, people in the Human Rights sub-secretariat's office, or even from the minority of judges who want to reopen these cases in the federal courts. They think it will help keep the pressure on to have these investigations overseas," Jorge Iturburu told me.

Hoping to overcome these difficulties, the lawyers and investigating judge flew to Buenos Aires expecting to receive help from Argentine judicial authorities. Upon their arrival, President Menem announced that the Argentine government would not cooperate, and the Argentine House of Representatives passed a resolution pointedly affirming that the cases had already been judged within Argentina. The Italian lawyers and investigating judge were left high and dry, with dozens of potential witnesses to see. They scrambled, calling on trade union and human rights contacts. "The lawyers were able to take statements from all the witnesses who had been scheduled to go before judges as part of the official rogatory procedure, either before the consulate or using other authentication," recalls Iturburu. "We turned all the statements over to the Italian investigating judge in his hotel room, and all that information became part of the record. And the Menem government looked bad for having snubbed the Italians."

The biggest threat to the developing legal investigation came at the end of 1995, when the prosecutor, Antonio Marini, asked the investigating judge to close all the cases given Argentina's lack of cooperation and thus the inability to obtain needed evidence. In addition, the prosecutor claimed that, according to the Argentine Congress declaration to this effect, the cases had all been judged in Argentina. The complainants replied that a political entity's blanket declaration (which was in turn based on the Argentine amnesty laws) couldn't bind the courts, and that only proof of a prior conviction or acquittal of the same defendants for the same acts would suffice. The prosecutor, they argued, had ample evidence before him of crimes that had never been tried anywhere else, but was refusing to look at it.

Iturburu and the complainants' lawyers began mobilizing to head off a decision to close down the case. Letters poured into the Justice Ministry from human rights groups. Eventually, the judge produced a split decision. On most of the charges, the record was not developed enough to proceed without cooperation from Argentina, and so those cases were to be closed. In eight cases, however, the existing record sufficed to proceed to trial.

From then on the pared-down case gathered momentum. A new prosecutor, Francesco Caporale, was much more enthusiastic than Marini had been. The Italian presidency, then in the hands of a center-left coalition, became a formal complainant in the case, as did a number of trade union confederations and the provincial governments of Emiglio-Romano and Sardinia, where several of the victims originated. Bringing the state into the case provided political backing and also solved some

of the perennial financial problems. "We never had any money," Iturburu told me.

As we got closer to trial, we realized that we were going to need some money to
pay the lawyers for their time. If the Italian presidency became a complainant,
it could hire the lawyers and they would get paid. So we arranged a meeting
between President Prodi's wife and some of the Grandmothers [of the Plaza de
Mayo] who were complainants in the case. Lita Boitano of the Mothers of the
Plaza de Mayo (Línea Fundadora) and Estela de Carlotto of the Grandmothers
went to Prodi's house, where they met him and ended up having a long conver-
sation. The president, on an official trip to Argentina soon after, met with family
members' groups there. When he returned he signed the presidency onto the
case.

Finally, in September 2000, trial began. Rome's maximum security
prison is a squat, ugly-modern building on the outskirts of the city. Its
courtrooms are often used for major criminal trials, because it is the
only facility where a jury can be sequestered. Over several months in
2000, two Argentine generals, Suárez-Mason and Riveros, and six under-
lings went on trial, in absentia, for the murders of Italo-Argentines during the mid-1970s. The case was by then seventeen years old. On a raised
dais, two professional judges and six lay judges and three alternates,
ordinary Italians, sat in black robes. Half were women; all listened
intently through the weeks of trial.

Witnesses described the modus operandi of the military and gave
expert testimony on how victims were identified. Dozens of witnesses
flew in from Argentina, and their testimony created a powerful record.
I watched the prosecution team put together over several days the jigsaw
puzzle of one woman's fate. Laura Carlotto, a history student from La
Plata, disappeared in 1977 along with her husband. She was pregnant at
the time. Among the witnesses were her mother, Estela de Carlotto, one
of the Grandmothers of the Plaza de Mayo, several ex-detainees who had
known her in the camps, a forensic anthropologist, and a journalist.

The president of the court asked questions regularly, although the lay
judges did not. The publicly appointed defense lawyers, younger than
the rest, objected to several witnesses' qualifications or testimony and
seemed to be trying hard to make sure the defendants, with whom they
had little contact, were adequately represented.

The court handed down sentences in December 2000. They found all
the defendants guilty of aggravated murder and kidnapping.[8] The 80-
page conviction lays out, in orderly detail, the evidence that each victim
was kidnapped and subsequently murdered after being detained in a
facility within the jurisdiction of one or more of the defendants. The
court rejected defense arguments that the killings were justified to combat a terrorist threat. Nor could the fact that the lower-ranked defen-

dants were obeying orders excuse them, because there is no obligation to obey a patently illegal order. Suárez-Mason was sentenced to life imprisonment and solitary confinement for three years. Riveros also received a life sentence, while the other four defendants received 24 years in prison each. Each victim was awarded civil damages of $200 million lira (some $100,000). The convictions were front-page news in Argentina. They were upheld on appeal.

Other Argentine cases followed. In June 1999, Italian prosecutor Caporale opened an investigation into the disappearances of Angela María Aieta and Giovanni and Susana Pegoraro, who gave birth to a daughter while prisoner at ESMA. (The daughter had been found and her appropriator jailed, but the baby-snatching case in Argentina had stalled because the girl, now a young woman, had refused to take a DNA test. Those responsible for kidnapping the parents were never tried.) The Pegoraro case had been one of those closed in 1995, but now the prosecutor argued that new evidence available to the Argentine courts made reopening feasible. The defendants included Admiral Emilio Massera, commander of naval operations Antonio Vanek, his lieutenant Héctor Antonio Febres, and infamous ESMA operatives Jorge Acosta, Jorge Raúl Vildoza and Alfredo Astiz (who, recall, was also wanted by the Spanish, French, and Swedes). Some of these men were under investigation, or had even been arrested, at home in connection with baby-snatching. The Italian complaints sought to complement local efforts by focusing on the crimes against the parents of the kidnapped babies—crimes then covered in Argentina by the amnesty laws. The Italian Ministry of Justice authorized the case a month later.

By 2001, Judge Claudio Tortora had amassed considerable files. The prosecutor, in anticipation of subsequent trial, asked the judge to request the arrest and extradition of Astiz and Vildoza, the only defendants not detained, on grounds that they were flight risks. The judge agreed, and sent the request to Interpol, who sent it to the Argentine Ministry of Justice, who sent it along to Judge María Servini de Cubría. Judge Servini has been handling a number of baby-snatching cases herself, including one involving Vildoza. She promptly issued an arrest order. Astiz turned himself in a few days later. Vildoza apparently remains in hiding.

The center-right Italian government of Silvio Berlusconi celebrated the arrest, comparing Astiz's detention with that of Slobodan Milosevic, who had been transferred to the International Criminal Tribunal in the Hague only days before. A public opinion poll showed that 62 percent of Argentines wanted Astiz extradited.[9] As it had in all other extradition cases involving military defendants, the De La Rua government denied the extradition request, on grounds that the extradition treaty between

Argentina and Italy did not allow extradition for crimes committed on Argentine territory.[10] After 44 days in detention, Astiz walked free again. But not quite as free as before: Judge Servini noted that the Italian charges included baby-snatching, and that if the dossier she received from Italy bore out these charges, (not covered by the amnesty laws) she would reissue her arrest order.

Germany: Full Circle at Nuremberg

The name Nuremberg is practically synonymous with international justice. The German city was the site of the International Military Tribunal, the court that tried the Nazi leadership after World War II. The Nuremberg Tribunal, despite its many faults, ushered in a new era: one where military and civilian commanders were individually responsible for the decisions they made that led to criminal acts, where carrying out orders was no defense, and where crimes committed by the leadership of a country against its own citizens were of international concern and not just internal affairs. Fifty-six years after the Nuremberg trials, another hearing on atrocious crimes committed in the context of a state policy of extermination took place in Nuremberg. This time, the suspects were Argentine military officers, the victims Germans or Argentines of German descent and the preliminary hearing part of pre-trial investigations before the local Nuremberg prosecutor.

The Argentine and German militaries have always been close. Argentina patterned its armed forces after those of the Kaiser. After World War II, hundreds of Nazis and Nazi sympathizers made their way to refuge in Argentina. During the 1970s, many of the military "operatives" involved in kidnappings, torture, and killings considered themselves Nazi sympathizers and followers. Concentration camps bore Nazi flags and emblems. Jorge Acosta, one of the most notorious torturers, wore a swastika and called himself a follower of Hitler. Jews were subject to especially vicious and humiliating treatment in the torture camps. Of those missing or killed during the military government, more than 10 percent were Jewish. Jews make up about 2 percent of the country's population.

Jewish immigration to Argentina started in the nineteenth century. The bulk of Jewish immigrants came, as did the Italians, in the late nineteenth and early twentieth century. After the U.S., Argentina was the second largest recipient of Jewish immigrants during the turn-of-the-century exodus. Another wave of Jews arrived fleeing Germany in the 1930s. These refugees, stripped of their German citizenship by a 1941 Nazi rule, settled permanently in Argentina. After the war, the refugees could regain their German citizenship if they affirmatively reclaimed it. Many did not.

One of those who fled the Nazis was Ellen Marx, a tall, gaunt, energetic woman in her eighties. Marx settled in Buenos Aires and raised a
family, including her daughter Leonor. On August 21, 1976, Leonor was
arrested and disappeared into the Argentine *nacht und nebel*—night and
fog—never to be seen again.[11] She was one of 85 German or Germano-
Argentines known by name who disappeared in Argentina during this
period, although the actual figure is no doubt higher. About half of
them were Jews.

"Our children grew up speaking Spanish and German. Many years
later, during the 1970s, the mother of Klaus Zieschank, who had also
disappeared, put together a group of family members to see what we
could do in Germany to get justice. We asked around, and in February
1999 a German private lawyer visited Argentina to take our statements,"
Ellen Marx told me. As a result of those visits, the lawyers filed criminal
complaints with the Nuremberg-Furth chief prosecutor's office against
41 former Argentine high-ranking officers.[12] The complaints named
eleven German or German-Argentine disappearance victims. Under
German law, German prosecutors can investigate cases where the victims
are German, and may ask a court to order the arrest of the accused in
conjunction with a request for extradition.

The lawyers acted out of political and moral solidarity, as pro bono
counsel. Wolfgang Kaleck, for instance, the German lawyer who visited
Ellen Marx, worked with a legal collective, the Republican Lawyers Association, involved in a range of anti-discrimination cases and other progressive causes. He had been involved in supporting Latin American
human rights issues since his student days, and knew the Latin American
exile and activist community well.

History has its own ironies and cruel jokes. For Ellen Marx, the final
irony came when the prosecutor's office informed her German lawyer
that he was thinking of dismissing four of the eleven cases—the four
where the victims' families were Jewish. The prosecutor argued that the
victims were not really German nationals because their parents' German
nationality had been lost during the 1930s and the parents, or the children, had never taken the necessary affirmative steps to reinstate it.
Unlike in Spain and elsewhere, in Germany the prosecutor must agree
to bring criminal complaints before a judge. A subsequent advisory
opinion of the Federal Supreme Court to the contrary notwithstanding,
the prosecutor refused to go forward. It took a public campaign in Germany to change the prosecutor's mind, but eventually he agreed to look
into these cases as well. He took some 60 testimonies at the German
Embassy in Buenos Aires, including that of Ellen Marx.

Other cases moved forward as well. A Coalition Against Impunity,
formed in 1998 during a visit to Germany by Nobel laureate Adolfo

Pérez Esquivel, began organizing testimony before the prosecutor. The coalition included church groups, lawyers, and exile groups. It brought cases involving both Argentine and Chilean victims, the Argentines in Nuremberg, the Chileans in Dusseldorf. The Dusseldorf prosecutor investigated the kidnapping, torture, and execution of five German citizens and fourteen Chileans of German descent. Once Pinochet returned to Chile, the German courts sent the case file back to Chile, prompting an investigation there. On March 27, 2001, the Chilean Supreme Court asked Judge Guzmán to open a special investigation into the German cases, which had never before been looked at by Chilean courts.

The Argentine cases took a different route. One involved Elisabeth Kasseman, the daughter of a prominent German theologian. She had come to Argentina to study and was a university student and translator when she was arrested in March 1977. She was arrested and interrogated together with another young woman named Dianna Austin, now a Presbyterian minister in Elmont, New York. In January 2001, Austin traveled to Nuremberg to give her testimony.[13]

She told how the two women had been arrested together and taken first to an army barracks in the Palermo district of Buenos Aires. Austin was detained for 14 hours, beaten, raped, and finally ordered out of the country. "We have nothing against her, but we have some ideological differences," an officer told Austin when she asked about Elisabeth. "He confirmed that they still had her in their custody." Austin returned to the U.S. and mobilized church pressure for her release, but to no avail. Kasseman's body, showing that she had been horribly tortured and shot in the back and neck, was recovered from a mass grave in June 1977 and returned to Germany for burial. Her parents were told she had died as a result of an armed confrontation between "subversives" and the police. They paid $22,000 to get her body back. She was twenty years old when she died.

Other testimony followed. Elena Alfaro, a death camp survivor now living in France, traveled to Germany to testify that she had seen Elisabeth Kasseman alive in the El Vesubio secret detention camp, also in Buenos Aires. An autopsy by a German forensic specialist confirmed she had been shot at point-blank range, making the "armed confrontation" story unlikely. The existence of a dead body allowed the prosecutor's office to charge murder. Under German law dating from the 1960s and 1970s prosecutions of ex-Nazis, murder has no statute of limitations. Disappearance, however, was more problematic. The crime of forced disappearance is part of Germany's new penal code, but that code could not apply retroactively. In those cases where no body was ever found, therefore, kidnapping or murder remained the only options. Kidnapping was subject to a long-expired statute of limitations, so the lawyers found themselves arguing that where the kidnapped person had never appeared, the cases should be treated like murder cases. This flipped on its head the argument lawyers were making in the French cases, where murder was subject to a statute of limitations but kidnapping could be considered a continuing offense. The variations in national law led lawyers to espouse wildly divergent legal theories in factually similar cases.

In March 2001, the Nuremberg-Furth court issued an arrest order and request for the extradition of retired general Guillermo Suárez-Mason, whose responsibility included the Palermo and El Vesubio camps. The court followed up with a similar request in early 2002 for former chief of the Federal Police Juan Bautista Sasiain and retired colonel Pedro Durán Sáenz, the commander of El Vesubio. Complainants' lawyers, backed by the prestigious Max Planck Institute, also argued that the court should charge the members of the Argentine junta, especially Videla and Massera, on the theory that they were the intellectual authors (*autores mediatos*) of the assassination by virtue of their organizational role.

In the Suárez-Mason case, Judge Gabriel Cavallo granted the request, but then by law had to send it on to the Foreign Ministry for a final determination. Like every other extradition request received involving the crimes of the military government, it was denied in November 2001. President Menem decreed that Argentina's "official doctrine" was to deny all such requests on national sovereignty grounds.[14] Incoming President De la Rua had pledged that he would let justice take its course, but he soon ratified the "official doctrine," as did his successor Eduardo Duhalde. Under De la Rua's decree, the Argentine government recognized no other state's right to try "dirty war"-related crimes committed on Argentine territory.[15] The denial of extradition was by now routine. It was the same response the Foreign Ministry had made to the Spanish, French and Italian courts.

But something unexpected happened. The German government challenged the summary denial of the extradition request in the Argentine courts. The attorney for the German government, Alberto Zuppi, had worked on the successful extradition to Germany of ex-SS member Joseph Schwammberger in 1989. He was now a law professor and a lawyer representing several European countries in their extradition efforts. He knew that the lack of a formal extradition treaty between the two countries had been no impediment in Schwammberger's case, so why should it be now? He argued to the courts that a blanket policy of no extradition for those crimes connected to the military government usurped the courts' proper role in extradition proceedings. Under Argentine extradition law, the executive branch gets two chances to consider an extradition request: first it can rule on its admissibility and the requirements of reciprocity, and second, after the courts have looked at the legal merits, it can deny it on grounds of national security or for other reasons. The executive branch, he argued, could validly deny extradition in a given case. What it couldn't do was establish a priori a blanket policy that refused the courts the opportunity to consider each request on its merits, once the request was formally admissible. The "official doctrine" law was also unlawful because Argentina had accepted a number of treaty obligations (starting with the Geneva Conventions, the Torture Convention, and the Inter-American Convention on Forced Disappearances) that required the prosecution of certain grave crimes no matter where committed.

At the same time, Germany challenged the government's allegation that Suárez-Mason was immune from all criminal process because he had been pardoned by President Menem. The government's view was that trying someone after a pardon would violate the *ne bis in idem* (double jeopardy) principle (which holds that a person cannot be tried twice for the same crime). Not so, said Zuppi: a pardon not preceded by a trial does not raise double jeopardy problems. On the contrary, the pardons were unlawful under Argentine law because there had been no prior conviction. They also violated Argentina's international obligations to extradite or prosecute. In summary, the German government asked that the extradition proceedings be reopened.

This was heady stuff. None of the arguments about pardons were new; Argentine lawyers had been making them for years. What *was* new was that the complainant was another government, arguing in the domestic courts of the state sheltering the suspects for its right to try the killers of its citizens. In other words, Germany's sovereign rights, not just Argentina's, were at issue here. A friendly government was questioning Argentina's compliance with its international law obligations, however gently and respectfully, using judicial, not diplomatic means.

The case epitomized the judicialization of interstate relations in at least the area of grave human rights violations. In June 2002, the Buenos Aires Federal Court accepted the complaint. With the advent of the Kirschner government in 2003, the point may have become moot. One of the new president's first acts in office was to repeal the "official doctrine" and declare that he will allow the extradition of those requested by European countries in these cases. Implicated military officers began announcing that, all things considered, they would rather be tried at home than in Europe, leading to further pressure to annul the amnesty laws in Argentina. At this point the place of trial is unclear, but the possibilities of some trial somewhere are greater than ever. If President Kirchner and the courts follow up, Nuremberg may again see a small measure of justice done in its courts.

Spain: Life After Pinochet's Departure

The Audiencia Nacional decisions of November 1998 allowed Garzón to go forward with the extradition request for Pinochet, which he did formally in December 1998 with results that are now well known. But the Chilean criminal complaint was not limited to Pinochet. The 36 names on it included, in addition to the secret police officials and military officers one might expect, a number of top civilian officials in the military government. The list was published in the Chilean newspapers, practically ensuring that no one on it would be doing much traveling outside the country any time soon.

On the Argentine side, Garzón proceeded to issue extradition requests for a number of the officers he had previously indicted. A group of 48 military and police officers were requested on December 1999,[16] and another group of 18 in September 2001. Like his counterparts in France, Sweden, Italy, and Germany, he received quick, positive responses from Argentine judges, followed by the executive branch's absolute refusal to grant extradition. In mid-2003, following President Kirchner's announcement that he would no longer oppose extraditions, Garzón again requested extradition. Judge Canicoba ordered the arrest of 45 military officers and one civilian. This time, however, the Spanish government intervened: the Foreign Minstry argued that Argentina was moving to try the men at home and refused to ask for their formal extradition.

In addition, the Argentine side of the case now had a live defendant, Adolfo Scilingo, sitting in a Spanish jail. Scilingo apparently thought that his imprisonment would be brief and that his contributions would eventually be recognized. However, Garzón's October 10, 1997 order did not limit his detention. He spent some three months in jail. Garzón then decided that, while it would be too harsh to keep his star defendant in jail awaiting trial for what might be many months, it would be foolish to leave him free to return to Argentina. He issued an order for bail that required Scilingo to remain in Spain, available to testify. Scilingo, jobless and broke, eventually challenged the travel restrictions. When the Spanish Constitutional Court agreed with him that there was no legal basis for them, Judge Garzón returned him to jail, declared his investigation into Scilingo's crimes complete, and asked a separate panel of judges to set a trial date.

Cavallo: A Torturer's Unexpected Journey from Argentina to Mexico to Trial in Spain

As luck would have it, another potential defendant in the Argentine case soon appeared. Ricardo Miguel Cavallo had worked at ESMA, first locating and picking up those tagged by the machinery of terror, and later as the man in charge of the "Fish Tank," a part of the camp where prisoners deemed susceptible to "reeducation" worked as slave laborers repairing stolen electronic booty, clipping newspapers, or keeping the camp clean. Ironically, because Fish Tank prisoners were not killed, more ESMA prisoners survived to testify against Cavallo than there would have been had he worked elsewhere.

Fish Tank survivors recall that one of the tasks Cavallo supervised was the fabrication of false identification papers so that military agents could travel freely. After he returned to civilian life, Cavallo turned this assignment into a career. His initial capital came from money that victims allege he and other Navy officers garnered from the Argentine terror machine practice of forcing detainees and their families to sign over deeds to property and bank accounts. With this stake, he and his associates established a business, TALSUD, that obtained contracts with the governments of Bolivia, El Salvador, Paraguay, Uruguay, and Zaire to create a variety of national licensing and vehicle registration services. The biggest feather in TALSUD's cap was a 1999 contract awarded to a consortium it headed to establish a national vehicle registry for Mexico.

Car theft is a serious problem in Mexico. In 1998, President Ernesto Zedillo convinced the Mexican Congress that it could cut costs and hinder the black market in cars by creating a national automobile registry that would be contracted out to private entrepreneurs. The new enterprise, named RENAVE (Registro Nacional de Vehículos or National Vehicle Registry), was controversial from the beginning. For one thing, it increased the fees Mexicans paid to register their cars, and in the waning days of the PRI government many ordinary Mexicans suspected corruption. For another, registration entailed giving a great deal of personal information to the government. Skeptics speculated that the whole operation was just a cover to facilitate the work of car theft rings.

Raúl Ramos Tercero, deputy minister of Mexico's Ministry of Commerce and Industrial Development (SECOFI), was responsible for running a fair and open public tender before awarding the RENAVE contract. Long before Cavallo's identity was revealed, competitors who lost out to the TALSUD consortium were crying foul. Ramos defended the process. TALSUD may not have been the lowest bidder, he argued, but it was the most innovative. The TALSUD-led consortium was the only competitor in the field to propose using smart card technology to identify vehicles and maintain a continuously updated database that could not only track a car's ownership history, but increase the likelihood of collecting on tax payments and fines.

While SECOFI may have been dazzled by the technological possibilities the smart card vehicle registration system offered, many state and local government officials were not. Led by Mexico City's opposition party mayor, they refused to participate. To counter public and political resistance, SECOFI went on the offensive in mid-2000. It enlisted Cavallo to appear in a series of TV ads and press conferences extolling the virtues of RENAVE. It was to be his undoing.

"We never saw the TV broadcasts," recounts Shula Ehrenberg, who fled to Mexico from Argentina in the 1970s and since has been active in expatriate groups seeking justice for the dirty war killers. "We had two people in our group who had been detained in the ESMA and knew Cavallo, but neither of them saw him on TV." But many others saw the broadcasts. Someone tipped off the editor of the respected daily Mexican newspaper *Reforma* to look into the past of TALSUD and its director. José Vales, *Reforma*'s Buenos Aires correspondent, began digging, carefully, since he had to check his story without setting off alarms that might prompt Cavallo to fly the coop.

Cavallo's resume listed his name as Ricardo Miguel Cavallo and showed professional activities dating back only to 1990. What had he done before that? When Vales's editor called to say that one of RENAVE's lawyers had let slip that Cavallo had a military past, Vales had the lead he needed. As recounted by Vales himself and by Argentine journalist Eduardo Anguita, Vales made his way to the Center for Legal and Social Studies (Spanish CELS), an Argentine think-tank started by human rights activists.[17] In the CELS library Vales found an old photo of someone named Miguel Angel Cavallo, taken in the 1970s by Victor Basterra, who had run the false I.D. shop as a prisoner in ESMA and had secretly kept photographs of its operatives. The photo also had a number: 6,275,013. Vales called his editor. The number matched the Argentine identification card Ricardo Miguel Cavallo had used to obtain his residency permit in Mexico. Vales then reviewed the lists of known perpetrators that appeared in several books published in the mid-1980s in Argentina. He found one that listed a Miguel Angel Cavallo, alias Serpico, or Marcelo, or Ricardo.

Vales then went to see an ESMA survivor, Mario Villani. Villani looked at the photos of Cavallo. "I'll never forget that face. It's the same guy." Vales checked with additional survivors. They all recognized the picture as one of the ESMA torturers. They showed him the I.D. number on one of the documents from Garzón's investigation. Vales's editor, meanwhile, had a Mexican police identification expert compare the 1970s photo with the current one; he too saw the same person. With that, *Reforma* had enough to go public. But before doing so, its editors decided to give Cavallo a chance to rebut the accusations. In a tense meeting with the editorial staff, Cavallo offered to return to Argentina immediately and bring back the documentation that would prove his innocence. On the day the story broke, August 24, Cavallo boarded a commercial flight to Buenos Aires. There were no direct flights that day, but the stopover in Cancún promised to be brief. No doubt the torturer breathed a sigh of relief.

The head of Interpol in Mexico, Juan Miguel Ponce Edmonson, read the *Reforma* story over his morning coffee. Ponce Edmonson had a particular interest in things Argentine: his father had been a friend of Juan Perón during Perón's years of exile, and his wife was Argentine. Ponce had followed the *Pinochet* case and knew that Spain had indicted Argentine military officers responsible for dirty war crimes. On a hunch, he decided to check the flights leaving that day for Argentina. He found that there was only one, via Cancún, and that Cavallo's name was on the passenger list. Cavallo had used a false name in Mexico and he was a serious flight risk. That was enough to arrest and hold him for 48 hours, but beyond that an arrest warrant would be needed. So far, none was outstanding. When the plane touched down in Cancún, Mexican Interpol agents removed Cavallo and placed him under arrest.

Meanwhile, Mario Villani in Argentina had not been idle. After his interview with Vales, the ESMA survivor called Carlos Slepoy in Spain. A number of ESMA survivors had testified in Spain concerning Cavallo's responsibility for murder, torture, and disappearance, including a few, like Pilar Calveiro, who traveled there from Mexico. Although he had not physically harmed her, Calveiro fingered Cavallo as someone who had been in charge in ESMA. So did many others. Nonetheless, when the Spanish indictments were issued, Cavallo's name was left off—not for lack of evidence against him but because of a clerical error. In mid-2000, there was no international arrest order for Cavallo.

Word of Cavallo's arrest in Mexico provoked a flurry of phone calls and e-mails between Spain, Mexico, and Argentina. It was August 24, the height of Europe's summer vacation season, when entire countries virtually shut down. Judge Garzón, like most lawyers, was out of town. With some effort, Slepoy managed to get a message through to him, but, unaware of the clerical error, all Garzón could do was direct the human rights lawyer to get the warrant from the substitute judge on duty. Slepoy took the next train back to Madrid from his own beach house.

"We talked by phone to Judge Ruíz Polanco, the substitute judge, who knew nothing about the case. To show you how little he knew, he asked for a clerk to bring the case file, and the clerk replied that he would need a derrick to move it; the file was enormous. He told us he would study the case, but given that it was Friday afternoon, he would probably not do anything but would wait until Garzón got back on Monday. By then it would be too late, the 48 hours would be over, and the police would have to free him," Manuel Ollé, a young criminal law specialist who represents some of the Argentine plaintiffs in the Spanish case recounted. The lawyers in the Argentine case, including Slepoy, Ollé, Enrique Santiago, and Virginia Sáenz of IU, put together requests for an immediate arrest warrant and extradition. Finally, Judge Ruíz Polanco promised to try to find Garzón and told Ollé to check back with him in the afternoon. By then the judge was busy dealing with the politically charged case of seven suspected ETA terrorists. Fearing their opportunity might be lost if the judge left, Ollé and his associates camped out in the hallway.

Throughout the day, the Spanish lawyers spoke by phone with the editors of *Reforma* and with Shula Ehrenberg in Mexico, assuring them that yes, the judge would decide on the warrant, although they were not sure how or when. "At one point in the afternoon, we overheard the Judge calling Interpol, and that gave us some hope." As they were waiting in the hallway, two representatives from the Mexican embassy came to Judge Ruíz's chambers. They apparently had learned earlier from Judge Garzón's office that Cavallo's name was not listed on the warrant and that Judge Garzón was unavailable. They informed their superiors in Mexico City that no action was forthcoming (which would have meant releasing Cavallo), but the *Reforma* newspaper editors, using their own channels, were telling Mexican officials otherwise. The latter ordered their embassy representatives to double-check with Judge Ruíz. According to Ollé, "Even though the door to his chambers was closed, we could hear the judge explaining the concept of universal jurisdiction to the two diplomats. That's when we thought we'd be OK." Judge Ruíz, it turns out, had recently grappled with the concept of universal jurisdiction and the meaning of genocide. He was the investigating magistrate for a case then before the Spanish courts involving the 200,000 deaths and 40,000 disappearances of mostly Mayan Indians in Guatemala (I discuss that case in Chapter 7). At ten o'clock that night, Ruíz Polanco signed a warrant for Cavallo's arrest and faxed it to Mexico. The next day, the Mexican attorney general's office asked for his arrest.[18]

Mexico has historically been one of the staunchest defenders of national sovereignty on the world stage, in major part because the country has faced regular incursions and interference from its northern neighbor. "Poor Mexico: so far from God and so close to the United States," has long been a popular refrain. Extraterritorial jurisdiction got a bad name in Mexico after the 1990 kidnapping of Mexican doctor

Humberto Alvarez-Machain in Mexico by bounty hunters working with the U.S. Drug Enforcement Agency, an action upheld by the U.S. Supreme Court.[19] (Alvarez-Machain was tried and acquitted on charges that he had helped kill a DEA agent, returned to Mexico, and sued the United States and the bounty hunters for damages.) The Mexican government had supported Chile in its assertion that Spain had no jurisdiction over Pinochet.

On the other hand, over the last few years Mexico had relaxed its tight grip on sovereignty by becoming part of the North American Free Trade Agreement and allowing the extradition of Mexicans to the United States to stand trial on drug charges. More significantly, on August 1, 2000, Mexicans elected, for the first time in seventy years, a president from an opposition political party. Vicente Fox, a former Coca Cola executive from the National Action Party (PAN), beat the official Institutional Revolutionary Party (PRI) candidate handily. Fox promised a new era of openness. His government would take over on November 1. Cavallo's arrest took place during the interregnum.

Shula Ehrenberg and Silvia Panebianco, another Argentine long-time resident of Mexico, determined not to let Cavallo escape justice, reactivated the networks of Argentines that had helped sustain them while in exile. They named their group "Genocide Never Again" and their website "cavallobehindbars" (cavalloentrerejas.org). Shula lost her first husband and her husband's entire family to the terror, and fled Argentina with her one-year-old daughter Natalia. Natalia, now college age, darkhaired and serious, is one of the leaders of HIJOS, an organization of children of the disappeared and killed in Latin America's dirty wars. She began to talk to other Mexican-based members of HIJOs, and they mounted noisy demonstrations in front of the Mexican prosecutor's office and at the jail. Panebianco, who had been a human rights activist before fleeing Argentina, now worked with groups fighting discrimination against AIDS patients; she brought the Mexican human rights movement out to lobby for Cavallo's extradition.

There was a nagging doubt in the activists' minds: who had tipped off the editor of *Reforma*? And why? The newspaper insisted that it was just a good job of investigative reporting, and others concurred. Vales says that an Argentine exile tipped off the Mexico City mayor's office, which called the paper.[20] But rumors and conspiracy theories, always part of Mexican politics, swirled around the Cavallo *affaire*. The most widely shared involved a vendetta by the "dinosaur" old guard of the PRI that wanted to pay back President Ernesto Zedillo for loosening up the political system and thereby losing the election for the PRI. An alternative theory held that Cavallo was incidental to a fight over RENAVE among Zedillo's ex-cabinet ministers. The tip-off was intended to sink RENAVE, which it seems to have done. A third variant was that the whole matter was a fight between rival car theft rings, one of which had ties to Cavallo.

When the Spanish extradition request arrived, officials in Zedillo's Foreign Affairs Ministry were torn. Many were uncomfortable about the potential implications for Mexican sovereignty and its relations with Argentina if Cavallo were extradited. At the same time, coming on the heels of the *Pinochet* case, no one wanted to be seen as harboring a Southern Cone torturer. To decide how to proceed, they turned to the calendar. Zedillo's Foreign Ministry quickly determined that the judicial decision would not be handed down until power had been transferred to Vicente Fox and the PAN. They gleefully stood by as the process got rolling. If there was to be any political fallout, it would come after they were gone.

Traditionally, extradition is a slow and cumbersome process, sometimes regulated by bilateral treaties, and designed for an age when travel and communications were sluggish and few criminals crossed national borders. Mexico and Spain had an extradition treaty, but unluckily for Cavallo, it was less slow and cumbersome than most. Notwithstanding its domestic human rights problems, Mexico has long taken pride in its reputation as the place where other countries' exiled political dissidents could find a home. This included offering refuge to Basque separatists that Spain preferred to have living on another continent. But the tacit arrangement backfired when suspected ETA members used Mexico as a launchpad for their attacks in Spain. Spain sought their extradition, and Mexico, sympathetic to the government's anti-terrorism aims, accepted its proposal for a Protocol amending the two states' extradition treaty. The Protocol, like the European Convention on Extradition, sped up the extradition process by requiring the extraditing state merely to ensure that certain formal requirements were met. The actual determination of whether evidence to try the person for the crimes charged exists was left to the state requesting extradition. The Protocol—the only one of its kind that Mexico has agreed to—became law in 1996.[21]

Meanwhile, in Spain, Judge Garzón and the lawyers for the Argentine victims of Cavallo went to work in the sweltering late August heat to meet a 60-day deadline to justify his extradition request. First, they sorted through the reams of testimony to find ESMA victims and, among those, any who had mentioned Cavallo as among their torturers. They forwarded names to the Argentine human rights groups, who also were digging through files. They prevailed on Julio Strassera, who had been the chief prosecutor in the trials of Junta leaders in Argentina, to go back to court to authenticate a copy of the part of the transcript of that trial dealing with the ESMA, so that it would be admissible in a Spanish court. The Argentines began lining up eyewitnesses and complainants to send notarized letters to Garzón via the Spanish Embassy in Argentina, detailing eyewitness accounts of Cavallo's participation in torture. Thelma Jara de Cabezas wrote that she had been kidnapped in 1979 and tortured by "Marcelo," who, as part of his work as an intelligence operative, traveled with her to Uruguay twice so that she could give press interviews and "prove" that political prisoners were not disappearing. Dozens of people wrote to say that while they had been detained in the ESMA they had often seen an officer known as "Serpico" or "Marcelo" planning and carrying out kidnappings or giving orders in the Fish Tank.

Some witnesses had already appeared before the court in Madrid: Juan Gasparini, for instance, testified how after days of being tortured at the ESMA he had been driven to a house where his wife, children, and a friend of his wife were staying, and watched as officers including Cavallo shot up the house, killing the two women before his eyes. While there were a few reports of direct torture by Cavallo, many of the testimonies reiterated his role in defining who was to be captured, who would be killed, and who would be set free. All this evidence was presented to Mexico, together with internal military documents, Garzón's previous decisions on ESMA, and prior witness testimony before the United Nations and in the trial of the junta leaders in Argentina. Altogether, Garzón listed 227 disappearances during the period Cavallo was an ESMA operations officer, 121 acts of torture, and 21 cases where Cavallo was directly implicated by witness testimony, including several involving victims of Spanish descent.

Mexican Judge Jesús Guadalupe Luna Altamirano was on weekend duty at the federal criminal court on the day in September the evidence from Spain arrived, so the case landed on his desk. Under the PRI government, important cases were decided politically, with the judge subtly (or not so subtly) nudged toward the proper decision. But now, with the government otherwise occupied in the most important transition in generations, no guidance was forthcoming, and the case raised questions to which no one had the answers. Cavallo's lawyers, business attorneys who worked for RENAVE, were not very helpful. Their first act was to file papers to prevent their client from being extradited to Argentina—the one place he would be protected from prosecution by the amnesty laws, and therefore the place he wanted to go. Luna, who knew extradition law but not international law, began a crash course, together with his clerks and aides. They borrowed books from the libraries of local human rights groups, spent hours poring over treaties, and in January 2001 issued an opinion that runs to 345 pages.[22] Although judicial decisions are not generally rendered in public, the judge invited six Argentine survivors, including Silvia Panebianco and Shula and Natalia

Ehrenburg, into the courtroom. They burst into applause and tears when they heard the opinion.

Luna's decision allowed Cavallo's extradition on the charges of genocide and terrorism. He found that Judge Garzón had probable cause to find that Cavallo was implicated in these crimes, as required by Mexican law and the Spain-Mexico extradition treaty. He relied on international treaties, including the Torture Convention, as well as Mexican and Spanish law, to ground extraterritorial jurisdiction. He followed the Spanish Audiencia Nacional's 1998 decision on the question of whether the fact that the Spanish law establishing extraterritorial jurisdiction came after the alleged crimes did not violate the maxim *nulla poena sine lege*. That law merely provided a procedural avenue and was not substantive.

Judge Luna refused to allow extradition on the torture charges. At the time the crimes were committed, Mexico's statute of limitations would have barred those charges from going forward and, whereas the current statute of limitations would have allowed prosecution, Luna held that the law most favorable law to the defendant had to be applied. Judge Luna's decision now went back to the Foreign Ministry for a final determination.

Judge Luna clearly was pleased with the notoriety that followed. "It's the first time any judge has allowed an extradition to a third country. It's made me the most famous judge in Mexico," he told me. A convert to the universal jurisdiction gospel, he has been giving talks to Mexican lawyers and attending human rights conferences. Shortly after his opinion was rendered he was promoted to the court of appeals.

On November 1, 2000, Vicente Fox was sworn in as president of Mexico. For his foreign minister he chose an internationally known writer and political pundit, Jorge Castañeda. Castañeda's most recent book critiqued the Latin American left's failures during the 1970s and 1980s, and he was well acquainted with Argentina's recent history. Castañeda and his team had a more open and proactive vision of Mexico's foreign policy. Rather than hide behind a wall of sovereignty and nonintervention, they wanted Mexico to play a more important role in a globalizing world, a role that included a greater emphasis on human rights. When Manuel Ollé and Carlos Slepoy came to Mexico in November 2000 at the invitation of Argentine exiles who took up a collection to pay for their airfares, Castañeda invited them to his home.

In February 2001, the Foreign Ministry approved Cavallo's extradition.[23] In addition to backing Judge Luna's decision to allow the genocide and terrorism charges, the ministry reinstated the torture charges, thereby allowing the case to go forward in Spain on the easier-to-prove grounds of torture. The Foreign Ministry decision refers extensively to Mexico's and Spain's treaty commitments in the human rights area, to the Torture Convention's requirement to prosecute, and to rules about nonprescriptability of crimes against humanity. But it rests, at heart, on an interpretation of Mexican criminal law. Mexican law allows for accumulation of charges, and the Foreign Ministry argued that if all the charges were looked at together, the longest statute of limitations (30 years for genocide) would apply to all of them. According to government lawyers, that interpretation was new, but had a solid basis in prior local law. "We had a first draft based on international law," one of the lawyers recalled, "but our criminal law specialists thought our judges would think it was written in Martian. So we focused on the domestic law arguments."

Although theoretically this was the last stage of the extradition process, Cavallo had one card left to play. He filed an *amparo*, a mainstay of Mexican law that provides for judicial review of allegations that the state has violated an individual's constitutional rights. Cavallo hired a new team of lawyers, including an Argentine criminal law specialist with close ties to the Argentine navy. He began telling the press that if he went to Spain he would take others down with him: it was not clear whether he meant his ex-military comrades in Argentina or his Mexican business associates or both.

Cavallo's lawyers tried a second-track strategy of trying to persuade Argentina to seek Cavallo's extradition on the grounds that if he was to be tried, he should be tried in Argentina. An Argentine judicial panel soon ruled that there was no case pending in an Argentine court under which a request for extradition could proceed. On the other hand, Argentina did request Cavallo's extradition to Mendoza, Argentina, to stand trial on charges of fraud relating to TALSUD's business practices. The Mexican government rejected this request as untimely and held that the Spanish request had priority because it was first in time. To the human rights activists, the Argentine request was a transparent attempt to invoke the "primacy" of the territorial courts to get Cavallo home, where he would be prosecuted for fraud but not for the much more serious disappearance and torture charges. The Mexico-Spain Extradition Treaty (in article 20) lists the relative gravity of the offenses, the place committed, the nationality of the offender, other treaty obligations, and the date of the respective requests as factors to take into account in deciding the priority of multiple requests. Under this balancing test, the courts decided the Spanish request took precedence.

On June 10, 2003, the Supreme Court threw out all Cavallo's claims and approved his extradition.[24] Mexico thus becomes the first country to formally extradite a suspect to another country for trial for crimes committed in a third country. The court ducked the issue of whether the Spanish courts had jurisdiction. Any such jurisdictional questions were for the requesting states' courts, not those of the requested state. As long as Spain had duly established courts of regular jurisdiction, that was enough under the Extradition Treaty. The court ratified Judge Luna's view of the statute of limitations, finding that under the Mexican law of the time the torture charges were time-barred, but the genocide and torture charges were not because they were brought within the applicable 20-year period. Finally, the Argentine amnesty laws did not apply outside Argentina, and in any case were violations of international law.

Cavallo, as of this writing, sits in a Spanish prison, and may join Adolfo Scilingo for trial. The Spanish public prosecutor, of course, again appealed Spain's jurisdiction over the cases, the Audiencia Nacional dismissed the appeal on March 26, 2001, and the case is currently before the Spanish Supreme Court. When trial will actually begin is anyone's guess. Meanwhile, Cavallo is one of the few Argentine torturers to have spent at least a few years in jail, which provides some comfort to his victims.

Chapter 6

Operation Condor Redux

By 1999, Judge Garzón's Spanish investigation into the links among the South American security forces during the 1970s began to bear fruit. His request to the U.S. authorities to provide documents on what the U.S. knew about repression in Argentina (and Judge García-Castellón's parallel request on Chile) eventually led to some interesting memos. Even more documents were declassified in February 1999, when President Clinton, at the request of a number of Congressional Democrats, ordered the CIA, State Department, and other agencies to review for release documents that might shed light on human rights abuses, terrorism, and other acts of political violence during and prior to the Pinochet era in Chile. Responses came from the State and Defense Departments, FBI, CIA, National Security Agency, and National Security Council. Although heavily redacted (entire pages were blacked out), the first batch included some 5,800 records, and a second batch, focusing on the Allende years, included some 1,100 documents. The third and final batch was released in November 2000 after agency opposition caused several delays (in the end, National Security Advisor Sandy Berger personally had to see to it the documents saw the light of day). In all, there were more than 16,000 documents, primarily relating to the later years of Pinochet's rule. A smaller batch related to Argentina.

Several memos confirmed what Martín Almada's search through the Paraguayan Archives of Terror had already revealed. The six Southern Cone governments—all military run or controlled—would, according to declassified memos, henceforth coordinate their "anti-subversive" activities, under the leadership of Chile's secret police and its director, Manuel Contreras. The security forces would share information, carry out combined operations, turn over suspected subversives to each other and even act outside the region to eliminate opponents.

A number of notorious cases, it turned out, fell within the rubric of Operation Condor. There were numerous disappearances of Uruguayans, Paraguayans, and Chileans in Argentina's Automotores Orletti detention camp. There was the killing of 119 Chileans whose bodies were dumped over the Argentine border; the crime was described as a firefight among rival subversive factions. There was the May 1976 assassination in Buenos Aires of the former president of the Uruguayan Chamber of Deputies, Héctor Gutiérrez Ruíz, and of Uruguayan former minister of education Zelmar Michelini. Four Uruguayan military officers had been accused of the crime and their extradition sought, but Argentine President Menem included them in his 1989 pardons, reportedly at the personal request of Uruguayan President Julio María Sanguinetti.[1] There was the killing of Bolivian General Juan José Torres, who nationalized the Bolivian tin mines as president in the early 1970s, was overthrown by General Hugo Banzer, and sought refuge in Argentina. A combined Argentine-Chilean-Bolivian task force assassinated him in Buenos Aires.

Then there were Condor's "third phase" operations. According to an FBI memo of September 28, 1976, combined secret teams from the Operation Condor states were to travel the world to pursue "terrorists" and their supporters and, if necessary, assassinate them. The memo pointed out that the 1976 car bomb killing of Orlando Letelier, Allende's foreign minister, and an associate in Washington, D.C., could well have been a "third phase" operation. Other assassinations also fit the pattern. There was, for example, the 1974 car bomb assassination in Buenos Aires of Chilean General Carlos Prats, who had been Allende's army chief, and his wife Sofia. There were the assassination attempts on exiled legislators Carlos Altamirano, in Madrid, and Bernardo Leighton, in Rome.

Based in part on the U.S. documents as well as the Paraguayan archives and information that came out of the Spanish investigation, human rights lawyers began going to court around the world. In Paraguay, Martín Almada and others in the National Pro-Human Rights Commission began compiling names and cases of Paraguayans who had disappeared into the maw of Operation Condor. In April 1997, they asked a local criminal investigating magistrate, Dr. Pedro Mayor Martínez, to look into the disappearance of Paraguayans in Argentina. They referred Martínez to Judge Garzón's indictment of Galtieri: "just as Argentine impunity cannot be exported to the Spanish people, so it cannot be exported to Argentina's neighbor, Paraguay," they argued. On February 26, 1999, Judge Martínez agreed to open an investigation into three of the disappearances. Federico Tatter had disappeared in Argentina in 1976, but his photo in the Paraguayan Archives showed him wearing the same clothes he had worn the day of his disappearance. Oscar Luis Rojas was Argentine, with Paraguayan parents, and had disappeared in Asunción. Ignacio Samaniego's name also appeared in the Archives, although he had disappeared in Argentina. Article 8.1(7) of Paraguay's penal code, the judge explained, allowed for universal jurisdiction over certain international crimes, including forced disappearances as defined in the Inter-American Convention on Forced Disappearances, ratified by Paraguay in 1996. Thus, neither the fact that the final stages of the crime had occurred in Argentina nor the lapse of time mattered. Judge Martínez opened an investigation. In time, a group of low-level police officers were tried, but the higher-ups remained largely beyond reach.

Operation Condor Back Home

In Argentina, Alberto Pedroncini decided the time was ripe to bring the Operation Condor case home. In November 1999, Pedroncini and three colleagues filed a complaint in Buenos Aires court on behalf of family members of Argentines, Chileans, Paraguayans, and Uruguayans who disappeared during the late 1970s.[2] The list of accused reads like a who's-who of ex-dictators and military brass: Generals Videla, Suárez-Mason, and Harguindeguy of Argentina; General Pinochet, former DINA head General Contreras, and his deputy Brigadier Espinoza of Chile; General Stroessner of Paraguay, his police chief, General Brites, and two colonels in charge of police and military intelligence; General Vapora, commander-in-chief of the Uruguayan army, and six of his officers; and General Hugo Banzer of Bolivia. The complainants included the families of Chileans, Paraguayans, and Uruguayans. The thread tying the cases together was that part of each crime took place on Argentine soil. Thus, Argentina had jurisdiction over the foreign defendants because the crimes were either initiated or partially carried out in Argentina, as well as under a theory of universal jurisdiction. With respect to these defendants, moreover, the Argentine amnesty laws simply did not apply—they were either commanders or not members of the Argentine military. The crimes charged included forced disappearance in violation of the Inter-American Convention on Forced Disappearances, illegal deprivation of liberty, and illicit association or criminal conspiracy.

The complaint landed in the chambers of Argentine Judge Rodolfo Canicoba Corral. In April and again in July 2001,[3] Judge Canicoba Corral issued indictments against the defendants for illegal association (conspiracy) and unlawful deprivation of liberty. He followed up with arrest warrants and extradition requests for the accused. He focused on the disappearance charges, holding that the crimes violated both national and international law. He used the recently ratified Inter-American Convention to hold that no barriers to prosecution, such as a statute of limitations, applied because disappearances are continuing crimes. He found that the defendants also conspired to commit aggravated kidnapping, torture, homicide, and forced disappearance through the criminal use of each state's apparatus.

General Videla, already convicted, pardoned, and now again under house arrest in the baby-snatching cases, appealed the arrest order. In May 2002, the Buenos Aires Court of Appeal affirmed.[4] The court considered the illegal association and unlawful deprivation of liberty claims within the context of crimes against humanity. It cited the 1968 UN Convention on the Non-Applicability of Statutes of Limitations, the London Charter that established the Nuremberg Tribunal, and the Rome Statute of the ICC. The crimes under discussion "transcend the individual victim, because by their very nature, they attack and deny the humanity of all. Essentially, all humanity is the victim." Article 118 of the Argentine constitution allowed the Argentine courts to prosecute crimes against customary law no matter where committed; jurisdiction was both territorial and universal, based on the nature of the crimes.

As to the illicit association charges, the court found that Videla was clearly part of the conspiracy at least while he led the military junta from 1976 to 1978. The crime of illicit association was charged at Nuremberg against the SS and other elite Nazi units, and the appeals court referred extensively to the Nuremberg legacy. As a result, Videla is potentially guilty of all crimes committed by co-conspirators.

The court rejected Videla's claim that the current prosecution was barred on double jeopardy grounds, because the Condor-related charges had never been aired. The statute of limitations was equally unavailing, especially since crimes against humanity are imprescriptable in international law. The Court of Appeals ordered the judge to create lists of victims of each nationality and then investigate their fate on a case-by-case basis, looking at whether there was a conspiracy to commit torture and murder. If warranted, the Court directed the trial judge to seek extradition.

Argentina's neighbors have been no more willing than Argentina itself to extradite suspects for trial abroad. Uruguay has refused Judge Canicoba's requests on grounds that its national amnesty law precluded prosecutions abroad as well as home. The Uruguayan foreign minister argued that the double criminality requirement was not satisfied since forced disappearances were not part of the penal code. Both arguments were legally suspect, but the Uruguayan government insisted it would not arrest those named in the Argentine warrants. The Bolivian Supreme Court was set to consider the extradition request for former General Banzer when he died on cancer in 2002. Chile and Brazil also eventually refused the Argentine judge's extradition requests. Judge Alberto Chaigneau of the Chilean Supreme Court ordered the arrest of Manuel Contreras pending consideration of Canicoba's extradition request, but the Supreme Court refused to extradite.[5] However, Judge Guzmán took up a complaint involving twenty Operation Condor-related disappearances, investigated, and charged Manuel Contreras and others. He also requested anew that the courts strip Pinochet of his parliamentary immunity.

Brazilian NGOs and legislators asked prosecutors to begin proceedings against ex-Paraguayan dictator Alfredo Stroessner, who lives in Brasilia. The Cardoso government refused to either extradite or prosecute, but activists hoped to convince the Lula government to be more sympathetic, so far without success. Nonetheless, the Brazilian Supreme Court authorized an Argentine judge to peruse the files of Brazilian security services. Brazilian authorities agreed to respond to requests for information on the Condor-related activities of the now defunct National Intelligence Service and the Federal Police. In addition, the Brazilian Congress demanded an investigation into the local military's role in Operation Condor and approved reparations for Brazilian victims of disappearances.

Operation Condor-related cases sprang up in Europe as well. In June 1999 a group of eleven family members of the disappeared visited Italian investigating magistrate Giancarlo Capaldo. Their relatives, Italo-Argentines and Italo-Uruguayans, had disappeared in Argentina or Brazil between 1974 and 1980. They accused Argentine General Cristino Nicolaides, navy Captain Luis D'Imperio, and Colonel Jorge Muzzio; Paraguayan police chief Pastor Coronel; and five notorious members of the Uruguayan security forces. Barely a month later, on July 9, 1999, the Italian Minister of Justice approved opening the investigation under article 8 of the penal code.

Witnesses started coming to Italy. Investigating magistrate Capaldo visited Judge Garzón in Madrid and Judge Le Loire in France, comparing notes and materials on Operation Condor. Another Italian prosecutor, Giovanni Salvi, traveled to Chile and France to trace the connections between the DINA and Operation Condor.

In March 2001 Italy indicted Videla, Galtieri, Viola, Massera, Suárez-Mason, and other leaders of the Argentine military government, as well as Pinochet, Contreras, and other DINA officials. Some 50 officials in all were now targets, most of them the same officials targeted by Operation Condor inquiries elsewhere. The inquiries differ because each focuses on the fate of specific victims.

Uruguay

The Operation Condor cases, spurred in turn by Judge Garzón's Spanish investigation, helped reopen the issue of impunity in Uruguay. The

1986 Law on the Expiry of the State's Punitive Capacity, the result of a deal between the military and the traditional political parties, had precluded any prosecutions for human rights abuses committed during the military regime. A coalition of human rights groups invoked a Uruguayan law that allows a referendum if a quarter of the electorate requests it to challenge the amnesty law, but a campaign of veiled threats and intimidation by the military sent the referendum to a narrow defeat in 1989. The failure exhausted and demoralized the human rights groups. Also, torture and arbitrary detention under inhumane conditions had been the norm in Uruguay, but only 30 or so people actually disappeared in the country. The immense majority of disappearances of Uruguayans—some 140, at last count—took place in Argentina.

A good part of the impetus to reopen the issue in Uruguay came from one man's quest for his missing grandchild. Juan Gelman is an Argentine poet and writer beloved throughout Latin America and Europe. He brought file folders full of information to Judge Capaldo in Italy. He also testified before Judge Garzón in Spain, on April 1, 1998. He told the judge how his son Marcelo, then twenty years old, and Marcelo's nineteen-year old wife Claudia were arrested and disappeared while Claudia was pregnant; how survivors saw them at Automotores Orletti, the Buenos Aires Operation Condor detention camp run jointly by Argentines, Chileans, and Uruguayans; how he received information that Claudia had been transferred to a prison in Uruguay to give birth; and how, to the best of his knowledge, the child was born between the end of November and beginning of December 1976. Mother and child were last seen accompanied by Uruguayan military officials Juan Rodríguez Buratti and José Arab, who ended up as defendants in the Argentine Operation Condor case. He told how he had begged the Uruguayan government to help him find his grandchild, to no avail.

Doors started opening with the election of Jorge Batlle as President in late 1999. In August, 2000 Batlle created a "Peace Commission" to look into the Uruguayan disappearance cases. He appointed commissioners including the archbishop of Montevideo, representatives of the country's political parties, labor groups, family members, and the government. The Commission had no subpoena power and no power to name names, but focused instead on finding the remains of the disappeared and identifying secret detention centers.

Batlle also agreed to look into the Gelman case. He met with the family members of the disappeared and assassinated, the first time the government had invited them to talk. Soon thereafter, Batlle announced that he had found Gelman's granddaughter. To protect her privacy, the name was not made public, but Gelman soon happily confirmed that he had met the girl, now a young adult, and that they had established a relationship. Gelman also announced that he knew his son's murderer: Captain Ricardo Medina Blanco.

Criminal complaints quickly followed. Operation Condor was one starting place. In September 2002, the families of twelve victims of Uruguayan authorities operating in Argentina in 1976 accused ten of the most notorious Uruguayan officers of kidnapping, illicit association, and child theft.[6] Their complaint also challenges Uruguay's 1985 amnesty law using the Argentine and Inter-American jurisprudence as precedent. In April 2002, criminal court judge Alvaro Franca agreed with the complainants that cases of forced disappearance (charged as kidnapping under Uruguayan law) and child-snatching are permanent crimes that continued beyond the 1985 amnesty. However, the judge chose not to reopen the cases himself, instead sending them back to the local courts where complaints had originally been filed with instructions to each court to determine if the long-closed files should be reopened.

Gaps in the amnesty law have been the other wedge for judges to begin to pry open the courts. For example, the amnesty law does not cover civil servants like Foreign Minister Juan Carlos Blanco. In October 2002, Judge Eduardo Cavalli charged Blanco with covering up the aggravated arbitrary detention and subsequent disappearance of Elena Quinteros, a thirty-one-year old teacher, and ordered him jailed pending trial.[7] Quinteros had been captured by the Uruguayan military, and in a desperate attempt to escape threw herself over the wall of the Venezuelan Embassy in Montevideo. Security forces stormed the embassy and dragged Quinteros out in front of dozens of witnesses. She was never seen again. Venezuela demanded her return, and Blanco apparently initially recommended that the government turn her over, but he was outvoted by the military. He then publicly announced that the Uruguayan government knew nothing about any such person—the basis for the cover-up charges against him.

In charging Blanco, the judge confronted the statute of limitations argument. As of 1996, the judge found, the Inter-American Convention on Forced Disappearances had become part of Uruguayan law. Even though at the time forced disappearance was not specifically a crime, the underlying conduct was covered by the Convention and not subject to a statute of limitations. And even if the statute had run long before 1996, the judge found that unless there was proof of the date of Quinteros's death, no prescription could apply.

Juan Bordaberry, the civilian figurehead of the military regime in its early days, also faced charges that he played a role in the assassinations of eight Communist Party militants, shot by police in 1972. An investigating magistrate, Rolando Vomero, found that the statute was tolled during the dictatorship years, when it was clearly impossible to bring a claim.

Cases that seemed long buried surfaced. A judge reopened the investigation into the deaths of Zelmar Michelini and Héctor Gutiérrez, popular politicians and potential presidents assassinated in 1976. The legislature, which now includes Michelini's son, began considering a bill to criminalize torture, forced disappearance, and other crimes against humanity. Retired military officers complained that they were heckled and spat on when they went to the store. Still, the military remains unrepentant. At the end of 2001, the current commander-in-chief, Lieutenant General Carlos Daners, told a TV audience: "the army will not apologize for anything it did."[8]

The "Third Phase" Cases: Prats, Letelier, Leighton

Soon after its creation in 1974, the Chilean secret police DINA had organized an even more secret Exterior Department, in charge of tracking and neutralizing opponents of the regime who had fled Chile. The Exterior Department also worked closely with other Southern Cone secret services, sharing agents, false identifications, and resources. Among the DINA's most spectacular actions outside Chile were the Prats and Letelier car-bombings in Argentina and the U.S. and the near-assassination of Bernardo Leighton in Rome.

The Spanish investigation renewed interest in these notorious cases. One reason was Garzón's focus on Operation Condor; another was the release of declassified U.S. documents. Judge Guzmán in Chile, in the course of his newly invigorated investigations, also produced declarations that shed light on the planning and execution of these cases. Whatever the combination of factors, the long dormant cases came alive again after 1998.

Letelier

Orlando Letelier was Allende's defense and foreign minister. After the coup he escaped and took up residence in Washington, D.C., where he remained an outspoken critic of the Pinochet regime. On September 21, 1976, as he was traveling to work with associates Michael and Ronni Moffitt, a powerful car bomb exploded, killing Letelier and Ronni Moffitt and leaving her husband Michael injured. The crime was the worst modern incident of foreign terrorism committed in a U.S. city before September 11, 2001. Three low-level operatives, Cuban exiles, were convicted in U.S. court, but the sentences were overturned. One of them, Guillermo Novo, was finally imprisoned in Panama in 2004 for trying to kill Fidel Castro. Two others were fugitives for over a decade. One, Virgilio Pablo Paz Romero, was living as a suburban father and anti-Castro activist in southern Florida. He was only picked up in 1991 after the television show *America's Most Wanted* aired a segment on the Letelier case and someone phoned in a tip to law enforcement. He was sentenced to twelve years in prison and released in 2001. DINA agent Michael Townley, a U.S. citizen, turned state's witness and provided details of the DINA's role in exchange for a reduced sentence and a place in the Federal Witness Protection Program. Another DINA operative, army Major Armando Fernández Larios, initially avoided U.S. prosecution by remaining in Chile. In 1987 he left Chile, pled guilty to accessory charges in the Letelier-Moffitt murders, and served only five months of a seven-year sentence before moving to southern Florida.

DINA head Manuel Contreras and his deputy were indicted, but Chile refused to extradite and chose to try them at home instead. The U.S. put enormous pressure on the Chilean government to solve this crime, even if all the others went unsolved. The killing was excluded from the terms of the 1978 amnesty law. Finally, in 1991, Chilean judge Adolfo Bañados began his own investigation into the case. Manuel Contreras and Pedro Espinoza were eventually found guilty of orchestrating the assassination and sentenced to seven and six years in prison respectively.[9] Contreras at first refused to serve jail time, but soon turned himself in to serve his time at Punto Peuco, a prison especially outfitted for his comfort.

Meanwhile, the families pursued civil compensation from the state. They filed and won a civil suit in U.S. courts in the early 1980s, but could not attach the only real property Chile owned in the U.S., the airplanes of LAN Chile, the national airline.[10] They then turned to the U.S. government to help them get the compensation owed them. In January 1992, Chile's civilian government finally accepted an international arbitration panel's order to pay $2.6 million in reparations to the Letelier and Moffitt families.[11]

In Washington, the Clinton administration applauded the convictions in Chile of Contreras and Espinoza for the Letelier assassination. Letelier, after all, had been a friend of many influential Democrats and a well-known figure in Washington circles, and the crime was committed in the heart of the U.S., not some far-off backwater. The newly released documents and Pinochet's arrest in London rekindled interest in the case, and especially in Pinochet's role in ordering the killing. FBI agents Robert Scherrer and Carter Cornick, who investigated the killing, and prosecutor Eugene Propper were all convinced that Pinochet was part of the plot. Yet without a confession from the general or his deputy they had no way to prove it. Furthermore, Pinochet at the time of the bombers' trial was a sitting head of state, and no one thought it was worth putting too much energy into putting together a case likely to fail on immunity grounds.

Technically, the Letelier case was never closed in the U.S. Indictments for Contreras and Espinoza have been outstanding since 1978. The still-open case provided an avenue to raise the issue again with the Justice Department. Sam Buffone, a lawyer who represented the Letelier and Moffitt families in their civil suit against the Chilean government in 1980–84, approached Attorney General Janet Reno after Pinochet's arrest in London, asking her to look into Pinochet's role more closely. Buffone, together with the Institute for Policy Studies where Letelier had worked and other Washington NGOs, argued that it was inconsistent to be demanding action against terrorism from other countries while ignoring terrorist outrages committed by foreign agents on U.S. soil.

In January 1999, Reno assigned a team of 20 U.S. Attorneys and FBI agents to take a new look, focusing on the links between Contreras and Pinochet. She also ordered the Justice Department to comply with the Spanish courts' requests under the U.S.-Spain mutual legal assistance treaty to provide documentation relevant to the Spanish prosecution of Pinochet, but she excluded anything that might support a Pinochet indictment in *Letelier.*

In March 2000, a delegation of FBI agents and U.S. prosecutors paid a well-publicized visit to Santiago. With press following them everywhere, the somberly dressed agents must have looked to the Chilean public like characters from a U.S. television series: there were few 6-foot-plus, bald African Americans in well-tailored suits on the streets of Santiago. The prosecutors and agents worked through a Chilean judge to question Contreras, Espinoza, and a number of other ex-officers. Espinoza's lawyer released an old statement in which he suggested that he was the fall guy for General Pinochet, while Contreras reiterated that his superior approved everything he did on a daily basis. The U.S. team returned to Washington and apparently recommended that Reno convene a grand jury, the first step toward issuing an indictment. During the subsequent internal discussions, the Clinton administration ended and the incoming Bush administration seemingly saw little point in moving forward.

Leighton

Orlando Letelier was only one of the DINA's targets in Operation Condor's "third phase." Bernardo Leighton, the head of the Christian Democrats and an outspoken Pinochet opponent, had fled to Italy after the coup with his wife Anita. In October 1975, he and his wife barely survived bullets to the back of the head, shot by an Italian fascist. Twenty years later, the Italian courts took up the Leighton case, and condemned Manuel Contreras to 20 years imprisonment and Raúl Iturriaga Neumann, who oversaw the DINA's foreign operations, to 18 years *in absentia* as the masterminds of the attack. The cases sat dormant for five years. It was not until 2000 that the Italian courts, perhaps seeing a new openness in the judiciary, asked the Chilean courts to extradite the two men. The lower courts willingly detained and questioned Iturriaga (Contreras was already in jail). On November 27, 2001, the Chilean Supreme Court declined to extradite the two men. The domestic prosecution of Iturriaga and the others would come not as a result of the Leighton assassination attempt, but as a result of the spectacular killing of Pinochet's one-time mentor and superior, General Carlos Prats.

Prats

In mid-1974, at one of his breakfast meetings with his deputy Contreras, Pinochet expressed the opinion that General Prats, who had been his predecessor, mentor, and boss as commander in chief of the Chilean Army, was a dangerous man. Contreras needed no more: he put the DINA's Exterior Department into operation to get rid of Prats. Prats had been loyal to Allende and to the Chilean military's constitutionalist tradition. As the crisis in Chile deepened, in August 1973, Prats decided to resign as army head to avoid continuing friction within the officer corps. He urged Allende to appoint Pinochet as army chief and Allende did so, largely on Prats's recommendation that his successor would be loyal to democracy. After the coup, Prats and his wife went into exile in Argentina. By September 1974, they were receiving death threats. Sofía Cuthbert Prats visited the Chilean Consulate in Buenos Aires to request passports for herself and her husband, but no travel documents were forthcoming. The Chilean consul later testified that when she checked with the Foreign Ministry about the status of the passport request, she was told that no passports would be issued—General Prats and his wife would not be allowed to escape. Three days later, a car bomb went off as General Prats pulled his car into his garage, blowing the couple nine stories into the air.

Although it was widely assumed at the time that the Chilean DINA had committed the crime, local court investigations went nowhere and the case was closed. Years later, with the FBI investigation into the Letelier bombing, and the Contreras trial in Chile, enough information came out for Argentine judge María Servini to reopen the investigation. "We couldn't use the evidence from the Letelier case directly because of plea bargains with the U.S.," Cecilia Prats, one of the couple's daughters, told me. "It took us five years to get Michael Townley [one of the Letelier bombers] to agree to testify. That opened up new vistas in the case."

The first arrest was a Chilean living in Argentina, Enrique Arancibia Clavel, who worked informally with Townley. Townley, then under U.S. federal witness protection, told the judge about his role in the Prats attack, naming Arancibia as one of the bombers and detailing the structure of the DINA's Exterior Department. "The case was reopened in 1991," the judge recalled. "We had information from prosecutors in Italy and Spain, from the U.S. prosecutors in Letelier, from the Paraguayan archives of terror. With that, the case began to crack. But it took a long time."

Judge Servini issued arrest warrants for Arancibia, Manuel Contreras, his deputy Pedro Espinoza, DINA Exterior Department head Raúl Iturriaga Neumann, Iturriaga's second-in-command José Zara Holger, and his brother Jorge Iturriaga Neumann, a DINA collaborator. Raúl Iturriaga and Zara, together with Townley, had been in Buenos Aires the day of the blast.

The defendants challenged the warrants on grounds that the statute of limitations had long since expired. Judge Servini, citing customary international law, found that the Prats murder formed part of a pattern of state-planned abuses that constituted a crime against humanity.[12] She cited the Nuremberg tribunals, the Universal Declaration of Human Rights, the Covenant on Civil and Political Rights, the Convention on Non-Applicability of Statutes of Limitations, and the more recent jurisprudence of the ICTY and ICTR to conclude that crimes against humanity had a special status in customary international law, which made them imprescriptable. The most recent statement of that fact, the judge noted, was the Rome Statute establishing the ICC. The crimes alleged fit squarely within the definition—they were systematic and carried out as state policy against a civilian population—and therefore no statute of limitations applied. On November 27, 2000, Arancibia Clavel was sentenced to life in prison for double murder and illicit association. In August 2004 the Argentine Supreme Court reaffirmed the sentence and the imprescriptability of crimes against humanity.

While Arancibia lived in Argentina, the rest of the defendants lived in Chile. (The one exception was Armando Fernández Larios, who lived in the U.S. In May 2002, Judge Servini asked the U.S. to extradite him. It is not clear whether the plea agreement that keeps him from being extradited back to Chile applies to third countries. In any case, Fernández had problems in the U.S., as we will see presently.) The Chilean government had been a complainant in the Arancibia prosecution, but seemed uninterested in going farther up the chain of command. Nonetheless,

Judge Servini turned her attention to interrogating the remaining defendants and preparing extradition requests. Several times during 2001, Servini and prosecutors in her office traveled to Santiago to interview those with knowledge of the case. On October 8, 2001, Servini issued indictments, arrest orders, and extradition requests for the five Chilean defendants for murder, illicit association, and crimes against humanity.[13] A Chilean judge initially approved the arrest warrants. While those cases were pending, Judge Servini took the next logical step: indicting Pinochet.

The Prats family had three daughters who were studying abroad when their parents were killed. For over a quarter century, as they raised their own families, they have sought their parents' killers. "We've been pursuing this case our whole lives," Cecilia Prats told me. "I was nineteen when it happened, and used to visit my parents on weekends. We stayed in Chile because we thought they would come home soon." They hired Chilean attorneys, Pamela Pereira and Hernán Quezada, who asked Judge Servini to issue an arrest warrant for Augusto Pinochet as head of the conspiracy. As with the other defendants, the judge found that no statute of limitations barred prosecution. In September 2001, the judge asked permission from the Chilean Supreme Court to interrogate Pinochet as a potential defendant and asked him to appoint defense counsel. The Court replied that before Pinochet could be questioned, he would have to be stripped of his parliamentary immunity—another *desafuero* process. Although the same court had approved removing Pinochet's immunity a month earlier, that decision was limited to a single case, *Caravan of Death*; with each new case the process had to be repeated. Servini immediately drafted a request and sent it, through the Argentine Foreign Ministry, on December 14. It never arrived in Santiago. Foreign Ministry sources explained that it had gotten "lost," although they weren't sure how. In May 2002, at the request of the Prats family lawyers, the Argentine judge resubmitted the *desafuero* request, but meanwhile, the Chilean Supreme Court had ruled that Pinochet was unfit to stand trial because of his deteriorated mental state. In November 2002, the Supreme Court denied the Argentine request on grounds that Pinochet's health made him unfit for preliminary judicial proceedings as well as trial.[14] The Court also eventually upheld the lower court's denial of extradition requests for the lower ranked defendants. Shortly thereafter, applying the "extradite or prosecute" rule, the Supreme Court ordered that the local investigations into General Prats's murder be reopened, and named the same former DINA officials as suspects.[15] They were charged and arrested in March 2003.

"We never thought we'd get this far in the investigation," says Cecilia Prats. "My sister Sofia went to the U.S. to testify in the Letelier case, to

Spain to testify in the case before Garzón, and to Italy to testify in the Leighton case—it was important to see the link among the three cases. It's a burden, we travel to Argentina a lot, plus people come up to us and tell us their stories. We want these cases clarified for us and for everyone, because even though there are many other cases that will not be solved, if these same people are judged in our case, that will be a form of justice for the others."

The U.S. Cases: Investigations, Civil Suits, and the Trial of U.S. Complicity

The U.S. was connected to events in Chile in many ways. U.S. citizens were victims of the regime, and the U.S. served as a refuge for a few notorious DINA operatives. In addition, the U.S. was deeply implicated in opposition to Allende and planning the coup. Subsequent Congressional hearings established that the U.S. goal was to "make the economy scream" in order to remove Allende and that the CIA was involved in a number of unsavory activities. In the post-coup years, the document releases of the late 1990s showed that the U.S. both knew about and played a role in Operation Condor. The terror network coordinated its activities through a U.S. encryption and communication system based in the Panama Canal Zone. The CIA admitted in September 2000 that DINA chief Manuel Contreras was a CIA asset between 1974 and 1977, and that he received an unspecified payment for his services. During these same years Contreras was known to U.S. officials as "Condor One."

The declassified U.S. documents also cast new light on the deaths of U.S. citizens Frank Teruggi and Charles Horman. Horman was one of the most famous victims of the 1973 coup, the subject of the film *Missing*. He and his colleague Teruggi were among the thousands killed in the Santiago stadium in the first weeks after the coup. The day before the coup, Horman, a journalist, had been in the coastal town of Viña del Mar, and had talked to some U.S. naval officers who boasted about their role in the upcoming coup. The film depicts his family's anguished search and the U.S. government's complete lack of sympathy with the plight of American citizens caught up in the coup. Joyce Horman, Charles's widow, has never stopped pressing the government for information on the case. She is convinced that Charles was killed because he knew too much.

A declassified State Department document from August 25, 1976 reads: "There is some circumstantial evidence to suggest U.S. intelligence may have played an unfortunate part in Horman's death. At best it was limited to providing or confirming information that helped motivate his murder by the GOC [government of Chile]. At worst, U.S. intelligence was aware that GOC saw Horman in a rather serious light and U.S. officials did nothing to discourage the logical outcome of GOC paranoia."[16]

With this document in hand, Joyce Horman hired lawyers in Chile (one of them is Fabiola Letelier, Orlando's sister) and in December 2000 filed a criminal complaint with Judge Guzmán against Pinochet and whoever else should turn out to be responsible for her husband's death. On May 14, 2002, Judge Guzmán staged a four-hour reenactment of the killings at the national stadium in the days immediately following the coup. He took advantage of the visit of *Missing* filmmaker Costa Gavras (in Chile to receive a government award) to ask him about his sources for the film. As a strange detail, Costa Gavras told the local press that this was not the first time he had worked with Judge Guzmán: as a young lawyer, the judge had been an extra on the set of the film *State of Siege*. "He's a much better judge than he was an actor," Costa Gavras told the press.

Guzmán also called in former U.S. consul Fred Purdy for questioning. Purdy, who many U.S. citizens resident in Chile in 1973 remember as coldly turning away their pleas for help, eventually retired to Chile, where he writes books on Chilean wine. The judge considered him an *inculpado,* or potential suspect, because he knew about the killings and did not try to stop them. Purdy angrily denied having any connection to the *Horman* or *Teruggi* cases or any responsibility for the fate of U.S. citizens in Chile at the time. Using a provision of Chilean law that allows the investigating judge to question two witnesses with contradictory stories at the same time (called a *careo* or confrontation), the judge confronted Purdy with Marc Cooper, a journalist for *The Nation,* who lived in Chile during the coup and, not surprisingly, remembered events differently. Purdy thus became the first former U.S. official to be questioned by a judge about the U.S. government role in human rights abuses in Chile.[17] In December 2003, Judge Guzmán indicted former security agent Rafael González as an accomplice in Horman's murder.

While Joyce Horman pressed her suit in Chile, other family members pursued those killers who had "retired" to the U.S. Remember Armando Fernández Larios? He was a notorious member of the DINA, involved in the Letelier and Prats murders, and involved in the infamous *Caravan of Death* case that that absorbed so much of Judge Guzmán's attention. He was also, by 1987, a resident of the state of Florida, selling car parts and living quietly after serving a short prison stint for his role in the Letelier assassination. Part of his deal with the U.S. government in exchange for his cooperation in that case was that he could not be extradited to Chile.

Fernández Larios's comfortable retirement was too much to bear for Zita Cabello-Barrueto. Her brother Winston was a twenty-three-year old economist when he was pulled out of prison by the Caravana military officers and killed. There was clear evidence that Fernández Larios was part of the mission that ordered the killings, and more and more evidence that he personally knifed Winston Cabello to death. Zita Cabello-Barrueto eventually moved to the U.S. and became a filmmaker and professor at the University of California. In 1999, she sued Fernández Larios in U.S. federal court for torturing and killing her brother.

"When Pinochet was arrested I approached the Center for Justice and Accountability [a San Francisco-based organization that brings lawsuits against torturers and helps torture victims] because they were collecting testimony from Chilean exiles in the U.S. to be sent to London to support the *Pinochet* extradition case. I asked what CJA did, and when they explained, I said I had a case." She had learned of the circumstances of her brother's death from a psychiatrist acquaintance who had interviewed Fernández Larios back in 1974, and after hearing that he was in the U.S., she hired a detective to track him down. To make out her legal case against him, she got leads, traveled to Chile, and started knocking on doors of ex-prisoners and ex-soldiers. She was not a lawyer, but she was, as she put it, a very good researcher, and she was only interested in knowing the story of one person's death, a young father with two children and a sister. She found the person who had drawn up the list of prisoners in the local jail to be killed, who told her regretfully that if he had taken her brother's name off the list, he would have had to put someone else's on. She found the driver of the truck who had taken the prisoners on their last ride. Some of these people had testified before Judge Guzmán, but others had not, and were willing to talk but not to testify. After a number of trips to Chile, she had about a half-dozen witnesses willing to tape depositions she could use in U.S. court.

In October 2002, on what would have been her brother's birthday, Zita Cabello-Barrueto returned to Chile. She placed an ad in the local papers inviting the public to a commemoration of Winston Cabello's life and recounting her lawsuit against Fernández Larios. Much to the family's surprise, over 300 people showed up at the Economics Faculty where years before Winston had been a student. The Cabello-Barruetos were moved, as strangers told anecdotes about Winston's life, and about the other students whose lives were cut short.

Back in the U.S., Cabello-Barrueto and her attorneys prepared for the upcoming jury trial. On October 17, 2003, a Florida jury awarded her and Winston's other family members $4 million in civil damages for torture, summary execution, and crimes against humanity. The suit was based in part on the Alien Tort Claims Act, which allows non-U.S. citizens to sue in cases of violations of the "law of nations." Some two dozen cases charge foreign officials with torture, extrajudicial killing, forced disappearance, crimes against humanity, war crimes, genocide, cruel, inhuman or degrading treatment, forced labor, and prolonged arbitrary detention. In 1992, Congress endorsed the idea of U.S. courts hearing these cases by passing the Torture Victims Protection Act, which covers torture and extrajudicial killing and can be brought by both U.S. citizens and noncitizens.[18]

In practice, few plaintiffs have ever collected damages. Most individual defendants have few assets in the United States, and states are generally immune from suit. In the mid-1990s, plaintiffs started using the ATCA to sue corporations for aiding and abetting forced labor, summary executions, rape, and torture. The corporate cases made it possible for winning plaintiffs to get real damages, but also (for that very reason) unleashed a swarm of lawyers, lobbyists, and conservative academics who attacked the very notion of the ATCA. The validity of the Act was before the U.S. Supreme Court in 2004, and the Bush II administration weighed in on the side of opponents of the statute. In the end, the Supreme Court upheld the validity of the law.

Fernández-Larios was a foot soldier in the campaign against Allende supporters in Chile. Heading the U.S. onslaught against Allende's Chile was National Security Advisor Henry Kissinger. Kissinger has written about his minute oversight of the government's Chile policy. So it is not surprising that judges in Spain, France, Argentina, and Chile would like to talk to him.

In the Horman case, Judge Guzmán sent out a letter rogatory in July 2001 asking Kissinger for any information he might have about the extent of U.S. government knowledge at the time of the murder. Predictably, he got no reply. A year later, Guzmán pointedly observed that not replying to his questions put Kissinger in contempt of court and subject to arrest if he traveled to Chile. On September 11, 2001, the anniversary of the military coup in Chile, a criminal case was filed in Chile naming several ex-Southern Cone leaders as well as Henry Kissinger, ex-CIA head Richard Helms, and his deputy Vernon Walters for their roles in Operation Condor. On the other side of the Andes, Judge Canicoba also wanted to talk to Kissinger about his role in Operation Condor. Kissinger decided to cancel a March 2002 trip to Brazil to receive an award, just in case.

But while avoiding South America might be easy for the head of a global consulting firm, it was more difficult for Kissinger to avoid traveling to Europe. Requests for his testimony began springing there up as well. French Judges Roger Le Loire and Sophie-Hélène Château wanted to talk to him about the U.S. role in the disappearances of French citizens in Chile and Argentina. Judge Le Loire sent a request for an interview to his deluxe Paris hotel when Kissinger visited France in 2001. He was interested in talking to Kissinger because Kissinger's signature was on declassified Plan Condor documents, including some that talked about eradicating communists like Miguel Enríquez. Enríquez, the Chilean leader of the MIR, had been closely linked to one of the French citizens whose disappearance Le Loire was investigating. The judge thought Kissinger might know something about the circumstances. Kissinger turned him down and promptly left the country, and the U.S. Embassy responded to Le Loire that any information he might need was property of the U.S. government and should be requested through government channels.

Judge Garzón in Spain wanted to talk to Kissinger about Operation Condor. When Kissinger showed up in London in April 2002, Judge Garzón asked British authorities to ask Kissinger if he would answer a few questions. The British did so, and reported back that Kissinger was not interested, that under British law they could not compel him to appear as a witness, and that Kissinger had referred all questions to the U.S. State Department. The State Department in turn told the press that Dr. Kissinger could answer no questions because he had immunity. "The U.S. department of state's defensive response to this inquiry can only raise questions about what Mr. Kissinger has to hide," Joan Garcés and Manuel Murillo, the Spanish lawyers representing General Pinochet's victims, said in an April 22, 2002 press release.

So far, judges wanted Kissinger as a witness, not a suspect in the crimes. Others argue that Kissinger is probably the biggest living war criminal not yet arrested for trial, and that it is incumbent upon those who profess a belief in global justice to not limit themselves to the former dictators of small countries but to take on the policymakers of rich and powerful states. As requests for testimony mounted, Kissinger faced a political campaign to expose and shame him, and perhaps to encourage prosecutions under a theory of command responsibility for war crimes. Christopher Hitchens, a journalist, wrote a political indictment, *The Trial of Henry Kissinger*, that was translated into several languages and a documentary;[19] an activist website, Kissinger Watch, tracks the ex-secretary's moves and the legal actions against him.

During Kissinger's same April 2002 London visit, a British human rights campaigner, Peter Tatchell, decided to test the limits of the law. He applied to Bow Street Magistrate's Court for an arrest warrant for Kissinger on grounds that the indiscriminate bombing of civilians, destruction of property, and environmental harms caused by the carpet-bombing and napalming of Vietnam, Cambodia, and Laos during the 1960s and early 1970s constituted war crimes actionable in a UK court.

Two days later, Judge Nicholas Evans, the same magistrate who had signed the arrest warrant for Augusto Pinochet, turned Tatchell's application down. Only the director of public prosecutions could actually initiate a prosecution for war crimes committed before 2001, and the prosecutor had indicated he was not interested in doing so. Although the judge recognized he could issue an arrest warrant on his own, he did not see the point, he wrote, if no prosecution was forthcoming. The evidence before him was not enough to issue the warrant, although the judge added that "I do not doubt the strength of feeling in him [Mr. Tatchell] and many others that justice requires that Mr. Kissinger should face the allegations made against him in a court of law."[20]

Kissinger's legal problems have come home as well. In September 2001 the son of Chilean General René Schneider sued Kissinger, Helms, and others in the District Court for the District of Columbia under the Alien Tort Claims Act, alleging that Kissinger and Helms were part of a conspiracy and had aided and abetted the Chilean right-wingers who murdered his father in 1970. General Schneider was commander-in-chief of the army and a staunch constitutionalist. Right-wing elements in the army concocted a plan to kidnap Schneider if Allende won the 1970 elections, spirit him out of the country, and blame the left. The U.S., through a "Track II" unofficial policy team at the National Security Council, provided arms and support to the plotters. According to U.S. documents Kissinger disavowed support for the plot (while leaving the arms and money for the plotters intact) about a week before it was scheduled to take place. Schneider was kidnapped, but the plan misfired and Schneider was killed. The U.S. never helped Chilean authorities find the killers, although declassified documents make clear that they knew who they were.

Kissinger's lawyers have contested the Schneider lawsuit on grounds that Kissinger was acting as an official U.S. policymaker and that therefore the suit is actually an attack on the U.S. government's policy on Chile and the courts have no business getting involved. Furthermore, the defendant argued that he had immunity for anything done in an official capacity.[21] The judge assigned to the case seems to be in no hurry to decide whether it can go forward.

The Schneider lawsuit may or may not prosper, but the idea that the powerful actors who fund, encourage, train, or otherwise make possible the activities of goon squads and rogue police or army units should be held accountable is gaining ground in a number of areas. With the development of these cases, the globalization of justice becomes more symmetrical, holding wrongdoers from both North and South accountable. Alien Tort Claims Act cases in the U.S. allege that multinational oil companies are aiding and abetting forced labor in Myanmar, shootings of unarmed demonstrators in Nigeria, and military crackdowns in the Indonesian province of Aceh.[22] Lawsuits in France charge the Total oil company with forced labor in Burma, a French forest products company with depredations in the Cameroon rainforest, and a French general who boasted of torture during the Algerian war (1954–62) with justification (*apologia*) of war crimes and crimes against humanity (this last case was dismissed). In the UK, lawsuits seek accountability from local manufacturers of implements used for torture. As these types of suits proliferate, they bring attention to the many links between the actions and omissions of powerful companies and governments and massive human rights violations. They also raise a host of questions about where to draw the lines. Somewhere between liability for simply investing in a country where abuses regularly occur (a position not even the most ardent human rights advocate defends) and taking an active role in the planning and execution of atrocities lies the appropriate standard for corporate liability. Somewhere between maintaining normal diplomatic and military ties with dictatorships and knowingly providing material assistance to state criminals lies the line a government cannot tread without incurring responsibility. Those lines are changing as you read these words, as concepts like joint venturers, agents, aiders and abetters, and co-conspirators become part of the lexicon of human rights groups and judges finding in the globalization of justice a fitting counterweight to economic globalization and military might.

Chapter 7

The Legal Legacy of Pinochet: Universal Jurisdiction and Its Discontents

The spectacle of Chile's once-powerful General Pinochet under arrest, and the favorable initial decisions from the House of Lords in Britain and the Audiencia Nacional in Spain, kindled new hopes in human rights advocates around the world. The courts of many countries were closed to investigations or lawsuits involving abuses by the local military or police, due to formal amnesty laws or informal threats, bribes, or other pressures. Maybe the *Pinochet* path was a viable alternative. Transnational prosecutions in the courts of other states, hitherto considered legally possible but more than a little fanciful, started looking much more interesting.

Cases began to arrive before the Spanish and Belgian courts because they had the most well-known laws allowing extraterritorial jurisdiction. Some were easy to dispose of. A group of Cubans and Chilean Pinochet supporters called on Judge Garzón to investigate Cuban president Fidel Castro, but the court quickly found that a head of state was immune from suit in Spanish courts while in office. Cases against Morocco's King Hassan II and Theodoro Nguema of Equatorial Guinea met the same fate. A case against former Communist Party head Santiago Carrillo was dismissed as well.

Other allegations were more promising. Four cases in particular before European courts seemed to be natural extensions of the *Pinochet* precedent. One involved the massacre of hundreds of thousands of Guatemalans, mostly Mayan indigenous people. Two others involved Africans: Hissène Habré, former dictator of Chad, and Abdulaye Yerodia Ndombasi, a high-ranking official in the Congolese government. A fourth involved Désiré Bouterse, former strongman of Suriname. Each would, in its own way, come up against the political and legal limits of prosecution based on universal jurisdiction. Together, they mark at least a temporary retreat from the initial euphoria of 1998.

Guatemala: Subsidiary Jurisdiction and the Narrowing of the Spanish Forum

Rigoberta Menchú, a Qu'iche Indian woman, won the Nobel Peace Prize in 1992 for her advocacy of indigenous peoples' rights. Menchú saw her own family decimated by Guatemala's counterinsurgency war, which left over 200,000 dead or missing from 1960 to 1996. According to the UN-sponsored Commission on Historical Clarification (CEH, after the Spanish acronym) that investigated the atrocities, the army and associated paramilitary groups targeted indigenous communities as well as student, labor and religious figures considered to support leftist guerrillas. More than 600 villages were completely destroyed, and some 40,000 people disappeared.[1] The figures made the Chilean and even the Argentine cases pale in comparison. Menchú began exploring the options in Spain. A number of people counseled patience. "Let's not overload the boat," Joan Garcés advised, at least while the outcome of the Pinochet extradition was pending. Others insisted that, on the contrary, the time was ripe to push the doors of the Spanish courts open even further.

In December 1999, Rigoberta Menchú, together with Guatemalan groups of family members of those killed, Spanish labor unions, and solidarity groups, filed a complaint before the Audiencia Nacional charging eight people with genocide, terrorism, and torture.[2] The suspects include five generals, two police chiefs, and a colonel, among them former presidents and defense and interior ministers. The most notorious is General Efraín Ríos Montt, who took power in a coup in March 1982 and over the next eighteen months implemented a scorched earth policy. Ríos Montt continued to dominate Guatemalan politics for years, as president of Congress and a losing candidate in the 2003 presidential elections. Like Pinochet, he remains defiantly unapologetic about waging what he considers to be a successful war on communist subversion. Another suspect, Donaldo Alvarez Ruíz, former interior minister and head of the police, is in hiding outside the country (many say in the U.S.), while a third lives in Venezuela. The rest are free in Guatemala; one has parleyed his expertise into a private security business, while another served as mayor of a small town.

The complaint focused on a number of incidents as exemplars of genocide. Rigoberta Menchú's own family history was one. Her mother and brother were publicly tortured and killed by the army. Her father was burned alive when he, together with other peasant leaders, sat in at the Spanish Embassy in 1980 demanding an end to repression in the Mayan highland communities. Over the ambassador's protests, police shot incendiary bombs into the embassy, starting a fire that killed 39 people, including eight members of the embassy staff. The Spanish Embassy fire provided one tie to Spain, but there were others. Three Spanish priests, Faustino Villanueva, José María Gran Cuerra, and Juan Alonso Fernández, were assassinated in Guatemala, and a fourth, Carlos Pérez Alonso, disappeared. Additional complainants referenced several army massacres and individual murder and disappearance cases.

The Guatemalan complaint had several strengths. The magnitude and drama of the massacres in Guatemala was undeniable. The underlying acts, at least in part, concerned Spain, and family members of the slain Spanish priests were complainants. A wide variety of Spanish organizations, especially the leftist union confederation Comisiones Obreras, had signed on along with Guatemalan groups—nineteen complainants in all. As a matter of legal theory, it was much simpler to charge genocide in the Guatemalan case than in the Southern Cone cases, as the facts showed a clear pattern of targeting ethnically distinct people and the UN Commission's findings on genocide and on the military's responsibility had already paved the way. The existing precedents on Chile and Argentina also seemed to indicate that the Spanish courts would be receptive to the claims.

Indeed, on March 27, 2000, Judge Guillermo Ruíz Polanco accepted the complaint and agreed to open an investigation.[3] In his ruling, the judge noted the connections to Spain and found that the accused were directly involved in the crimes charged. "The events reported clearly show the appearance of genocide. And that is sufficient for now," said the judge's ruling. The genocide charges included both the targeting of ethnic Mayans and the intended elimination of a part of the "national" group due to its perceived ideology. The judge, like Judge Garzón before him, found that Spanish jurisdiction was appropriate because the local courts had not acted. While Guatemala had "original territorial jurisdiction," it was not exclusive.

In the absence of the honorable and effective exercise of [territorial] jurisdiction, it must be replaced by courts—such as Spain's—that uphold the universal prosecution of crimes against human rights. . . . There is no reason to presume that the petition for justice before the Spanish courts was made with caprice or frivolity. . . . Despite the big words, the reticence of states in the issues under consideration forces the victims of crimes against humanity, their heirs, their families and their legal representatives to bear a costly international legal pilgrimage due to the passivity—if not the complicity—of the territorial judges who should assume these cases in the first place.

Once Ruíz Polanco found jurisdiction, evidence gathering began. Documentary evidence began to pour in—newspaper articles, reports of exhumations of mass graves, death certificates. But by mid-2000 the political and legal climate had chilled noticeably in Spain. Pinochet had gone home and the Argentine and Chilean cases, while still open, assumed a lower profile. Bombings and assassinations carried out by the Basque separatist group ETA had nerves on edge. Furthermore, the International Criminal Court (ICC) now looked as if it might become a reality in the near future. Even though under the Court's statute it would not be able to consider pre-2000 crimes and thus would never consider the Guatemalan case, still, public opinion attributed more power to the nascent court than it actually had. The local press and pundits worried publicly about a deluge of cases turning the Spanish courts into a "mini-ICC" that would solve all the world's problems except Spain's. Ruíz Polanco began to reflect some of these hesitations. The judge demanded a hefty bond to admit a Guatemalan co-complainant. He refused to add more potential defendants and held off on hearing more than a few live witnesses.

Despite its strengths, Guatemala was a harder case in many ways than the earlier Southern Cone ones. Far less was known internationally about the atrocities in Guatemala, and Ríos Montt had never assumed the iconic status of a Pinochet. Europeans had protested U.S. intervention in Central America, but never in the numbers nor with the intensity that greeted the 1973 coup in Chile. There were far fewer Guatemalans than Argentines and Chileans living in exile in Spain and throughout Europe. Guatemalans who did live in Spain tended to be less educated and far less integrated into Spanish society, with less ability to move the necessary levers of politics and public opinion. In particular, there were no Guatemalan-related lawyers and activists living in Spain who could serve the "bridging" roles that Joan Garcés, Gregorio Dionis, and Carlos Slepoy had played in the Southern Cone cases. There was no one who had at once the intimate knowledge of recent Guatemalan history, the personal passion to pursue justice, and the ability to navigate Spanish law, politics, and public relations. Instead, the legal team had Guatemalan human rights lawyers based in Guatemala, Spanish and Argentine labor and criminal law specialists with limited knowledge of Guatemala (including eventually Slepoy and Galán from the Argentine legal team), and a non-lawyer liaison from the Menchú Foundation trying to knit it all together. The case got much less publicity, and while a sizable number of long-standing Spanish solidarity groups signed on as *acción popular*, the widespread support from Parliament, the press, and intellectuals that characterized the earlier cases was missing.

Guatemalan realities counseled caution as well. The transition from military rule there was far from complete and human rights activists and lawyers were continually threatened and harassed. The posture of the Guatemalan courts was murky. The 1996 Guatemalan Law of National

Reconciliation granted amnesty to those involved in the war, but, in response to UN urging, it excluded cases of genocide, torture, and disappearances (but not necessarily massacres).[4] The local courts up to that time had refused to apply the law in cases involving human rights violations, so there was no formal impediment to prosecution. Rather, courts had found ways to fail to investigate, to leave cases in legal limbo and to release defendants on obscure technicalities. The few convictions for human rights-related crimes were of the rank and file, not the higher-ups. Judges, prosecutors, and victims' lawyers were routinely threatened, and the system was notoriously corrupt. It was a case of de facto rather than de jure impunity.

Local groups pursued cases before the domestic courts despite the obstacles, including a case charging genocide against the same set of defendants. There was at first little coordination between the groups spearheading local actions and those focusing on the Spanish case, although it improved over time.

According to some observers, Menchú had launched her complaint precipitously, both to influence upcoming elections in Guatemala and because she feared that the Spanish forum might close. The complaint itself included vastly disparate incidents with no tight common thread among them, and relied heavily on the CEH's findings and the church-authored REHMI report on human rights violations. Any investigating magistrate would have been daunted by the thought of managing this case. Despite these difficulties, the Guatemalan complainants were confident that the Spanish courts would support them just as they had supported their Southern Cone counterparts.

Just as he had in the Southern Cone cases, the public prosecutor objected to the Spanish court's jurisdiction. Some of his arguments were identical to the earlier ones: the facts didn't support charges of genocide or terrorism; Spanish courts had no extraterritorial jurisdiction; this was retroactive application of law; a domestic amnesty law precluded prosecution. Others were specific to the Guatemalan situation: a diplomatic settlement between Spain and Guatemala meant that the Spanish Embassy massacre was not actionable; the 1996 peace accords provided for sufficient domestic truth seeking. On May 4, 2000, prosecutor Pedro Rubira appealed Ruíz Polanco's acceptance of jurisdiction.[5]

Over the summer of 2000, the Audiencia Nacional, acting as an appeals court, agreed that given the importance of the case they would hear it in full rather than sit as a panel. The public hearing, set for November 30, carried over to the next day. Thirteen days later, just before the Christmas holidays, the court ruled against the Guatemalans.[6] It held that "for the moment" Spanish courts had no jurisdiction over the alleged crimes, and that the case should be closed. The judges gave two reasons. First, while the Spanish courts could consider genocide and terrorism committed elsewhere by non-Spaniards, any such inquiry had to be subsidiary to the state where the crimes took place. Other national courts could act only if there were clear legal impediments to prosecution, or if judges were "subject to pressure from official or de facto powers that create a climate of intimidation or fear making it impossible to carry out the judicial function with the serenity and impartiality required." Second, since the CEH had only published its report in 1999 and the Law of National Reconciliation permitted genocide prosecutions, there was insufficient evidence in the record that the Guatemalan courts were not able or willing to do the job themselves. Therefore, Spanish courts should stay out of the case. It was not difficult to see the decision as a signal that the courts were uninterested in broadening the opening provided by the Southern Cone cases. Others alleging genocide need not apply.

The decision sparked a vigorous debate among the lawyers and complainants groups. Now what? There were two options: appeal or wait and refile the case. Appeal was to the Spanish Supreme Court, widely considered more conservative than the Audiencia Nacional. Pursuing an appeal was risky. Not only could the court close off the possibility of ever refiling the Guatemalan case in Spain, but it could overturn the existing jurisprudence of the Argentine and Chilean cases, destroy the pending cases against Scilingo and Cavallo, and close off many if not all future possibilities of access. For some people, an appeal would give the public prosecutor, and by extension the Aznar government, just the opportunity they had been waiting for. Far better, these people said, to document better both the inactivity of the Guatemalan courts and the exact contours of the case, and then go back to the investigating judge, who was obviously sympathetic, and start again. Others argued that in Guatemala this would be seen as an admission of defeat, and would discourage those trying to break through the wall of impunity at home. Moreover, it would leave intact a crabbed interpretation of the Spanish law on extraterritorial prosecution of genocide, one that ignored the text of Spanish law. An appeal would also open up the possibility of further appeals to the Constitutional Court or, eventually, the European Court of Human Rights, where a more favorable decision might be possible. It was important to push as far as possible, and not give up so easily, said these advocates. After a series of personal and e-mail consultations among the lawyers, experts, and complainant groups, the latter position prevailed and an appeal was filed.

The Supreme Court, recognizing the importance of the issue, agreed to hear the case *en banc* (as a whole), and heard oral argument in July 2002. A decision expected in September 2002 was put off indefinitely as rumors of internal disagreement swirled. On February 25, 2003, over two years after the Audiencia Nacional decision, the fears of those who doubted the wisdom of an appeal came partially true.[7] The Spanish Supreme Court, by a vote of 8–7, overturned in part the Audiencia Nacional decision and gutted Spain's universal jurisdiction law. The majority held, in short, that only cases with a clear tie to Spain could proceed. The case was reopened and remanded to pursue investigations into the possible torture of Spanish citizens in the 1980 Embassy massacre, and the torture of the four Spanish priests killed by the military in 1980 through 1982. All the genocide and terrorism charges and the torture charges against non-Spaniards were dismissed. While the Spanish courts remained open for cases involving victims of Spanish ancestry (and perhaps for refugees residing in Spain), as a situs for universal justice they were no longer an option.

The majority opinion largely follows the arguments of the Spanish government's prosecutors' office. The opinion first quickly disposes of the Audiencia Nacional's inquiry into the availability of an alternative forum which, the Court found, was inappropriate. "Basing subsidiarity on the real or apparent inactivity of local courts implies a judgment of one state's courts about the ability to administer justice of the similarly situated organs of another sovereign state." While such an "unable or unwilling" inquiry might be appropriate for an ICC, national courts should not be making these kinds of judgments, which could have an important effect on foreign relations and should be left to the political branches.

Next, the majority construed the 1948 Genocide Convention. The court found, as the Southern Cone cases had held, that article 6 of the Convention was not limited to territorial and international criminal jurisdictions. However, article 8 directs states to respond to genocide occurring outside their borders by going to the UN, not by exercising universal jurisdiction. The presence of a UN mission showed that the UN knew about conditions in Guatemala, yet had failed to create an ad hoc tribunal along the lines of those in Yugoslavia or Rwanda.

The heart of the matter, for the majority, was that article 23.4 of the LOPD, despite its apparent clarity, could not be so open-ended as to allow criminal investigations based on news of crimes being committed anywhere in the world. Spanish law had to conform to other principles of international law, including respect for other states' sovereignty and the principle of non-intervention in the internal affairs of other states. Extraterritorial jurisdiction, when not authorized by the UN or specifically regulated by treaty, required a point of contact with national interests. The majority cited cases from the German and Belgian courts, and the ICJ's *Arrest Warrant (Congo v. Belgium)* case (discussed later), in support of these propositions. The court pointed to the "extradite or prosecute" provisions of a number of treaties, including the Torture and Terrorism Conventions, as requiring the presence of the defendant to proceed when there is no other type of national interest (like the protective principle or active or passive personality principles) involved. A connection to a state interest, the majority opined, creates legitimacy and rationality in international relations and respect for the non-intervention principle. What is more, this connection to a national interest should exist in the principal charges against the defendant, not just in related or ancillary ones. For that reason, all the genocide charges were bad—none of the defendants were present and there was no allegation that genocide had been aimed at Spaniards as a group. Only the torture charges, to the extent they involved Spanish citizens, could stand, because the Convention Against Torture allows for passive personality jurisdiction.

The seven dissenters started from the position that universal jurisdiction in cases of genocide was necessary to avoid impunity, and that in such cases the state acted in representation of the international community. The majority's view was too restrictive and, therefore, "incompatible with the treatment of this grave crime in our internal law and in international law." It ignored the legislative intent and the language of article 23.4, as well as international law. It confused passive personality and universal jurisdiction, left any extraterritorial prosecution of genocide practically impossible, confused the treaty-based section (g) of the statute with the rest, and converted the minimum requirements of treaties into a maximum. On international law, the majority ignored a later, and contrary, German Supreme Court decision, misconstrued the ICJ's *Arrest Warrant* case (which had only dealt with immunity), ignored the Belgian court's subsequent upholding of a non-presence-based universal jurisdiction law in *Sharon*, and failed to cite a number of other relevant cases (including the British House of Lords decision in *Pinochet*) in support of Europe's widespread acceptance of a broad view of universal jurisdiction.

The dissent answered the majority's concern about chaos in the international system by superimposing a necessity criterion, such that no extraterritorial intervention was needed where the domestic courts were doing the job. That criterion, however, could not be based on the court's inactivity, which was too hard to measure and too politically charged at an early stage in the proceedings. Rather, any limits had to come from a flexible, prudential rule of reason aimed merely at practical concerns like the potential effectiveness of an investigation and extradition request or a potentially high burden on the Spanish courts. For the dissenters, a tie to Spain was merely an aid in applying this rule of reason, not a jurisdictional prerequisite. In this case, they found more than enough links to Spain to justify the Spanish courts' intervention. The countries were linked by historic, social, linguistic and jurispruden-tial ties. The crimes at issue involved Spanish citizens, not as victims themselves of genocide, but as victims targeted because they were defending others from genocide. This case was a paradigmatic example of those where Spain *should* exercise its jurisdiction: there would never be a more compelling case. "If there is no nexus in this case, then a nexus requirement becomes a mere pretext to exclude or suppress uni-versal jurisdiction in all genocide cases." That, the dissenters argued, should not be done.

A second case reaffirmed the need for a tight nexus requirement. On March 8, 2004, a panel of the Spanish Supreme Court reaffirmed its *Guatemala* holding in a case involving Chilean General Hernán Brady.[8] The Court allowed the case to move forward because the victim, Car-melo Soria, was of Spanish nationality. The repetition means that the Court's limited view of universal jurisdiction now has jurisprudential value.[9] It will be followed when it decides pending challenges to Spanish jurisdiction in the cases of Argentine torturers Adolfo Scilingo and Ricardo Cavallo.[10] If so, trial should be allowed to proceed, as there were numerous victims of Spanish descent killed or disappeared in the Naval Mechanics School (ESMA) where the two men worked.

The Court also grappled with the argument that the Spanish courts were "subsidiary" to the territorial courts or an international criminal court. On May 20, 2003, a three-judge panel of the Spanish Supreme Court affirmed the dismissal of a case alleging genocide, terrorism, tor-ture, and arbitrary detention against ex-presidents Alan García and Alberto Fujimori, ex-General Vladimiro Montecinos, and other high-ranking government officials in Peru.[11] The Peruvian complaint, like the Guatemalan, was based on the universal jurisdiction provisions of Span-ish law and argued that the Peruvian courts were not investigating the crimes. The panel's decision backtracked slightly from the harshness of the majority's ruling in the *Guatemala* case. It restated the Spanish courts' ability to judge genocide cases based on universal jurisdiction, and reaffirmed the Audiencia Nacional's rulings in the Argentine and Chilean cases.

The panel in the Peru case characterized the issue as one not of sub-sidiarity but of the "principle of necessity of jurisdictional intervention." To evaluate necessity, the Court considered whether the territorial courts were exercising *effective* jurisdiction. It looked to whether the events at issue were *in fact* the subject of prosecution, without attempting to analyze why or why not or to evaluate the existence of a state of de facto impunity. In the Peruvian case, investigations against several of the defendants were proceeding in local courts, and suspects were in jail or had fled the jurisdiction (the case with ex-president Fujimori). Thus, for the time being, Spanish prosecution was inappropriate.

Bouterse and the Conservatism of National Law

Not all the countries in Latin America were once colonies of Spain or Portugal. Suriname, for instance, was a Dutch colony. Many Surinamese over the years migrated to the Netherlands, and Surinamese residents often had dual nationality. Suriname was governed during the early 1980s by a military regime that brooked no dissent. On the night of December 8, 1982, fifteen people, including one Dutch national, were arrested, tortured, and summarily executed by the military government, under the command of Désiré Bouterse. The victims were prominent opposition figures. The official story was that they had been arrested for plotting a coup and shot while trying to escape, but witnesses contradicted the "attempted escape" theory.

Relatives of the victims, unable to get a hearing in Suriname, asked the Amsterdam Court of Appeals to order prosecution of Bouterse in the Netherlands.[12] Unlike Spain, the Netherlands has no procedure for victims to initiate criminal proceedings directly, although they can join in to ask for compensation once an investigation starts (and can appeal a prosecutor's decision not to prosecute). The Court, facing a novel issue, asked international law expert John Dugard to advise whether the customary law on torture or crimes against humanity would allow the court to prosecute these acts, especially given the fact that the Netherlands only became a party to the Convention Against Torture (and passed its implementing legislation) after the acts in question. This was, of course, the same issue that had troubled the House of Lords in *Pinochet* in the extradition context. The Court of Appeals, based on Dugard's reply, backed the position of Lord Millet in *Pinochet III*.[13] The court allowed the prosecution because torture violated Dutch law on assault, as well as customary international law, long before 1982, and all the Torture Convention did was codify the existing rules and create a new procedure. Therefore, retrospective application of the Convention's rules on extraterritorial jurisdiction did not violate the principle of legality or nonretroactivity of law. Furthermore, the Court added, there were good reasons to allow prosecution of this case in the Netherlands: the case would not be prosecuted at home, the events in question had shocked public opinion in the Netherlands, some of the victims had Dutch nationality (Netherlands law, like Spanish, does not contemplate jurisdiction based simply on the victims' nationality), and the complainants live in the Netherlands. The Dutch courts had a good claim to jurisdiction.[14]

On September 18, 2001, the Dutch Supreme Court reversed.[15] The court found that under the Netherlands legal system, retrospective application of the 1988 Torture Act would violate the principle of legality. The court found that, while torture may have been a crime under Dutch law and customary international law before that time, the courts could do nothing about it because they had no extraterritorial jurisdiction before the Torture Convention implementing legislation was passed. This exactly paralleled the majority's view in *Pinochet III*. Even though Dutch law theoretically allowed the direct incorporation of international law into national law, customary (unwritten) international law did not override contrary statutory provisions. The Court (mis)read the customary law at issue to be the possibility of retroactive application of the prohibition on torture. The court looked to the legislative history of the implementing law to support its holding that it could not apply before 1989. The court also chose to apply the statute of limitations in force for domestic assault, which had long since passed. The more extended statute of limitations applicable to torture, like the substantive offense, was only codified after the events in question and so could not be applied retroactively. Thus the statute of limitations barred the prosecution.

The "retroactivity" problem has two variants: when the conduct investigated took place before the investigating state ratified the treaties that allow for extraterritorial jurisdiction, or when it happened before the domestic laws changed to authorize extraterritorial prosecutions, codify crimes, or extend statutes of limitations. The Dutch courts have not been alone in grappling with the question of whether either of those two cases constitutes "retroactive" or ex post facto application of law, which would violate the basic principles of legality. There has been no unanimous response.

Those courts that have not found retroactivity an insurmountable obstacle follow the reasoning of the Dutch Court of Appeals, distinguishing between the underlying criminal conduct and the provisions allowing for extraterritorial jurisdiction over that conduct. The reason for insisting on nonretroactive justice is that defendants must have adequate notice of what conduct is prohibited, and governments must not be allowed to come along after the fact and criminalize politically inconvenient acts or actors. But in cases of torture, disappearance, and mass murder, it is difficult to imagine that notice of criminality is lacking, and indeed, the underlying acts have been prohibited in national and international law for quite some time. As a matter of international law, at least the prohibitions on genocide, war crimes, and crimes against humanity (including systematic torture) date back over fifty years. Therefore, this is not *retroactive* but *retrospective* law. The Spanish courts followed this approach in the Chilean and Argentine cases.

The Supreme Court also limited the reach of the Dutch Implementing Act of the Torture Convention. Article 5 extends the courts' jurisdiction to "any person who commits outside the Netherlands one of the offenses described," but the *Bouterse* court read the section to require a "point of contact" with the Netherlands, either presence or nationality/residence. Meanwhile, as with other transnational investigations, this one too triggered a preliminary judicial proceeding in Suriname. The Court of Appeals noted that if such a domestic proceeding were to prosper, it would suspend the Dutch proceedings. To date, however, the Surinamese case seems not to have progressed.

The Hissène Habré case and the Politics of Prosecution

Chileans and Argentines prosecuted in Spain, Rwandans in Belgium— the pattern seemed obvious to those opposed to transnational prosecutions. "It's an act of colonialism," thundered the right-wing National Renovation Party in Chile.[16] Indeed, it did seem like a group of developed country, often ex-colonial country, courts were judging a group of developing country defendants. This imbalance may necessarily be a fact of life, at least for now—after all, it is easier to keep track of dictators who travel to rich countries, where the exile and activist networks that sustain investigations tend to be strongest—but it is an uncomfortable fact. A truly universal system of justice would be more balanced.

So it was with great interest that Reed Brody, advocacy director of the New York-based organization Human Rights Watch, listened to Delphine Djiraibe. Djiraibe, president of the Chadian Association for the Promotion and Defense of Human Rights, wanted help in bringing Chad's former dictator Hissène Habré to justice for massive violations of human rights.[17] From 1982 to 1990, Habré periodically targeted various ethnic groups, killed political prisoners, and ran a political police accused of torture and murder. A subsequent Truth Commission accused his regime of committing crimes against humanity, although it was unable to investigate fully. The new, post-1990 government was headed by Habré's former chief of staff and defense minister, and it was naturally disinclined to investigate or prosecute the crimes of its predecessor. A Chadian Association of Victims of Political Repression and Crime had compiled dossiers on 792 cases, but had been unable to advance domestic prosecutions. Most interestingly, Habré had fled, not to a European country, but to Senegal. This would be the first attempt to prosecute a former African head of state in his place of refuge. If it

worked, there was a long line of other African dictators and their hench-
men who were then living in nearby states, including Idi Amin of
Uganda (living in Saudi Arabia) and Mengistu Haile Mariam of Ethiopia
(living in Zimbabwe), who might begin to feel unwanted in their new
homes.

Brody and the Chadians agreed that Senegal seemed a promising
place to bring a case based on universal jurisdiction. It had a relatively
independent judiciary, a stable democracy, and had demonstrated leadership in human rights. It was the first country to ratify the Statute of
the ICC, and had been a party to the Torture Convention since 1986. A
successful prosecution could serve as an example to other African states
that Africa could deal with its own, and dispel the notion that only ex-
colonial powers were interested in bringing dictators to justice.

Reed Brody, in a 2001 article, tells what happened:

International researchers visited Chad twice, where they met the remaining
faithful of the moribund Association of Victims who provided them with the
thousands of pages of documentation they had prepared in 1991, and had kept
in hiding when the government changed its mind on digging up the past. Working in secret, because of fears that someone, including Chadian officials, might
tip off Habré who could then flee Senegal for a more protective shelter, the
researchers were introduced to victims and potential witnesses and sought documentation of Habré's crimes. Meanwhile, Human Rights Watch quietly organized a coalition of Chadian, Senegalese and international NGOs to support the
complaint, as well as a group of Senegalese lawyers to represent the victims. The
coalition decided to bring the case as a private prosecution rather than presenting the evidence to Senegalese authorities and requesting a state prosecution.[18]

Seven Chadians and the Victims Association filed a complaint on January 25, 2000 in Dakar Regional Court charging Habré with torture, bar-
barous acts (a crime under Senegalese law), and crimes against
humanity, including forced disappearances. By chance, the case fell to
investigating magistrate Demba Kandji, who had advanced education
and training in international human rights law. Kandji moved quickly to
get the state prosecutor's advice, to hear testimony, and to summon
Habré and indict him on initial charges of being an accomplice to torture, leaving open the possibility of further charges to follow. Judge Kandji sent letters rogatory to Chad, asking a Chadian judge to interview
witnesses there, and heard testimony from ex-political prisoners who
told of Habré's visits to prisons and presence during torture sessions.

The victims' initial euphoria was short-lived, however. In February,
Habré's lawyers filed a motion to dismiss the case before the Court of
Appeals, alleging lack of jurisdiction. More ominously, the Senegalese
press began portraying the ex-dictator as the victim of a French-Ameri-
can plot and not such a villain after all. There were indications that

Habré was spending some of the millions he was accused of stealing from Chad in the public relations effort. "We learned that you have to build the case in public opinion before building it at court. We started doing this too late, and Habré's lawyers and friends got there first," recounted Pascal Kambale, a lawyer for the complainants, at a conference in March 2001.[19]

The political climate soon got worse. In March 2000, Senegal elected a new president, Abdoulaye Wade, whose advisor on justice issues was none other than Habré's defense counsel. The government's attitude toward the prosecution quickly worsened. Government attorneys, previously supportive of the complainants, now supported dismissal. The Superior Council of Magistrates, headed by the president, transferred Judge Kandji off the investigation to a new post and promoted the appeals court judge hearing the case. The signs were clear and accurate. On July 4, 2000, the appeals court dismissed the charges against Habré.

The court found that Senegalese courts had no jurisidiction over extra-territorial torture. Senegal had ratified the Torture Convention, but it had never made the prosecution of torture part of its domestic criminal law, and therefore the Convention's obligations to extradite or prosecute suspected torturers were not effective in local courts. The court rejected the argument that Senegal's constitution automatically made international treaties part of domestic law, finding that although that may generally be true, penal law, because it can affect individual liberties, requires full translation into the penal code. The court also rejected the use of the customary international law prohibiting crimes against humanity, because, like torture, these crimes had not been codified as such in the local penal code. Months later, on March 20, 2001, the Cour de Cassation affirmed.[20]

The case, like *Bouterse*, was a clear reminder of the unfinished state of affairs in international law. True, Senegal was a leader in signing and ratifying treaties, but without domestic implementing laws, it was hard to make use of them in the local courts. One of the lessons of *Habré* in Senegal is that even civil law judges will be much more comfortable, especially in the criminal setting, if substantive treaty provisions have been translated to the penal and procedural codes, with appropriate penalties attached. Even where judges could, under domestic law, apply customary international law principles, most (although not all) will be reluctant to do so in a case involving individual criminal defendants. They want codification.

Moreover, law was uncomfortably subject to political decisions to quash cases: the *New York Times* July 21 editorial on the case denounced what "looks suspiciously like interference from the country's new president." The Executive Branch in Senegal had achieved what Spain's conservative government could not: sink a judicial inquiry.

While to date governments seem to be much more willing to intervene to quash than to promote investigations, the Senegalese experience in the Habré case highlighted one of the key worries of skeptics on universal jurisdiction: governments could equally push courts to investigate where such investigation was not warranted. After all, not all courts are equally independent or equally free of pressure or equally solicitous of the rights of the accused and the victims. In the hands of the wrong court, a prosecution could turn into either a witchhunt or a whitewash. On the other hand, the same is true for prosecutions based on any other ground of jurisdiction. Most politicized or unfair trials are run-of-the-mill territorial affairs, and in these no one argues that the courts have no jurisdiction. Instead, rules to determine what constitutes a fair trial, basic but still meaningful, can be found in the core global and regional treaties on human rights and the dozens of Guidelines, Principles and other such documents crafted by international lawyers and judges over the years.[21] The rules specify such bedrock principles as an independent judiciary, the accused's right to a lawyer and to not incriminate himself, the rule against ex post facto charges, and the like. If states implementing universal jurisdiction fail to respect those rules, they can be challenged and criticized just as they would be for any other type of prosecution.

The victims and their supporters, horribly disappointed by the Senegalese dismissal, took solace in the increased visibility of the issue within Chad. As in Chile and Argentina, the transnational prosecution galvanized local efforts. In September, the president of Chad met with the Association of Victims, expressed his disappointment with the decision, and promised support for their cases within Chad and access to previously inaccessible evidence. In October 2000, seventeen victims lodged criminal complaints for torture, murder, and disappearances against members of the former political police. Dozens of cases filed against individual torturers have followed. Initially dismissed on grounds that a 1993 law ousted the regular courts of jurisdiction, in April 2001 the Constitutional Council reinstated the complaints and found that the 1993 law should be withdrawn.[22] In May 2001, the Chadian government authorized NGO researchers to search the former secret police premises. They found thousands of archived pages documenting the repression, which are now being analyzed for future prosecutions. The continuing limits of domestic prosecution became clear early on, however, when the office of the prosecutor handling the file was ransacked, and victims' lawyer Jacqueline Moudeïna was attacked and badly injured by a potential defendant.

With the help of the international committee of NGO supporters (including Human Rights Watch and the International Federation for Human Rights), the victims' association decided to continue with efforts to investigate and try Habré outside Chad. The Belgian courts seemed the best possibility: Belgium had excellent legislation on universal jurisdiction and French-speaking magistrates. The only problem was that any Belgian investigation was likely to take some time. Meanwhile, with no outstanding warrant against him, Habré was free to go, and likely to quickly find a more sheltered haven.

The human rights lawyers sought ways to pressure the Senegalese authorities to keep Habré in his adopted home until a Belgian warrant could be issued. They lobbied the Committee Against Torture, a United Nations expert body in charge of monitoring compliance with the Torture Convention, to find that Senegal's compliance with the treaty depended on not letting Habré slip away.[23] Eventually, UN Secretary General Kofi Annan issued a personal plea to the Senegalese president. With international scrutiny and criticism of the Senegalese courts growing, President Wade agreed that Senegal would hold Habré pending an extradition request from a Belgian judge.

The *Habré* case in Belgium was assigned to investigating magistrate Daniel Fransen. In the spring of 2002, he traveled to Chad to investigate the charges against Habré. Survivors of torture and secret detention came to the worn courthouse in N'Djamena, the Chadian capital, to testify before Fransen. He also traveled to the sites of mass graves and five hidden detention centers, including one on the grounds of the ex-presidential compound. He moved around the dusty capital with a prosecutor, four Belgian policemen, and a court clerk. The judge's visit again energized the victims. "Before, everyone thought we were just a bunch of crazy people. Now, they can see that Habré could go on trial for his crimes," Souleymane Guengueng, now the head of the victims' association, told a Canadian reporter.[24]

Reed Brody accompanied Judge Fransen in Chad. He recalls one particular incident involving Ismael Hachim, an ethnic minority prisoner held for seventeen months in a covered-over swimming pool turned underground prison. When Hachim got out of jail upon Habré's overthrow, the officers who had arrested him told him that it was Touka Haliki, Habré's director of intelligence, who had ordered his arrest and torture. It was only in 2001, when Hachim got access to his personal secret police file, that he could be sure. Haliki, still a police supervisor, was one of those Judge Fransen called in to testify, and when Haliki denied involvement in the persecution of the Zaghawa minority group, the judge called Hachim to encounter Haliki face-to-face. When Haliki still claimed his innocence, Hachim whipped out the document in which Haliki ordered his arrest and another in which Haliki signed off on Hachim's interrogation. "In that moment, he became very small, and I became very tall," explained Hachim to all who would listen."Even if he is never prosecuted, I now feel like some justice has been done. That's what this is really about, isn't it?"[25]

The case against Habré in the Belgian courts continues as of this writing. Both Senegal and Chad have indicated that they have no objection to an extradition request from Belgian authorities. But the case is one of only three to survive the 2003 reform of Belgium's universal jurisdiction law.

Yerodia, Sharon, and the Reform of Belgium's Universal Jurisdiction Law

The 1999 Belgian law went farther than any other to date. It allowed "pure" universal jurisdiction, that is, jurisdiction that does not require the presence of the defendant to open an investigation. It also allowed anyone, even plaintiffs who did not live in Belgium, to bring charges, and it explicitly ruled out any immunity from prosecution, even for sitting heads of state. Predictably, it generated a great deal of business for the Belgian criminal courts. An early complaint, originally filed in November 1998 (at the same time as the Belgian complaint against Pinochet) charged Abdulaye Yerodia Ndombasi with grave breaches of the Geneva Conventions and crimes against humanity. The complainants were mostly Congolese exiles living in Belgium; five were Belgian citizens. They charged that, as part of the Laurent Kabila government's efforts to expel an ethnically Tutsi rebel force in the Eastern Democratic Republic of the Congo (DRC), top officials in that government, including Kabila himself, Yerodia Ndombasi, and two others, publicly called for acts of violence against the "invaders." Some of their incendiary speeches were captured on TV tape. Their calls were soon answered by a wave of lynchings, arrests, and persecution of Tutsis throughout the DRC.

After a year's investigation and with the approval of the state prosecutor, on April 11, 2000, Judge Vandermeersch issued an arrest warrant for Yerodia as author or co-author of war crimes and crimes against humanity. There was only one small problem: at the time he issued the warrant (although not when the acts took place) Yerodia was foreign minister of the DRC. Judge Vandermeersch recognized the potential awkwardness of a foreign minister trying to do his job with an Interpol warrant out for his arrest. He noted that while under Belgian law there was no reason to preclude the ability of the courts to try the case, execution of the arrest warrant had to be stayed while the suspect was a state representative on an official visit. To do otherwise would impermissibly gum up the works of international diplomacy and tread on the rights of the state, not just the individual. However, there was a point to issuing the warrant even if it could not be executed: it allowed the judge to compile a dossier of information about the alleged crime that would be available once the defendant no longer held a diplomatic post. Vandermeersch also notified the Congolese courts of the case, but they made no effort (not surprisingly) to open their own investigation.

The DRC did react, however. On October 17, 2000, the Congolese government filed a complaint with the International Court of Justice, the venerable tribunal for legal disputes between states. It accused Belgium of overstepping its authority, violating the customary law principle that a state may not exercise its authority on the territory of another state, and trampling on the rules about the immunity of foreign ministers from suit. It asked the court to tell Belgium to quash the arrest warrant.

By the time the case came before the court, Yerodia was no longer part of the Congolese government and that government had dropped its objections to universal jurisdiction in general to focus on the immunity issue. Belgian lawyers argued that since Yerodia was no long entitled to immunity, the case was moot and should be dismissed. Not so, said the DRC. It was still an affront to them that their foreign minister had been so badly treated, and the arrest warrant was still pending against him.

The ICJ decision, announced on Valentine's Day, February 14, 2002, vindicated the DRC position.[26] The Court ordered Belgium to rescind the arrest warrant against Yerodia. The Court, against the wishes of some of the judges, focused entirely on the immunity issue. A majority found that customary law protected sitting heads of state, heads of government and diplomats in their personal capacities. It also covered sitting foreign ministers who needed to travel freely in order to carry out their duties. In other words, they enjoyed a functional immunity from civil or criminal suit in another country. The presence of specific provisions denying immunity in international instruments like the Statutes of the ad hoc tribunals and the ICC only covered those specific tribunals and did not apply to national courts.

This was arguably not true at all, since many of the immunity-denying instruments were aimed at national as well as international courts. However, the Court then went much further, muddying up again the little bit that the House of Lords had left reasonably clear. First, the Court ignored the nature of the charged crimes and the customary law that certain international crimes had to be prosecuted no matter who the suspect was. Second, the ICJ found four situations under which immunities under international law would not bar prosecution: when the national state institutes proceedings against its own officials; when it waives their immunity before another state; when the case is before an international criminal court; or, "in respect to acts committed prior or subsequent to his or her period of office, as well as in respect of acts committed during that period of office in a private capacity."

The first two were unlikely to arise: after all, if the home state were willing to prosecute, what would be the point of going elsewhere? The language about private acts was particularly problematic. How would it apply in the case of a Pinochet or other high-ranking official? Did the Court's language about private acts mean that they could be tried for murder committed during a fit of pique, but not for a deliberate policy of state-sponsored murder? Could torture or summary execution ever be "private" when their definition involves persons acting in an official capacity? Even international crimes that do not explicitly require an element of official action as part of the crime would usually be carried out as part of an ex-minister's public, not private, functions. If read to preclude prosecution in those cases, the Court's decision set the law back decades and contravened much national and international jurisprudence (and state diplomatic efforts) on the subject.

A trio of judges on the Court, each with a long and distinguished career protecting human rights, saw the problem clearly. In a separate opinion,[27] they tried to minimize the damage by suggesting that international crimes, by their very nature, could never constitute anything but private (unofficial) acts, and so no issue of immunity arose once the personal immunity of a sitting minister or head of state no longer applied. Therefore, former heads of state, ministers and the like could be arrested and tried for such acts. If this is true, then the Court's decision creates no great impediment to current practice, but the terminology deeming large-scale ethnically or politically motivated killings "private" remains both unnecessary and a little strange.

The *Arrest Warrant* case left for another day the question of whether universal jurisdiction was an unacceptable infringement on sovereignty. That day was not long in coming. On December 9, 2002, the Congo (Brazzaville, next door to the DRC) filed a complaint in the ICJ arising from the prosecution in France of its President, Minister of the Interior, Inspector General of the Army and and captain of the presidential guard, on charges of crimes against humanity and torture stemming from the killing and disappearance of over 350 refugees on the shores of the Congo River in May 1999 (known as the "disappeared of the Beach" case).[28] The army inspector general, Norbert Dabira, had a house in France that he visited regularly, which allowed a local French magistrate to open a criminal investigation. The case, as framed, directly challenged the French effort to use universal jurisdiction to prosecute the defendants "for crimes allegedly committed in connection with the exercise of his powers for the maintenance of public order." The case is ongoing as this book goes to press.

While the *Yerodia* case returned to the Belgian indictment chamber to determine whether a new arrest warrant was in order, new cases took center stage. Several of them were explosive. Cumulatively they would determine the fate of the 1999 law. Rather than focus on obscure defendants in little-known conflicts, they forced the Belgian courts to metaphorically stick their head into the lion's mouth of global politics, with predictable results. Of these, perhaps the most explosive was the case filed against Israeli Prime Minister Ariel Sharon.

The *Sharon* case began on June 18, 2001, when 23 Lebanese-Palestinian complainants, only one resident in Belgium, filed a complaint against Ariel Sharon, at the time defense minister and now prime minister of Israel, and Amos Yaron, then the commander of Israeli forces in Lebanon and now CEO of the Israeli Defense Forces, along with other Israeli military officials and members of the Phalange Lebanese militia. The complaint alleged that Sharon, Yaron, and the others had committed war crimes, crimes against humanity, and genocide by allowing Lebanese militiamen to murder hundreds of innocent civilians in the Sabra and Shatila refugee camps during Israel's 1982 invasion of Lebanon. They pointed as evidence to an Israeli commission of inquiry that had found Sharon "indirectly responsible."

The Belgian investigating magistrates recognized full well the explosive political implications of investigating Israel's head of state, but felt constrained by the requirements of Belgian criminal procedure to open a file, after first getting the approval of the state prosecutor. The decision set off an outcry. The *Sharon* case seemed the worst possible test case: a high-profile, powerful, controversial defendant, a current head of state, no ties to Belgium to speak of, no cooperation from the state where the defendant resided or where the crimes were committed. As Israel pointed out, the Israelis had delved extensively into the case, Sharon had lost his job, and there had been at least an implicit decision that criminal prosecution was not warranted. On the other hand, there was plenty of evidence tying the suspects to awful crimes. How could the complainants' lawyers tell their clients that their suffering and the loss of their family members was too politically sensitive and not worth trying every possible legal avenue to redress?

In a June 26, 2002 decision, the Brussels Court of Appeals first reaffirmed that a law establishing Belgian jurisdiction over international crimes committed outside Belgium by non-Belgians (that is, under universal jurisdiction) was not per se invalid. It was, however, subject to the requirement that the defendant be present on Belgian soil.[29] Ariel

Sharon, presumably, was not to be found in Belgium. In that case, the court found, the case could not be heard and should be dismissed. The Court of Cassation in February 2003 confirmed the dismissal, but now on immunity grounds, following the ICJ majority opinion. However, it allowed the case against other defendants, including Amos Yaron, to go forward.

The *Sharon* case raised the profile of Belgium's universal jurisdiction law and its potential for discomfiting the powerful. More high-profile cases found their way into the courts. In the context of the buildup of war in Iraq and fierce European opposition to U.S. government actions there, a group of Iraqis in March 2003 sued former president George H. E. W. Bush, Richard Cheney, Colin Powell, and Norman Schwarzkopf for bombing an air raid shelter in Baghdad during the 1991 Gulf War.[30] In May, another complaint accused General Tommy Franks and other U.S. officials of war crimes committed during the 2003 invasion of Iraq.[31]

This was too much. Even Foreign Minister Michel, a supporter of the Belgian law, called the Franks suit an abuse of the law. With the U.S. threatening to pull NATO meetings out of Belgium and Defense Secretary Donald Rumsfield publicly fuming at Belgian effrontery, the Parliament acted. Since January 2003, the Belgian Senate had been working on a series of amendments to the law. Now the legislature quickly passed a sweeping package of changes designed to curb the use of the Belgian courts. In August 2003, in the face of continuing U.S. pressure the incoming government coalition agreed to amend the law still further, to make it even more difficult to use in cases not related to Belgium through nationality or the place of the crime.

One change harmonized Belgian law with the international law on immunity (that is, the ICJ decision in the *Arrest Warrant* case). The most important changes concern the issues of links to the forum, executive discretion, and the relationship to other jurisdictions.[32] A case cannot be opened unless there is a link between the crime and Belgium: either the suspect must be Belgian, or the victim must be Belgian or resident in Belgium for at least three years, or a treaty (e.g., the Torture Convention) must require prosecution, for example when the suspect is present in Belgium. Victims can now file suit directly (as *partie civil*) only if the accused is Belgian or lives in Belgium. Otherwise, the decision to investigate lies entirely with the state prosecutor or, in some cases, the office of public prosecutions. The prosecutor is obliged to proceed unless, among other reasons, in the interests of justice and in keeping with Belgium's international obligations, the case should instead be brought in another jurisdiction, where the administration of justice is independent and impartial. The decision not to proceed cannot be challenged. These last provisions seemed tailormade to get rid of the cases against Israelis and Americans and likely to produce negotiations over what the interests of justice consist of in every new case.

Belgian and international lawyers and NGOs protested that the law was being gutted based simply on U.S. antipathy to any kind of international justice, and that the proposed reforms went too far. A few pending cases, including *Habré*, were "grandfathered in" because the investigations were at an advanced stage, but most were not.

Tightening Up State Control: Links and Presence

Along a number of different axes and in a number of countries, the law has been reduced and tightened up. Both judges and legislators seem to be reacting to a sense that universal jurisdiction without specified limits is too unbounded, too subject to confusion when more than one jurisdiction can prosecute the same course of conduct. In an effort to create an orderly process of prioritization faced with the theoretical possibility of multiple prosecutions for the same course of action, Spain and Belgium, through different means, have in effect superimposed a nationality tie (or at least something close to it) on something they are still calling universal jurisdiction. The partial closing of the Spanish and Belgian forums leaves few states with universal jurisdiction provisions that do not require either the presence of the defendant or a nationality (or at least long-term residency) link. The German universal jurisdiction law, for example, on its face requires no link to Germany in cases of genocide, crimes against humanity and war crimes. However, section 153f of the Code of Crimes Against International Law directs the public prosecutor to excercise discretion to avoid cases where there is no tie to Germany (nationality, presence, or anticipated presence), and to defer to an international court or to a state with ties to the crime, the defendant, or the victim that intends to extradite. The law does, however, allow cases without a nationality or presence link in extraordinary circumstances.[33] South Africa and Canada allow universal jurisdiction where either the perpetrator or victim is a citizen or resident or the perpetrator is present.[34]

The practical effect on existing cases may not be great. In the Argentine, Chilean and Guatemalan cases in Spain, for instance, there are Spanish victims; in Belgium, the ongoing Rwandan and Chadian (Habré) cases, among others, involve Belgian citizens and long-time residents. But the conceptual effect is much more serious. The re-imposition of a nationality tie in effect negates the whole point of universal jurisdiction, reducing it to a simple variant on passive personality jurisdiction. There are in general preferences in the law for judicial forums with close ties, of some sort, to the subject matter of a case, out of practical concerns for the ability of a court to actually try the case. But if universal jurisdiction exists at all because these crimes are of concern to all states, why should any additional tie be necessary as a jurisdictional prerequisite? Most international criminal law treaties simply require states either to extradite suspects to a country that will investigate and, if necessary, try them, or to do the job themselves. Either one is fine. Here it seems that the difference between the prudential "rule of reason" of the Spanish Supreme Court dissenters and the jurisdictional prerequisite of the Spanish majority and the Belgian legislator is the difference between some universal jurisdiction and jurisdiction that is universal in name only.

The question whether a defendant needs to be present in the jurisdiction of the court, and at what stage, goes to the heart of what universal jurisdiction is about. Completely unmoored prosecutions seem too open to potential abuse, too much a case of complainants shopping for a forum. But at what point does the defendant have to be present? Can a court investigate, issue a warrant, request extradition of the defendant, and then satisfy the presence requirement through extradition? If, as is likely, extradition is denied, the case is ended, but the further result is a legal obligation (known as *aut dedere aut judicare*, or extradite or prosecute), at least under several relevant treaties like the Convention Against Torture, to pursue the case at home. After all, if the defendant has to be present for the judicial process to commence, it will be difficult to ever get to the arrest stage, as ex-dictators and torturers are unlikely to linger somewhere long enough for a conscientious judge to put a dossier together, at least once they get wind of an investigation. Universal jurisdiction, under that scenario, will still play a constructive role, but it will be very much to ensure that dictators stay home, that there is no foreign safe haven for such people, not to see that they are actually brought to justice. Nor can courts put together the evidence and testimony that might jump-start a domestic prosecution if the "investigate and extradite" route is closed. Under a "presence of the defendant" rule, the Pinochet case would never have happened. Recall that British human rights groups had tried four times to start a prosecution against him on various trips to the UK, but each time he had left before the slow machinery of the justice system (and the requisite political will) could be brought to bear. Without the Spanish extradition request, it would have been much more difficult to put that machinery into operation.

Many countries—more than 120, according to a 2001 Amnesty International study[35]—have some universal jurisdiction provisions, and most of these do not specify one way or the other whether the defendant needs to be present at the start. More recent universal jurisdiction provisions, enacted as states bring their law into conformity with the Rome

Statute, show no clear pattern, although a majority require presence when there is no other tie.[36] There seems to be no clear rule on presence under the little existing customary law that *allows* states to prosecute. Treaties are similarly split: while the Geneva Conventions grave breaches provisions have no presence requirement, treaties covering everything from torture to hijacking to attacks on diplomats start from the premise that the defendant is present. Other forms of jurisdiction do not require the defendant's presence to investigate or charge. To take a current example, the Al-Qaeda bombings of U.S. embassies in Kenya and Tanzania in 1998 resulted in a series of convictions in U.S. courts, but the first named defendant is still at large: the case caption is *United States v. Osama Bin Laden*. It is hard to imagine precluding investigation until the defendant was present in the forum.[37] Yet why should these cases be different?

There are valid concerns that judges will be overwhelmed with the expense and time involved in preparing arrest warrants and extradition requests that are unlikely to prosper. Also, complainants and their lawyers may be tempted to bring charges under these circumstances simply for the publicity value, or to make a timely political point (a charge that could be leveled easily against the Belgian cases against U.S. officials, for example). Where an extradition treaty leaves proof of a defendant's guilt to the requesting state, the burden will be considerably lessened. Perhaps a useful role for NGOs would be to compile lists of witnesses and evidence against likely suspects, files that can be submitted on short notice to investigating magistrates or prosecutors. Not knowing whether such a file exists and could be quickly exploited would at least provide some disincentives to Riviera retirements and shopping sprees for *génocidaires*. But on balance, for transnational prosecutions to play a useful role either as deterrent or catalyst, courts' ability to do some pre-presence investigation seems to be a prerequisite.

Territorial and Transnational Prosecutions

The relationship of the transnational forum to the domestic one is complex. First are the concerns, previously mentioned, about unfair trials and double standards between strong and weak countries. More fundamentally, does universal jurisdiction only come into play as a backstop when national courts cannot or will not act? Even if you agree with the general premise that, where possible, domestic courts are better at judging questions of mass crimes on their own territory—they have more knowledge of the situation, access to the evidence, ability to change local perceptions and power balances—that still leaves open the thorny questions of capacity. Everyone agrees that under some circumstances, the local courts cannot do the job, especially where the suspects are still powerful or the courts compromised. How should one court decide whether another country's judiciary is unable or unwilling to act, or adequately criminalizes the acts and provides due process?

One approach, adopted by the Spanish Audiencia Nacional in the Guatemalan case seems to apply a version of the "unable or unwilling" standard. First, see if there are legal impediments to prosecution, like amnesty laws. If not, see if fear and intimidation might keep judges from doing their job even without a formal law. The approach illustrates some of the potential problems and unknowns. What if the formal impediments to prosecution come not from an amnesty law, but from other legal devices like statutes of limitation, immunities, or repeated procedural maneuvers by defendants? Will a foreign court be willing and able to wade through all the possible veiled impunity devices of someone else's law? Perhaps so, with assistance from the parties. But does such a rule merely ensure that new dictators will protect themselves from prosecution not through the amnesty laws common in the 1970s and 1980s (and increasingly discredited now), but through less formal, more deadly devices that create a de facto rather than legal impunity?

The Guatemalan case shows how difficult it is for courts to judge de facto impunity. Why did the court pick 1999 (the year the Historical Clarification Commission issued its report) as the baseline, rather than the beginning of civilian government (1986) or the beginning of the "peace process"? (1996). If one of those dates had been the jumping-off point, the inactivity and hostility of the local courts would have been much more salient. How long should the transnational court (or the ICC, for that matter) wait to see if domestic action is forthcoming? How many cases need to be underway before the courts are given a pass? Will a few (how many?) "emblematic" cases do, or do most cases have to be investigated? What if the local courts are willing to condemn the lower-level triggermen but not the higher-ups who gave the orders? For this reason, the Supreme Court in the Peruvian case abandoned the effort, looking simply to whether the events at issue were *in fact* the subject of prosecution, without attempting to analyze why or why not or to evaluate the existence of a state of de facto impunity. This creates a more workable bright-line rule, but also leaves open the possibility that all possible forums will be de facto closed to complainants.

On the other hand, requiring complainants to show that trial at home is impossible creates tensions among lawyers and NGOs who will need to work together to present the case. The tensions are, in a sense, the flip side of the dilemma that transnational prosecutions create for the governments of the "target" country: to argue that it is illegitimate to try the suspect abroad, they have to allow trial at home. Conversely, it is hard for complainants to show that trial at home is impossible while at the same time participating in or encouraging efforts to open up at least some space for domestic investigations—which is, after all, one of the aims of transnational prosecutions in the first place. This dilemma was present in the Chilean case as well. Experts were providing affidavits to Judge Garzón assuring him that it was impossible to bring a successful complaint against Pinochet in Chilean courts, even as day to day those complaints began to pile up, due in no small measure to the catalytic effect of Garzón's investigation. In an application of the Heisenberg uncertainty principle to law, the very success of the foreign investigations changes the domestic conditions that give rise to them and the attitudes of the actors involved. Eventually, complainants must choose the most promising forum, but forcing them to do so prematurely can choke off useful pressure for change. It can also force victims who are often scattered around the world to concentrate their resources on a single place, which may prove much more difficult for them.

Multiple investigations in competing jurisdictions raise a number of difficulties. Extradition requests from a number of investigating states for the same defendants have to date been solved through a combination of a "first in time, first in line" rule and a preference for states with which the extraditing state has a relevant treaty, and these rules seem by and large to be adequate. Extradition requests from the territorial state subsequent to a transnational indictment raise the question of the genuineness of the inquiry: in the Cavallo case, for example, Argentine courts opened investigations based on lesser charges in a transparent attempt to bring the defendant home. Even when both investigations and prosecutions are carried out in good faith, at what point should the case be transferred back to the territorial forum, and what guarantees should the transnational forum request that a domestic court will see it through? What about the existing investigative file, the witness statements and the like? Some witnesses might be willing to testify abroad, but not be happy about having their statements transferred to a domestic court they are reluctant to trust. There is also the issue of judicial economy: at some point, the balance of equities shifts to finishing trial where the investigation has begun.

A final problem is that not all de jure amnesties are alike. The Chilean and Argentine decisions hold that an amnesty, especially one condemned by regional and global human rights bodies, will not impede prosecution of beneficiaries who stray outside their borders. The French Cour de Cassation agreed in the *Ould Dah* case, finding that recognition of a domestic amnesty would undermine the principle of universal jurisdiction.[38]

But what about amnesties that make nonprosecution contingent on truth-telling, contrition, or community service? The South African example is the clearest case of a conditional amnesty law that was widely supported internationally and had significant domestic backing. If a beneficiary of that amnesty were to travel, say, to Belgium, would he be subject to potential prosecution for committing crimes against humanity?

A first answer might be to say that such scenarios should arise rarely, because the amount of support and resources it takes to mount a credible transnational prosecution presupposes at least a significant amount of support from victims groups and human rights organizations at home, which would not be forthcoming if a conditional amnesty had widespread legitimacy. Post-South Africa, conditional amnesty-type laws in places like Rwanda and East Timor have excluded organizers, planners, or leaders in genocide, crimes against humanity, and serious war crimes. They have, instead, turned to alternative forms of punishment and accountability for low-level offenses, while insisting on punishment for the worst crimes.

Nonetheless, these are not complete answers. In reality, as with the determination of whether the courts are capable of acting, both the ICC and transnational prosecutions *do* take decisions about the validity and legitimacy of amnesty and pardon laws out of the purely national ambit. International law provides some guidelines for judges: blanket amnesties, self-amnesties granted by the perpetrators, and amnesties that do not require disclosure of the facts require no deference. In closer cases, a fact-specific inquiry will be needed. As Garth Meintjes and Juan Méndez suggest, the proportionality between the political aim sought and the means employed, combined with absolute prohibitions on amnesty for the most serious international crimes, may be the best we can do in terms of general rules.[39] It will be up to judges in transnational cases (as well as at the ICC) to evaluate whether the application of a particular contingent amnesty law (or alternative punishment measure) to specific facts passes muster and therefore makes a transnational prosecution inappropriate.

Stepping Forward, Stepping Back

So should activists have restrained themselves, not pushed the envelope of universal jurisdiction quite so hard, in hopes of not triggering a backlash by states? By targeting highly visible current heads of state and by bringing dozens of cases at once, mostly in the two venues that seemed most accessible (Belgium and Spain), activist lawyers did indeed "overload the boat" while the process was still new, highly controversial, and fragile. A more prudent strategy would have waited until the courts had enough experience with low-level defendants in more straightforward cases to make the more controversial ones seem firmly rooted in normal judicial practice. The result, in the short run, is a loss of momentum from the heady days of 1998.

In the end, though, the effect may be salutary, as courts and legislatures have to iron out some of the stickier points of transnational investigations and prosecutions, making it easier for other legislatures and courts to follow in their wake. Futhermore, the ebbs and flows of transnational prosecutions follow the natural evolution of any new regime. Linear progress is seldom the way of such things.

Indeed, by 2003 a number of universal jurisdiction cases involving relatively low-ranking offenders living in Europe were underway. In part, these cases were newly possible because the crimes took place after the date of implementation of the Torture Convention in most European states. For example, in September 2003, Dutch authorities arrested Sebastian Nzapali, a former colonel in the Zairian army under Mobutu known then as the "king of the beasts," and accused him of torture and rape committed in 1995 and 1996, using the 1988 implementing legislation to the Torture Convention. Nzapali, who had been living in the Netherlands since 1998, was tried and convicted on the torture charges in Rotterdam in March 2004. He was acquitted on the rape charges and sentenced to thirty months in prison.

In addition to Ely Ould Dah, the Mauritanian alleged torturer, cases in France include two Algerians, the mayor of a small town and his brother, members of the Algerian Relizane Militias. The two were indicted on March 30, 2004, by a Nimes investigating judge for torture and crimes against humanity stemming from a terror campaign against civilians between 1994 and 1997. The two brothers had moved to France, and the prosecutor initiated an investigation in 2003, bringing witnesses from Algeria to testify before the magistrate. The brothers have been released on bail awaiting trial.

Some progress has indeed been made. The *Pinochet* cases established the legitimacy of transnational prosecutions based on both universal and passive personality jurisdiction, at least under some circumstances. They showed that the existing universal jurisdiction laws could actually be used, and touched off a new willingness by advocates and courts to use them. They made clear that there are some limits to the immunity of government officials when hauled before national courts accused of international crimes, even if we still debate exactly where those limits are. They strengthened the idea that proper accountability for such crimes is the business of justice everywhere, and that domestic laws enshrining unfair trials or shielding perpetrators are subject to outside scrutiny and cannot per se bind foreign courts. They yielded landmark jurisprudence in the highest national courts of a handful of countries, jurisprudence that both draws from international courts and ideas and feeds back into them.

Yet there has been perhaps less progress than might be hoped for. The outer limits of what law can do when confronted with power are not fixed, but they do take time to expand: for now, current heads of state and figures who retain influence in powerful countries may be beyond the pale.

The danger is not that politically motivated courts will run amok, but that complainants will overreach. It is true that advocates and victim groups may have complex motivations for launching complaints—it is hard to doubt that some complainants in the *Sharon* case wanted to embarrass the Israeli government and remind the world of the past perfidies of its leader. But so what? Most human endeavor is marked by multiple agendas and interests. All that can usefully be said is that advocates, prosecutors, and human rights groups should exercise care in recognizing and understanding these multiple agendas. The fact that they exist is not reason enough to limit the courts to cases involving unknown, powerless or uncontroversial protagonists, although it may counsel greater strategic selectivity.

In the best of circumstances, a cohesive group of lawyers and activists would plot out, step by determined step, how and where to bring the cases that would systematically expand the outer limits of international law. They might look for models to the way the NAACP plotted the fall of Jim Crow laws in the U.S. South over at least two decades in the mid-twentieth century.[40] But although there is communication and coordination among many of the lawyers involved in these cases, the days are long gone when any single group can define and enforce limitations on appropriate cases. Someone out there will always want to try something new and audacious, even if it makes bad law. The resulting ups and downs are the price to be paid for a decentralized, global process largely driven by victims' groups. The very nature of transnational prosecutions makes them opportunistic, supplemental, ad-hoc. They will never be the only mechanism for achieving justice. But they are one piece of the emerging architecture, an architecture with a number of pillars.

Enter the ICC

The U.S. pressure on Belgium to gut its universal jurisdiction law seemed particularly galling because it dovetailed with larger U.S. efforts to derail international justice, particularly the implacable U.S. opposition to the nascent International Criminal Court, which had at the time barely appointed judges and a prosecutor. The advent of the ICC changed how transnational investigations and prosecutions fit into the larger picture.

The International Military Tribunal at Nuremberg was not the first international court to try war crimes: the first such trial was in the Middle Ages. But in the wake of World War II the idea took hold that there should be a way to try individuals for the worst crimes even when their home state was not willing or able to do so. The 1948 Genocide Convention contemplated an international criminal court, but the idea soon foundered on the rising Cold War. It wasn't until the heady days of the post-Communist, post-Gulf War New World Order that the idea was successfully refloated. Trinidad and Tobago proposed a court to try drug dealers and war criminals, but the drug dealer idea morphed over the course of the 1990s into a court that would deal with a very small group of very bad international crimes: genocide, crimes against humanity, and certain war crimes. The International Law Commission prepared a draft and the UN set up a Preparatory Commission, which worked for nearly three years. At the end, in a marathon five-week session in June and July 1998, the delegates of 120 countries and some 175 nongovernmental organizations hashed out the Rome Statute creating an International Criminal Court. Four years later (record time by international treaty standards), the required sixty countries had agreed to sign on to the Court, and it formally came into being.[41]

The drafters of the ICC statute were not working completely from scratch. They had a wealth of experience to draw on from the two ad hoc international criminal tribunals. These tribunals had been one of the first innovations in a post-Cold War world. As conflict raged in the Balkans in the early 1990s and TV viewers recoiled to see emaciated concentration camp inmates in the heart of a Europe that had in living memory vowed "never again," the UN Security Council created an International Criminal Tribunal (ICTY) to investigate and judge individuals charged with war crimes, crimes against humanity, or genocide in the former Yugoslavia. A year later, the slaughter of more than three quarters of a million Rwandans, mostly of the Tutsi minority (and the rest majority ethnicity Hutus who opposed the killing), and most by their neighbors using hoes and machetes, led to calls for the UN to treat African genocide as seriously as European. The result was the International Criminal Tribunal on Rwanda (ICTR), based in Arusha, Tanzania. Both ad hoc tribunals, as Security Council creations (under the Council's Chapter VII powers to act in the face of threats to peace), could compel the cooperation of any UN member state—assuming the Council and its members were willing to back up the tribunals.

It is not easy to create a new court from scratch and imbue it with the necessary law, procedure, and rules of evidence. These had to be a blend of the world's major legal systems, especially the civil law systems of Europe (and ex-European colonies like Rwanda) and the common law systems that were familiar to many of the judges, prosecutors, and financial backers of the tribunals. The tribunals also had to have offices, judges, clerks and bookkeepers. The office of the prosecutor needed its own lawyers, investigators, vehicles, computers, translators, and the like. Defense counsel had to be recruited from the private bar. Cooperative arrangements had to be made for seeking and requesting the surrender of suspects and for a jail to hold them in. Appropriate penalties had to be devised. This is not the place to tell the story of how all those things happened, with their fits and starts, ups and downs, in the history of the two ad hoc tribunals. They did happen, and the cumulative experiences of setting up and running the tribunals gave a big boost to the architects of the ICC.[42]

Like the ad hoc tribunals, the ICC sets up a three-part structure, with a panel of eighteen judges who represent all regions, men and women, experts in criminal law and international law. A prosecutor's office along with the Security Council and a State Party can decide to initiate investigations into any set of events happening after (but not before) July 1, 2002. A Registry administers the Court. The Security Council can request investigation into any situation that it decides comes within the Court's mandate; if the Prosecutor or a State Party wants to start an investigation, either the state where the crimes allegedly took place or the state of nationality of the defendant has to be a party to the treaty (or accept the investigation on a one-time basis). The prosecutor, as a further check against any overly aggressive tendencies, must also get permission from a panel of judges before starting an investigation on his or her own. There are no official immunities and no statutes of limitations. Commanders are responsible for their subordinates' acts, and obeying orders is a defense in only very limited circumstances. The Rome Statute also sets out elaborate rules for the conduct of an investigation and trial, and for appeal.

Unlike the ad hoc tribunals, the ICC will not have first pick of the cases it wants to try. Instead, it will act as a backstop, stepping in only if national courts are "unable or unwilling" to investigate. The definition of "unwilling" in article 17 of the court's statute includes cases involving sham proceedings, excessive delays, a compromised judiciary, or other cases of apparent shielding of potential defendants. "Unable" is more straightforward: a state is unable to act if "due to a total or substantial collapse or unavailability of its national judicial system, it is unable to obtain the accused or the necessary evidence and testimony."

In the best possible scenario, the Court will have almost no business at all. The threat of an ICC investigation will be enough to push domestic courts to look into the alleged crimes and domestic governments to give the courts the leeway to do so, hoping to avoid the stigma of having its courts labeled inoperative. In a sense, the Court's objective is the same as that of a transnational investigation: to jumpstart stalled or obstructed domestic justice. Its main weakness lies in its jurisdictional requirements. The state of either nationality or territoriality (usually the same) must be a party to the treaty; violators who stay at home are only at risk if the Security Council wants them or their own government turns them in (or perhaps if their government in an earlier era became a party and the current regime neglected to back out). A Pinochet or a Saddam Hussein is likely to remain beyond the reach of the court, at least while still in power. The Court's main business will likely come from newly empowered "post-transition" governments wanting the internationals to bear the cost, and the political heat, of prosecutions of deposed and disgraced ex-leaders. The number of countries that have recently suffered from civil wars ratifying the ICC Statute indicates that at least some post-conflict governments see the Court's potential along these lines.

Does the advent of the ICC make transnational prosecutions obsolete? In a word, no. The significant limitations on the court's jurisdiction, in terms of both timing and state consent, mean that many cases will never even get near the ICC. Even for those cases that are technically within the court's purview, the Prosecutor will have to focus on a few crucial situations, leaving many cases untouched. Resources are likely to be inadequate. At the same time, the heightened expectations created by the advent of the Court are likely to vastly increase the demand for justice, though it may take some time for national courts to take up the challenge. Transnational prosecutions have the potential to fill the gap, to take up the many cases the ICC will be unable to hear, and to act as an adjunct and multiplier of the emerging international criminal jurisprudence.

There is nothing in the Rome Statute that would keep the national courts of third-party states from acting, and some indication that their action takes precedence over the ICC. Article 17 of the ICC statute talks about "a State which has jurisdiction over" a case as having first crack under the complementarity provisions. So if a case were properly before a transnational court on the basis of universal (or victim-nationality-based) jurisdiction, that state could, by choosing to go forward, oust the ICC of jurisdiction. This makes sense in an overall scheme where the ICC remains the court of last resort. Transnational courts act as a second line of defense, allowing the ICC to focus on those cases where, for instance, head of state immunity allows only an international court to proceed. Only if the burden is thus distributed does the ICC have a chance of meeting the (unrealistically?) high expectations now heaped on it.

Institution-Building and Networking Approaches

A two-track approach to international justice seems to be emerging. On the one hand are the new institutions of global justice, built from the ground up. On the other is the networking approach, featuring a (to date still small) group of existing national courts and webs of international and national lawyers and organizations that coalesce around specific transnational prosecutions. The two approaches largely complement each other, but they do have different strengths and weaknesses. Alongside these approaches are an increasingly varied array of noncriminal mechanisms.

As the International Criminal Court, the pinnacle of the "institution-building" approach, comes on line, the *Pinochet* cases provide important lessons and insights that can help the new court be useful to the victims of terrible crimes. The "institution-building" approach to global justice is of a piece with other twentieth-century institution-building, including the United Nations itself, the International Court of Justice, the World Trade Organization, the World Bank and International Monetary Fund, and a host of specialized international and regional agencies and courts. Institution-building is integral to channeling and controlling the unbridled global marketplace, and to coordination and orderly relations among states. States voluntarily surrender a small (in reality, smaller for some countries than others) proportion of their sovereignty to these institutions in exchange for benefits and a say in their management, runs the theory. These institutions each require new rules (created by treaty), new personnel, new dispute resolution procedures, entire new international regimes. They are an integral part of the phenomenon we often refer to as globalization.

Globalization, of course, has its discontents. Critics complain that new global institutions are undemocratic, that they privilege rich countries and rich interests within rich countries, that they ignore the effects of their decisions on the poor and on the planet's health, and that the underlying social contract binding government to the governed at the national level does not exist internationally. Others excoriate the bureaucracy, enforced mediocrity, and sluggishness of global institutions. They demand a "globalization from below," a bubbling up of ideas and policy choices from civil society in every particular place, to balance and legitimize the top-down inaccessibility of many global institutions.

Institutions of global justice, no matter how noble and well-intentioned, may well suffer from many of the same defects as other top-down global efforts. As a treaty-based institution, the ICC is a creature of states, subject to the least-common-denominator politics of state consensus and the power of large states to threaten and bribe where necessary. The formal independence of the judges and prosecutor insulates the Court to some extent, but cannot change the fact that it will be dependent on states for its budget and its muscle. U.S. opposition to the Court only exacerbates these problems.

Top-down institution-building efforts may also suffer from the lack of grounding in a specific local reality. The experience of the ad hoc tribunals provides some indication of the kinds of problems we might encounter. Both tribunals have suffered from being far, geographically and culturally, from their "target" populations. A lack of publicity (and in parts of the former Yugoslavia, heavily self-censored media during the 1990s) and of radio coverage of the trials meant that for the average Bosnian, Serb, Croat, or Rwandan the tribunals were no more than a far-off, unintelligible abstraction, if that. Add to these the problems inherent in any criminal proceeding: they are drawn-out, focused on detail, and hard to make accessible to the public. There may well have been a connection between the tribunals' activities and, say, the inability of certain local thugs (who might worry about Tribunal indictments) to continue to hold local office—but it is not clear that connection was apparent to the average townsperson.

The ad hoc tribunals have also been a mixed blessing for domestic efforts and local institutions. The local courts have not been the beneficiaries of anywhere near the resources and expertise they needed to become meaningful participants in justice at home. In the former Yugoslavia, few domestic prosecutions occurred and those that did were problematic. By 2002, it was clear that domestic prosecutions were necessary, but there were continuing squabbles about who should be in charge and how to ensure the safety and security of witnesses.

In Rwanda, these problems were even worse. The tribunal seat was in Arusha, Tanzania, a long, bumpy jeep ride (or, for those few who could afford or even imagine it, a short plane ride) away. Proceedings were in English and French, and translators to the local Kinyarwandan usually failed to make the context of motions and holdings intelligible to the local population. While the tribunal spent tens of millions on trials of most of the top ringleaders—as of the end of 2002, eleven cases had been completed and cases against sixty others were in progress or pending—the local courts confronted the impossible task of sorting out over 100,000 prisoners detained in festering local jails.

For witnesses and the families of victims, the tribunals could prove frustrating. Exhumations and interviews of family members, asked to recall details of their loved ones' clothing and characteristics, for instance, were carried out with the sole purpose of evidence-gathering, leaving family members to complain that their need to reclaim the body for proper burial was decidedly secondary.[43] Witness protection was offered, but only while the witness was testifying. In Rwanda, a number of potential witnesses were killed before investigative methods improved. The prosecutorial strategy has been largely a "top-down" one, where the victims and witnesses play little active part. Relations between the Rwanda tribunal and victims' groups in the country have been strained at best. A recent report found that women rape victims were especially upset that prosecutors had never prepared them adequately for the rigors of cross-examination, and had not explained how they fit into prosecutorial strategy. Judges and court personnel, they felt, were disrespectful and aloof. A 2003 study of witnesses before the Yugoslav Tribunal also pointed out areas where prosecutors had been seriously neglectful of their witnesses.[44]

Victims at the Center

It is striking to compare the mixed impact of the ad hoc tribunals on victims and on local justice processes with the seemingly much greater and less ambiguous impact of the transnational investigations recounted in this book. Those transnational efforts, done at a fraction of the cost, relied for their effectiveness on existing national courts and on a network of complainants, NGOs and lawyers in a number of countries. Moreover, the impact seemed to occur even when the defendants were indicted or charged but unlikely to ever be extradited for trial.

Why? One answer has to do with the *agency* of victims and survivors. Rather than play passive roles in litigation driven by prosecutors, the victims and witnesses, and their organizations and attorneys, were the driving forces behind the cases. Once the cases were open, people spontaneously wrote to the investigating magistrate telling their story or asking if they could testify if they traveled to see him. There were limits to who could participate—a few would-be complainants were turned down on grounds that no one in the human rights community had ever heard of them and they were suspected of simply wanting access to the case file—but they were very broad limits. The cases stirred imaginations and opened possibilities precisely because they seemed decentralized, less controllable by state interests, more, if you will, acts of imagination.

Structural characteristics of these transnational prosecutions led to this sense of empowerment. The cases used existing courts and judges and needed no special political will on the part of states to proceed. Setting up international institutions requires resources and support that can only come from states, but that also makes the institutions (even with adequate safeguards for their formal independence) dependent on state will and appropriations. In contrast, at the national level investigations can be undertaken as a matter of routine, where legal factors are more likely to predominate over the political ones, at least initially. The onus then is on the executive branch of a state, in particular the foreign affairs office, to step in and derail an investigation, not to put into action the machinery to start one. Although it can be done (as the Senegalese *Habré* case shows), there is a political price to pay for appearing to interfere with the independence of the courts. Eventually, the executive branch can weigh in, at the stage of extradition or the appeal of an indictment, but at that point the initial fact-finding, the outlines of the case, have already been laid down.

All the cases studied here involved continental systems that allow individuals to initiate an investigation and to take part through the mechanism of the *partie civile*. In a 1997 report to the UN on principles to combat impunity, the Human Rights Sub-Commission reporter, Louis Joinet, endorsed this approach. "Although the decision to prosecute lies primarily within the competence of the State, supplementary procedural rules should be introduced to enable victims to institute proceedings, on either an individual or a collective basis, where the authorities fail to do so, particularly as civil plaintiffs. This option should be extended to nongovernmental organizations with recognized long-standing activities on behalf of the victims concerned."[45] It is disturbing to note that the trend in Europe since 2002 has been in the opposite direction, to remove victims' initiative and place discretion to begin investigations entirely in the hands of a state prosecutor.

Common law countries do not have investigating magistrates who look into charges of crimes, but prosecutors who have full discretion to decide whether to press charges. Far fewer transnational prosecutions are likely to arise in these systems. Nonetheless, we allow some measure of the victim autonomy provided by the *partie civile* system by encouraging tort suits (for wrongful death or injuries suffered) in cases of crime. In the United States, Alien Tort Claims Act suits, like the one against Caravan of Death member Fernández Larios, seem to provoke something of the same positive response in plaintiffs. The use of these mechanisms and the development of similar ones in other common-law countries need to be protected and expanded.

In part in reaction to the experiences of the ad hoc tribunals, the ICC takes a more victim- and witness-friendly approach. There is a Victims and Witnesses Unit, in charge of witness security and protection and assistance to victims and families. Victims can be represented before the court and can ask to present their views at trial. They can also be present at preliminary hearings, make their views known, and be notified if the prosecutor decides not to go forward. While not quite the same as the *partie civile* procedure, it is also a long way from the prosecutorial model of the common law and the ad hoc tribunals.

The judges will play a large role in regulating how and to what extent victims participate during pre-trial procedures and at trial, including whether and how they can question witnesses and access documents. The Rules of Procedure establish the presumption that victims will be able to be heard, receive copies of the case file, and attend hearings.[46] Unlike the ad hoc tribunals, the ICC rules reflect an increasingly-shared view that the interests of the victims may not always line up with those of the prosecution, and that victims need their own voice and defenders. Where there are many victims (with many possible lawyers) the victims can be asked to agree on joint representation, and if they cannot agree, the registrar can do it for them. During a subsequent reparations hearing, victims (and their attorneys) will be able to participate fully.

For the first time, the ICC envisions a central role for reparations to victims. Article 75 of the Rome Statute tells the Court to craft rules on reparations for victims. The Court can, upon request or on its own motion, decide on the amount of damages and the form of reparations. Reparations will be paid by individual perpetrators, but not by states. The statute also creates a trust fund for victims, which can be used to distribute awards, including collective reparations, when there are large numbers of victims. Judgments, however, will have to be collected from national courts, and it is not clear how that will work. It is also not clear where the money will come from (perhaps some perpetrators have findable secret bank accounts, but how many?), or whether the Court will have the capacity to identify victims and distribute funds.

It is much too early to tell how these provisions will be used in practice. If taken seriously by judges and prosecutors, they could go quite some way toward bringing the international proceedings closer to the people most affected by the crimes. There is a large amount of discretion left to the judges, prosecutor, and registry to craft, in practice, the Court's relationship with victims and their representatives. There will be inevitable tensions between the needs of prosecutors and the needs of victims and witnesses. The transnational cases teach that the Court must take victim empowerment and agency seriously in everything it does, and especially during the pre-trial, investigative phases, if it is to truly aid victims and their communities.

Much will depend as well on whether the ICC sees transnational cases as allies, competitors, or even vestiges of a now unnecessary past. The Court should use the advantages of a decentralized approach. Decentralization allows a number of experienced investigative judges, each working with the same corpus of international law but with their own national procedures and implementing acts, to develop a jurisprudence of international criminal justice "from below." This jurisprudence will be, no doubt, heavily influenced by the work of the ad hoc and other international criminal tribunals and the ICC, but it will multiply the number of unanswered questions that can be tackled. The decentralized, organic development of jurisprudence is likely to generate the kinds of debate and even disagreement among courts, based on concrete factual situations, that over time allows the working out of complex issues of law and policy. It also corresponds to the way other enforcement mechanisms have evolved in the human rights field: through multiple, overlapping forums, where the number of possible routes of redress offsets the weaknesses of each individual mechanism and allows events to be viewed through multiple prisms. At the dawn of a new enforcement regime, this approach may better lead to bringing multiple talents to bear and devising solutions that have been tested in practice.

Admittedly, fostering a proliferation of transnational cases reduces the chances that like cases are treated alike (at least during some initial period), and runs the risk of creating bad national precedents. The trade-off, though, is a large number of domestic judges grappling with international criminal law and procedure, internalizing and domesticating this law and the human rights and humanitarian law that comes with it. That domestication is likely to lead to wider and better application of human rights law and international criminal law more generally. It will better put perpetrators and would-be perpetrators on notice of where the limits are. It may also prove a far greater deterrent to crimes against humanity and their ilk if would-be *génocidaires* know that their acts are being watched, and may be judged, in many different places, subject to many different sets of political and legal constraints, not just one.

Chapter 8

The Actors Behind the *Pinochet* Cases

The cases described in this book involve broad coalitions of actors making law, influencing foreign affairs, and changing the domestic political calculus in the countries that were the "target" of the litigation as well as in the countries where the cases were brought. They provide insights into how these coalitions were formed and the tensions and synergies that affected them. Social scientists have attributed a major role to such coalitions in driving international relations. The cases also provide new windows into the role of exile and diasporic communities as agents of political change in their "home" and "host" countries. They help clarify the specific role of national judges in making international law effective on the national level, and in the seeds of a global judicial culture. Finally, they raise questions as to the meaning and pace of transitions to democracy. This chapter explores some of the lessons learned.

Actors and Activists: Transnational Advocacy Networks and "Spirals" of Change

Chile and Argentina have long been textbook examples of the effective interplay between the international and national spheres of action. Chile has for many years had a well-organized movement pushing for justice within the country. The 1973 coup and the atrocities that followed it galvanized a nascent human rights movement into action. The Comité Pro-Paz and its successor, the Vicaría de la Solidaridad, played key roles in amassing the information on human rights violations that would undergird later investigations. Groups like the Vicaría used their ties with churches and human rights groups worldwide to disseminate information on the violations and to create moral outrage about them. Pressured by international human rights groups, the UN Human Rights Commission for the first time sent a fact-finding mission, and the criticisms of the Chilean junta by the UN, the Inter-American Commission on Human Rights, and Amnesty International led to increasing use of country-specific scrutiny.[1] It also set the stage for a decade of campaigns against torture. The growing isolation of the Pinochet regime as a human rights pariah, and the impact this had on Chile's military and economic ties to powerful countries and international financial institutions, eventually prodded the Pinochet regime to move beyond simple denials of the facts. It stopped massive disappearances, renamed and reorganized the DINA, and allowed some very limited political concessions. This in turn emboldened human rights activists inside and outside the country, who pushed for further concessions, ending in the 1989 plebiscite that ousted Pinochet and led to elections.

In Argentina as well, respected campaigners like Emilio Mignone and organizations like CELS and SERPAJ sprung up during and after the dictatorship years to document and denounce human rights violations. Nobel Prize laureate Adolfo Pérez Esquivel was tireless in bringing the plight of Argentines to international forums; the Inter-American Commission's 1979 visit, and the efforts of the UN human rights staff in Geneva, including the creation of the UN Working Group on Disappearances, also brought key pressure to bear on the Videla regime for a winding down and eventual end to massive disappearances.[2] The Mothers and Grandmothers of the Plaza de Mayo were instrumental as well, especially in defining and advocating for a "right to identity" for children that was later enshrined in international treaties.[3]

Social scientists describe this interplay in terms like "boomerangs" or "spirals." For example, political scientists use a "boomerang" model to explain how human rights norms affect state policy, even in states that have no particular interest in the protection of human rights.[4] It works like this. Human rights violations in the Southern Cone created activists who went outside a closed domestic political system to find allies and pressure points abroad. They used the power of ideas like human rights, and the ability to name violations, fact-find about them, and create moral outrage to make their case on the international level. International institutions like the UN and the Inter-American Human Rights Commission took up complaints of violations, leading to political, economic, and moral pressure from powerful states (in Europe and North America) as well as these institutions to open up, thus in turn creating more domestic political space, which encouraged more human rights related organizing at home. A series of such inside-outside-inside "boomerangs," with increasing concessions by governments and increasing pressure from activists inside and out, creates a spiral of increasing internalization and institutionalization of human rights norms.[5]

This model depends on the activities of groups of nongovernmental activists both in the "target" country and outside, willing to pressure their own governments, to initiate judicial proceedings, and to lobby international institutions. Social scientists have long studied the emergence and increasing influence of these networks, which are composed

of like-minded committed and knowledgeable "actors working internationally on an issue, who are bound together by shared values, a common discourse, and dense exchanges of information and services."[6]
These "transnational advocacy networks" of activists transmit ideas and
norms from one country to another, create joint campaigns, and work
together to create pressure on recalcitrant governments.

The story I tell fits this model well, but with variations. In the post-
dictatorial era, domestic activists turned to the international stage
because the domestic courts were closed to them and other branches of
government were unable or unwilling to pry them open. In addition to
international institutions, these individuals and groups turned to the
domestic judiciary of other countries, invoking the norms of international law. They had to master not only the language of international
law and diplomacy, but the rules of other legal and political systems,
with the help of networks including international NGOs and local solidarity and legal groups. The focus on using the courts meant a prepon-
derant role for lawyers and judges, each with their own professional
norms and ethos. Their efforts in turn stimulated human rights activists
and lawyers, politicians, and, as a result, judges, to push cases forward
on the domestic front, which in turn opened up information that was
useful in new and expanded transnational prosecutions. Time and time
again, the results of investigations begun in Europe prompted investigations in Latin America and Africa, which prompted new investigations
in other Latin American and African states. Extradition requests from
Europe, even when denied, had the same result. At times, investigations
in one Latin American country led to new investigations elsewhere in
Latin America. At the same time, these transnational prosecutions
changed the societies where the courts were located. They both influenced and were influenced by the direction of international law itself.
They fit nicely into the idea of a "justice cascade" in Latin America, a
confluence of internal and external factors reaching a tipping point
after which change comes more rapidly and decisively.[7]

The "boomerang/spiral" model is a tighter fit with Chile than with
Argentina. In Chile, the domestic courts had never been open, although
by 1998 judicial reform was starting to have some effect. The push from
outside was clearly a major (although not the only) driver for change.
Argentina, in contrast, had tried the leaders of the military juntas and
had initiated dozens of other investigations before the process was cut
off by the *punto final* and due obedience laws and by Menem's pardons.
The lower courts were open to innovative strategies based on both
domestic and international law, and activists knew how to "set up"
domestic change through international work and pressure. As examples,
consider the Grandmothers' work on the "right to identity" internation-

ally, which was then used in the domestic child appropriation cases, or Carmen Lapacó's complaint to the Inter-American Commission on Human Rights, which then served as the impetus for the "truth trials." Rather than a one-way account of pressure from outside affecting domestic events, in Argentina the inside and outside activist coalitions worked both spheres simultaneously, applying pressure where and when needed.[8]

The loose alliance of lawyers, human rights activists, social service providers, family members of the disappeared, journalists, and academics on three continents that began to take shape around pushing for trials had many of the attributes of a transnational advocacy network. It is easy to conclude from these connections among the groups that the *Pinochet* litigation and its aftershocks were the product of a vast conspiratorial network, well oiled and articulated and able to foil the will of governments throughout the world. Indeed, there were prodigious feats of transcontinental cooperation involved. These were made possible in part by new technologies, especially the Internet, which amplified the network's ability to react quickly and concentrate resources at key moments. Finding dozens of victims of torture in Chile after 1988 and getting their evidence before Judge Garzón so that he could bring it before the British courts, all in large part done in the short time between the House of Lords decision in March 1999 and the extradition hearing in September, was probably the most impressive feat. It could not have been done without preexisting contacts and correspondence among the various lawyers and local human rights groups. Sifting through the wealth of declassified U.S. government documents, or the reams of police files in the Archive of Terror in Paraguay, to find the nuggets that would fuel Operation Condor-linked prosecutions in numerous countries required a high degree of cross-border cooperation and coordination. So did getting that information authenticated and translated so that a local judge could use it, and into the hands of the appropriate lawyers and investigating magistrates. There are many other examples.

It is possible, however, to overstate the amount of organization and coordination involved. This was no tight, centralized operation but a dispersed series of individuals and small groups loosely bound by common goals and mutual acquaintances who came together over time around specific campaigns and opportunities. Recall, for instance, that both the Argentine and Chilean complainant groups in Spain discovered that a case had been filed through reading the newspaper. Serendipity plays a large role in this story: that Judge Garzón should have ended up with the case, that Andy McEntee of Amnesty International London should have worked on Chile in the past, that a Mexican newspaper should have turned up Ricardo Cavallo's past as a torturer in a story originally looking for corruption and self-dealing. All these cannot be ascribed to the work of human rights networks. The networks involved are still in their very early stages, but they knew how to take advantage of events and how to communicate.

Exiles and Diasporas as Political Actors

Accounts of transnational advocacy networks and their ability to create change focus on domestic activist groups, but many of the activists in this story were exiles or former expatriates come home, and the story highlights the role of diasporic communities and solidarity activists. The dictatorships that gave rise to groups of family members of the disappeared also provoked mass exoduses, people fleeing the secret police, the death squads, or the slow death of economic disaster. Tens of thousands of exiles and refugees flooded out of Latin America, making their way largely to Europe and North America. Some 50,000 Argentines now reside in Spain as do thousands of Chileans. Others ended up in Sweden, France, Italy, Britain, and the United States. And unlike migrations from Central America and Africa, these exiles were largely middle class, educated and savvy. Most quickly figured out how to get things done in their new circumstances. Despite new careers and often new families, many kept alive the dream of creating a new, democratic homeland. They formed solidarity groups, transmitting information about their old homes to the new country, asking for international pressure on the dictators, bringing speakers, mobilizing politicians, and raising funds for opposition groups and humanitarian aid. Even with the advent of civilian government, many chose to stay in their adopted country, while traveling regularly to see family and friends back home and maintaining an interest in home-country politics. They made common cause with local people who had long-standing family or personal ties to Latin America, people like Joan Garcés, Sophie Thonon, Andy McEntee, or Wolfgang Kaleck.

Here is another facet of globalization, or transnationalization, at work. The communities that organized the Piquete de Londres or pressured the Mexican government to extradite Ricardo Cavallo could be characterized as diasporas, pushed out of their original homeland and bound together by a persistent common identity as Chileans or Argentines, fans of *empanadas* and *cueca* or *bife* and *tango*. Especially with the advent of the Internet, these diasporas maintain close contact with home, reading the local newspapers and keeping up with local politics. While the term diaspora may originally have had an ethnic element, as in the case of Jews or Armenians, it now encompasses a wider range of diasporic groups.[9] These groups' aim was not to overthrow the existing government, but to mobilize inside and outside resources to change "home state" policies through legal action and its attendant publicity. These diasporas used the courts, not the electoral system or other means, to advocate for human rights in their homelands.[10] They were a force to be reckoned with by the Southern Cone regimes they aimed to influence, and by the European governments where they resided. They influenced politics in their "host state," mobilizing public opinion and making it more difficult for governments to publicly oppose transnational investigations and extradition.

Lawyers as Transnational Actors

Another distinguishing factor in this story was the predominance of lawyers. Public interest lawyering has always played a key role in social struggles—think of Thurgood Marshall in the U.S., Shirin Ebadi, Iran's 2003 Nobel Peace Prize winner, or Nelson Mandela in South Africa. In Latin America, courageous attorneys risked their own lives to file countless habeas corpus petitions asking for the government to own up to detaining disappeared people—dozens of them disappeared themselves in the process. Over the years lawyers represented political prisoners, filed petitions and, increasingly, turned to international forums to press their case. In the corridors of the Inter-American and UN Commissions on Human Rights and at conferences for academics and activists, they began meeting and comparing notes and strategies. In 1996, for instance, as the Spanish litigation was getting under way, there were conferences on strategies to combat impunity in Madrid and Santiago, where many of the driving forces behind the cases in this book either presented or listened in the audience.

Lawyers differ from NGOs. Public interest lawyers, especially, share both an ideological commitment and a set of professional knowledge and norms. The former made the lawyers an integral part of the transnational advocacy groups. The latter, however, made them operate more like an epistemic community,[11] whose power derives from specialized knowledge common to the community's members. Lawyers had preexisting professional associations and networks. The amount and quality of these professional contacts varied: the academics and barristers who argued the cases in the UK, for instance, all knew each other through professional law associations and conferences (indeed, lawyers on opposing sides in the case had been or, in another case, would become, law partners). The lawyers who represented the complainants directly tended to have more contacts with the relevant human rights activist communities. Over time, and in large part as a result of these cases, the lawyers developed their own caucuses and coalitions that carried over into a number of continuing legal projects focused on universal jurisdiction and on the ICC.

Moreover, the two roles—advocate and expert—were often in tension, as lawyers struggled with how closely to identify with their clients and how far to push the envelope of existing law. It was the combination of the attributes of a network participant, with its focus on information provision and mobilization of pressure, and of an epistemic community member, with its claim to specialized, dispassionate knowledge (of international law, in this case) that made the lawyers such a potent force.

As for their clients, attempting to force justice through the courts had the advantage of being able to tap into a prestigious and accepted language, the language of law. But it had significant disadvantages. Timing problems created exhaustion and impatience. Exhaustion when detention (of Pinochet, of Cavallo, of Olivera) required almost round-the-clock work to find the necessary judges, translate and send the necessary paperwork, and respond to events. Impatience with the slow pace of normal judicial procedure, where hearings take months to schedule, judges take their time to rule, and extradition requests sit unanswered for months while complainants, witnesses, and defendants grow older.

Furthermore, the results to date have been inconclusive. There were investigations, arrest warrants, indictments, extradition requests, but as of mid-2004 the only final guilty verdicts have come in trials in absentia and civil lawsuits. That will change if the Scilingo and Cavallo cases come to trial in Spain and as the domestic investigations in Chile and Argentina reach their conclusion. But by and large, it was the investgation, indictment, and arrest order that mattered. And that defined the limits of what could be achieved.

The criminal investigations acted in part like declaratory judgments: a way to put the evidence together, to have it evaluated by an expert and publicly validated in judicial pronouncements. In that sense, they share with truth commissions, "truth trials," and other types of sanctions an emphasis on telling the story. They provide a nice illustration of the argument that it is fair process, at least as much as outcome, that determines victim satisfaction with a judicial process.[12]

Judges, Transgovernmental Networks, and the Domestication of International Law

Traditional international relations theorists focus on the interests and actions of states: the UK arrests Pinochet, Spain seeks his extradition. But states are not monolithic. New scholarship over the last decade or so has started to pry open the "black box" of the state, exploring how different branches of government, or even agencies within a single branch, can pursue different, and sometimes conflicting, international agendas.[13] Think how often, for example, the U.S. State and Defense Departments can work at cross-purposes.

One of the important lessons of these cases is that judges do not necessarily respond to the same pressures, or interests, as the executive branches in their own country, even when it comes to cases with foreign policy implications. At times, the executive branch strenuously or quietly objected to the actions of its own judiciary (Spain and Argentina in the first category, Chile in the second). Of course, even in the best democracies the judicial branch is not immune from societal influence or political change, nor should it be. The question then becomes how judges perceive the incentives and pressures on them that make them pursue highly controversial human rights cases even in the face of executive branch opposition.

In part, judges are open to using the laws of war and of human rights precisely because they are couched in the language of law, a language that is familiar. There is a professional pride involved in applying new law, even new international law, that judges express. On the other hand, the cases are also couched in the familiar language and rhythms of criminal investigation. These are not human rights judges but criminal law magistrates, whose daily fare involves traffickers, smugglers, murderers, and the like, and who know how to put together evidence and request extradition. They are not limited to the canons of rights discourse, but deal in the language of the criminal law, generally subject to less molding from the political branches. But professional inclination cannot alone explain why the investigating magistrates in these cases agreed to take on difficult and time-consuming tasks that were almost certain to bring them controversy.

One response foregrounds the position of some judges as "norm entrepreneurs."[14] In each country under study, it is possible to trace how one or a couple of judges have been in the vanguard of applying international human rights law to domestic cases. Almost all these "norm entrepreneur" judges, it turns out, have either studied or lived in other countries or have participated in extrajudicial activities that connected them to colleagues elsewhere and allowed a process of mutual enrichment to take place. To cite some examples: Judge Leopoldo Schiffrin (who brought the idea of crimes against humanity into Argentine jurisprudence) studied international law in Germany. Judge Gabriel Cavallo (who wrote the first decision overturning the Argentine amnesty laws) had studied international law as a law student and later participated in human rights courses in the U.S. and elsewhere. Judge Carlos Cerda, the courageous Chilean jurist who first reinterpreted the amnesty law in the 1980s and was sanctioned for it, got an advanced degree from the faculty of Louvain, Belgium, and a doctorate in legal philosophy from Paris. Judge Juan Guzmán in Chile grew up as the son of a diplomat/poet and was educated in France, England, the U.S., Argentina, and Chile. Judge Baltazar Garzón in Spain has long championed the cause of indigenous peoples under international law and has become a tireless supporter of the International Criminal Court. Judge Damien Vandermeersch in Belgium is an academic expert on international criminal and humanitarian law, teaching seminars and writing scholarly articles on the subject. Academic training and personal interests thus predisposed some key judges toward using international law when they got the chance. In turn, these judges have shared their expertise around the world, participating in trainings, seminars and conferences as experts and innovators in international law, inspiring new generations.

Transnational advocacy networks influence the work of judges through changing the context in which they work, for example, through strengthening and publicizing international complaint mechanisms. Increasing familiarity with international institutions for the protection of human rights made judges more amenable to using international law in their own courts. Judge Cavallo specifically pointed to the role of the Inter-American Human Rights Commission, with its complaint mechanism, as an important avenue for increasing human rights awareness among the judiciary and bar. "People began to hear of the Commission because you could file complaints, and because of their 1979 visit to Argentina. It raised consciousness, especially among criminal lawyers," he told me. Another avenue has been legislative. The key step has not been ratification of treaties: rather, it was the raising of human rights treaties to constitutional rank that precipitated a new attention to these treaties among the judiciary in Argentina. In a number of cases (Argentina, Chile, Belgium) academic writing laid out the legal theories ultimately adopted years before judges got a chance to apply them to a concrete case. In several cases (Spain, Senegal, Argentina, the UK) *amicus curiae* or intervenor briefs or memos based on international law and presented by international human rights organizations have helped shape judicial decisions.

Over time, the human rights movement also affected judges by recognizing their contributions to the development of human rights law. The judges in these cases won human rights awards, were interviewed regularly by the press, were invited to academic and activist conferences, and generally raised their profile both at home and abroad. Often, for trial-level criminal investigative magistrates, this was the first time they had received such attention for their work. It can't help but have made work in this area more enticing. Indeed, both Judge Garzón in Spain and Judge Guzmán in Chile were reprimanded and criticized for comments on human rights-related issues that were a product of their high public profiles; their supporters complained that judicial colleagues were just jealous.

Contact with complainants also made judges more open to forging ahead. Judge Guzmán of Chile readily recounts how he only became aware of the magnitude and depth of suffering caused by the military's actions when he began receiving family members of the dead and disappeared and traveling around Chile seeking secret burial sites. Judge Garzón has also talked about how moved he has been by the stories of survivors and victims, many of whom work with groups of family members. Judge Le Loire assigned paramount importance to the effect of his investigation on the French family members of victims. "If the families feel like justice was done, it doesn't matter whether the ultimate conviction resulted from my investigation or if my work triggered other investigations. The important thing is that the families feel that I've done my job."

Judges also have their own transgovernmental networks. Investigating judges communicate with each other largely in the course of concrete case-driven needs. Judge Cavallo of Argentina, for example, had talked to Judge Garzón of Spain before 1996 in the context of a run-of-the-mill drug trafficking extradition case. When the time came to discuss Garzón's request to extradite ex-military officers from Argentina to stand trial in Spain, communication was easier because of the earlier contact. Judges Le Loire of France and Garzón of Spain had worked together on ETA cases. Judges in several instances maintained direct links in order to skirt the cumbersome and easily derailed formal procedure for transmitting evidentiary and extradition requests. Judges have also compared notes: Guzmán of Chile has talked to both Garzón of Spain and Le Loire of France about common legal issues affecting their overlapping cases. Le Loire also shared information with Italian judges on the methods of the Chilean secret service. In a number of cases, the judges visited each other informally to advance investigations, especially when official channels were slow or obstructionist.

At the level of Supreme Courts and constitutional courts, there is a more formal infrastructure of meetings and congresses. In addition, courts explicitly cite to each other, approving or distinguishing the holdings of other courts in an ongoing judicial dialogue.[15] These front-line investigating magistrates didn't hold congresses—several told me they were too busy for such things—but they did borrow from each other in concrete cases and make use of similar principles to push the boundaries of their national law. They used comparative and international law extensively, both to convince national audiences of the legitimacy of their actions and self-consciously to develop the international law on the subject. They cited each other's findings of fact and found similar solutions to problems like the "retroactivity" of treaty or statutory provisions. Of course, such borrowing was far more common among judges from similar legal systems, especially those, like Spain and the countries of Latin America, where the same language was used. The British courts tended to cite cases from other common-law jurisdictions, especially the U.S. There was some crossover—for example Argentine courts cited U.S. court decisions—but this seems to be a general characteristic of Argentine law rather than one specific to human rights-related cases.

Spiraling On: Dynamic Effects in the "Outside" State

Most writing on transnational advocacy and norm institutionalization focuses on the "inside" or target state—the state where the human rights violations took place. But these cases show that transnational prosecutions are both affected by, and in turn affect, the "outside" states from whence the pressure for change originates.

Transnational prosecutions raise risks of embarrassment and interference with commercial and diplomatic relations that diplomats tend to avoid if possible. Yet in each of the countries where transnational investigations or extradition procedures originated, there were countervailing internal pressures that led the governments to a more neutral position, or at least to mitigate their opposition. All these countries had a more or less sizeable and organized human rights lobby, and most had taken positions supporting criminal investigations in the Bosnian and Rwandan cases. Several, including France, Germany, Senegal, and the UK, were vocal supporters of the ICC. Beyond that, many of these investigations caught the governments in transition. In Belgium, Mexico, Spain and the UK, the cases arose just before or during a transition to a government of the opposing party, creating a situation where the new government wanted to distinguish itself from the old one, and where officials of the old government were less worried about creating future problems for the foreign ministry. In Spain, even once the conservative Aznar government took power, it was a minority government, dependent for its survival on the regional parties from the two most politically progressive regions of Spain (Cataluyna and the Basque Country), and so careful not to assume too aggressive an opposition to a popular cause. In Italy, Germany and the U.S. the cases were given new impetus under relatively progressive administrations.

On the other hand, the cases may have influenced a hardening of attitudes towards transnational, and international prosecutions. In the U.S., for example, the attempts to question Henry Kissinger no doubt helped solidify opposition to the International Criminal Court in both the legislative and executive branch.

The evolution of the cases created a secondary effect in the societies where the courts operate. Because they were high-profile and controversial, they raised the prominence of human rights and international law at home, suggesting that issues of impunity and accountability are important global concerns. Judges became more open to applying international law. The UK House of Lords, for example, in the next case it considered after *Pinochet*, a refugee law case, was much more liberal in applying international refugee law than it had been in the past, due in part at least to a new sensitivity to human rights issues.[16] Complainants in several European countries began looking more seriously at the possibilities of bringing resident human rights violators (individual and corporate) to book.

Beyond judges, the transnational investigations raised the issue of accountability for past violations more generally. This effect was clearest in Spain. The question of why Spain should prosecute the dictators of other countries, when the crimes of the Spanish Civil War remained unexamined, eventually came home to roost. The Spanish Parliament unanimously, for the first time, on November 20, 2002 agreed to honor the memory of "those men and women who were victims of the Spanish civil war, as well as those who suffered the repression of the Francoist dictatorship."[17] The Chamber of Deputies called on the government to recognize and provide economic and social assistance to those exiled by the war and to those Spaniards sent abroad as children. It also called on the government to assist with the ongoing exhumation of hundreds of mass graves.[18]

In Mexico, the demise of one-party PRI rule and the rise of several figures connected with the human rights movement to positions of power was clearly the driving force behind a new willingness to look into the crimes of the past. Nonetheless, journalists and political observers have pointed to the role of the Pinochet and Cavallo investigations in inspiring efforts to investigate the killings of students and peasants in Mexico in 1968, 1971 and throughout the 1970s. As of now, a Special Prosecutor is looking into the crimes, and ex-presidents and generals have been called in to testify. In November 2003, the Mexican Supreme Court found that the statute of limitations did not bar investigation and prosecution of 1970s-era disappearances, as these constitute continuing crimes.[19] As with most social phenomena, it is impossible to draw a single cause-effect line between Garzón's investigations in the Southern Cone and the renewed interest in domestic accountability, but surely the renewed national and international debate on accountability played a role in bringing long-dormant issues to the forefront.

Transitional Moments and Transnational Prosecutions

The concept of a "transition to democracy" became common currency in the 1990s. Books, articles and whole institutions grew up around the notion that the period of time after a repressive regime is toppled or a civil war ended and before new, more democratic institutions are consolidated presents special challenges and special needs. Everything is in flux: the new regime needs to signal a clear break with the past, but not change so far or so fast that the wheels of government screech to a halt. The remnants of the ancien régime may still wield considerable military or political power that must be somehow accommodated. Victims clamor for truth, justice, and redress. International support is at its height, but international attention will soon shift to the next crisis spot.

In these transitional situations, the prevailing wisdom has been that the new government should move quickly to establish mechanisms for dealing with the past. Once the "transitional moment" passes, it will be much harder to garner internal and external support for whatever combination of policies the government chooses, whether it be trials, truth commissions, cleansing of the bureaucracy or security forces, or reparations and commemorations. What's more, writers have emphasized the need for quick closure to painful, unresolved issues arising from conflict or repression. Governments need to act within about a one-year window, I wrote in 1995, "before the new government loses the widespread legitimacy it enjoys, before the political unity engendered by opposition to the old regime evaporates and apathy sets in, before the old guard can reorganize, and before the new government is overwhelmed by intractable economic and social problems."[20] Before international support dries up, NGOs drift and burn out, potential defendants and witnesses die or fall ill, and burgeoning common crime occupies the time of prosecutors and courts, I might add now.

I still believe there is a great deal of truth to these arguments. But the cases considered here complicate the picture. They show that government cannot decree the end of a transition. Not only are attempts to sweep the past under a rug of silence, even a partial one, contrary to emerging international law, they are just not going to work. Attempted transitions that try to close down the questions of truth, justice and redress too soon, will not hold. The unresolved or untouched issues will rise, becoming their own unburied, unquiet ghosts. And it may be that at least some aspects of justice prove easier to attain after time has distanced the actors, and the society, from the events in question.

Neither the Chilean nor the Argentine governments ignored the issue of transitional justice. The Chileans had the Truth and Reconciliation Commission, the trial of Contreras and Espinoza for killing Orlando

Letelier, and a substantial reparations program. Argentina went farther, investigating the disappearances in the CONADEP, trying the heads of the military juntas (although later pardons undermined some the practical effect) and providing reparations to many of the victims and their families. They then, in effect, declared the transition over and democracy its own reward. It is now clear that in a globalized world where both victims and victimizers travel and information travels even faster, such national declarations are not definitive.

Rather, it seems that calls for justice are periodic or cyclical, perhaps corresponding to generational change. It is no accident that most domestic trials of Nazis in postwar Germany happened in the early 1960s, when the first postwar generation came of age. It took the French two generations to confront their own history of collaboration, and it took the Spanish almost thirty years after Franco's death to apologize officially to the victims of Francoism, and nearly forty for the U.S. government to pay reparations for Japanese internment. So it is not surprising that now, twenty-odd years after the events, Chileans and Argentines should reopen the questions left unanswered in the immediate aftermath of the transition.

Waiting does have its advantages. Witnesses (and lawyers and judges) are less fearful for their personal safety or that of their family. It takes a while for people to be convinced that democracy is not simply an interlude between repressive episodes, especially where that's been the norm. The wall of silence that keeps terror-stricken communities from talking even within families, much less publicly, takes some time to dissipate. It is surprising how many of the witnesses in the cases, or how many of the exiles settled in Europe, had never before spoken of their torture or trauma. Time, in these cases, clearly does not heal all wounds—but it may make them easier to talk about.

With the passage of time, some perpetrators may have pangs of conscience or feel a need to clear their name or the name of their outfit, or at least not to be the fall guy for the higher-ups. A number of the military officers who decided to speak to judges in the 1990s said they did so because they felt their institutions had not been personally supportive, or had not taken institutional responsibility for their acts. Within the armed forces, those most implicated in crimes retire, and in the face of new institutional needs and challenges their influence wanes. The armed forces itself tends to lose the ability to define the national agenda, although clearly this was much less the case in Chile than in Argentina.

Judges may also have less of a personal stake in trying the crimes of the past. Most obviously, because many will be untouched by old battles and unable to suffer guilt pangs from their inaction in desperate times. This may lead to a willingness uncharacteristic of earlier judges to follow the evidence wherever it goes. The role of the judiciary as such may be stronger. This is, of course, one of the reasons to hold trials in the first place: to strengthen the rule of law and show that the current government is one "of laws, not of men." But early in a fragile transition, the courts may not be strong enough or independent enough to challenge executive decisions to close off prosecutions. That was certainly the case in Latin America in the 1980s and early 1990s. It may take the combination of judicial reform, experience with constitutionalism and judicial review, and outside example that finally pushes the courts to act. That takes time.

Perhaps we should decouple the notion of trials from that of transition.[21] Trials of wrongdoers from the prior regime may continue well beyond any "transitional" phase. The justifications for such trials, therefore, would have to be found somewhere beyond the usual rationales for trials in a transitional context: reestablishing the rule of law, providing an example that the new government differs from the old, avoiding the settling of scores against groups rather than culpable individuals. Ten to twenty years after the fact, these rationales will not stand. What then remains are the retributive, deterrent and victim-focused rationales for prosecutions: they are useful to right a social balance broken by offenders, to dissuade others from similar behavior, to substantiate and reinforce international rules, and, perhaps, to provide surcease and satisfaction to victims. The claims of justice, while more modest, are still quite powerful.

What lessons does a rethinking of "transition" suggest? These, at least: post-conflict governments should not count on a quick, self-contained transition period, but should expect periodic eruptions of the past into the present; blanket amnesty laws or other attempts to manufacture an end to discussion about the past are doomed, at least in the long run; it is key to create the conditions for prosecutions, but not invariably to prosecute all the leaders (or followers) of the old regime immediately, no matter what their crimes. In practice, transitional governments can phase in dealing with the past over a period of time, designing a multiphased, multilayered strategy on the basis of adequate consultation. Early on, they should focus on preserving evidence and on not foreclosing future options through blanket amnesties or the like. Removing the organizers and implementers of abuse from positions of power at the local level as well as nationally will keep them from sabotaging a new regime's plans or, as is often the case, serving as the basis of emerging criminal gangs. The creation of a credible factual record, through truth commissions or some equivalent mechanism, is also an early task, as is ensuring the basic material needs of survivors and a start to rebuilding of communities and communal ties. Increased attention to distributive justice, as well as rule of law, would enrich the toolkit of transitional justice practitioners enormously.[22] The question for transitions then becomes, not whether or not to prosecute or compensate, but in what time frame and under what conditions, and in what combination of national, transnational, and international forums. The answer to these questions will vary too much for general prescriptions to be useful. Transnational prosecutions will rarely be a centerpiece of such efforts, but they will often be a necessary component.

The larger question of the utility of prosecutions at all, anywhere, now or later, remains to be answered. The question is easiest to answer in the negative: a complete *lack* of prosecutions does seem to impede efforts at social reconstruction or reconciliation, and to act as a festering wound in the body politic. There is little empirical evidence for the view that trials either do or don't affirmatively help, in part because it's hard to pull apart the effects of a trial itself from its attendant record-creating, publicity and discussion-generating effects, and easy to speculate about other social measures that would generate similar discussion.[23] The answers may also vary considerably among cultures; other regions may see courts and trials as less central to justice. Nonetheless, the insistence of both international law and victims' groups in many places that only a formal airing of the charges against at least the ringleaders in cases of crimes against all humanity should provide some guide.

Final Word: The Meaning of the *Pinochet* Litigation

Transnational cases are quite rare, even after the *Pinochet* cases and their progeny. Even fewer transnational cases result in full trials, and fewer still in convictions. It remains to be seen whether universal jurisdiction will wither or bloom as a basis for proceedings.

The power of these cases does not come solely, or even, I suggest, mainly, from the capacity to capture errant dictators and torturers. Nor does it come from the possible salutary deterrent effects, either on atrocities or, at the least, on post-atrocity travel. In any case, these effects are next to impossible to measure in more than anecdotal terms. Rather, the primary value lies in the ability of a transnational investigation to prompt investigations and prosecutions at home. Through focusing world attention, through forcing the government to defend its judiciary, through empowering and strengthening domestic human rights lawyers and activists, transnational prosecutions time and time again have jump-started stalled or non-existent processes of accountability.

The aim of transnational prosecutions should therefore be primarily to set in motion real domestic processes of investigation and potential prosecution of those who are the target of the transnational action. If that is the objective, then those contemplating bringing transnational cases should focus on the conditions that will facilitate this outcome. Throughout this book, I have tried to indicate some of those conditions. In assessing the impact of the *Pinochet* litigation, it is hard to untangle the effects of the litigation itself from the attendant public debate. In the wake of the arrest, a dozen new books (mostly in Spanish) rehearsed Pinochet's past and the arguments for and against his prosecution. These books, and movies and TV specials on the same subject, circulated widely throughout Latin America. People who had never talked about their torture, or the effects of exile, or even their ambivalence about the coup, now opened up to family, friends and, in some cases, neighbors. A thousand intimate discussions of politics and personal fate followed. It may be that provoking these small, local discussions is the best starting point for real reconciliation, and public interventions should be judged on how well they propel discussion rather than shut it off . Measured on that scale, the *Pinochet* cases were a rousing success.

In the end, it was ordinary people, acting mostly on their own time and their own dime, who made the *Pinochet* cases a landmark in international law and a symbol for both dictators and *génocidaires* and for their survivors. It will be ordinary people, organized into various and ever-changing groups, who will hold states to their promises to respect and ensure basic human rights. And it is ordinary people who, again and again and again, until it's not necessary any more, will demand justice, of the national and international and transnational kind.

Notes

Chapter 1. The Beginning

1. Pilar Urbano, *Garzón: El hombre que veía amanecer* (Madrid: Plaza and Janes, 2000), 483.

2. *Israel v. Eichmann*, 36 *Int'l. L. Rep.* 5 (Israel, Dist. Ct., Jerusalem 1961).

3. The Amnesty International study, "Universal Jurisdiction: The Duty of States to Enact and Implement Legislation," AI Index IOR 53/002-018/2001 was released on CD-Rom in September 2001.

4. Matilde Artés's story is in Fernando Mas, *De Nuremberg a Madrid* (Madrid: Grijalbo, 1999), 32; Eduardo Anguita, *Sano juicio: Baltasar Garzón, algunos sobrevivientes y la lucha contra la impunidad en Latinoamérica* (Buenos Aires: Sudamericana, 2001), 174; Rita Arditti, *Searching for Life: The Grandmothers of the Plaza de Mayo and the Disappeared Children of Argentina* (Berkeley: University of California Press, 1999), 107.

5. Judge Garzón describes this testimony in his indictment of Admiral Leopoldo Galtieri, *Orden de Prisión Provisional Contra Galtieri*, Juzgado No. 5, Audiencia Nacional, March 25, 1997, available at http://www.derechos.org/nizkor/arg/espana/autogalt.html.

6. Mas, *De Nuremberg a Madrid*, 52.

7. *Orden de Prisión Provisional Contra Galtieri*.

8. Urbano, *Garzón*, 502.

9. Juan Gasparini, in Norberto Bermúdez and Juan Gasparini, *El testigo secreto* (Buenos Aires: Vergara, 1999), 39, puts the amount at $70 million. José Navas, spokesperson for IU in the Foreign Affairs Commission of the Spanish Congress of Deputies, gave a figure of $7 billion, as cited in Mas, 163.

10. *El Mercurio*, June 26, 1997, quoted in Paz Rojas, Víctor Espinoza, Julia Urquieta, and Hernán Soto, *Tarda pero llega: Pinochet ante la justicia española* (Santiago: LOM, 1998), 23.

11. Rojas et al., *Tarda pero llega*, 27.

12. Urbano, Garzón, 505.

13. Memo from case files, also reproduced in Rojas et al., 132.

Chapter 2. The Adventures of Augusto Pinochet in the United Kingdom: A "Most Civilized Country"

1. The defendant, Mohamed Ahmed Mahgroub, was charged with torture. The case was dropped in May 1999 with no further explanation from the Scottish prosecutor. Redress, "Universal Jurisdiction in Europe," available at www.redress.org.

2. *Al-Adsani v. Government of Kuwait*, 107 I.L.R. 536 (1996); *Al-Adsani v. United*

Kingdom, European Court of Human Rights, Application No. 35763/97, Judgment, November 21, 2001.

3. In Pilar Urbano, *Garzón: El hombre que veía amanecer* (Madrid: Plaza and Janes, 2000), 522, among others.

4. On the Pinochet family ties to arms dealing and manufacturing, see, among others, Tito Drago, *El Retorno de la ilusión: Pinochet el fin de la impunidad* (Barcelona: RBA Actual, 1999), 19–22.

5. European Parliament, Resolution on the arrest of General Pinochet in London, B4-0975/98, October 22, 1998.

6. Concluding observations of the Committee Against Torture: United Kingdom, November 17, 1998, UN Doc. A/54/44, para. 77 (f).

7. Quoted in Luis A. Salinas, *The London Clinic* (Santiago: LOM, 1999), 68.

8. Drago, *El Retorno de la ilusión,* 164.

9. Salinas, *The London Clinic,* 58.

10. Hugh O'Shaughnessy, *Pinochet: The Politics of Torture* (New York: NYU Press: 2000), 169.

11. Juan Francisco Coloane, *Britannia y un general* (Santiago: LOM, 2000), 174.

12. Reed Brody and Michael Ratner, eds., *The Pinochet Papers: The Case of Augusto Pinochet in Spain and Britain* (The Hague: Kluwer, 2000), 61.

13. Decision of the High Court of Justice for England and Wales, *In re Pinochet,* October 28, 1998, para. 80, reproduced in Brody and Ratner, 89.

14. Recollections of the participants; see also Eduardo Anguita, *Sano juicio: Baltasar Garzón, algunos sobrevivientes y la lucha contra la impunidad en Latinoamérica* (Buenos Aires: Sudamericana, 2001), 279–88.

15. The Chilean case, dated November 5, 1998, is reproduced in English in Brody and Ratner, *The Pinochet Papers,* 95, along with the companion Argentine case, dated November 14, 1998, in Spanish at www.derechos.org/nizkor/arg.

16. Control Council Law No. 10, Punishment of Persons Guilty of War Crimes, Crimes Against Peace and Against Humanity, December 20, 1945, art. II(1)(c).

17. William A. Schabas, "Problems of International Codification: Were the Atrocities in Cambodia and Kosovo Genocide?" *New England Law Review* 35 (Winter 2001): 287.

18. Decision by the Appellate Committee of the House of Lords, *In re Pinochet,* November 25, 1998 (hereafter *Pinochet I*).

19. Urbano, *Garzón,* 533.

20. Decision by the Appellate Committee of the House of Lords, *In re Pinochet,* January 15, 1999 (hereafter *Pinochet II*).

21. David Robertson seems to take this position. "The House of Lords as a Political and Constitutional Court: Lessons from the Pinochet Case," in *The Pinochet Case: A Legal and Constitutional Analysis,* ed. Diana Woodhouse (Oxford: Hart, 2000), 17–40.

22. Evadne Grant, "Pinochet 2: The Questions of Jurisdiction and Bias," in Woodhouse, *The Pinochet Case,* 41–61, p. 61.

23. Transcript of the hearings, day 2, Tuesday, January 19, 1999, p. 52.

24. Decision by the Appellate Committee of the House of Lords, *In re Pinochet,* March 24, 1999 (hereafter *Pinochet III*).

25. See, e.g., *Timurtas v. Turkey,* Case No. 23531/94, European Court of Human Rights, June 13, 2000, and other similar cases.

26. Urbano, 535, 545; Drago, *El Retorno de la ilusión,* 189.

27. *El Mercurio*, August 1, 1999.

28. *El País*, August 3, 1999, 8.

29. Judgment, In the Bow Street Magistrates' Court, *The Kingdom of Spain v. Augusto Pinochet Ugarte*, October 8, 1999, reproduced in Brody and Ratner, *The Pinochet Papers*, 397.

30. British medical report on Augusto Pinochet, reproduced in Brody and Ratner, *The Pinochet Papers*, 447.

31. Press statement, reproduced in Brody and Ratner, *The Pinochet Papers*, 412.

32. Brody and Ratner, *The Pinochet Papers*, 414.

33. Decision of the High Court of Justice for England and Wales, *R. v. Secretary of State for Home Department, ex parte The Kingdom of Belgium*, February 15, 2000, reproduced in Brody and Ratner, *The Pinochet Papers*, 417.

34. Comments of Spanish Doctors on British Medical Report, February 18, 2000, reproduced in Brody and Ratner, *The Pinochet Papers*, 461.

35. Letters from the Home Office to the Spanish, Belgian, Swiss, and French Ambassadors, March 2, 2000, reproduced in Brody and Ratner, *The Pinochet Papers*, 465.

36. Ernesto Ekeizer traces the diplomatic efforts in *Yo, Augusto* (Madrid: Aguilar, 2003). See also Hugh O'Shaugnessy's reporting in the *Guardian* for 1999 and 2000.

37. Antonio Remiro Brotóns, *El Caso Pinochet: Los límites de la impunidad* (Madrid: Biblioteca Nueva Política Exterior, 2000), 194.

38. Remiro Brotóns, *El Caso Pinochet*, 194.

Chapter 3. The Investigations Come Home to Chile

1. *The Mirror*, March 3, 2000.

2. The Criminal Procedure code was amended in 2000 to create a separate prosecutor's office and defense counsel, and an oral-based trial. Ley 19.696, October 12, 2000. That system only applies to crimes committed after its entry into operation. The methods of judicial control have also changed recently, with the creation of a Judicial Ethics Council, but it remains to be seen whether the result will be a more or less politicized judiciary.

3. Alejandra Matus's book, *El Libro negro de la justicia chilena* (Buenos Aires: Verso, 1999), was banned in Chile, and its author fled the country after criminal charges were filed against her for violations of the State Security law. In 2000, a parliamentary attempt to eliminate the law failed.

4. *Caso Miguel Estay Reyno and others*, Santiago, October 7, 1986.

5. Matus, *El Libro negro*, 47–52.

6. Arzobispado de Santiago, Fundación Documentación y Archivo de la Vicaría de la Solidaridad, *Situación de los derechos humanos durante el Segundo Semestre de 1996*.

7. *Caso Poblete Cordova*, Rol. No. 469-98, Corte Suprema, September 9, 1998. There is a technical problem with this argument. The grave breaches provisions of the Geneva Conventions, and the obligation to prosecute offenders, are placed in the sections on international armed conflict, not civil wars. No decision of the Chilean courts has focused on the distinction.

8. See, for instance, Hernán Montealegre Klenner's argument in *La Seguridad*

del estado y los derechos humanos (Santiago: Academia de Humanismo Cristiano, 1979).

9. For instance, *Caso Romo Mena*, Corte Suprema, October 26, 1995.

10. See, for instance, *Caso Uribe Tamblay et al.*, Corte Suprema, August 19, 1998; *Caso Quinones Lembach*, Corte Suprema, October 6, 1998; *Caso Eugenia Martínez*, Corte Suprema, November 11, 1998.

11. *Caso Contreras Maluje*, Corte Suprema, October 26, 1998. Other disappearance cases reopened by the Supreme Court on grounds that the amnesty could not yet be applied include Berrios, Barrientos, Moraga, 24 farmers disappeared in Paine, and 8 MIR militants disappeared in Valparaíso. See Arzobispado de Santiago, *Situación de los derechos humanos durante el Primer Semestre de 1998*; *Segundo Semestre de 1998*.

12. Resolución del Ministro de Fuero Juan Guzmán Tapia, June 8, 1999.

13. Corte Suprema de Chile, July 20, 1999.

14. Although the public was barred, the newspaper *La Nación* ran a special supplement on May 28, 2000, with a blow-by-blow account of the hearings.

15. *Diario La Segunda*, June 5, 2000.

16. Judge Guzmán's original indictment was issued December 1, 2000; the Court of Appeals reversed him on December 11. The Supreme Court agreed with the Court of Appeals (and reversed Guzmán) on December 20.

17. Pinochet's arrest produced a spate of indignant books with names like Patricio C. Parodi Pinedo's *El Secuestro del general* (The Kidnapping of the General) (Santiago: Antártica Quebecor, 1990), which made variations on these arguments.

18. Declaración Pública de Abogados de Derechos Humanos Rechazando la Mesa de Diálogo, June 17, 2000, available at http://www.derechos.org/nizkor/chile/doc/mesa2.html.

19. Corte Suprema, July 1, 2001.

20. Corte Suprema, October 14. 2002. Guzmán kept 5 of the 99 consolidated case files originally under his jurisdiction.

21. Arzobispado de Santiago, *Situación de los derechos humanos durante el Primero Semestre de 2002*.

22. Corte de Apelaciones de Santiago, August 6, 2002.

23. Judge Guzmán ordered the case against Contreras closed on June 22, 2002, and was upheld by the Supreme Court. On June 2, 2003, Judge Guzmán ordered five lower-ranked officers indicted and detained in the case.

24. FASIC, Lista de Querellas Actualizada, available at http://www.fasic.org.

25. Sebastian Brett, "Discreet Path to Justice? Chile, Thirty Years After the Military Coup," *Human Rights Watch* (September 2003), available at http://www.hrw.org/americas. A draft text of the law is available at http://www.memoriayjusticia.cl/espanol/sp-home.html.

26. *Caso Barrios Altos (Chumbipuma y otros v. Peru)* sentence of March 14, 2001.

27. Quinta Sala de la Corte de Apelaciones de Santiago, *s/ recurso de Fernando Laureani Maturana y Miguel Krassnoff Marchenko (Caso Miguel Angel Sandoval)*, January 5, 2004, para. 53.

Chapter 4. Argentina: Truth and Consequences

1. Jaime Malamud-Goti, *Game Without End: State Terror and the Politics of Justice* (Norman: University of Oklahoma Press, 1996).

2. Judgment, No. 23, Cámara Federal de Apelaciones en lo Criminal y Correccional, December 5, 1985, 26 I.L.M. 317 (1987) (appeals court); *Causa* 13, Corte Suprema, December 30, 1986, Revista de Jurisprudencia Argentina, no. 5513, April 29, 1987.

3. These were Generals Camps and Riccheri. Marcelo Sancinetti and Marcelo Ferrante, *El Derecho penal en la protección de los derechos humanos* (Buenos Aires: Hammurabi, 1999), 341.

4. *Camps*, Corte Suprema, June 22, 1987.

5. William C. Prilliman, *The Judiciary and Democratic Decay in Latin America* (Westport, Conn.: Praeger, 2000), 123.

6. Prilliman, *The Judiciary and Democratic Decay*, 128.

7. *In re Miguel Angel Ekmekdijian c. Gerardo Sofovich*, Corte Suprema, July 7, 1992; Sancinetti and Ferrante.

8. *Schwammberger, Josef Franz Leo s/solicitud de extradicción*, Corte Suprema, CSJN Fallos 313: 257, March 20, 1990.

9. *Priebke, Erich s/solicitud de extradicción*, Corte Suprema, CSJN Fallos 318: 2148, November 2, 1995.

10. The Italian case itself raised the question of retroactivity of law that has bedeviled this type of prosecution. The Italian Military Tribunal originally held that Priebke could not be charged with genocide because it had only become a crime under Italian law in 1967. After a public outcry, the civilian courts reversed the ruling, finding that under international law, crimes such as Priebke's were war crimes and/or crimes against humanity, and so covered by the customary law (indeed, jus cogens) rule of non-applicability of statutes of limitations. Corte di assise di Roma, *Sentencia condenatoria del Gral (R) Carlos Guillermo Suárez Masón, Gral (R) Santiago Omar Riveros y otros por crímenes contra ciudadanos italianos en la República Argentina*, December 6, 2000, available at http://www.derechos.org/nizkor/italia/sent.html.

11. *Priebke.*

12. Brief as *amicus curiae* of CEJIL and Human Rights Watch/Americas, June 1995, available at http://www.nuncamas.org/document/document.htm.

13. *Privaciones ilegales de libertad en el centro clandestino de detención Club Atlético (Lapacó Case)*, Cámara Federal de Apelaciones en lo Criminal y Correccional, Sala II, October 14, 1997.

14. *Suárez Mason, Carlos Guillermo s/homicidio, privación illegal de la libertad, etc.*, Corte Suprema, CSJN, S.1085, September 29, 1998.

15. *Urteaga, Facundo Raúl c. Estado Nacional—Estado Mayor Conjunto de las FF.AA.*, Corte Suprema, CSJN, U. 14.33, October 15, 1998.

16. *Alicia Consuela Herrera et al.*, case nos. 10.147 et al., 1992–93 Ann. Rep. Int.-Am. Comm'n H. Rts. 41 (1993).

17. *Las Hojas Massacre Case*, case no. 10.287, 1992–93 Ann. Rep. Int.-Am. Comm'n. H. Rts. 88 (1993) (El Salvador); *Hugo Leonardo et al.*, case nos. 10.029 et al., 1992–93 Ann. Rep. Int.-Am. Comm'n H. Rts 154 (1993) (Uruguay); *Garay Hermosilla et al.*, case no. 10.843, 1996 Ann. Rep. Int.-Am. Comm'n H. Rts. 156 (1997) (Chile).

18. *Caso Barrios Altos (Chumbipuma Aguirre y otros v. Peru)*, sentence of March 14, 2001.

19. *Carmen Aguiar de Lapacó v. Argentina*, case no. 12.059, Report 21/00, OEA/Ser.L/V/II.106 Doc. 3 rev. at 340 (1999).

20. *Schwammberger, J. F. L. s/extradicción*, Cámara Federal de la Plata, Sala III penal, No. 41.979, August 30, 1989, voto del Dr. Schiffrin.

21. Cámara Federal de Apelaciones de La Plata, case no. 1098, Res. 140/99, November 1, 1999.

22. Cámara Federal de Apelaciones de La Plata, case no. 1098, Res. 168/99, December 14, 1999; see also revision by the full appeals court, April 25, 2000.

23. That court hears challenges to criminal law rulings. Cámara Nacional de Casación Penal, Causa No. 1996—Sala IV, *Julian Oscar, s/recurso de queja*, September 13, 2000.

24. Mónica Gutiérrez, "Encuentro de abogados que actúan en casos de derechos humanos," *Página 12*, Buenos Aires, April 23, 2001.

25. *La Nación*, "No se podrá demoler la ESMA, lo confirmó la Corte Suprema; puede tener 'pruebas valiosas'," February 14, 2001.

26. See Rita Arditti, *Searching for Life: The Grandmothers of the Plaza de Mayo and the Disappeared Children of Argentina* (Berkeley: University of California Press, 1999).

27. *Videla, Jorge Rafael y otros s/presunta infracción a los articulos 146, 293 y 139 inciso 2 del Codigo Penal*, Causa No. 1284/85, Juzgado Federal No. 1 Criminal y Correccional de San Isidro, a cargo del Dr. Roberto José Marquevich, resolution of May 14, 1997, at 2847 et sec. (Bianco).

28. All these cases are described in the Marquevich indictment of Videla, *Videla, Jorge Rafael y otros*, resolution of July 13, 1998.

29. *Videla, Jorge Rafael y otros*, at 2869.

30. *Videla, Jorge Rafael, s/recursos de apelación y nulidad*, Resolution of the Cámara Federal de Apelaciones en lo Criminal y Correccional, Sala I, September 9, 1999.

31. *Nicolaides, Cristino y otros s/sustracción de menores*, No. 10326/96, Juzgado Nacional en lo Criminal y Correccional No. 7, Secretaria No. 13, Dr. Adolfo Luis Bagnasco, September 22, 1999.

32. *Astiz, Alfredo s/nulidad*, No. 16.071, Cámara Federal de Apelaciones en lo Criminal y Correccional, Sala II, May 4, 2000.

33. A description of the Court of Appeals decision is at "Los Represores de la ESMA confirmados en prisión," *Página 12*, January 11, 2002, available at http://www.pagina12.com.ar/2001/01-12/01-12-29/pag12.htm.

34. *Simon, Julio, del Cerro, Juan Antonio s/sustracción de menores de 10 anos*, No. 8686/2000, Juzgado Nacional en lo Criminal y Correccional No. 4, Dr. Gabriel Cavallo, March 6, 2001, available at www.derechos.org/nizkor/arg/ley/juezcavallo03mar.htlm. The underlying baby-snatching case is *Landa, Ceferino s/ procesamiento con prisión preventiva*, No. 16.425, February 25, 2000, confirmed by the Federal Appeals Court on May 11, 2000.

35. *Extradition of Suárez-Mason*, 694 F. Supp. 676; 1988 (N.D. Calif., April 27, 1988).

36. *Cavallo* decision of March 6, 2001, 27.

37. *Cavallo*, 74.

38. *Astiz, Alfredo y otros s/delito de accion Pública*, No. 7.694/99, Juzgado Nacional en lo Criminal y Correccional No. 12, Dr. Claudio Bonadío, October 1, 2001.

39. *Incidente de apelación de Simon, Julio*, No. 17.889, Cámara Federal de Apelaciones en lo Criminal y Correccional, Sala II, November 9, 2001.

40. *Sobre la inconstitucionalidad y nulidad de las leyes de Obediencia Debida y Punto Final*, Res. No. 586/02, Juzgado Federal No. 1 de Santa Fe, Dr. Reinaldo Ruben Rodríguez, August 14, 2002; Cámara Federal de Salta, *Causa Cabezas, Daniel Vicente y Otros s/ Denuncia—Palomitas—Cabezas de Buey*, Expte. de Cámara No. 027/03, July 29, 2003.

41. *Verbitsky, Horacio-C.E.L.S. S/Inconstitucionalidad de las leyes N 23521 y 23492, en relacion: Desaparición forzada de personas-torturas y homicidios agravados en hechos ocurridos en la localidad de Margarita Belén, Chaco el 13/12/ 76,* No. 306/01, Juzgado Federal de Chaco, Dr. Carlos Skidelsky, March 6, 2003.

42. Dictamen del procurador general de la Nación en contra de las leyes de Obediencia Debida y Punto Final en la Causa S.C.S. 1767; L. XXXVIII, *Simon, Julio Hector y otros s/privación ilegítima de la libertad, etc.,* No. S.C.S. 17768 (Caso Poblete), August 29, 2002. An almost identical brief was filed in the Conrado Gómez case.

43. Supreme Court President Julio Nazareno resigned on June 27, 2003 to avoid impeachment, as did Judge Guillermo López. Judge Moliné O'Connor was removed by the legislature and Judge Adolfo Vásquez faces impeachment. President Kirchner appointed Professor Raúl Zaffaroni, one of the country's foremost penal law specialists and anti-impunity campaigners, and proposed Carmen Argibay, then a judge at the International Criminal Tribunal for the Former Yugoslavia, to the Court along with another woman.

44. Law 23.040, December 29, 1983. The Supreme Court upheld the law on December 30, 1986.

Chapter 5. The European Cases

1. A summary of the case may be found in English at Luc Reydams, Belgian Tribunal of First Instance of Brussels (investigating magistrate), November 8, 1998, *A.J.I.L.* 93 (July 1999): 700.

2. That story is told in Tina Rosenberg, *Children of Cain: Violence and the Violent in Latin America* (New York: Morrow, 1991), 79–81.

3. Rosenberg, *Children of Cain,* 132.

4. *Alfredo Astiz,* March 16, 1990, Cour d'Assises de Paris.

5. On the prosecution of Ould Dah, see www.fidh.org; on crimes against humanity, see *Fédération National des Déportées et Internés Résistants et Patriots v. Barbie,* 78 ILR 124 (Cour de Cassation 1985); 100 ILR 330 (Cour de Cassation 1988); *Boudarel, George* (Cour de Cassation Crim., Apr. 1, 1993, *Gaz. Pal.* 1993, 281); *Touvier,* 100 ILR 338 (Cour de Cassation 1992).

6. See *La Nación,* February 21, 2001;

7. Quoted in "Olivera quedó libre por 'error' de la Justicia," *Página 12,* February 21, 2001.

8. Corte di assise di Roma, December 6, 2000, Spanish version at http// www.derechos.org/nizkor/italia/sentencia.html.

9. *La Nación* On-line, July 2, 2001.

10. *Página 12,* July 3, 2001.

11. The details of her case, along with the Nuremberg proceedings, can be found (in German) at www/menschenrechte.org/Koalition/htm.

12. Bundesgerichtshof, decision of October 20, 1999, cited in Dr. iur. Florian Jessberger, "Prosecuting International Crimes in Domestic Courts: A Look Back Ahead," December 8, 2001 (unpublished paper, Humboldt-Universitat zu Berlin.)

13. "Presbyterian Torture Survivor to Testify About Friend's Death in Argentine 'Dirty War': Minister from New York Takes Witness Stand in Nuremberg," *Presbyterian Church of USA News,* January 17, 2001.

14. Decree 111/98 was specific to the Spanish investigation and prohibited

all judicial cooperation as well as extradition. See http://www.u-j.info/index/134018.

15. Decree 1581/2001, Cooperación Internacional en Materia Penal, December 5, 2001, denied judicial assistance or extradition in any inquiry into the 1976–83 period crimes covered by the amnesty laws.

16. *Auto pidiendo orden de arresto internacional,* December 30, 1999; Auto of 10 Oct. 1997.

17. In addition to his articles for *Reforma,* Vales published a book, *Ricardo Cavallo: Genocidio y corrupción en América latina* (Buenos Aires: Norma, 2003). See Anguita, *Sano juicio,* chap. 7.

18. Oficio PGR/0583/2000, August 25, 2000, Procuraduría General de la República. Cavallo was ordered detained the next day.

19. *United States v. Alvarez-Machain,* 504 US 655 (1992), *Alvarez-Machain v. United States,* 284 F.3d 1039 (9th Cir. 2002), reversed,—US—(2004), June 29, 2004.

20. Vales, *Ricardo Cavallo,* 417, 426–28.

21. Treaty of Extradition and Mutual Assistance in Penal Matters between the United Mexican States and the Kingdom of Spain, entered into force July 1, 1980; Protocol to the Treaty of Extradition, entered into force September 1, 1996.

22. *Extradition No. 5/2000,* Decision of January 11, 2001, Judge Jesús Guadalupe Luna Altamirano, Juez Sexto de Distrito en Procesos Penales Federales en el Distrito Federal, available on www.derechos.org/nizkor/arg/cavallo.

23. Acuerdo de la Secretaría de Relaciones Exteriores, February 2, 2001.

24. Suprema Corte de Justicia, *Caso Cavallo,* June 10, 2003, available at www.scjn.gob.mx/inicial.asp.

Chapter 6. Operation Condor Redux

1. Human Rights Watch, *Argentina, Reluctant Partner,* December 2001, available at http://www.hrw.org/americas.

2. Querella, November 8, 1999, reproduced in *El Mostrador,* April 18, 2000, www.elmostrador.cl.

3. Juzgado Nacional en lo Criminal y Correccional Federal No. 7, Case 13.445/1999, decisions of April 11, 2001 and July 10, 2001.

4. *Videla, Jorge R. s/procesamiento,* Cámara Federal de Buenos Aires, Causa 33714, Sala I, May 23, 2002 (appeals court).

5. Corte Suprema, Sala II, Penal, March 27, 2002; also in Human Rights Watch, *Argentina, Reluctant Partner,* chap. 9.

6. The complaint was filed September 4, 2001 in the Montevideo Juzgado Penal de Turno.

7. Judge Eduardo Cavalli, Juez Letrado de Primera Instancia en lo Penal, October 18, 2002.

8. *Agenda Confidencial,* Channel 12 TV program, December 30, 2001, reported at www.comcosur.com.uy.

9. *S/sentencia de Manuel Contreras y Pedro Espinoza,* Corte Suprema, May 30, 1995.

10. The litigation spawned several decisions: *Letelier v. Republic of Chile,* 488 F.Supp. 665 (D.D.C., March 11, 1980); *Letelier v. Republic of Chile,* 502 F.Supp. 259 (D.D.C., November 5, 1980); *De Letelier v. Republic of Chile,* 567 F. Supp. 1490

(S.D.N.Y., July 28, 1983); *Letelier v. Republic of Chile*, 748 F.2d 790 (2nd Cir., 1984), cert. denied 471 U.S. 1125 (1985).

11. Decision with regard to the dispute concerning resonsibility for the deaths of Letelier and Moffitt, 31 I.L.M. 1 (1992).

12. Judge Servini's auto of November 17, 2000; affirmed by the Cámara Federal de Buenos Aires, May 22, 2001.

13. Judge Servini requested the preventive detention of the defendants on October 8, 2001, in a decision affirmed by the Cámara Federal de Buenos Aires on December 18, 2001.

14. The Chilean Supreme Court refused twice to extradite Pinochet: on August 6, 2001 they said his immunity needed to be removed; on November 8, 2002 they definitively refused to extradite.

15. The Chilean Supreme Court decided not to grant extradition to the remaining defendants on December 2, 2002, but ordered local courts to reopen the Prats case in Chile. On January 23, 2003, the Prats daughters filed a criminal complaint, thus becoming a party to the ongoing criminal investigation. For a chronology of events, see www.memoriayjusticia.cl/english.

16. Marc Cooper, *The Nation*, June 3, 2002. The memo can be found in the National Security Archive's declassified materials on Chile, at http://www.gwu.edu/~nsarchiv/news/19991008/.

17. Cooper, *The Nation*, June 3, 2002.

18. Both the statute and the original ATCA are at 28 U.S.C. 1350.

19. Christopher Hitchens, *The Trial of Henry Kissinger* (New York: Verso, 2001); the movie *The Trials of Henry Kissinger* was produced by Icarus Films, New York, 2002.

20. Bow Street Magistrates Court, District Judge Nicolas Evans, April 24, 2002.

21. *René Schneider et al. v. Henry Kissinger et al.*, Civ. No. 01-1902 (HHK), U.S. District Court for the District of Columbia. The Motion to Dismiss by the government, acting as Kissinger's attorney, was filed November 9, 2001.

22. The cases are, respectively, *Doe v. Unocal Corp.*, *Bowoto v. Chevron Corp.*, and *Doe v. Exxon-Mobil Corp.* Information on them can be found at http://www.earthrights.org. As of this writing, none have gone to jury trial.

Chapter 7. The Legal Legacy of Pinochet: Universal Jurisdiction and Its Discontents

1. Commission on Historical Clarification, *Memory of Silence*, February 25, 1999, available at www.hrdata.aaas.org/ceh/report/english.

2. Presentation of complaint, No. 331/99, before Juzgado Central de Instrucción no.1 de la Audiencia Nacional, December 2, 1999.

3. Auto of March 27, 2000.

4. Ley de Reconciliación Nacional, Decree 145-96, December 18, 1996.

5. Diligencias Previas No. 331/99, May 4, 2000; there is a prior motion to reconsider, dated March 29, 2000. The basic documents through 2000 are contained in Fundación Rigoberta Menchú Tum, *Jurisdicción Universal para el Juzgamiento del Genocidio en Guatemala* (México: FRMT, 2001).

6. *Caso Guatemala (Rigoberta Menchú Tum)*, Audiencia Nacional (Sala penal), December 13, 2000, available at http://www.icrc.org/ihl-nat.nsf and http://www.derechos.org/nizkor/guatemala.

7. Tribunal Supremo, *Caso Genocidio en Guatemala*, February 25, 2003, available at http://www.derechos.org/nizkor/guatemala/doc/gtmsent.html.

8. Tribunal Supremo, *Caso Hernán Brady Roche*, March 8, 2004, available at http://www.derechos.org/nizkor/chile/juicio/brady.html.

9. Article 1(6) of the Civil Code holds that jurisprudence (court decisions) complement doctrine when the Supreme Court has established them "repeatedly."

10. Ricardo Cavallo was extradited from Mexico and ordered jailed pending trial by the Audiencia Nacional on June 29, 2003. Adolfo Scilingo was arrested in Madrid, and his case was ordered ready for trial on June 27, 2003. Both men have appealed to the Supreme Court.

11. Tribunal Supremo, *Caso Genocidio en Perú* (No. 712/2003), available at http://www.universaljurisdiction.info/index/128118.

12. The complaint was originally filed in 1996, alleging murder. On May 13, 1997, the Public Prosecution Service decided not to prosecute, and the complainants appealed that decision on June 13 and 27. Originally the complaint was based on the Dutch nationality of the defendant, but an examining magistrate found on July 30, 1999, that he did not have Dutch nationality. The case then went back to the court of appeals on the torture charges.

13. Opinion of C. J. R. Dugard, requested by the Court of Appeal of Amsterdam, July 7, 2000.

14. Court of Appeal of Amsterdam, November 20, 2000, Institute's Collection No. 5013, Elrono. AA8395, available at http://www.rechtspraak.nl. For commentary, see Jann K. Kleffner, "Jurisdiction over Genocide, Crimes Against Humanity: War Crimes, Torture and Terrorism in the Netherlands," Amsterdam Center for International Law, in *Crimes internationaux et jurisdictions nationales: Etude comparée*, ed. Antonio Cassese and Mireille Delmas-Marty. (Paris: Presses Universitaires de France, 2002).

15. Supreme Court of the Netherlands, Criminal Div., No. 00749/01 (CW 2323), September 18, 2001.

16. Quoted in Patricio C. Parodi Pinedo, *El Secuestro del general* (Santiago: Antártica Quebecor, 1990), 153.

17. Many of the documents related to the Habré prosecution, in English and French, may be found on the Human Rights Watch website, http://www.hrw.org.

18. Reed Brody, "Justice Comes to Chad," March 20, 2002, available at http://www.hrw.org/editorials/2002/justicetochad.htm.

19. Speech at American University, Washington School of Law, Conference on the Pinochet Case, March 2001.

20. Cour de Cassation du Senegal, Première chambre statuant en matière pénale, Arrêt n' 14 du 20-3-2001 Pénal, *Souleymane Guengueng et autres contre Hissène Habré*, March 20, 2001, available at http://www.hrw.org/french/themes/habre-cour_de_cass.html.

21. For example, International Covenant on Civil and Political Rights, art. 14; American Convention on Human Rights, art. 8; African Charter on Human and Peoples' Rights, art. 7.

22. Conseil Constitutionnel, Decision No. 002/PCC/SG/001, available at http://www.hrw.org/french/themes/habre-decisionduconseil.html.

23. See http://www.hrw.org/french/themes/habre-cat.html.

24. Marcus Gee, "Evil on Trial, Part I," *Toronto Globe and Mail*, June 8, 2002.

25. Brody, "Justice Comes to Chad."

26. *The Arrest Warrant case (Democratic Republic of Congo v. Belgium)*. The decision is available on the ICJ website, http://www.icj-cij.org, and also at www.u-paris2.fr/cij/icjwww/idocket/iCOBE/ iCOBEcr/icobe_icr_2001-11_20011019.PDF.

27. Separate Opinion of Judges Higgins, Buergenthal, and Koojimans.

28. *Case of Certain Criminal Proceedings in France (Republic of the Congo v. France)*, application of December 9, 2002, available at http://www.icj-cij.org/icjwww/idocket/icof/icoforder/icof_iapplication_2 0020209.pdf; Order of 17 June 2003, Request for Provisional Measures, available at http://www.icj-cij.org/ic www/idocket/icof/icoforder/icof_iorder_20030617. PDF.

29. 10th Chamber, Cour d'Appel de Bruxelles, *Sharon and others*, June 26, 2002, available at http://www.universaljurisdiction.info/index/cases/cases/Belgium_Sharon_cas e/case_Doc_Summaries/101492,0.

30. Complaint of March 18, 2003; see Belgian Cour de Cassation, dismissal of September 24, 2003, available at http://www.universaljurisdiction.info/index/129351.

31. Complaint of May 12, 2003, available at http://www.stopusa.be/1Campagne/Proces-Franks/PROCES-complaint_against_Tommy_Franks.htm#_Toc 43649523.

32. For a summary and analysis, see Human Rights Watch, "Belgium: Questions and Answers on the 'Anti-Atrocity' Law," June 2003, available at http://www.hrw.org/campaigns/icc/belgium-qna.pdf.

33. Draft Code of Crimes Against International Law, sec. 153f. The Draft Code entered into force on June 30, 2002. The text of the law can be found at http://www.bmj.bund.de/frames/eng/service/legislation_plans/10000582/index.html.

34. See article 8, Crimes Against Humanity and War Crimes Act of Canada (2000); article 2(3), Implementation of the Rome Statute of the ICC Act of South Africa (2002).

35. The study is available at http://web.amnesty.org/web/web.nsf/pages/int_jus_uj_legal_memorandum, or on CD-ROM. See also Luc Reydams, *Universal Jurisdiction: International and Municipal Legal Perspectives* (Oxford: Oxford University Press, 2003).

36. A person present in Canada suspected of previously committing one or more ICC crimes, pursuant to article 8 of the Crimes against Humanity and War Crimes Act Act "may be prosecuted" if "after the time the offence is alleged to have been committed, the person is present in Canada.". In contrast, article 8 of the New Zealand International Crimes and International Criminal Court Act 2000 provides for universal jurisdiction over war crimes within the jurisdiction of the International Criminal Court, occurring on or after October 1, 2000, or over acts which would have constituted crimes in New Zealand at the time they occurred had it taken place in New Zealand. Section 8 (3) expressly provides that the accused does not need to be present in New Zealand at the time he or she is charged.

37. *United States v. Bin Laden*, 132 F. Supp. 2d 168 (S.D. N.Y. 2001). Thanks to Diane Amann for this idea.

38. Cour de Cassation, *Ely Ould Dah case*, October 23, 2002, available at http://legal.apt.ch/MECHANISMS/International_Justice/Universal%20Jurisdiction/France%/20-%20Germany%20-%20UK/fr-ca%20e;u%20ould.htm.

39. Garth Meintjes and Juan E. Méndez. "Reconciling Amnesties with Universal Jurisdiction," *International Law Forum* 2 (2000): 76.

40. That story is told in Richard Kluger, *Simple Justice: The History of Brown v.*

Board of Education and Black America's Struggle for Equality (New York: Knopf, 1975).

41. On the creation and operation of the ICC, see William A. Schabas, *An Introduction to the International Criminal Court* (Cambridge: Cambridge University Press, 2001); Geoffrey Robertson, *Crimes Against Humanity: The Struggle for Global Justice* (London: Viking, 1999).

42. See Elizabeth Neuffer, *The Key to My Neighbor's House: Seeking Justice in Bosnia and Rwanda* (New York: Picador, 2002); John Hagan, *Justice in the Balkans: Prosecuting War Crimes in the Hague Tribunal* (Chicago: University of Chicago Press, 2003); Virginia Morris and Michael Scharf, *The International Criminal Tribunal for Rwanda* (New York: Transnational Press, 1998).

43. Eric Stover and Rachel Shikegane, "The Missing in the Aftermath of War: When Do the Needs of Victims' Families and International War Crimes Tribunals Clash?" *International Review of the Red Cross* (December 2002).

44. See Letter to ICTR Prosecutor Carla del Ponte from Coalition for Women's Human Rights in Conflict Situations, March 12, 2003, available at http://www.ccr-ny.org/v2/reports/docs/DelponteLetter.pdf; Eric Stover, *The Witnesses: War Crimes and the Promise of Justice in the Hague* (Berkeley: Human Rights Center at the University of California, 2003; Philadelphia: University of Pennsylvania Press, 2005).

45. Final Report on the Question of Impunity for Violations of Human Rights (Civil and Political Rights), prepared by Louis Joinet in accordance with resolution 1996/119 of the Subcommission for the Prevention of Discrimination and Protection of Minorities, 49th Sess., Agenda Item 9, UN Doc. E/CN.4/Sub.2/1997/20/Rev. 1 (2 Oct. 1997), principle 18.

46. International Criminal Court, Rules of Procedure and Evidence, Rule 91.

Chapter 8. The Actors Behind the Pinochet *Cases*

1. Marc Bossuyt, "The Development of Special Procedures of the United Nations Commission on Human Rights," *Human Rights Law Journal* 6 (1985): 179.

2. Iain Guest, *Behind the Disappearances: Argentina's Dirty War Against Human Rights and the United Nations* (Philadelphia: University of Pennsylvania Press, 1990).

3. Rita Arditti, *Searching for Life: The Grandmothers of the Plaza de Mayo and the Disappeared Children of Argentina* (Berkeley: University of California Press, 1999). The right to identity is part of the Convention on the Rights of the Child.

4. Margaret Keck and Kathryn Sikkink, *Activists Beyond Borders: Transnational Advocacy Networks in International Politics* (Ithaca, N.Y.: Cornell University Press, 1998).

5. Thomas Risse and Kathryn Sikkink, "The Socialization of International Human Rights Norms into Domestic Practices: Introduction," in *The Power of Human Rights: International Norms and Domestic Change*, ed. Thomas Risse, Stephen C. Ropp, and Kathryn Sikkink (Cambridge: Cambridge University Press, 1999), 18–35.

6. Risse and Sikkink, "The Socialization of International Human Rights Norms."

7. Ellen Lutz and Kathryn Sikkink, "The Justice Cascade: The Evolution and

Impact of Foreign Human Rights Trials in Latin America," *Chicago Journal of International Law* 2 (2001): 1, 29–30.

8. Kathryn Sikkink has called Argentina a case of "insider-outsider coalitions."

9. Khachig Toloyan, "Rethinking Diaspora(s): Stateless Power in the Transnational Moment," *Diaspora* 5 (1996): 3–86.

10. Yossi Shain and others discuss the role of these communities in influencing electoral politics. See Yossi Shain, "The Mexican-American Diaspora's Impact on Mexico," *Political Science Quarterly* 114 (Winter 1999).

11. Peter M. Haas, ed., *Knowledge, Power and International Policy Coordination*, Studies in International Relations (Columbia: University of South Carolina Press, 1997), originally special issue, *International Organization* 46, 1 (1992); see also Lutz and Sikkink, "The Justice Cascade."

12. See, for example, Thomas R. Tyler, *Why People Obey the Law* (New Haven, Conn.: Yale University Press, 1990).

13. Andrew Moravcsik, "Taking Preferences Seriously: A Liberal Theory of International Politics," *International Organization* 51 (1997): 513–53; Anne-Marie Slaughter et al., "International Law and International Relations Theory: A New Generation of Interdisciplinary Scholarship," *American Journal of International Law* 92 (1998): 367.

14. Martha Finnemore and Kathryn Sikkink, "International Norm Dynamics and Political Change," *International Organization* 52 (1998): 887.

15. Christopher McCrudden, "A Common Law of Human Rights? Transnational Judicial Conversations on Constitutional Rights," *Oxford Journal of Legal Studies* 20 (2000): 499; Anne-Marie Slaughter, "Judicial Globalization," *Virginia Journal of International Law* 40 (1999–2000): 1103.

16. Judgments—*Islam (A.P.) v. Secretary of State for the Home Department; Regina v. Immigration Appeal Tribunal and Another Ex Parte Shah (A.P.)* (Conjoined Appeals), March 25, 1999. Of course, the entry into force of the 1998 Human Rights Act also played a large role in this increased sensibility.

17. Resolution, Spanish Chamber of Deputies, November 20, 2002.

18. "Spain Begins to Confront Its Past," *Christian Science Monitor*, February 6, 2003, available at http://www.csmonitor.com/2003/0206/p06s01-woam.html.

19. On November 26, 2003, a judge in Guerrero province issued an arrest warrant in a disappearance case, after the Supreme Court overturned a lower court decision on the statute of limitations issue. Information at www.hrw.org/press/2003/11/mexico112603.htm.

20. Naomi Roht-Arriaza, "Conclusions," in *Impunity in International Law and Practice*, ed. Naomi Roht-Arriaza (Oxford: Oxford University Press, 1995).

21. Thanks to Alexandra Hunneus for developing this idea.

22. Rama Mani, *Beyond Retribution: Seeking Justice in the Shadows of War* (Oxford: Polity Press, 2002). Mani's framework gives equal weight in post-conflict societies to building the rule of law, rectificatory justice, and distributive justice and shows how the three are interrelated.

23. See Laurel Fletcher and Harvey M. Weinstein, "Violence and Social Repair: Rethinking the Contribution of Justice to Reconciliation," *Human Rights Quarterly* 24, 3 (2002): 573–639, on the lack of empirical data; Mark Osiel, *Mass Atrocity, Collective Memory, and the Law* (New Brunswick, N.J.: Transaction Publishers, 1997) and Jose E. Alvarez,. "Crimes of States/Crimes of Hate: Lessons from Rwanda," *Yale Journal of International Law* 24 (1999): 365, on the discussion-provoking effects of trials.

Bibliography

Abrams, Jason. "The Atrocities in Cambodia and Kosovo: Observations on the Codification of Genocide." *New England Law Review* 35 (Winter 2001): 303.

Acuna, Carlos H. "Guarding the Guardians in Argentina: Some Lessons About the Risks and Benefits of Empowering the Courts." In *Transitional Justice and the Rule of Law in New Democracies*, ed. A. James McAdams. Notre Dame, Ind.: University of Notre Dame Press, 1997.

Alonso, Camilo Marks. "Impunidad y tribunales chilenos." Mimeo, Vicaría de la Solidaridad, September 3, 1990.

Alvarez, Jose E. "Crimes of States/Crimes of Hate: Lessons from Rwanda." *Yale Journal of International Law* 24 (1999): 365.

Amnesty International. "Universal Jurisdiction: The Duty of States to Enact and Implement Legislation." AI Index IOR 53/002-018/2001. CD-Rom. September 2001.

Anguita, Eduardo. *Sano juicio: Baltasar Garzón, algunos sobrevivientes y la lucha contra la impunidad en Latinoamérica.* Buenos Aires: Sudamericana, 2001.

Arditti, Rita. *Searching for Life: The Grandmothers of the Plaza de Mayo and the Disappeared Children of Argentina.* Berkeley: University of California Press, 1999.

Arzobispado de Santiago, Fundación de Documentación y Archivo de la Vicaría de la Solidaridad. *Informes Semestrales.* 1996–2001.

Azocar, Pablo. *Pinochet: Epitafio para un tirano.* Madrid: Editorial Popular, 2000.

Bassiouni, M. Cherif. "Universal Jurisdiction for International Crimes." *Virginia Journal of International Law* 42 (2001): 81–162.

Bermúdez, Norberto and Juan Gasparini. *El Testigo secreto.* Buenos Aires: Javier Vergara, 1999.

Bossuyt, Marc. "The Development of Special Procedures of the United Nations Commission on Human Rights." *Human Rights Law Journal* 6 (1985).

Bradley, Craig M. *Criminal Procedure: A Worldwide Study.* Durham, N.C.: Carolina Academic Press, 1999.

Brett, Sebastian. "Discreet Path to Justice: Chile, Thirty Years After the Military Coup." *Human Rights Watch* (September 2003).

Brody, Reed. "The Prosecution of Hissène Habré—An 'African Pinochet'." *New England Law Review* 35 (2001): 321.

Brody, Reed and Michael Ratner, eds. *The Pinochet Papers: The Case of Augusto Pinochet in Spain and Britain.* The Hague: Kluwer, 2000.

Brysk, Alison. "From Above and Below: Social Movements, the International System, and Human Rights in Argentina." *Comparative Political Studies* 26 (1993): 259–85.

Cassese, Antonio and Mireille Delmas-Marty, eds. *Crimes internationaux et jurisdictions nationales: Étude comparée.* Paris: Presses Universitaries de France, 2002.

Centro de Estudios Legales y Sociales (CELS). *Derechos humanos en la Argentina, informe anual 1997, 1998, 1999, 2000, 2001.* Buenos Aires: Editorial Universitaria de Buenos Aires.

Cohen, Robin. "Diasporas and the Nation-State: From Victims to Challengers." *International Affairs* 72 (July 1996): 507–20.

Coloane, Juan Francisco. *Britannia y un general.* Santiago: LOM, 2000.

Comisión Nacional sobre la Desaparición de Personas (CONADEP). *Nunca más: Informe de la Comisión Nacional sobre la Desaparición de Personas.* Buenos Aires:Universitaria de Buenos Aires, 1986.

Correa Sutil, Jorge. "The Judiciary and the Political System in Chile: The Dilemmas of Judicial Independence During the Transition to Democracy." In *Transition to Democracy in Latin America: The Role of the Judiciary,* ed. Irwin Stotzky. Boulder, Colo.: Westview Press, 1993.

———. "No Victorious Army Has Ever Been Prosecuted . . .': The Unsettled Story of Transitional Justice in Chile." In *Transitional Justice and the Rule of Law in New Democracies,* ed. James McAdams. Notre Dame, Ind.: University of Notre Dame Press, 1997.

Davis, Madeleine. *The Pinochet Case: Origins, Progress, and Implications.* Institute of Latin American Studies Research Papers 53. London: University of London, Institute of Latin American Studies, 2000.

Dinges, John. *The Condor Years: How Pinochet and His Allies Brought Terrorism to Three Continents.* New York: New Press, 2004.

Dorfman, Ariel, *Exorcising Terror: The Incredible Unending Trial of General Augusto Pinochet.* New York: Seven Stories Press, 2002.

Drago, Tito. *El Retorno de la ilusión: Pinochet el fin de la impunidad.* Barcelona: RBA Actual, 1999.

Ekaizer, Ernesto. *Yo, Augusto.* Madrid: Aguilar, 2003.

Dayenoff, David Elbio. *De la Querella al sobreseimiento.* Buenos Aires: García Alonso, 2001.

Feitlowitz, Marguerite. *A Lexicon of Terror: Argentina and the Legacies of Torture.* New York: Oxford University Press, 1998.

Finnemore, Martha and Kathryn Sikkink. "International Norm Dynamics and Political Change." *International Organization* 52 (1998): 887–917.

Fletcher, Laurel and Harvey M. Weinstein. "Violence and Social Repair: Rethinking the Contribution of Justice to Reconciliation." *Human Rights Quarterly* 24, 3 (2002): 573–639.

Folgueiro, Hernán and Pablo F. Parenti. *Persecución penal de graves violaciones de los derechos humanos.* Cuadernos de Doctrina y Jurisprudencia Penal 9. Buenos Aires: Ad-Hoc Villela, 2003.

Fundación Rigoberta Menchú Tum. *Jurisdicción universal para el juzgamiento del genocidio en Guatemala.* México: FRMT, 2001.

Gourevitch, Philip. *We Wish to Inform You That Tomorrow We Will Be Killed with Our Families.* New York: Picador Press, 1999.

Grant, Evadne. "Pinochet 2: The Questions of Jurisdiction and Bias." In *The Pinochet Case: A Legal and Constitutional Analysis,* ed. Diana Woodhouse. Oxford: Hart, 2000. 41–61.

Guest, Iain. *Beyond the Disappearances: Argentina's Dirty War Against Human Rights and the United Nations.* Philadelphia: University of Pennsylvania Press, 1990.

Haas, Peter M., ed. *Knowledge, Power, and International Policy Coordination.* Studies in International Relations. Columbia: University of South Carolina Press, 1997. Originally special issue, *International Organization* 46, 1 (1992).

Hagan, John. *Justice in the Balkans: Prosecuting War Crimes in the Hague Tribunal.* Chicago: University of Chicago Press, 2003.

Hannum, Hurst. "International Law and Cambodian Genocide: The Sounds of Silence." *Human Rights Quarterly* 11 (1989): 82–138.

Hitchens, Christopher. *The Trial of Henry Kissinger.* New York: Verso, 2001.

Keck, Margaret and Kathryn Sikkink. *Activists Beyond Borders: Advocacy Networks in International Politics.* Ithaca, N.Y.: Cornell University Press, 1998.

Kleffner, Jann K. "Jurisdiction over Genocide, Crimes Against Humanity: War Crimes, Torture and Terrorism in the Netherlands." Amsterdam Center for International Law. In *Crimes internationaux et jurisdictions nationales: Etude comparée,* ed. Antonio Cassese and Mireille Delmas-Marty. Paris: Presses Universitaires de France, 2002.

Kluger, Richard. *Simple Justice: The History of Brown v. Board of Education and Black America's Struggle for Equality.* New York: Knopf, 1975.

Kornbluh, Peter. *The Pinochet File: A Declassified Dossier on Atrocity and Accountability.* New York: New Press, 2003.

Lippman, Matthew. "The Drafting of the 1948 Convention on the Prevention and Punishment of the Crime of Genocide." *Boston University International Law Journal* 3 (1984): 1–65.

Lira, Elizabeth. "Mesa de diálogo de derechos humanos en Chile, 21 de agosto 1999–13 de junio de 2000." In *Nuevo gobierno: Desafíos de la reconciliación, Chile, 1999–2000,* ed. Facultad Latinoamericana de Ciencias Sociales. Santiago: FLACSO, 2001.

Lozada, Salvador Maria. *Los Derechos humanos y la impunidad en la Argentina, 1974–1999.* Buenos Aires: Nuevohacer, 1999.

Lutz, Ellen and Kathryn Sikkink. "International Human Rights Law and Practice in Latin America." *International Organization* 54 (Summer 2000): 633–59.

———. "The Justice Cascade: The Evolution and Impact of Foreign Human Rights Trials in Latin America." *Chicago Journal of International Law* 2, 1 (2001).

Macedo, Stephen, ed. *Universal Jurisdiction: National Courts and the Prosecution of Serious Crimes Under International Law.* Philadelphia: University of Pennsylvania Press, 2004.

Malamud-Goti, Jaime. *Game Without End: State Terror and the Politics of Justice.* Norman: University of Oklahoma Press, 1996.

Mani, Rama. *Beyond Retribution: Seeking Justice in the Shadows of War.* Oxford: Polity Press, 2002.

Marks, Stephen P. "The *Hissène Habré* Case: The Law and Politics of Universal Jurisdiction." In *Universal Jurisdiction: National Courts and the Prosecution of Serious Crimes Under International Law,* ed. Stephen Macedo 131–67. Philadelphia: University of Pennsylvania Press, 2004.

Martín de Pozuelo, Eduardo and Santiago Tarín. *España acusa.* Madrid: Plaza Janes, 1999.

Mas, Fernando. *De Nuremberg a Madrid.* Madrid: Grijalbo, 1999.

Matus Acuña, Alejandra. *El Libro negro de la justicia chilena.* Buenos Aires: Verso, 1999.

McCrudden, Christopher. "A Common Law of Human Rights? Transnational Judicial Conversations on Constitutional Rights." *Oxford Journal of Legal Studies* 20 (2000).

Meintjes, Garth and Juan E. Méndez. "Reconciling Amnesties with Universal Jurisdiction." *International Law Forum* 2 (2000).

Méndez, Juan E., Martín Abregú, and Javier Mariezcurrena. *Verdad y justicia: Homenaje a Emilio F. Mignone.* San José, Costa Rica: IIDH, 2001.

Mera Figueroa, Jorge. *El Decreto-ley 2.191, de amnistia, y los derechos humanos.* Academia de Humanismo Cristiano, August 1989.

Montealegre Klenner, Hernán. *La Seguridad del estado y los derechos humanos.* Santiago: Academia de Humanismo Cristiano, 1979.

Montoya, Roberto and Daniel Pereyra. *El Caso Pinochet y la impunidad en America latina.* Buenos Aires: Pandemia, 2000.

Moravcsik, Andrew. "Taking Preferences Seriously: A Liberal Theory of International Politics." *International Organization* 51 (1997): 513–53.

Morris, Virginia and Michael Scharf. *The International Criminal Tribunal for Rwanda.* New York: Transnational Press, 1998.

Neuffer, Elizabeth. *The Key to My Neighbor's House: Seeking Justice in Bosnia and Rwanda.* New York: Picador, 2002.

Osiel, Mark. *Mass Atrocity, Collective Memory, and the Law.* New Brunswick, N.J.: Transaction Publishers, 1997.

O'Shaughnessy, Hugh. *Pinochet: The Politics of Torture.* New York: New York University Press: 2000.

Ostergaard-Nielsen, Eva. "Diasporas in World Politics." In *Non-State Actors in World Politics,* ed. Daphne Josselin and William Wallace. Hampshire, UK: Palgrave, 2001.

Parodi Pinedo, Patricio C. *El Secuestro del general.* Santiago: Antártica Quebecor, 1990.

Plataforma Argentina Contra la Impunidad. *Simposio contra la impunidad y en defensa de los derechos humanos, Barcelona, 24–25–26 de octubre 1997.* Barcelona: Icaria, 1998.

Prilliman, William C. *The Judiciary and Democratic Decay in Latin America.* Westport, Conn.: Praeger, 2000.

Remiro Brotóns, Antonio. *El Caso Pinochet: Los límites de la impunidad.* Madrid: Biblioteca Nueva Política Exterior, 2000.

Reydams, Luc. *Universal Jurisdiction: International and Municipal Legal Perspectives.* Oxford: Oxford University Press, 2003.

Risse, Thomas, Stephen C. Ropp, and Kathryn Sikkink. *The Power of Human Rights: International Norms and Domestic Change.* Cambridge: Cambridge University Press, 1999.

Risse, Thomas and Kathryn Sikkink. "The Socialization of International Human Rights Norms into Domestic Practices: Introduction." In *The Power of Human Rights: International Norms and Domestic Change,* ed. Thomas Risse, Stephen C. Ropp, and Kathryn Sikkink. Cambridge: Cambridge University Press, 1999. 18–35.

Robertson, David. "The House of Lords as a Political and Constitutional Court: Lessons from The Pinochet Case." In *The Pinochet Case: A Legal and Constitutional Analysis,* ed. Diana Woodhouse. Oxford: Hart, 2000. 17–40.

Robertson, Geoffrey. *Crimes Against Humanity: The Struggle for Global Justice.* London: Viking, 1999.

Roht-Arriaza, Naomi. "Conclusions." In *Impunity in International Law and Practice,* ed. Naomi Roht-Arriaza. Oxford: Oxford University Press, 1995.

Rojas Aravena, Francisco and Carolina Stefoni Espinoza. *El "Caso Pinochet": Visiones hemisféricas de su detención en Londres.* Santiago: FLACSO, 2001.

Rojas, Paz, Víctor Espinoza, Julia Urquieta, and Hernán Soto. *Tarda pero llega: Pinochet ante la justicia española.* Santiago: LOM, 1998.

Roniger, Luis and Mario Sznajder. *The Legacy of Human Rights Violations in the Southern Cone: Argentina, Chile, and Uruguay.* Oxford: Oxford University Press, 1999.

Rosenberg, Tina. *Children of Cain: Violence and the Violent in Latin America.* New York: Wm. Morrow, 1991.

Salinas, Luis A. *The London Clinic.* Santiago: LOM, 1999.

Sancinetti, Marcelo and Marcelo Ferrante. *El Derecho penal en la protección de los derechos humanos.* Buenos Aires: Hammurabi, 1999.

Schabas, William A. *Genocide in International Law: The Crimes of Crimes.* Cambridge: Cambridge University Press, 2001.

———. *An Introduction to the International Criminal Court.* Cambridge: Cambridge University Press, 2001.

———. "Problems of International Codification: Were the Atrocities in Cambodia and Kosovo Genocide?" *New England Law Review* 35 (Winter 2001): 287.

Scherer García, Julio. *Pinochet: Vivir matando.* México: Nuevo Siglo Aguilar, 2000.

Shain, Yossi. "The Mexican-American Diaspora's Impact on Mexico." *Political Science Quarterly* (Winter 1999): 114.

———. *The Frontier of Loyalty: Political Exile in the Age of the Nation-State.* Middletown, Conn.: Wesleyan University Press, 1989.

Slaughter, Anne-Marie. "Judicial Globalization." *Virginia Journal of International Law* 40 (1999–2000).

———. "A Typology of Transjudicial Communication." *University of Richmond Law Review* 29 (1994): 99.

Slaughter, Anne-Marie et al. "International Law and International Relations Theory: A New Generation of Interdisciplinary Scholarship." *American Journal of International Law* 92 (1998): 367.

Slepoy, Carlos. "Jurisdicción universal: Subsidiariedad o concurrencia?" *Punto y Seguido* 1 (February 2000).

Stern, Brigitte. "International Decision: French Tribunal de grande instance (Paris)." *American Journal of International Law* 93 (1999): 696.

Stover, Eric. *The Witnesses: War Crimes and the Promise of Justice in the Hague.* Berkeley: Human Rights Center at the University of California, 2003. Philadelphia: University of Pennsylvania Press, 2005.

Stover, Eric and Rachel Shikegane. "The Missing in the Aftermath of War: When Do the Needs of Victims' Families and International War Crimes Tribunals Clash?" *International Review of the Red Cross* (December 2002).

Toloyan, Khachig. "Rethinking Diaspora(s): Stateless Power in the Transnational Moment." *Diaspora* 5 (1996): 3–86.

Tyler, Thomas R. *Why People Obey the Law.* New Haven, Conn.: Yale University Press, 1990.

Urbano, Pilar. *Garzón: El hombre que veía amanecer.* Madrid: Plaza and Janes, 2000.

Uribe Arce, Armando and Miguel Vicuña Navarro. *El Accidente Pinochet.* Santiago: Sudamericana 1999.

Vales, José. *Ricardo Cavallo: Genocidio y corrupción en América latina.* Buenos Aires: Norma, 2003.

Vargas, Edmundo. "Visits on the Spot: The Experience of the Inter-American Commission on Human Rights." In *International Law and Fact-Finding in the Field of Human Rights,* ed. Bertram G. Ramcharan. Boston: Nijhoff, 1982.

Verdugo, Patricia. *Los Zarpazos del puma.* Santiago: LOM, 1989. Published in English as *Chile, Pinochet, and the Caravan of Death.* Miami: North-South Center Press, 2001.

Walleyn, Luc. "Victimes et témoins de crimes internationaux: Du droit à une protection au droit à la parole." *International Review of the Red Cross* 84 (March 2002): 845.

Woodhouse, Diana, ed. *The Pinochet Case: A Legal and Constitutional Analysis.* Oxford: Hart, 2000.

Specialized Web Sites

http://www.web.amnesty.org/pages/int_jus_uj
http://www.cavalloentrerejas.org
http://www.cels.org.ar
http://www.derechos.org/nizkor
http://www.fasic.cl
http://www.fidh.org
http://www.hrw.org
http://www.legal.apt.ch
http://www.memoriajusticia.org
http://www.nuncamas.org
http://www.tni.org/pinochet
http://uj-info.org
http://www.universaljurisdiction.info

Interviews (1999–2003)

Martín Abregú
Rosario Aguilar
Pedro Aylwin
Jimmy Bell
Myriam Bell
Judge Gerardo Bernales
Geoffrey Bindman
Lita Boitano
Laura Bretal
Sebastian Brett
Zita Cabello-Barrueto
Estela de Carlotto
Sherman Carroll
Carlos Castresana
Nelson Caucoto
Judge Gabriel Cavallo
Judge Carlos Cerda
Ana Chávez
Eduardo Contreras
George D'Allemagne
Viviana Díaz
Gregorio Dionis
Nicole Druilly
Marga Durán
Shula Ehrenberg
Carlos Esposito
Eduardo Fungairiño
Joan Garcés
Antonio García
Judge Enrique García Bacigalupo
Roberto Garretón
Judge Baltazar Garzón

Amb. Juan Manuel Gómez Robledo
Juan González
María José Guembe
Hugo Gutiérrez
Judge Juan Guzmán Tapia
Jorge Iturburu
Judge Milton Juica
Wolfgang Kaleck
Judge Roger Le Loire
Fabiola Letelier
Elizabeth Lira
Graciela Lois
Estela López Funes
Judge Jesús Luna Altamirano
Jorge Magasich
Giancarlo Maniga
Ellen Marx
Fernando Mas
Andy McEntee
Fiona McKay
Clare Montgomery
Judge Sergio Muñoz
Manuel Ollé
María Luisa Ortíz
Silvia Panebianco
Alberto Pedroncini
Min. Eduardo Peña Haller
Alicia Pierini
Cecilia Prats
Hernán Quezada
Verónica Reyna
Alcira Ríos
Paz Rojas
Beatrix Roux
Hugo Ruíz
Héctor Salazar
Philippe Sands
Enrique Santiago
Judge Leopoldo Schiffrin
Judge María Servini
Virginia Shoppée
Carlos Slepoy
Stefaan Smis
Julio Strassera
Sophie Thonon
Judge Damien Vandermeersch
Carolina Varsky
Roberto Vásquez
Marta Vedío
José Zalaquett

Index

Abregú, Martín, 98
Accountability for past human rights violations, ix–xii, 222–23
Acosta, Jorge, 21, 25, 113, 133–34
Ad hoc tribunals versus transnational prosecutions, 203–7. *See also* ICTY; ICTR
Aguilar, Rosario, 118, 121
Al-Adsani v. United Kingdom, 33
Alfonsín, Raúl, viii, 15, 97, 99, 117, 130
Alien Tort Claims Act (ATCA), 114, 165–66, 168, 205
Almada, Martín, 30, 150, 151
Al-Qaeda, 4, 5, 193
Alsina, Joan, 94
Altamirano, Carlos, 151
Alvarez Ruíz, Donaldo, 171
Alvarez-Machain, Humberto, 144
American Convention on Human Rights, 99, 103
Amiel-Baquet, Marcel-René, 125
Amin, Idi, 182
Amnesty International, 10, 31, 32, 37, 40, 50–54, 59, 192, 208, 211; and Lord Hoffmann, 50–54
Amnesty laws, 194–96, 222. *See also* Argentine amnesty laws; Chilean amnesty laws; Uruguay
Andreu, Federico 10, 33, 47
Annan, Kofi, 185
APDH. *See* Permanent Association of Human Rights
Appiani, Jorge, 128
Arancibia Clavel, Enrique, 161
Archives of Terror, 30, 150, 211
Arduino, Adolfo Mario, 38
Arellano Stark, Sergio, 74–77, 84
Argentina: constitutional reform, 99; double jeopardy, 111; judiciary and corruption, 97–99; Junta trials, viii, 97, 98; official doctrine on extradition, 137; relationship with European countries,

10, 16, 122, 129; right to truth, 101–8; transitional justice, 209, 221
Argentine amnesty laws, 97–98, 100, 102–3; annulled, 117; and *Camps* decision, 97–98; declared unconstitutional, 113–17; exceptions to, 108–13; and Mexico, 149; and Spain, 49–50
Argentine Human Rights Association of Madrid, 10
Arrest Warrant (Congo v. Belgium), 176–77
Artés, Matilde, 14, 29, 110
Asociación Libre de Abogados, 10
Association for Human Rights, La Plata, 104–5
Association of Families of the Disappeared, Argentina, 108
Association of Family Members of the Detained-Disappeared, Chile (AFDD), 38–39, 68, 81, 86
Association of Family Members of Those Executed for Political Reasons, Chile, 81
Association of Free Lawyers (ALA), 10
Association of Relatives and Friends of French Citizens Disappeared in Argentina, 122–23
Astiz, Alfredo, 112, 202; and France, 122–24; and Italy, 123, 133–34
ATCA. *See* Alien Tort Claims Act
Audiencia Nacional (Spain) 3, 44–50, 171, 174–75
Austin, Dianna, 136
Aylwin Azócar, Patricio, viii, 71, 72
Aznar, José María, 15, 59

Bagnasco, Adolfo, 111–12
Balza, Martín, 97
Bañados, Adolfo, 158
Banzer, Hugo, 151–53
Barcella, Lawrence, 25
Bartle, Ronald, 42–43, 60–61
Batlle, Jorge, 155

Bautista Sasiain, Juan, 137
Beausire, William, 40, 83
Beauthier, Georges, 118
Belgium: case against Pinochet, 62–63,
    118–21; customary international law,
    120–21; *Habré* case, 185–86, 191, 205;
    Rwanda cases, 119, 191; *Sharon* case,
    177, 189–90, 198; starting a case, 119–
    20, 190; suit against British Home
    Office, 62–63; suits against U.S. officials,
    190; universal jurisdiction, 120, 186,
    189–91; *Yerodia* case, 186–87, 189
Berger, Sandy, 150
Berlusconi, Silvio, 133
Bianco, Norberto Atilio, 108
Bignone, Reynaldo Benito, 111
Bindman, Geoffrey, 32, 40, 50, 53
Bingham of Cornhill, Thomas Henry,
    Lord, 43, 53
Blair, Tony, 36, 64
Blanco, Juan Carlos, 156
Boitano, Lita, 132
Bolivia, 151, 153
Bonadío, Claudio, 113, 115
Bonaparte, Laura, 13
Bordaberry, Juan, 156
Bouterse, Désiré Delano, 170, 179–81
Brady, Hernán, 178
Brazil, 153, 154
British case against Pinochet: actors in,
    39–40; additions to extradition request,
    59; bias in *Pinochet II*, 52–54; crimes
    charged, 41–43; double criminality, 57;
    economic effects, 36, 65; extradition
    hearing, 60–61; final decision not to
    extradite, 62–63; House of Lords, *Pino-
    chet I*, 50–51; House of Lords, *Pinochet
    III*, 56–58; immunity, 35, 43–44, 51, 55,
    57; intervenors, 43, 50; legal fees, 41, 44;
    Piquete de Londres, 37–39; political
    effects, 64–66; prior attempts to prose-
    cute, 32–33; release of medical exams,
    63
Brody, Reed, 181, 182, 185
Browne-Wilkinson, Nicholas, Lord, 56–57
Buffone, Sam, 159

Cabello, Winston, 165
Camps, Ramón, 97, 106, 157, 160, 175–76;
    decision, 97, 103

Canicoba Corral, Rodolfo, 139
Cañón, Hugo, 107
Capaldo, Giancarlo, 154–55
Caporale, Francesco, 131, 133
Caravan of Death, 27, 74–77
Carroll, Sherman, 39–40
Cassidy, Sheila, 40
Castañeda, Jorge, 147
Castillo, Jaime, 87
Castillo White, Rubén, 76
Castresana, Carlos, 2, 9, 15
Castro, Fidel, 170
Caucoto, Nelson, 85
Cavallo, Gabriel, 114–15, 120, 137, 215–17
Cavallo, Ricardo Miguel, 140–49, 178, 211,
    214; decision on extradition to Spain,
    147; Mexican Foreign Ministry approval
    of extradition, 147–48; multiple extradi-
    tion requests, 148; Spanish arrest war-
    rant, 143
CELS. *See* Center for Legal and Social
    Studies
Center for Justice and Accountability
    (CJA), 165
Center for Legal and Social Studies
    (CELS), 101, 114–16, 141, 209
Central Intelligence Agency (CIA), 150,
    163
Cerda, Carlos, 71, 82, 215
Cezón, Carlos, 70
Chad, 181–82, 184–85
Chadian Association for the Promotion
    and Defense of Human Rights, 181
Chadian Association of Victims of Political
    Repression, 181, 184
Chanfreau, Alphonse, 125
Chávez, Ana, 10, 17, 18
Chile: arbitration with Spain on Pinochet
    extradition, 59–60; coup and dictator-
    ship, ix, 208; and German cases, 206;
    and Pinochet prosecution, 85; response
    to extradition requests, 232; and Span-
    ish investigation, 25, 64–65; and Rettig
    Commission, viii–ix, 72, 87, 220; transi-
    tional justice, 220–21
Chilean judiciary: advances in cases after
    2001, 83, 85, 93–96; decisions on prose-
    cution of Pinochet, 81, 82, 84, 92, 93;
    early cases, 69–72; military courts, 72,
    94; reforms, 72–73, 90

Chilean law, 69, 76; amnesty law, 70–74, 77, 82, 90, 94, 103; amnesty law and Spain, 49; and international treaties, 73, 80; legislators' limited immunity, 79
CIA. *See* Central Intelligence Agency
CJA. *See* Center for Justice and Accountability
Claudet-Fernández, Jean-Yves, 125–26
Clinton, William, 150
CODEPU. *See* Commission on the Defense of the Rights of the People
Comité Pro-Paz, 208
Commission on Historical Clarification (CEH), 171
Commission on the Defense of the Rights of the People (CODEPU), 59
Committee Against Torture, 185
Complainant access to courts and standing: Belgium, 181; Chile, 69; France, 123–24; Netherlands, 179; Spain, 5, 11–12
CONADEP. *See* National Commission on the Disappeared
Continuing crime theory, 61, 74, 77, 111, 219
Contreras, Eduardo, 68, 93
Contreras, Manuel, 13, 25, 94, 95, 126, 154, 163, 220; Leighton assassination attempt, 160; Letelier car bombing, 70, 158, 159; Operation Condor, 152, 153; Prats assassination, 160–61
Convention Against Torture and Other Cruel, Inhuman or Degrading Treatment or Punishment, 8, 32, 37, 40, 43, 49, 56, 57, 60, 99, 124, 138, 147, 177, 179, 182, 183, 190, 192, 197
Convention on the Non-Applicability of Statutes of Limitations to War Crimes and Crimes Against Humanity, 100, 153, 161
Convention on the Prevention and Punishment of the Crime of Genocide, 8, 43, 46–48, 99, 176, 199
Cook, Robin, 64, 118
Cooper, Marc, 164
Cornick, Carter, 158
Coronel, Pastor, 154
Crimes against humanity, 46, 48, 100, 111, 114, 120, 124, 148, 153, 161, 165, 179, 186

De Carlotto, Estela, 132
De La Rua, Eduardo, 133, 137

Del Cerro, Juan Antonio, 114
Del Ponte, Carla, 24
Democratic Republic of the Congo (DRC), 186–88
Detention centers: Automotores Orletti, 30, 109, 150, 155; Campo de Mayo, 108–10, 117; Cuatro Alamos, 83; Club Atlético, 101; El Olimpo, 173; El Vesubio, 137; José Domingo Cañas, 83; La Escuelita, 107; Navy Mechanics School (ESMA), 20, 22, 101, 108, 117, 122, 140, 142 ; Pozo de Banfield, 104, 110; Venda Sexy, 83; Villa Grimaldi, 77, 78, 83, 127
Díaz Araneda, Patricio, 77
Díaz, Viviana, 86, 90
Directorate for National Intelligence (DINA), Chile, 25, 51, 75, 70–71, 73, 77–78, 83, 93–95, 125, 152, 154, 157–64
Dionis, Gregorio, 8, 10, 173
Djiraibe, Delphine, 181
Domon, Alice, 122
Drouilly, Nicole, 37–39
Duffy, Peter, 82
Dugard, John, 179
Duquet, Léonie, 122
Durán Sáenz, Pedro, 137
Durán, Marga, 10

Ebadi, Shirin, 213
Ehrenberg, Shula, 141, 144, 146–47
Eichmann, Adolf, 7, 99
Enríquez, Edgardo, 35
Erize Tisseau, Marie Anne, 127–28
Espinoza, Pedro, 71, 77, 95, 152, 158, 161, 220
ESMA. *See* Detention centers, Navy Mechanics School
ETA (Basque), 3, 28, 124, 145
Etchecolatz, Miguel, 106
European Parliament, 39
Evans, Nicholas, 35, 168
Exiles: Chilean in UK, 37–38: Latin American, 212–13
Extortion, and Argentine amnesty laws, 112–13
Extradition, 127, 139, 151–54, 158, 160, 161, 164, 186, 192, 195, 210; Argentine policy, 127, 133–34, 137–39; *aut dedere aut judicare* (extradite or prosecute),

Extradition (*continued*)
162, 177, 192; Mexico-Spain protocol,
145, 148; UK, 57. *See also* British case
against Pinochet

Family Members of the Disappeared in
Argentina (Familiares), 10
FASIC. *See* Foundation for Social Assistance
of the Christian Churches
Febres, Héctor Antonio, 133
Fernández Larios, Armando, 77, 158, 161,
164–66
Ferreyro, Miguel Angel, 106
FIDH. *See* International Federation for
Human Rights
Foundation for Social Assistance of the
Christian Churches (FASIC), 1, 25, 59,
70, 79
Forced disappearance, 74, 113, 114, 124,
136–37, 151, 152, 156
Fox, Vicente, 144, 147
France: Argentine cases, 124; *Astiz* case,
122–24; Chilean cases, 124, 126–27;
Ould Dah case, 124, 195, 197; and Pino-
chet arrest, 125; universal jurisdiction,
188–89, 197. *See also* French law
Franco, Rubén, 111
Fransen, Daniel, 185
Frei Ruíz-Tagle, Eduardo, 36, 37, 64, 67, 87
Freiler, Eduardo, 111
French law: criminal procedure, 123, 125,
127, 137; torture, 124; trial in absentia,
123
Fujimori, Alberto, 178, 179
Fungairiño, Eduardo, 27–28, 44
Furci, Miguel Angel, 109

Galán, José Luís, 10, 45
Galtieri, Leopoldo, 19, 20
Garcés, Joan, 4, 13, 31, 33, 38, 42, 45, 55,
171, 173, 212
García-Castellón, Manuel, 13, 14, 25, 27,
31, 33, 35
Garretón, Roberto, 26, 86, 87, 125
Garzón, Baltazar, 2, 3, 14, 18, 24, 28–29, 34,
35, 41, 42, 50, 51, 56, 59, 85, 86, 107,
110, 112, 114, 120, 124, 126, 139, 141–
43, 145, 147, 150, 151, 154, 156, 157,
163, 167, 195, 170, 195, 211, 216, 217
Garzón, Cristina, 107

Gasparini, Juan, 21, 146
Gelman, Juan, 30, 155–56
Geneva Conventions, 8, 73, 76, 82, 120,
123, 138, 186, 193
Genocide, 1, 72, 100, 172; Guatemala, 171,
172; Spain, 46–48
Genocide Convention. *See* Convention on
the Prevention and Punishment of the
Crime of Genocide
Gentilli, Marcello, 130
Germany, 332; Argentine cases, 134–39;
extradition challenge denial in Argen-
tine courts, 137–39; Chilean cases,
135–36; law, 135–37
Globalization, 168–69, 202, 212, 217
Goff of Chieveley, Robert Lionel, Lord, 57
Gómez, Conrado Higinio, 112, 115
González, Felipe, 3, 12, 15, 36, 60
González, Jorge Raúl, 24
Granados, Carlos, 14–15
Grandmothers of the Plaza de Mayo, 14,
108–9, 114, 132, 210
Guatemala: genocide of Mayan Indians,
171, 172; human rights cases, 173–74;
judiciary, 174; Spanish Audencia Nacional decision, 174–75, 194; Spanish com-
plaint, 171–73; Supreme Court decision,
175–78
Guengueng, Souleymane, 185
Gutiérrez Ruíz, Héctor, 151, 157
Guzmán Tapia, Juan, 70, 76, 83, 91, 93, 136,
216, 217; and France, 126; Caravan of
Death, 76–79, 82–84, 165; *Horman* case,
163–64, 166; Operation Condor, 154,
157

Habré, Hissène, 170, 181–83, 185–86, 191,
205
Hachim, Ismael, 185–86
Hagelin, Dagmar, 122
Haliki, Touka, 185–86
Harguindeguy, Albano Jorge, 152
Hassan II, 170
Head of state immunity. *See* Immunity
Herreros, Isabelo, 10, 17, 22
Hertz, Carmen, 75, 76
Hoffman, Leonard, Lord, 51–55
Hope of Craighead, Lord, 57
Horman, Charles, 163
Horman, Joyce, 163–64

Human Rights Networks, 208–9, 211–12, 216
Human Rights Watch, 40, 181, 182, 185
Hutton, James Brian, Lord, 57

IACHR. *See* Inter-American Commission on Human Rights
ICC. *See* International Criminal Court
ICJ. *See* International Court of Justice
ICTR. *See* International Criminal Tribunal on Rwanda
ICTY. *See* International Criminal Tribunal for the Former Yugoslavia
Immunity, diplomatic, 34, 51, 167; foreign ministers, 186–88; head of state, 43, 44, 51, 57, 120, 186–88, 190. *See also* British case against Pinochet; Pinochet
Insulza, José Miguel, 26, 59
Inter-American Commission on Human Rights (IACHR), 102–3, 109, 115, 208, 209, 211, 213, 216
Inter-American Convention on Forced Disappearances, 95, 138, 152, 156
Inter-American Court of Human Rights: *Barrios Altos* decision, 95; *Velásquez* decision, 101
International Court of Justice (ICJ), 187, 202; *Arrest Warrant Case (Congo v. Belgium)*, 176, 187–88, 190; *Republic of Congo v. France*, 188
International Criminal Court (ICC), 48, 198–202, 214, 218, 219; jurisdiction, 194, 196; limits, 200–203; reparations, 206; Rome statute, 153, 161, 182, 192–93, 199–200; and victims, 205–6
International Criminal Tribunal for the Former Yugoslavia (ICTY), x, 133, 199, 203–4
International Criminal Tribunal on Rwanda (ICTR), xi, 199, 203–4
International Federation for Human Rights (FIDH), 185
International law, domestic applicability of, 42, 57, 80, 86, 95, 99, 114–15, 129–30, 179–80, 183; Argentine cases, 129–34; *Olivera* case, 128–29; Priebke extradition, 100; *Sharon* case, 189; *Suárez-Mason/Riveros* case, 132–33
Iturburu, Jorge, 130–32
Iturriaga Neumann, Jorge, 161

Iturriaga Neumann, Raúl, 160, 161
Izquierda Unida (Spain), 10, 12, 17
Izurieta, Ricardo, 87

Jacquard, Alexis, 122
Jews: and Argentina, 134–35; and German prosecutions, 135
Jiménez, Tucapel, 93
Joinet, Louis, 205
Jones, Alun, 41, 43, 44, 56
Judges, as social actors, 214–18
Judicial cooperation, 191, 217–18
Jurisdiction: passive personality, 7, 121–22, 179, 191; territoriality principle, 7, 152. *See also* Universal jurisdiction

Kaleck, Wolfgang, 135, 212
Kambale, Pascal, 183
Kandji, Demba, 182, 183
Kasseman, Elisabeth, 136
Kirchner, Néstor, 116–17, 139
Kissinger, Henry, 40, 166–68, 218; *Schneider* case, 168; trial, 167
Kissinger Watch, 167
Klein, Georges, 124, 127
Kornbluth, Peter, 125

Labrador family, 19
Lagos, Joaquín, 79
Lagos, Ricardo, 20, 67, 69, 88, 90, 91, 94
Landa, Ceferino, 114
Lapacó, Carmen, 101–3; and IACHR, 102–3, 211
Lavin, Claudio, 76
Lawyers, as social actors, 213–14
Le Loire, Roger, 124–27, 154, 166–67, 217
League for Peoples' Rights, Italy, 129
League of the Rights of Man, France, 118
Leighton, Bernardo, 25, 77, 126, 151, 157, 159–60, 163
Letelier, Fabiola, 164
Letelier, Orlando, 25, 30, 70, 77, 108, 118, 151, 157–59, 162, 164, 221
Literas, Gustavo, 130
Llidó, Antonio, 14, 94
Lloyd of Berwick, Lord, 51
Lois, Graciela, 10, 108
Longeira, Pablo, 80
Luna Altamirano, Jesús Guadalupe, 146, 147

Mandela, Nelson, 213
Maniga, Giancarlo, 130
Marín, Gladys, 68, 75, 81
Marquevich, Roberto, 108, 110–11
Marshall, Thurgood, 213
Martínez, Pedro Mayor, 151–52
Marx, Ellen, 135–36
Mas, Fernando, 13, 15
Massera, Emilio, 21, 24, 111, 112, 133
Matus, Alejandra, 69
Matutes, Abel, 59, 64
McEntee, Andy, 32, 42, 211, 212
McKay, Fiona, 41, 43
Medical Foundation for the Care of Victims
  of Torture, 39
Menchú, Rigoberta, 171, 174
Menem, Carlos, 98, 99, 137, 210; Italian
  investigation, 131; pardons, 99, 151
Menéndez, Luciano, 107
Mengele, Joseph, 99
Mengistu, Haile Mariam, 182
Mesa de Diálogo, 87–90, 92, 93; armed
  forces self-investigation, 91; public dec-
  laration, 89
Mexico: investigation of past abuses, 219;
  law, 145, 147–49; national sovereignty,
  143; politics, 144, 145, 147
Michelini, Zelmar, 151, 157
Mignone, Emilio, 101, 209
Millet, Peter, Lord, 57
Moffitt, Michael, 157
Moffitt, Ronni, 70, 157
Montgomery, Clare, 41, 54
Moren Brito, Marcelo, 77, 95
Mothers of the Plaza de Mayo, 9, 17, 122,
  132, 209
Moudeïna, Jacqueline, 184
Muñoz, Sergio, 85, 94
Murillo, Manuel, 14, 167

National Commission on the Disappeared
  (CONADEP), 9, 17, 104, 221
National Commission for the Right to Iden-
  tity, 109
National Commission on Truth and Recon-
  ciliation (Rettig Commission), viii–ix,
  72, 87, 220
National Vehicle Registry (Mexico)
  (RENAVE), 140, 141, 146
Nazis, 134–35; and Argentina, 99–100
Netherlands, 179–81

Nguema, Theodoro, 170
Nicholls, Clive, 41, 50
Nicholls of Birkenhead, Lord, 51
Nicolaides, Cristino, 111, 154
Nieto, Carlos, 10
Nongovernmental organizations (NGOs),
  208–12; objectives, 54–55. See also indi-
  vidual NGOs
Nuremburg, International Military Tribu-
  nal at, 11, 134, 139, 161, 199
Nzapali, Sebastian, 197

Olivera, Jorge, 128–29, 214
Ollé, Manuel, 69, 143, 147
Operation Albania, 73, 94
Operation Condor, 29, 33, 126, 150–69,
  211; Argentine, 152–53; cases, 150–51;
  Italian, 154; Paraguayan, 151–52; third
  phase, 151, 157–63; U.S. documents,
  150, 163; Uruguayan, 154–56
Ould Dah, Ely, 124, 195, 197

Panebianco, Silvia, 144, 146
Paraguay, 30, 109, 150–52
Pavelic, Ante, 99
Pedroncini, Alberto, 111, 152
Pereira, Pamela, 87–90, 162
Pérez Esquivel, Adolfo, 9, 19, 135–36, 209
Pérez, Fran, 10, 17
Permanent Association of Human Rights
  (APDH), 10
Perón, María Isabel, 20
Peru, genocide case in Spanish court,
  178–79
Pesle, Etienne, 125
Phillips of Worth Matravers, Lord, 57
Pinochet Ugarte, Augusto, 1, 26, 32, 35, 36,
  41, 59, 92–94; arrest in London, 35–37;
  Caravan of Death, 74, 78; complaints in
  Chile, 68–69; and France, 121, 126, 127;
  health, 61–63, 80, 84, 92–93; indictment
  in Caravana case, 83–84, 92; Operation
  Condor, 152, 154, 158–59; return to
  Chile, 68; revocation of immunity, 78–
  82, 92–93, 162; and UK, 36, 41–44,
  50–66; UK cases in other courts, 177,
  179, 197, 219
Poblete, Claudia Victoria, 113
Poblete Córdova case, 73–74
Poblete, Sergio, 26
Ponce Edmonson, Juan Miguel, 142
Prats, Carlos, 26, 127, 151, 160–63

Prats, Cecilia, 162–63
Priebke, Erich, 100, 169
Propper, Eugene, 158
Purdy, Fred, 164

Quezada, Hernán, 162
Quinteros, Elena, 156

Radice, Jorge, 113
Ramírez Montesinos, Vicente, 19
Ramírez Pineda, Luís, 126–27
Ramos Tercero, Raúl, 140
Rebolledo, Enrique, 76
Redress trust, 41, 43
Reforma, 141, 142
RENAVE. *See* National Vehicle Registry
Reno, Janet, 26, 159
Republic of Congo v. France, 188
Retroactivity and retrospectivity, 49, 57, 61, 74, 76, 114–17, 120, 147, 180–81
Rettig Commission. *See* National Commission on Truth and Reconciliation
Reyes, Verónica, 1, 25, 70, 79
Ribeiro, José Osvaldo, 126
Right to truth, 101–3, 106, 108
Ríos Montt, Efraín, 171, 173
Ríos, Alcira, 108, 109, 114
Rivera Matus, Juan Luis, 91
Riveros, Omar, 110, 132–33
Rodríguez Espoz, Jaime, 81
Rolón, Juan Carlos, 113
Rubira, Pedro, 45, 174
Ruíz Polanco, Guillermo, 142, 172, 174

Salazar, Héctor, 87, 88, 90
Salgado, Juan Carlos, 87, 89
Salvi, Giovanni, 126, 154
Sanguinetti, Julio María, 151
Santiago, Enrique, 10, 33, 45, 143
Saville of Newdigate, Mark, Lord, 57
Scherrer, Robert, 158
Schiffrin, Leopoldo, 103–6, 215
Schneider, René, 168
Schwammberger case, 103–4
Schwammberger, Joseph, 99–100, 103–4, 137
Scilingo, Adolfo, 22, 24, 97, 139, 178, 214
Senegal, 181, 184, 186; case against Habré, 181–83; restraining Habré from leaving, 185
Service for Peace and Justice (SERPAJ), 9, 10, 17, 209

Servini de Cubría, María: child stealing cases, 111; and Italy, 133–34; *Prats* case, 160–62
Sharon, Ariel, 189
Sierra, Sola, 38
Silva Iriarte, Mario, 75
Silva, Patricia, 75
Simón, Julio Héctor, 114
Slepoy, Carlos, 9, 10, 14, 17, 21, 23, 45, 142, 147, 173
Slynn of Hadley, Gordon, Lord, 51
Soria, Carmelo, 5, 14, 26, 94, 178
Spain: arbitration with Chile on Pinochet extradition, 60; Argentine arrest orders, 20, 24–25, 139; Argentine complaint, 6–8; Argentine investigation, 16–20, 24–25; Audiencia Nacional, 3, 44, 175; Chilean complaint, 13; Chilean investigation, 25–26; Civil War, 219, 221; doctors' response to Pinochet medical exam, 62–63; government response to Latin American complaints, 15, 59, 60, 62, 65; Guatemala case, 171–78; judiciary, 16; jurisdiction over Chilean and Argentine cases, 6–7, 45–50; Peru case, 178–79; Public Prosecutor's Office, 16, 27, 28, 174; societal reactions to transnational cases, 29, 173, 218–19
Spanish law: criminal complaints, 5, 11–12; terrorism, 48–49; universal jurisdiction, 6–7, 45–50, 175, 176
South Africa, x, 196
Statute of limitations, 74, 100, 111, 113, 121, 124, 129, 136, 147, 148, 152, 156, 161
Stealing of children, 14–15, 31, 106, 108–12, 133–34; birthing wards in detention centers, 110; role of DNA, 109–10
Steyn, Johan, Lord, 51
Strassera, Julio, 18, 145
Straw, Jack, 51, 58, 62–64, 67, 80
Stroessner, Alfredo, 152, 154
Suárez-Mason, Carlos Guillermo, 110, 114, 117, 132–33; and Germany, 136–38; Operation Condor, 152, 154
Suriname, 179–81
Sweden, 122
Switzerland, 121, 122

TALSUD, 140
Tatchell, Peter, 167

Terrorism. *See* Spanish law
Teruggi, Frank, 163
Tetzlaff, Hernán, 109
Thatcher, Margaret, 1, 36, 67
Thonon, Sophie, 123, 128, 212
Torres Silva, Fernando, 27, 93
Torres, Juan José, 29, 151
Torture. *See* Convention Against Torture
  and Other Cruel, Inhuman or Degrad-
  ing Treatment or Punishment
Total Oil Company, 169
Townley, Michael, 158, 161
Transitional justice, ix–xi, 220–24
Transnational advocacy networks, 209–14;
  exiles as, 212–13; lawyers as, 213–14
Transnational prosecutions: actors in, 211;
  agency of victims and survivors, 204–7;
  effect on domestic investigations and
  prosecutions, 209–10, 218–19, 223–24;
  judges and, 214–18; structural characteristics, 194–95
Truth trials, 104–8

Union of Progressive Prosecutors, 2, 4, 10
United Kingdom, 36, 37, 39, 64; law and
  legal system, 32, 54; *See also* British case
  against Pinochet
United Left. *See* Izquierda Unida
United Nations Human Rights Commission, 205, 208, 209, 213
United States: and Chilean coup, 163–64;
  support of Spanish investigation, 25–26,
  150
Universal jurisdiction, 7, 192, 223–24; 2003
  amendments to law, 190, 198; Argentina, 152; Belgium, 186–91; Canada,
  191; Congo (Brazzaville) case, 188, 197;
  due process concerns, 184, 193; France,
  197; Germany, 191; inability or unwill-
  ingness of domestic courts, 176, 193–96;

influence of executive branches, 183–
  84, 186; Netherlands, 179, 197; nexus to
  forum state, 176, 178, 191; Paraguay,
  151–52; presence of defendant, 177,
  189, 191–93; South Africa, 191; Spain, 6,
  46, 70, 71, 172, 175–79, 194, 196. *See also*
  individual countries
Urteaga, Facundo, 102
Uruguay, 154–57; amnesty law, 103, 155;
  cases, 156, 157; double criminality, 153;
  Gelman case, 155–56; Peace Commission, 155; response to extradition
  requests, 153

Valdés, Juan Gabriel, 60, 64
Vales, José, 141–44
Vandermeersch, Damien, 119–21, 186, 216
Vanek, Antonio, 133
Vapora, Julio, 152
Vedio, Marta, 105
Vicaría de la Solidaridad, 70, 208
Victim-centered justice, 204–7
Videla, Jorge Rafael, 98, 110–12; Operation
  Condor, 152–53; systematic plan, 110,
  112
Vildoza, Jorge Raúl, 25, 133
Villagra, Hiram, 81
Villani, Mario, 20, 24, 141, 142

Whamond, Francis, 113
Wilson, Richard, 47

Yaron, Amos, 189, 190
Yerodia Ndombasi, Abdulaye, 170, 186–87,
  189

Zalaquett, José, 80, 87
Zara Holger, José, 161
Zedillo, Ernesto, 140, 144
Zuppi, Alberto, 127, 137

Acknowledgments

This book is the product of four years of research. It could not have been completed without the many people who shared information, expertise, stories, documents, and dreams. Those interviewed, who are listed in the Bibliography, were generous with their time and knowledge. I am especially grateful to all the people who sent me cases (often unpublished), and for access to archival materials at CELS in Argentina, CODEPU, FASIC, and FUNVISOL in Chile, the International Secretariat of Amnesty International in London, and the offices of Enrique Santiago and of Equipo Nizkor in Madrid. I also learned a great deal from the participants at many conferences on these themes over the last four years, including conferences on the *Pinochet* case in London and Washington, D.C. A number of people tried to teach me something about their domestic law. Where the lessons didn't take and I've got it wrong, the responsibility is entirely mine.

The research was generously supported by a grant for Research and Writing from the John D. and Catherine T. MacArthur Foundation, and a grant from the United States Institute of Peace. Of course, the opinions, findings, and conclusions or recommendations in this book are mine alone and do not reflect the views of the United States Institute of Peace or any other source of support. I also benefited from a stint as the Harry and Lillian Hastings Research Chair at my institution, the University of California's Hastings College of Law.

Many people reviewed portions of the manuscript and gave helpful comments. They include Judge Juan Guzmán Tapia, Elizabeth Lira, Juan Méndez, Javier Mariezcurrena, Hernán Folguiero, Fiona McKay, Christopher Hall, Joan Garcés, Carlos Castresana, Sophie Thonon, Wolfgang Kaleck, Diane Amann, Kathryn Sikkink, Stacie Jonas, and Patricia Sellers. I had excellent research assistance from Heather Robert, Deborah McCrimmon, Amanda Clarke, and Carlos Campos. I especially thank Deborah McCrimmon for struggling with the index. Bert Lockwood, Peter Agree, and Ellie Goldberg at Penn Press helped get the book into print. Ellen Lutz, incisive reviewer and dear friend, read the whole manuscript, provided comments, and helped talk me through the rough spots. My husband suffered through weeks of single parenting, late nights, and other manifestations of my obsession with this project. He and my children, thankfully, shared my sense that the story was worth telling. For that I am profoundly grateful.